Violence on the Job

Identifying Risks and Developing Solutions

Edited by Gary R. VandenBos and Elizabeth Q. Bulatao

American Psychological Association
Washington, DC

Published by
American Psychological Association
750 First Street, NE
Washington, DC 20002

Copies may be ordered from
APA Order Department
P.O. Box 92984
Washington, DC 20090-2984

In the United Kingdom and Europe, copies may be ordered from
American Psychological Association
3 Henrietta Street
Covent Garden, London
WC2E 8LU England

Typeset in Century Schoolbook by EPS Group Inc., Easton, MD

Cover designer: Jennifer Pritchard, Washington, DC
Printer: Data Reproductions Corporation, Rochester Hills, MI
Technical/production editor: Edward B. Meidenbauer

Library of Congress Cataloging-in-Publication Data
Violence on the job : identifying risks and developing solutions / edited by Gary
    R. VandenBos and Elizabeth Q. Bulatao.
        p.   cm.
    Includes bibliographical references and index.
    ISBN 1-55798-389-5
    1. Violence in the workplace.   I. VandenBos, Gary R.   II. Bulatao,
Elizabeth Q.
HF5549.5.E43V546   1996
658.4′73—dc20   96-9143
                                                                                        CIP

British Library Cataloguing-in-Publication Data
A CIP record is available from the British Library.

Printed in the United States of America
First edition

Contents

Contributors

David G. Alexander, *George Meany Center for Labor Studies, Silver Spring, MD*
David Bargal, *Paul Baerwald School of Social Work, The Hebrew University School of Social Work, Jerusalem*
Julian Barling, *School of Business, Queen's University, Kingston, Ontario*
Robert A. Baron, *Rensselaer Polytechnic Institute, Troy, NY*
Joel E. Bennett, *Texas Christian University, Fort Worth, TX*
Elizabeth Brondolo, *Department of Psychology, St. John's University, Jamaica, NY*
Barbara Burr, *U.S. Department of Labor, Occupational Safety and Health Administration, Washington, DC*
David F. Bush, *Villanova University, Villanova, PA*
John Dignam, *Federal Bureau of Prisons, Washington, DC*
Richard J. Driscoll, *National Institute for Occupational Safety and Health, Cincinnati, OH*
Thomas J. Fagan, *Federal Bureau of Prisons, Washington, DC*
Georgina J. Flannery, *Newton Free Library, Newton, MA*
Raymond B. Flannery, Jr., *Department of Psychiatry, Harvard Medical School, Boston, MA*
Robert Folger, *Tulane University, New Orleans, LA*
Susan Fox, *U.S. Department of Labor, Occupational Safety and Health Administration, Washington, DC*
Caroline Freeman, *U.S. Department of Labor, Occupational Safety and Health Administration, Washington, DC*
Lucy N. Friedman, *Victim Services, New York, NY*
Neil B. Guterman, *Columbia University School of Social Work, New York, NY*
M. Annette Hanson, *Department of Psychiatry, Harvard Medical School, Boston, MA*
Joseph J. Hurrell, Jr., *National Institute for Occupational Safety and Health, Cincinnati, OH*
Maria Imperial, *Victim Services, New York, NY*
Srinika Jayaratne, *University of Michigan School of Social Work, Ann Arbor, MI*
Thomas Jellife, *New York City Department of Transportation*
Dennis L. Johnston, *Behavior Analysts and Consultants, Inc., Stuart, FL*
Judith L. King, *University of Alabama at Birmingham*
Joseph A. Kinney, *National Safe Workplace Institute, Charlotte, NC*
John G. Kurutz, *United States Postal Service, Washington, DC*
Marilyn Lewis Lanza, *Edith Nourse Rogers Memorial Veterans Hospital, Bedford, MA, and Boston University School of Public Health*
Wayne E. K. Lehman, *Texas Christian University, Fort Worth, TX*
Bernard A. McCann, *Laborers' Health and Safety Fund of North America, Washington, DC*
Elizabeth Melhado, *St. John's University, Jamaica, NY*
Peter R. Neville, *Victim Services, New York, NY*
John Nicoletti, *Nicoletti-Flater Associates, Lakewood, CO*
P. Gavan O'Shea, *Villanova University, Villanova, PA*
Walter E. Penk, *Department of Psychiatry, Harvard Medical School, Boston, MA*
Christopher J. Quinn, *New York City Department of Transportation*

David A. Root, *Employee Assistance Program, Hughes Aerospace and Electronics Co., Fullerton, CA*

David A. Safran, *Deval Star, Inc., Psychological Research and Consulting, New York, NY*

John Santasine, *U.S. Department of Labor, Occupational Safety and Health Administration, Washington, DC*

Kelly Spooner, *Nicoletti-Flater Associates, Lakewood, CO*

Brian W. Sugden, *Health Management Systems of America, Washington, DC*

Aldo J. Tartaglini, Jr., *Deval Star, Inc., Psychological Research and Consulting, New York, NY*

Susan Brown Tucker, *Victim Services, New York, NY*

Wendy Tunick, *Department of Psychology, St. John's University, Jamaica, NY*

John M. Violanti, *Department of Criminal Justice, Rochester Institute of Technology, Rochester, NY*

Thomas W. White, *U.S. Department of Justice, Federal Bureau of Prisons, Kansas City, KS*

Karen A. Worthington, *National Institute for Occupational Safety and Health, Cincinnati, OH*

Mark D. Ziska, *Hughes Aerospace and Electronics Co., Fullerton, CA*

1

Workplace Violence: Its Scope and the Issues

Elizabeth Q. Bulatao and Gary R. VandenBos

The American preoccupation with crime has come indoors. As dramatic stories about workplace violence have inundated the media, shock at crime in the office has supplemented hysteria about crime in the streets. But despite the explosion of concern, workplace violence is not a new phenomenon, but an enduring aspect of what appears to be a stable trend in crime.

Determining the actual facts about workplace violence is difficult. There is no agreement on what constitutes workplace violence. Misinformation and myth have followed in the emotional wake of recent workplace violence incidents. In this introduction, we will present an overview of the book, as well as underline the key facts about the incidence, importance, and costs of workplace violence.

Definitions

Homicide is the most dramatic component of workplace violence, and the premature loss of human life always justifies concern. In several industry groups and several occupations, homicide is more frequent than any other cause of fatal workplace injuries. This is true in the retail trade, in finance and insurance, and in service industries, but it is also true for executives and managers (Jenkins, Kisner, et al., 1993). Homicides were the second leading cause of worker deaths in 1994 (Bureau of Labor Statistics, 1995c).

Nonetheless homicide actually makes up a very small percentage of workplace violence, and of all homicides that occur in a given year, workplace homicide occurs the least. In 1992, only about 1 out of 650 workplace acts of violence involved homicide. And, those workplace homicides represented only 4% of all homicides in that year.

Given the proportionally small role of homicide in workplace violence, it is important to understand what workplace violence actually covers. Researchers and government officials are still struggling toward a consensus definition. Essentially they face three issues: (a) how broadly to define violence, (b) how to define the workplace, and (c) whether to focus on the link between violence and work.

The first issue is how broadly to define violence. A fairly narrow definition is that of Kraus, Blander, and McArthur (1995). In a review of government data, professional journals, and publications from private companies, they focus only on physical assaults, defined as

> an unlawful attack, or attempted attack, by one person upon another for purpose of inflicting severe or aggravated bodily injury. Assault often involves use of a weapon or other means likely to produce death or great bodily harm. Here, assault incidents are limited to those involving physical injury and thus exclude rape, verbal assault, harassment, and related outcomes (p. 358).

For a slightly broader definition, one could instead follow the National Crime Victimization Survey and consider all "violent acts, including physical assaults and threats of assault, directed toward persons at work or on duty" (Jenkins, 1996b, p. 1). Essentially this covers all crimes of violence, including homicide, rape, robbery, and simple and aggravated assault.

A still broader definition would cover all crimes in the workplace, including thefts and "household-type" crimes, each of which outnumber crimes of violence by more than 3 to 1. Household-type crimes involve incidents such as loss of a motor vehicle in a company parking lot or garage; they should not be confused with crimes committed at the victim's home. Victimless crimes—drug and alcohol abuse, illegal gambling, and prostitution—are potentially additional types of workplace crime that could be included.

Some researchers attempt to encompass all destructive acts, including even lapses in etiquette. Thus, Folger and Baron (chapter 3, this volume), for example, look at

> any form of behavior by individuals that is intended to harm current or previous coworkers or their organization. Thus, our definition includes instances of *workplace violence* but also encompasses many other forms of aggression—everything from spreading negative rumors about target individuals or their protégés, through withholding information or resources needed by targets or even purposely failing to return phone calls from them. (p. 52)

Folger and Baron's term *workplace aggression* can be used to encompass the broad class of incidents they describe. In order to focus the following discussion more sharply, however, it is useful to maintain a somewhat more narrow definition of workplace violence as referring to actual crimes of violence in the workplace: homicide, rape, robbery, and simple and aggravated assault. Nonviolent crime (theft, household-type crime, victimless crime) would be excluded, but it could be covered under the intermediate category of *workplace crime*.

The second issue is how to define a workplace. Workplaces are not only offices or factories. Some workers, such as policemen and taxi drivers, work on the streets, and others, such as plumbers and visiting nurses, work in the homes of their customers. One could thus argue that some victims of workplace violence carry their "workplaces" along with them.

Therefore, any incident of violence while working or on duty is an incident of workplace violence. Even this is not an entirely adequate definition of workplace, in terms of some of the definitions of workplace violence, however. It excludes, for instance, a suicide occurring off the job but directly precipitated by job stress. It also leaves somewhat problematic the classification of such incidents as thefts of unoccupied offices, where the victim is not at work. Nonetheless, though it has its limits, the most convenient way to identify workplace violence appears to be to refer to *crimes of violence that occur in the workplace or while the victim is at work or on duty* (Jenkins, 1996b). In some of the chapters that follow, however, somewhat different definitions may be used.

The third issue is whether workplace violence should be confined to incidents that are actually related to the victim's work. One specific reason to stress this link is the existence of mandated occupational safety and health standards that govern prevention of, response to, and liability for work-related injury but exclude injury at work that is somehow unrelated to the employee's duties. For instance, personal or domestic disputes that spill into the workplace would not be considered work-related. In addition, some courts have held that an assault on an employee in a company's parking lot is not work-related and not the employer's responsibility—but other courts have held differently, often because of the specific circumstances of a case (Mountain States Employers Council and Nicoletti-Flater Associates, 1994). The potential for extended legal debate about whether an assault did or did not "arise out of the employment" or merely took place "in the course of employment" (Thomas, 1992) makes it difficult to determine in a clear and predictable manner whether a particular incident is work-related. For this reason, it is inconvenient to define as workplace violence only those incidents that are certifiably work-related. Nevertheless, one can introduce, at least notionally, an additional category of incidents, *work-related violence*, overlapping with workplace violence. In some cases this category will be narrower than workplace violence, but in other cases it may possibly be broader. Figure 1 illustrates this distinction, as well as the earlier distinctions that have been made among different concepts, showing how the key concepts overlap.

Estimates of Workplace Violence

Given the complicated nature of these definitions, it is not surprising that the public both overestimates and underestimates the importance of workplace violence. The more potent reason for overestimation, perhaps, is how the media covers specific workplace violence incidents.

Through the Media's Lens

Media coverage has elevated workplace violence into a distinct category of crime, associated in the public mind with vengeance wreaked by dis-

4   BULATAO AND VANDENBOS

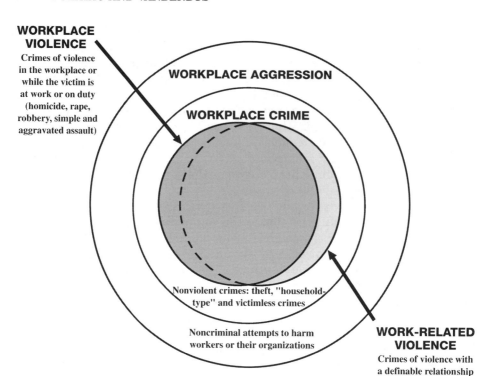

Figure 1. Concepts related to workplace violence.

gruntled and often berserk employees or former employees on their superiors and coworkers. Unfortunately, stilted reporting of such dramatic incidents—driven by the media's need to attract attention and make stories meaningful to the individual while sparing them complicated explanations—often fail to communicate the full context or put incidents in proper perspective.

Undoubtedly the media have found a responsive chord in people's concerns about the unpredictability of so many aspects of life and their inability to understand and control so much of what goes on around them. Journalists speculate that workplace violence reflects the stresses of an increasingly harsh business environment, proliferating layoffs, and disgruntled workers (Kraus et al., 1995). Easy access to guns and abuse of drugs and alcohol are often seen as exacerbating factors for workplace violence, as for other forms of violence. These sometimes overheated concerns have to be tempered by consideration of actual statistics, which have accumulated gradually over the past decade and a half.

Workplace Homicide

Early studies of workplace homicide. The Occupational Safety and Health Act, passed by the U.S. Congress in 1970 to assure safe and healthful working conditions, has contributed to the gradual accumulation of data on workplace violence. The Act was primarily concerned with hazards pertaining to industrial machinery and toxic chemicals; it made no mention of protecting workers from violence. By the 1980s, however, some reports on the frequency and circumstances of workplace injury due to violence began to appear (Kraus et al., 1995; Thomas, 1992). In 1982, a report from the Centers for Disease Control and Prevention discussed homicide among the causes of work-related deaths. In 1984, researchers from British Columbia and Oklahoma described the relative importance of work-related homicides among all occupational fatalities (cited in Kraus et al., 1995). In 1987, the *American Journal of Public Health* featured two epidemiological reports on incidence and features of homicides in work settings (Davis, 1987; Kraus, 1987). Other limited studies by criminologists, epidemiologists, and retail industry observers followed, focusing on sectors traditionally viewed as at highest risk (Thomas, 1992).

Prompted by these studies and their own assessments, the National Institute for Occupational Safety and Health (NIOSH) began to systematically collect data about violence-related occupational fatalities in the late 1980s (Kraus et al., 1995). In 1992, federal researchers devised standard criteria ("Operational Guidelines for Determination of Injury at Work") for use by medical examiners and coroners to determine workplace homicide (NIOSH, Centers for Disease Control and Prevention, 1993 [Appendix I]).

Statistics on workplace homicide. Two national surveillance systems now exist for workplace homicide. The first is the National Traumatic Occupational Fatalities surveillance system, maintained by NIOSH. This Occupational Fatalities system uses death certificates for workers 16 years of age or older from the 50 states and the District of Columbia to determine the cause of a workplace death. The system has some limitations because death certificates capture only about 81% of occupational injury deaths and provide little data about the circumstances. In addition, industry and occupation information listed on death certificates agrees only 60–75% of the time with actual employment status at the time of death (U.S. Department of Health and Human Services [DHHS], 1994).

The second system is the Bureau of Labor Statistics (BLS) National Census of Fatal Occupational Injuries, which compiles fatality data from multiple state and federal administrative sources, including death certificates, workers' compensation reports and claims, reports to various regulatory agencies, medical examiner reports, and news reports. Source documents are matched to ensure each fatality is counted only once. To verify that a fatality occurred at work, at least two independent source documents must agree, or, on rare occasions, a follow-up questionnaire is used (BLS, 1995c).

For the period 1980–1992, the NIOSH Occupational Fatalities system recorded 9,937 workplace homicides—close to 800 a year, for an average annual workplace homicide rate of 0.7 per 100,000 workers (Jenkins, 1996b). Over the 1980s, the rate declined, but it took an upward turn in the 1990s. In 1989 homicide was the third leading cause of job-related deaths, and in 1990, NIOSH data indicated that workplace homicides had surpassed accidents with machinery (Jenkins, 1996a). Bureau of Labor Statistics data also show that in 1993 and 1994, workplace homicide was the second leading cause of job-related deaths, and was approaching the numbers for job-related deaths in motor vehicles in frequency (BLS, 1994b, 1995c).

Drawing on a wider range of reports, the BLS Census of Fatal Occupational Injuries reports 40% higher workplace homicide figures: 1,044 for 1992, 1,074 for 1993, and 1,071 for 1994. Job-related homicides constituted 16% of all fatal injuries to workers in 1994 (BLS, 1995c).

Risk factors for workplace homicide. Crime plays a larger role when a workplace injury is fatal than when it is not. Of 6,588 job-related fatalities in 1994, 16% were homicides (BLS, 1995c), whereas of the 2.3 million job-related injuries (resulting in days away from work) in 1992, only 1% were due to violent acts (Toscano & Weber, 1995).

Although the NIOSH Occupational Fatalities system may give different figures from the BLS Census of Fatal Occupational Injuries, several researchers confirm that the two surveillance systems identify similar industries and occupations as high-risk and assign similar demographic characteristics to victims (Castillo & Jenkins, 1994; Jenkins, 1996b; Toscano & Weber, 1995; Windau & Toscano, 1994).

The risk of becoming the victim of a workplace homicide is particularly high for some industries and occupations. Table 1 shows that homicide was the leading cause of fatal occupational injuries in three industry groups and four occupational groups in 1980–1989 (Jenkins, Kisner, et al., 1993). Additional NIOSH Occupational Fatalities data show that between 1980 and 1992, the greatest number of homicides occurred in retail trade (38% of the total) and service industries as a whole (17%) (Jenkins, 1996).

For the last part of this period, 1990–1992, Jenkins (1996b) lists the rates for more narrowly defined high-risk industries: taxicab service, 41.4 per 100,000 (a rate almost 60 times the national average work-related homicide rate of 0.70); liquor stores, 7.5; detective-protective services, 7.0; gasoline service stations, 4.8; and jewelry stores, 4.7. The largest number of deaths occurred in grocery stores (330 over the 3 years), eating and drinking places (262), taxicab service (138), and justice and public order (137). The 1990–1992 rates reflect an increase over the 1980–1989 rates for taxicab service, detective-protective services, grocery stores, and jewelry stores, but a decrease in rates for gasoline service stations, justice and public order, and hotels and motels. Rates for both periods remain the same in eating and drinking places. It is also noteworthy that homicide figures for sales supervisors and proprietors increased from a rate of 2.8 per 100,000 workers in 1983–1989 to 3.3 per 100,000 workers in 1990–1992.

Given the extensive media coverage of particular incidents, special mention should be made about workplace homicides in U.S. Postal Service

Table 1. Leading Causes of Fatal Occupational Injuries, Selected Industries and Occupations, 1980–1989

Industry or occupation	Leading cause	Rate per 100,000	Second leading cause	Rate per 100,000	All fatal injuries: rate per 100,000
Retail trade	Homicide	1.66	Motor vehicle	.39	2.89
Service	Homicide	.61	Motor vehicle	.54	2.81
Finance, insurance, real estate	Homicide	.39	Motor vehicle	.30	1.37
Occupation					
Sales	Homicide	1.36	Motor vehicle	.59	2.81
Service	Homicide	.97	Motor vehicle	.60	2.94
Executive, administrative, managerial	Homicide	.90	Motor vehicle	.63	3.59
Clerical	Homicide	.18	Motor vehicle	.18	.62

Source: Jenkins, E. L., Kisner, S. M., Fosbroke, D. E., Layne, L. A., Stout, N. A., Castillo, D. N., Cutlip, P. M., & Cianfrocco, R. (1993, August). *Fatal injuries to workers in the United States, 1980–1989: A decade of surveillance. National Profile.* Washington, DC: U.S. Government Printing Office, DHHS (NIOSH) Publication Number 93–108, pp. 10, 19.

facilities. Are postal workers at great risk of violence, particularly from disgruntled coworkers? An analysis of NIOSH National Traumatic Occupational Fatalities (NTOF) surveillance system data (U.S. DHHS, 1994) showed that neither the Postal Service industry nor postal occupations were among the groups at highest risk. For the period 1983–1993, the workplace homicide rate for the Postal Service, 0.63 per 100,000 workers, was just under the workplace homicide rate for all occupations from the NTOF. Coworkers appear to be disproportionately responsible for homicides that do occur in the Postal Service, but this needs some qualification. From 1983 to 1989, 20 out of 35 work-related homicides were committed by coworkers or former coworkers, but 14 of these occurred in a single incident.

The majority (80%) of workplace homicide victims in 1980–1992 were men, who face three times as high a risk as women. However, because women face fewer occupation hazards—working more rarely with heavy machinery or at elevations—homicide accounts for 42% of occupational injury deaths among them, in comparison to 11% among men. Most female victims worked in retail trade (46%) and service (22%) industries; most male victims worked in retail trade (36%); service industries (16%); public administration (11%); and transportation, communication, and public utilities (11%) (Jenkins, 1996b).

Older workers (65 years and over) had the highest homicide victimization rate—more than twice that for workers in the 55–64 age group. This was true for both males and females. Jenkins and colleagues attribute this pattern to the perception that older persons are "softer" targets and to their lesser ability to survive injuries (Jenkins, 1996b; Jenkins, Layne, & Kisner, 1992).

Minority groups have a higher risk of homicide—one fourth of homicide victims are Blacks, Asian Americans, and other minorities, although they make up only one eighth of the labor force. According to Toscano and Weber (1995), part of the reason for this is the concentration of minorities in occupations with high homicide rates (driving taxis, managing small stores, etc.).

The majority (76%) of work-related homicides between 1980 and 1992 were committed with a firearm, and 12% were attributed to wounds inflicted by cutting or piercing instruments.

Contrary to popular opinion, the predominant motive in workplace homicides was neither anger nor passion—as may appear from well-publicized events—but robbery. Toscano and Weber (1995) report that

> robberies and related crimes, usually committed by persons unknown to the victims, accounted for three-fourths of the 1,063 homicides at work in 1993 compared to one-seventh committed by disgruntled coworkers, clients, or personal acquaintances (p. 1).[1]

Even counting homicides in the course of robbery, however, workplace homicide is still a small proportion of all workplace violence. Comparing the estimated 1,044 workplace homicides in 1992 with the 668,000 incidents of workplace violence estimated from the National Crime Victimization Survey (see Table 2) suggests that, as noted earlier, only 1 in 650 workplace crimes of violence involved homicide. To put it differently, 99.8% of the victims of workplace violence survived.

Nonfatal Workplace Violence

Nonfatal workplace violence is less dramatic, receives much less attention, and may be even substantially understated in existing statistics (Toscano & Weber, 1995). National Crime Victimization Survey data for 1987–1992 indicate that over half of all victimizations sustained at work were not reported to the police (Bachman, 1994). Workplace assault victims tend not to report crimes committed by offenders with whom they have some relationship. In addition, among certain groups, crimes that contain elements of assault are viewed as part of everyday life and are consequently overlooked or not considered important enough to mention. Moreover, assault, a major category of nonfatal workplace violence, is recalled less accurately by survey respondents than any other crime measured by the National Crime Victimization Survey (Bureau of Justice Statistics, 1994).

Early studies of nonfatal workplace violence. Data on nonfatal workplace violence has accumulated only gradually, and the available research

---

[1]In August 1995, BLS updated the figure to 1,071 homicides, out of a total of 6,331 fatal work injuries (BLS *News*, August 3, 1995, p. 5 [footnote to Table 1]).

Table 2. All Crimes and Workplace Crimes, 1992

Type	All crimes		Workplace crimes		
	N	% occurring at work	N	%	Rate per 100,000 workers[a]
All types	32,979,340	15.1%	4,992,100	100.0%	4,245
Crimes of violence	5,964,090	11.2%	668,000	13.4%	568
Rape	131,530	6.0%	7,900	0.2%	7
Robbery	1,113,300	4.8%	53,400	1.1%	45
Aggravated assault	1,594,210	11.5%	183,300	3.7%	156
Simple assault	3,125,030	13.6%	425,000	8.5%	361
Crimes of theft	12,197,890	18.2%	2,220,000	44.5%	1,888
Personal larceny with contact	478,170	0.0%	0	0.0%	0
Personal larceny without contact	11,719,710	18.9%	2,215,000	44.4%	1,884
Household-type crimes	14,817,360	14.2%	2,104,100	42.1%	1,789
Burglary	4,757,420	23.9%	1,137,000	22.8%	967
Household larceny	8,101,150	9.2%	745,300	14.9%	634
Motor vehicle theft	1,958,780	11.1%	217,400	4.4%	185

Note: Excluded are homicides and victimless crimes, which are not covered by the NCVS. Figures may not add up to totals because of rounding.

Source: Bureau of Justice Statistics, 1994, p. 79.

[a]The rate is based on an assumed 117.6 million employed civilian workers in 1992 (Bureau of Justice Statistics, 1995a, p. 16).

has focused largely on the riskiest occupations. Some early work in the mid-1980s (Block, Felson, & Block, 1984) involved calculating crime victimization rates by occupation from the National Crime Survey (later renamed the National Crime Victimization Survey). Analyses of 108,000 victimization incidents among the employed (reported in 2 million interviews between 1973 and 1981) identified occupations at highest risk for robbery and assault as law enforcement officers, recreation and amusement workers, gardeners and groundskeepers, garage and gas station attendants, newsboys, athletes and related workers, social and recreational workers, busboys, taxi drivers and chauffeurs, and dishwashers. However, the data did not distinguish crimes of violence happening in the workplace and outside the workplace (Castillo, 1995), and the authors could not determine if risk was associated with the nature of the work or with the lifestyles of people doing the job.

The location of the crime was better determined in the 1982 Victim Risk Supplement to the National Crime Victimization Survey, allowing Lynch (1987) to restrict analysis to workplace incidents. Predicting victimization at work with multivariate models based on demographic variables and workplace characteristics, Lynch determined that risk of workplace victimization was less a function of the occupation itself than of the specific task the victim performed. In particular, risk was associated with tasks that involved considerable public accessibility, mobility, and handling of money. Confirmatory findings were reported by Collins and Cox (1987), who used a 1983 crime survey of District of Columbia residents.

Studies using workers' compensation data for such states as Ohio, Virginia, and Washington have presented similar findings (e.g., Alexander, Franklin, & Wolf, 1994; Hales, Seligman, Newman, & Timbrook, 1988; Seligman, Newman, Timbrook, & Halperin, 1987; Thomas, 1992; see Castillo, 1995, for a review). As with the victim studies, the groups at highest risk are found to be those in law enforcement and employees in such service industries as gas stations, hotels and motels, food stores, and restaurants and bars. Among other miscellaneous findings are the fact that, in Ohio, risk was highest among workers in the 20–34 age group. In Washington state, the majority of sexual assaults were reported by women working alone, the majority of the rapes were committed by strangers, and neither robbery nor the use of weapons commonly accompanied rape. All these studies, however, rest on somewhat fragile data (Castillo, 1995). Numbers of incidents tend to be small. Coverage is limited because workers' compensation excludes part-time or casual workers, taxi drivers, the self-employed, and government employees. Such state requirements as minimum numbers of workdays lost before a claim can be filed further limit coverage. And debates on the work-relatedness of assaults may have been used to quash filing of some claims and bias the samples (Castillo, 1995; Thomas, 1992).

Other studies have focused on the frequency and circumstances of assaults in specific industries and occupations: health care settings (Bensley, Nelson, Kaufman, Silverstein, & Kalat, 1993; Lipscomb & Love, 1992; Lusk, 1992; Mahoney, 1991), social service agencies (Civil Service Employees Association, 1993; Bowie, 1989; Rowett, 1986), convenience stores (Erickson, 1991; Schreiber, 1991), and law enforcement (Federal Bureau of Investigation [FBI], 1992; Uchida, Brooks, & Koper, 1987). These studies are useful in suggesting workplace-specific prevention strategies (Castillo, 1995).

Current data sources on nonfatal workplace violence. Three recent surveys provide the best current national data on nonfatal workplace violence: (a) the Bureau of Justice Statistics (BJS) *National Crime Victimization Survey* (NCVS) (Bastian, 1995; BJS, 1994); (b) the BLS *Annual Survey of Occupational Injuries and Illnesses* (BLS, 1994a, 1995b); and (c) Northwestern National Life's *Fear and Violence in the Workplace: A Survey Documenting the Experience of American Workers* (1993). (The main report on the Northwestern survey is reprinted in this volume as Appendix A.)

The 1993 NCVS is the latest available survey in a series of annual surveys of a nationally representative sample of 50,000 households (about

100,000 persons aged 12 years and older). Beginning in 1979, the NCVS underwent a decade-long redesign to improve its ability to measure victimization in general as well as difficult-to-measure crimes, such as rape, sexual assault, and domestic violence. The May 1995 BJS *Bulletin* (Bastian, 1995) presents the initial data from the redesigned NCVS: 1993 victimization estimates and first retabulations of 1992 data. The *Bulletin* cautions against comparing estimates before and after the redesign. The NCVS explicitly excludes homicide and victimless crime.

The BLS Survey of Occupational Injuries, unlike its Census of Fatal Occupational Injuries, is based on a field survey rather than a compilation of data from varied sources. The survey covers some 250,000 private industry establishments annually, excluding the self-employed, small farmers, and government workers. Thus law enforcement is not covered, nor health care and community workers employed by a government agency. The survey only counts injuries serious enough to result in lost workdays.

Undertaken by a private agency, the 1993 Northwestern National Life Survey was an attempt at a comprehensive assessment of the effects of workplace violence. A sample of 600 full-time U.S. workers responded to a 15-minute telephone interview in July 1993. Self-employed workers and the military were excluded from the sample. This survey has the most quoted statistics in the workplace violence literature. Its results are often cited, by human resource professionals and the media alike, as evidence of the pervasiveness and scope of workplace violence and of the need to develop prevention strategies. However, the survey was based on a very small sample, and has various other shortcomings. Methodological details and even actual frequencies are poorly reported. The response rate was probably around 30–40%, as researchers estimated after the survey (Larson, 1994). Nonresponse or other sample biases may be responsible for the fact that managers and professionals appear overrepresented (39% of the sample, but only 27% in the U.S. labor force) and service workers underrepresented (7% of the sample, versus 14% in the labor force) (Castillo 1995).

Estimates of nonfatal workplace violence. The three surveys provide data that could, in principle, be complementary, but the inconsistencies across the surveys suggest that, at a minimum, one should be careful to specify which survey provides a particular figure.

The NCVS data for 1987–1992 show that, on the average each year for this period, nearly one million U.S. residents 12 years of age and older reported being victims of violent crime at work or on duty (including rape, robbery, and simple and aggravated assault) (Bachman, 1994).[2] For 1992, the number was 668,000, which represents less than 1% of the labor force (Table 2).

---

[2]Crime data for 1993 using the redesigned NCVS survey are available, but as noted above, the 1993 data cannot be properly compared with earlier survey data before the redesign (Bastian, 1995, p. 6).

Simple assaults, which comprised over two thirds of workplace violent crimes, resulted in injuries to one out of every seven victims; aggravated assaults resulted in injuries to one out of every five victims; and robberies resulted in injuries to one out of every four victims (Kraus et al., 1995). All in all, slightly fewer than 160,000 victims suffered injuries (aside from rape), and 10% of these required medical care. It appears that more than half of all victimizations were not reported to the police. Of those not reporting, 40% considered the incident minor or a private matter and 27% said they had reported the incident to another official, such as a company security guard (Bachman, 1994).

The 1992 Survey of Occupational Injuries, on the other hand, reported 22,400 nonfatal workplace assaults. This is well below the NCVS figure. If one takes from the NCVS estimate only those suffering some injury and, among these, selects only those who probably reported the incident, one is still left with a figure at least three times as large as that from the Survey of Occupational Injuries. This survey, therefore, is not the appropriate source for an overall estimate and is not designed to cover representative incidents.

The Northwestern survey, on its part, suggests even higher victimization rates than NCVS. Of the 600 full-time workers surveyed, 3% reported being physically attacked some time between July 1992 and July 1993, three times the rate in the NCVS. The small size and other shortcomings of the Northwestern survey should be borne in mind. The survey does include information on incidents involving what was labeled above as workplace aggression: 19% of respondents reported threats of physical harm, and 7% reported being harassed. The survey also queried respondents about workplace violence experienced at any time in their lives, an interesting question but one with potential recall biases. Of the 600 respondents, 55% reported some form of workplace aggression during their lifetime: 15% claimed they had been physically attacked on the job, 21% had been threatened, and 19% had been harassed.

NCVS data show that 61% of victimizations occurred in private companies and 30% in government work settings, federal, state, or local. Given that government employees are only 18% of the U.S. labor force, their overrepresentation among victims may be due to a few particularly risky occupations, such as public safety personnel. At-work or on-duty victimizations mainly occurred in commercial establishments (23%); on public property such as streets and parks (22%); in offices, factories, or warehouses (14%); or in restaurants, bars, or nightclubs (13%) (Bachman, 1994). The Survey of Occupational Injuries provides a different but not inconsistent classification of incidents by industry. The industries having the highest number of assaulted workers were service (64%) and retail trade (21%). Among assault victims in the service industry, 27% of victims worked in nursing homes, 13% worked in social services, and 11% worked in hospitals.

NCVS reports that 32% of victims faced armed offenders, almost a third of whom had a handgun. The Survey of Occupational Injuries adds much more detail about the nature of the incidents (though, because of coverage, much of this detail may not be generalizable to all workplace violence incidents). Almost two thirds of nonfatal assaults occurred in service industries such as nursing homes, hospitals, halfway homes, and establishments providing residential care and other social services. The typical nonfatal assault covered in this survey was an encounter between a patient and nursing staff in a health care institution. Almost half (47%) of these nonfatal assaults were incidents involving hitting, kicking, or beating; another 23% involved such specified acts as rape and threats; 11% involved squeezing, pinching, scratching, and twisting; and 3% involved shootings (which accounted, by contrast, for 82% of fatal workplace assaults in 1992) (Jenkins, 1996b; Toscano & Weber, 1995).

According to NCVS, among persons victimized while working, men were more likely than women to experience a violent crime (but both sexes were just as likely to become the victims of theft at work). Men were also more likely to be attacked by a stranger (58% of victims), whereas women were more likely to be attacked by someone known to them (60%). The Survey of Occupational Injuries, by contrast, suggests that women outnumber men, by 56% to 44%, among assault victims. Given this female majority, one finds as expected that the assailant was, in the majority of cases, someone known to the victim, though 19 times out of 20, not one known "intimately"—not a husband, ex-husband, boyfriend, or ex-boyfriend. Of assault victims of both sexes in service industries, 45% reported the source of injury was a health care patient, 31% identified another person (e.g., visitor or robber), and 6% identified a coworker or former coworker. The Northwestern survey similarly suggests that assault by strangers was not the predominant risk. Of the 89 workers who had been physically attacked at work at some point in their lives, 44% reported being attacked by a customer or client, 30% by coworkers or former employee; 24% by strangers, and 3% by someone else.

The Northwestern survey is the only one to report victim reactions. The majority of the 328 cases experiencing workplace violence (attack, threat, or harassment) over their lifetime reported that the incident affected them negatively—victims were angry, fearful, stressed, intimidated, or depressed; work lives were disrupted; and some were physically injured or became ill. A few respondents did deny any negative effect on their lives. Interestingly, most workers perceived the major causes of workplace violence to be general social problems—alcohol and drug abuse, layoffs and firings, poverty, the availability of guns, and violence on TV or in the movies. Less than 35% of all workers attributed workplace violence to pressure on the job, overly controlling management, and conflicts with coworkers. The report on the Northwestern survey also argues that highly stressed workers are at greater risk of workplace violence, the experience of which leads to higher burnout rates. Good prevention programs can make a difference: Companies with effective grievance resolution, harassment prevention, and security programs had workers who reported less job dissatisfaction, lower burnout rates, and less frequent stress-related illness than did companies without such programs.

Significance

Government officials and corporate leaders are giving more attention to workplace violence. A specific focus on this problem is desirable for several reasons. First, it has distinct consequences, financial and otherwise, for corporate America. Although rare overall, workplace homicide is now the second leading cause of fatal occupational injuries. It may not often result from conflict between employees, but it still affects worker morale and corporate productivity. This is a dimension of workplace insecurity that feeds on and adds to business worries.

Second, the circumstances of workplace violence differ from the circumstances of violent crime in general. For instance, 75% of workplace homicides in 1993 were robbery-related, in contrast to only 9% of all homicides in the U.S. population (Jenkins, 1996b). As a consequence, the majority of workplace homicide victims did not know their assailants, whereas half of all homicide victims did.

Third, prevention of certain types of events is possible but requires tailored measures. Specific factors in the workplace are associated with the risk for workplace violence: contact with the public, the handling of cash, working alone or in small groups, working late at night or very early in the morning, working in high-crime areas, guarding valuable property or possessions, and working in community settings. Appropriate security measures and specific prevention efforts could therefore reduce the problem of workplace violence (e.g., Jenkins & Castillo, 1993; Jenkins, 1996b; U.S. DHHS, 1994).

Recognizing the significant risk of job-related violence faced by health care and social service workers, the U.S. Department of Labor Occupational Safety and Health Administration (OSHA) recently issued *Guidelines for Preventing Workplace Violence for Health Care and Social Service Workers* (OSHA, 1996; the Guidelines are reprinted in full in Appendix B, this volume). The guidelines are advisory in nature. Employers are encouraged to use the guidelines in providing a safe and healthful work environment through effective violence prevention programs adapted to each organization's needs and resources.

Costs of Workplace Violence

The costs of workplace violence appear particularly high. Bachman (1994) has calculated the annual cost of workplace violence for 1987–1992 using NCVS data. During this period, workplace victimizations (rape, robbery, and simple and aggravated assault, excluding homicide) resulted in half a million employees missing a total of 1,751,100 days of work, or an average of 3.5 days per crime. This resulted in over $55 million in lost wages annually, not including days covered by sick and annual leave. Injured victims bore higher costs, losing about 11 uncompensated days per incident.

For 1992, the BLS Survey of Occupational Injuries reports somewhat similar estimates. Nonfatal violent acts involving "hitting and kicking" resulted in an average of 5 days away from work for victims. For nonfatal gunshot wounds, most of the victims were men, and they needed on average 30 days away from work to recuperate (Toscano & Weber, 1995).

For the Federal Government workforce alone, Fiscal Year 1993 saw 2,185 cases of workplace violence recorded by the Office of Workers' Compensation Programs (OWCP). Of the nonfatal cases, 1,222 involved time lost from work, with the highest rates, among 30 federal departments and agencies, being for the Department of Justice and the Department of Veterans Affairs (Freeman, Fox, Burr, & Santasine, chapter 10, this volume).

In the case of corporations, Wheeler and Baron (1994) report that for one electronic company (the Elgar Corporation), one tragic shooting incident cost the company an estimated $400,000, beyond costs covered by insurance, plus an estimated premium increase of $100,000 annually for workers' compensation. The General Dynamics corporation spent an estimated $1.2 million after an employee killed and wounded several fellow workers, in addition to expenses covered by insurance. And the corporation continued to incur costs 12 months after the incident.

These estimates of costs are fragmentary. Much remains to be learned about the financial consequences of workplace violence. In fact, as Castillo (1995) notes, "To date, research into nonfatal workplace violence has been sketchy, and there are critical gaps in information" (p. 225).

Societal Roots of Workplace Violence

Does the level of workplace violence reflect the level of violence in the society as a whole? It is difficult to say: Given the paucity of data for other industrial countries, the societal comparisons that would be needed are mostly not possible. Perhaps a plausible connection can be made. On the other hand, societal violence in the U.S. does not appear to be on the increase, whereas concern about workplace violence does.

From a global perspective, if one looks beyond the workplace, the U.S. appears to be a relatively violent society, though not a world leader. World Health Organization (WHO) data on homicide put the U.S. far above most Westernized industrial societies, but below the former Soviet Union and a variety of developing societies, including Mexico and Colombia. Homicide rates (per 100,000) in the U.S. of 15.9 for males and 4.2 for females compare unfavorably with rates in Finland (4.6 and 2.4), Ireland (0.8 and 0.4), and Germany and the United Kingdom (in both cases, under 1.5 for males and under 1.0 for females). On the other hand, rates are worse in the Russian Federation (24.9 and 6.7) and Mexico (31.5 and 3.5) (Dobrin, Wiersema, Loftin, & McDowall, 1996).

Fear of violence, indeed, has been an American preoccupation for several decades. From a historical perspective, the themes of rage and violence, always pervasive in American social history and popular culture, have always fascinated the public. Violent crime generates not just fear but also morbid curiosity, humor, and perverse glamour. Crime is a spectator sport—from Jesse James to Bonnie and Clyde to the O. J. Simpson trial. The media highlights this spectacle by selectively covering highly dramatic examples of violent crime and conveying its message in a manner that simultaneously generates fascination and increased concern in the average citizen. Advances in media technology have made crime more immediate and dramatic rather than making citizens better informed about its causes and consequences.

Nevertheless, overall violent crime is not rising (though there are troubling trends in such areas as the younger age of offenders). In analyzing crime trends from 1972 to 1993, Blumstein and Heinz (1995) note that most people would be surprised to learn that murder and robbery, the most serious violent crimes, "have been oscillating around strikingly flat trends" (p. 3) for two decades. Rates for these crimes have remained within fairly confined ranges of 200–250 per 100,000 people for robbery and 8 to 10 per 100,000 for murder.

> Both the murder and the robbery rates peaked in about 1980 (as the baby boomers began to emerge from the high-crime ages), declined through the early 1980s, and then climbed again during the late 1980s with the spawning of the crack epidemic and the "war on drugs." Over this period, there is no statistically significant trend for murder, and a slight upward trend for robbery (an annual increase of 3.0 robberies per 100,000, or 1.35 percent of the mean robbery rate over the 22 years). (Blumstein & Heinz, 1995, p. 3)

In 1994, criminal offenses (excluding arson) totaled 13.99 million, down 1% from the 1993 figure of 14.14 million. The number of persons murdered in 1994 was estimated at 23,305, the lowest since 1989. The 1994 total, although 23% above the 1985 level, was 1% below 1990 and 5% below 1993 (FBI, 1995, pp. 5, 14).

Workplace violence may, indeed, reflect societal violence in general. But even if societal violence appears to be stable or abating at the moment, the data on workplace violence are not adequate at this time to allow us to draw the same conclusion about it.

Behavioral Perspectives on Workplace Violence

Workplace violence can also be viewed as individual behavior, with particular psychological roots and occurring in a specific situational context. Some writers have discussed workplace violence from this perspective. Most such reports specifically addressing workplace violence usually have been case studies or accounts of personal experiences in workplace violence prevention rather than systematic research on the interaction between personality and situational causes. Nonetheless, these reports provide useful leads.

One interesting summary was provided by Hoad (1993), who covered the British literature on workplace violence—implying, incidentally, that societally distinctive factors cannot be entirely to blame. A violent incident in a workplace is seen as the culmination of stressful interaction, aggravated by a vicious cycle of misconceptions, frustration, and anger. Some prevention professionals emphasize that violence is the last recourse of the powerless, who feel that their justifiable complaints are being ignored and that asserting one's rights in a calm and rational manner is futile. Obviously, we would add, the individuals' personal history with violence is highly relevant, as is their understanding and interpretation of violent acts against them, and their explanation and justification of their violent acts against others. Clearly, the beliefs one has formed about the world, how it operates (and why), and human behavior influence how one interprets and responds to future events.

In Hoad's (1993) summary of the most common causes of workplace violence in the United Kingdom, the following factors appear to have the most relevance:

1. *Feeling aggrieved.* A sense of being treated unfairly, whether real or imagined, may give rise to violence (see Folger & Baron, chapter 3, this volume).

2. *Being forced to wait* causes irritation and frustration. If some other stimulus, such as another person's behavior, acts as an "anger-eliciting cue," a violent reaction may result (see Felson & Tedeschi, 1993, or Tedeschi & Felson, 1994, for a full description of the societal interactionist approach).

3. *Perceived intrusions into private life.* People who have already experienced loss of self-esteem as a result of reprimands, layoffs, the need to apply for a loan, or the frustrations of job-hunting, may view personal or searching questions as demeaning to their dignity.

4. *Prejudice*, racial or sexual, may contribute to violent outbursts against members of another group.

5. *Staff attitudes.* Violence may occur if one staff member is seen as a threat to another, and an interchange spirals out of hand (see Toch, 1992, 1993, and Toch & Adams, 1994, for illustrations of the differences between encounters ending in violence and those ending without violence).

6. An *uncomfortable physical environment* may combine with other possible factors to create a potentially violent situation.

7. *Alcohol* may act as a depressant, reducing control over irresponsible behavior (see Bennett & Lehman, chapter 5, this volume).

8. *Mental instability* can lead to erratic behavior and irresponsible conduct.

Parallel to these attempts to describe the causes of violence have been attempts to predict it, most often in a non-workplace context. Early attempts were not too successful. Monahan (1981) provided the best summary of research up to 1981, which led him to conclude that "even in the best of circumstances ... psychiatrists and psychologists seemed to be wrong at least twice as often as they were right" (Monahan, 1984, p. 1). However, Monahan also suggested ways in which violence prediction might be improved: deemphasizing clinical prediction, for instance, and focusing on short-term prediction in community settings rather than long-term prediction in custodial institutions. Summaries of more recent research have become more positive. After reviewing 19 selected empirical studies, Chaiken, Chaiken, and Rhodes (1994), in a National Research Council report, concluded that

> Violence can be predicted, meaning that within a given population we can assign different probabilities of violence to population members based on the characteristics of those members. . . . Nevertheless, there are significant concerns with the validity, reliability, and accuracy of predictions. (pp. 279–280)

A more extensive review by Mossman (1994) of 44 published studies looked at both the sensitivity and specificity of predictions and concluded that, though far from perfect, predictions are substantially more accurate than expected by chance. Mossman also noted that, as Monahan suggested, clinical observation did not improve the combined sensitivity and specificity of predictions beyond what they would be based on an individual's past behavior.

Some attempts at prediction of workplace violence specifically have been made using a cognitive model. Akers, Krohn, Lanza-Kaduce, and Radosevich (1979) hypothesized that a person who defines deviant behavior as acceptable or justified is more likely to engage in it. Two subsequent studies attempted to test this hypothesis. Terris (1979) gave the Personnel Security Inventory-6 to employees of several companies and analyzed the results in relation to whether they admitted, on preemployment polygraph examinations, having been involved in previous violent incidents. The violence attitude scale of the inventory was strongly related to admitting previous violent behavior, including fighting, brawling, and the use of force or weapons. Jones (1980) also studied employees from several companies and found that the violence attitude scale predicted two factors extracted from verbal admissions: an argument factor and a physical assault factor. Jones concluded that an employee's tolerance for violence can be assessed through psychological tests, which provide a statistically reliable predictor of on-the-job aggression. Jones suggested that job applicants with a cognitive predisposition to violence can still be hired but should not be placed in jobs that are frustrating or demanding or that require considerable customer contact.

Violence is easier to predict in some situations than others, and workplace violence may be among the more difficult areas in which to make firm individual predictions. Predictions at the group level may appear relatively easy, but for workplace violence the infrequency of serious incidents, even when they are better reported, impedes generalization (Kuzmits, 1992). In addition, the accuracy expected from a group prediction is insufficient if the prediction is meant to apply to an individual and to affect his or her prospects. Personal histories can help in prediction but are not enough. Criminal records help predict violent behavior within 5 years of release from prison, but not within a few weeks of release from a mental health clinic. A history of violence in one's family background during childhood can help predict violent behavior in general during adulthood, but not on the job in the next 6 months. In general, repeat violence by one adult is considerably easier to predict than an initial violent act (Chaiken et al., 1994).

Predictive exercises have generally dealt with only one component of workplace violence, that attributable to employees, former employees, clients, or customers. Workplace violence due to strangers, violence in the course of robberies in the workplace, and violence as part of rape in the workplace have received less research attention, although they make up a larger proportion of workplace violence as a whole. These types of workplace violence need more systematic examination, as several chapters in this book attempt to provide.

Psychological Issues in Workplace Violence

The information on workplace violence available to date is clearly insufficient. Nonetheless, it confirms that workplace violence is indeed a serious matter worth sustained attention. Many interpretations and approaches to dealing with workplace violence reflected in other longstanding psychological research traditions may be relevant. The current state of knowledge is such that tentative understanding and initial preventive efforts are reasonable, while simultaneously conducting rigorous empirical evaluations and developing theoretical perspectives.

The following chapters develop the psychological perspective on workplace violence, highlighting the approaches to understanding and prevention that appear most promising and providing data where available. The chapters in Part I deal with psychological theories and analyses of workplace violence, in Part II with patterns and correlates of workplace violence, in Part III with specific high-risk occupations, and in Part IV with organized approaches to prevention and management of workplace violence. An introduction appears at the beginning of each Part and attempts to provide a concise summary. In the remainder of this section, we will provide an overview of the kinds of issues that the book as a whole tries to address.

What are the psychological roots of workplace violence? This is the central question for Part I. Can insights on workplace violence be gleaned from the long tradition of psychological research on aggression? Is workplace violence learned behavior, and does social learning theory have much to say about it? Are existing psychological theories adequate to address the phenomenon, or are there important areas of workplace violence outside the parameters of such theoretical constructs? Definitive answers to all these questions cannot be offered at this time, but the chapters in Part I attempt to address each of them with the best knowledge available.

Part II addresses less lofty but more specific questions. What behavioral and social patterns are related to workplace violence? What role in workplace violence is played by alcohol? By domestic abuse? By interpersonal conflict? By stress on the job? Do "dead-end" jobs in fact involve higher risk of death or injury from violence? Of the many possible questions about patterns and correlates of workplace violence, these have received some attention from psychologists and other behavioral scientists, and some empirically based insights are laid out in Part II.

Certain occupations, as we have stressed in this introduction, are at considerably higher risk of workplace violence than most others. What makes this so, and what psychological effects does it have on the workers? Part III ranges over a variety of high-risk occupations, attempting to answer questions of this type. Some questions addressed in particular chapters in Part III are:

- Among workers in high-risk occupations, are there systematic individual differences in exposure to risk? Can such differences be linked to personality style or other individual characteristics?
- Do some workers systematically underestimate the degree of their exposure to workplace violence? What factors differentiate those who underestimate and those who overestimate violence potential?
- How do workers in high-risk occupations deal with having been assaulted? In the helping professions, for example, can it produce dysfunctional role conflict?
- For some occupations, can the risk increase if you do your job well?
- Should suicide be viewed as workplace violence under some conditions? Is it affected by predisposing factors similar to those for other forms of violence?
- Are occupational risks specific to American culture, or are there cross-cultural parallels?

The grim situations considered in Part III contrast with much more positive questions for Part IV. Can workplace violence be prevented, and its consequences for individuals, their families, and businesses mitigated? What general psychological principles must be kept in mind in designing workplace violence prevention and management programs? Who should be involved? Is broad worker participation in a program necessary, or will physical security measures suffice? Are there existing models of programs that appear to be effective? The chapters in Part IV provide some answers to these issues. But, given what is not known, and what is still to be learned about workplace violence, none of the programs suggested should be taken as the final word or the ultimate solution.

This book attempts to contribute some behavioral insights on the issue of workplace violence and ways to reduce the risk. But a lot more multidisciplinary work needs to be done in refining data collection, analyzing causes and correlates, studying specific situations, and assessing outcomes of prevention efforts to ensure the security of the workplace. The process of doing this has begun in the past two decades, and this volume will hopefully further that process.

References

Akers, R., Krohn, M., Lanza-Kaduce, L., & Radosevich, M. (1979). Social learning and deviant behavior: A specific test of a general theory. *Sociological Review, 44*, 636–655.

Alexander, B. H., Franklin, G. M., & Wolf, M. E. (1994). The sexual assault of women at work in Washington state, 1980 to 1989. *American Journal of Public Health, 84*, 640–642.

Bachman, R. (1994, July). Violence and theft in the workplace. *Crime Data Brief: National Crime Victimization Survey.* Washington, DC: Bureau of Justice Statistics, U.S. Department of Justice.

Bastian, L. (1995, May). *Bulletin. Criminal victimization 1993* (National Crime Victimization Survey). Washington, DC: Bureau of Justice Statistics, U.S. Department of Justice.

Bensley, L., Nelson, N., Kaufman, J., Silverstein, B., & Kalat, J. (1993). *Study of assaults on staff in Washington State psychiatric hospitals.* Olympia, WA: State of Washington Department of Labor and Industries.

Block, R., Felson, M., & Block, C. (1984). Crime victimization rates for incumbents of 246 occupations. *Sociology and Social Research, 69*, 442–451.

Blumstein, A., & Heinz, H. J., III. (1995, July). Youth violence, guns and the illicit-drug industry. In National Institute of Justice, *Trends, risks, and interventions in lethal violence: Proceedings of the Third Annual Spring Symposium of the Homicide Research Working Group.* Research Report (pp. 3–15). Washington, DC: U.S. Department of Justice, Office of Justice Programs.

Bowie, V. (1989). *Coping with violence: A guide for the human services.* Sydney, Australia: Karibuni Press.

Bureau of Justice Statistics, U.S. Department of Justice. (1994, March). *Criminal victimization in the United States, 1992* (National Crime Victimization Survey Report, NCJ-145125). Washington, DC: Author.

Bureau of Labor Statistics, U.S. Department of Labor. (1994a, April 26). *News. Work injuries and illnesses by selected characteristics, 1992* [news release]. Washington, DC: Author.

Bureau of Labor Statistics, U.S. Department of Labor. (1994b, August 10). *News. National census of fatal occupational injuries, 1993* [news release]. Washington, DC: Author.

Bureau of Labor Statistics, U.S. Department of Labor. (1995a, January). *Employment and earnings.* Washington, DC: Author.

Bureau of Labor Statistics, U.S. Department of Labor. (1995b, April 26). *News. Work injuries and illnesses by selected characteristics, 1993* [news release]. Washington, DC: Author.

Bureau of Labor Statistics, U.S. Department of Labor. (1995c, August 3). *News. National census of fatal occupational injuries, 1994* [news release]. Washington, DC: Author

Castillo, D. N. (1995, July). Nonfatal violence in the workplace: Directions for future research. In C. Block & R. Block (Eds.), *Trends, risks, and interventions in lethal violence: Proceedings of the Third Annual Spring Symposium of the Homicide Research Working Group* (pp. 225–235). Washington, DC: U.S. Department of Justice.

Castillo, D. N., & Jenkins, E. L. (1994, February). Industries and occupations at high risk for work-related homicide. *Journal of Occupational Medicine, 36*, 125–132.

Chaiken, J., Chaiken, M., & Rhodes, W. (1994). Predicting violent behavior and classifying violent offenders. In A. J. Reiss, Jr., & J. A. Roth (Eds.), *Understanding and preventing violence. Volume 4. Consequences and control* (pp. 217–294). Washington, DC: National Academy Press.

Civil Service Employees Association. (1993). *A matter of life and death: Worksite security and reducing risks in the danger zone.* Albany, NY: Author.

Collins, J. J., & Cox, B. G. (1987). Job activities and personal crime victimization: Implications for theory. *Social Science Research, 16*, 345–360.

Davis, H. (1987). Workplace homicides of Texas males. *American Journal of Public Health, 77*, 1290–1293.

Dobrin, A., Wiersema, B., Loftin, C., & McDowall, D. (1996). *Statistical handbook on violence in America*. Phoenix, AZ: Oryx.

Erickson, R. (1991). Convenience store homicide and rape. In National Association of Convenience Stores, *Convenience store security: Report and recommendations* (pp. 16–18). Alexandria, VA: National Association of Convenience Stores.

Federal Bureau of Investigation. (1992). *Killed in the line of duty: A study of selected felonious killings of law enforcement officers*. Washington, DC: U.S. Department of Justice.

Federal Bureau of Investigation. (1995). *Crime in the United States 1994* (Uniform Crime Reports). Washington, DC: U.S. Department of Justice.

Felson, R. B., & Tedeschi, J. T. (Eds.). (1993). *Aggression and violence: Social interactionist perspectives*. Washington, DC: American Psychological Association.

Hales, T. H., Seligman, P. J., Newman, S. C., & Timbrook, C. L. (1988). Occupational injuries due to violence. *Journal of Occupational Medicine, 30*, 483–487.

Hoad, C. D. (1993). Violence at work: Perspectives from research among 20 British employers. *Security Journal, 4*, 64–86.

Jenkins, E. L. (1996a). Workplace homicide: Industries and occupations at high risk. *Occupational Medicine: State of the Art Reviews, 11*, 219–225.

Jenkins, E. L. (1996b). *Violence in the workplace: Risk factors and prevention strategies* (DHHS [NIOSH] Publication Number 96–100). Washington, DC: Government Printing Office.

Jenkins, E. L., & Castillo, D. N. (1993). NIOSH occupational homicide data. In U.S. Department of Justice, *Questions and answers in lethal and non-lethal violence. Proceedings of the second annual workshop of the Homicide Research Working Group. FBI Academy, Quantico, Virginia, June 13–17, 1993* (pp. 99–102, National Institute of Justice Research Report NCJ 147480). Washington, DC: U.S. Department of Justice.

Jenkins, E. L., Kisner, S. M., Fosbroke, D. E., Layne, L. A., Stout, N. A., Castillo, D. N., Cutlip, P. M., & Cianfrocco, R. (1993, August). *Fatal injuries to workers in the United States, 1980–1989: A decade of surveillance. National Profile* (DHHS [NIOSH] Publication Number 93–108). Washington, DC: U.S. Department of Health and Human Services.

Jenkins, E. L., Layne, L. A., & Kisner, S. M. (1992). Homicide in the workplace: The U.S. experience, 1980–88. *American Association of Occupational Health Nurses Journal, 40*, 215–218.

Jones, J. W. (1980, June). Attitudinal correlates of employee violence. *Journal of Security Administration, 3*, 42–47.

Kraus, J. F. (1987). Homicide while at work: Persons, industries, and occupations at high risk. *American Journal of Public Health, 77*, 1285–1289.

Kraus, J. F., Blander, B., & McArthur, D. L. (1995). Incidence, risk factors and prevention strategies for work-related assault injuries: A review of what is known, what needs to be known, and countermeasures for intervention. *Annual Review of Public Health, 16*, 355–379.

Kuzmits, F. E. (1992, Spring). Workplace homicide: Prediction or prevention. *SAM Advanced Management Journal, 57*, 4–7.

Larson, Erik. (1994, October 13). Trigger happy: A false crisis: How workplace violence became a hot issue. *The Wall Street Journal*, p. A1.

Lipscomb, J. A., & Love, C. C. (1992). Violence toward health care workers: An emerging occupational hazard. *American Association of Occupational Health Nurses Journal, 40*, 219–228.

Lusk, S. L. (1992). Violence experienced by nurses' aides in nursing homes: An exploratory study. *American Association of Occupational Health Nurses Journal, 40*, 237–241.

Lynch, J. P. (1987). Routine activity and victimization at work. *Journal of Quantitative Criminology, 3*, 283–300.

Mahoney, B. S. (1991). *Victimization of Pennsylvania emergency department nurses in the line of duty*. Unpublished doctoral dissertation, Pennsylvania State University.

Monahan, J. (1981). *The clinical prediction of violent behavior*. Washington, DC: U.S. Government Printing Office.

Monahan, J. (1984). The prediction of violent behavior: Toward a second generation of theory and policy. *American Journal of Psychiatry, 141*, 1–15.

Mossman, D. (1994). Assessing predictions of violence: Being accurate about accuracy. *Journal of Consulting and Clinical Psychology, 62*, 783–792.

Mountain States Employers Council & Nicoletti-Flater Associates. (1994). *Violence goes to work: An employer's guide*. Denver and Lakewood, CO: Author.

National Institute for Occupational Safety and Health, Centers for Disease Control and Prevention. (1993, August). *Fatal injuries to workers in the United States, 1980–89: A decade of surveillance*. Washington, DC: U.S. Department of Health and Human Services.

Northwestern National Life, Employee Benefits Division. (1993). *Fear and violence in the workplace: A survey documenting the experience of American workers*. Minneapolis, MN: Author.

Occupational Safety and Health Act of 1970. U.S. Public Law 91-596 (December 29, 1970).

Occupational Safety and Health Administration, U.S. Department of Labor. (1996). *Guidelines for preventing workplace violence for health care and social service workers*. Washington, DC: Author.

Rowett, C. R. (1986). *Violence in social work: A research study of violence in the context of local authority social work*. Cambridge, England: University of Cambridge Institute of Criminology.

Schreiber, F. B. (1991). 1991 national survey of convenience store crime and security. In *Convenience store security: Report and recommendations* (NACS report, pp. 12–15). Alexandria, VA: National Association of Convenience Stores.

Seligman, P. J., Newman, S. C., Timbrook, C. L., & Halperin, W. E. (1987). Sexual assault of women at work. *American Journal of Industrial Medicine, 12*, 445–450.

Tedeschi, J. T., & Felson, R. B. (1994). *Violence, aggression, and coercive actions*. Washington, DC: American Psychological Association.

Terris, W. (1979). Attitudinal correlates of employee integrity: Theft-related admissions made in a pre-employment polygraph examination. *Journal of Security Administration, 2*, 30–39.

Thomas, J. L. (1992). Occupational violent crime: Research on an emerging issue. *Journal of Safety Research, 23*, 55–62.

Toch, H. (1992). *Violent men: An inquiry into the psychology of violence*. Washington, DC: American Psychological Association.

Toch, H. (1993). *Living in prison: The ecology of survival*. Washington, DC: American Psychological Association.

Toch, H., & Adams, K. (1994). *The disturbed violent offender*. Washington, DC: American Psychological Association.

Toscano, G., & Weber, W. (1995, April). Violence in the workplace. *Compensation and working conditions*. Washington, DC: U.S. Department of Labor, Bureau of Labor Statistics.

Uchida, C. D., Brooks, L. W., & Koper, C. S. (1987). Danger to police during domestic encounters: Assaults on Baltimore County police, 1984–86. *Criminal Justice Prevention Review, 2*, 357–371.

U.S. Department of Health and Human Services. (1994, August 19). Occupational injury deaths of postal workers—United States, 1980–89. *Morbidity and Mortality Weekly Report, 43*, pp. 587, 593–595.

Wheeler, E. D., & Baron, S. A. (1994). *Violence in our schools, hospitals and public places*. Ventura, CA: Pathfinder Publishing of California.

Windau, J., & Toscano, G. (1994, February). Workplace homicides in 1992. *Compensation and Working Conditions*, pp. 1–8.

Part I

The Problem of Workplace Violence

Introduction

These three chapters (Chapters 2–4) attempt to provide meaning and theoretical context to the statistics on workplace violence. Barling provides a model of workplace violence grounded in social learning theory. He looks for the causes of violence in contextual and personal factors and in their interaction, specifically in stress produced in the individual by the work situation. Work stress, he argues, can be tied to context (i.e., to specific objective, quantifiable workplace events). The effect of these stressors depends on the individual's perception of them, and may lead to psychological or even physical strain. The direct outcome of violence for the victim, on the other hand, is immediate mood and cognitive distraction. Resulting from this direct outcome are a number of possible indirect outcomes, including emotional exhaustion, depression, psychosomatic complaints, accidents, and turnover intentions. The severity of direct and indirect outcomes depends on the victim's perceptions, which in turn are based on several dimensions of the violent event itself that combine in some additive fashion.

An alternative theoretical approach is taken by Folger and Baron, who derive their theory from the extensive research on human aggression and the growing body of literature on the causes and effects of felt injustice. For them, workplace violence and aggression result from a complex interplay among several factors: recent changes in work settings, such as restructuring and downsizing; employee reactions to such changes, including perceptions of unfairness and feelings of resentment; and certain personal characteristics, such as the tendency to attribute others' actions to hostile intent. Their analysis leads them to propose measures to reduce workplace aggression, focusing primarily on avoiding or at least reducing perceptions of unfair treatment.

White provides not a theory but a call for careful analytical examination of the issue of workplace violence, to confront public misperceptions of its magnitude with the statistical facts. Workplace violence has become a major social issue despite limited information about it. What information exists has not always filtered through to the public. Indeed, as the introductory chapter to this book notes, few people recognize that violence against workers by their coworkers is a relatively minor part of workplace violence, which more frequently involves assaults or threats from strangers. The limited understanding of the phenomenon needs to be taken into account when psychologists and other professionals attempt to design ways to prevent workplace violence and manage its effects. Professionals also need to become more aware of the legal issues involved and the potential liabilities when they attempt to intervene.

2

The Prediction, Experience, and Consequences of Workplace Violence

Julian Barling

The workplace is one location in which many people typically have felt safe, at least safe from the reality of violence in the rest of their environments. However, workplace violence is on the rise, and the workplace is no longer a safe haven from the ills of society (Leather, Cox, & Farnsworth, 1990; McLean Parks & Kidder, 1994). Although some employees, by the nature of their jobs (e.g., police), might reasonably expect to encounter violence at work, more and more employees in supposedly low-risk jobs are experiencing the effects of violence (Hill, 1988). Homicide in the workplace, the most severe form of workplace violence, is the fastest growing form of murder in the United States (Anfuso, 1994; Stuart, 1992), and murder is now the single most common cause of death on the job in New York State. Murder also is now the leading cause of death in the workplace for women and the third most frequent cause for men (Anfuso, 1994; Toufexis, 1994).

The overwhelming magnitude of this trend toward workplace violence cannot be overstated. A 1993 survey conducted by Northwestern National Life Insurance suggested that more than 2 million employees suffer physical attacks at work each year and that more than 6 million are threatened in some way at work (see Anfuso, 1994; also see Appendix A, this volume). As alarming as these data are, they probably underestimate the magnitude of the problem: It has been known for some time that five incidents of violence occur against employees for each one that is reported (Lion, Snyder, & Merrill, 1981). Recent research also has suggested that any effects of workplace violence are far more widespread than considered previously (e.g., Hall & Spector, 1991; Schwarz & Kowalski, 1993; Sutker, Uddo, Brailey, Vasterling, & Errera, 1994).

Most of this research has concentrated on the prevalence and incidence of workplace violence and on the demographic characteristics of the

Preparation of this chapter was supported by grants from the Social Sciences and Humanities Research Council of Canada, the Advisory Research Council, and the School of Business, Queen's University, Kingston, Ontario, Canada. The comments of Helen Sandys-Wunsch, Lianne Greenberg, and Kevin Kelloway throughout various stages of the preparation of this chapter are acknowledged.

victims and perpetrators. By contrast, much less research has been conducted on the predictors and outcomes of workplace violence. The findings that do exist are frequently contradictory because of the inconsistency of the definition and lack of an adequate measurement tool across studies.

The aims of this chapter are threefold. First, possible predictors of workplace violence are discussed. Second, a brief conceptualization of the psychological experience of workplace violence is presented. Finally, the personal and organizational consequences of violence in the workplace are considered. At a general level, the discussion of the predictors and outcomes of the workplace violence, together with a consideration of the psychological experience of workplace violence, also serve as an agenda for future research.

Toward a Conceptualization of Workplace Violence

The use of the term *workplace violence* is remarkably varied in the literature, leading to confusion and incomparable results between studies (Lanza, Kayne, Hicks, & Milner, 1991). Often, some type of severe bodily injury is considered symptomatic of violence, but this approach is problematic because it reflects only a small portion of workplace violence (Slora, Joy, & Terris, 1991) and implies erroneously that violence should be defined according to its effects. A more appropriate approach describes workplace violence in terms of behaviors that range from the least physically injurious (e.g., pushing and shoving) to the most severe (e.g., assault and murder; Slora et al., 1991).

The primary focus in this chapter is on physical aggression or violence in the workplace rather than on "psychological aggression." In developing this chapter, however, I could not ignore completely psychological violence in the workplace for several reasons. First, psychological violence in the workplace is more frequent than physical violence. In a study of 136 men, 82%, 74%, and 76% admitted to some form of psychological violence against coworkers, subordinates, and supervisors, respectively (Greenberg & Barling, 1995). By contrast, only 2 of the 136 respondents reported using physical aggression at work. Second, and perhaps more important, on the basis of research from the literature on family violence, it is apparent that incidents of psychological violence precede physical aggression (Murphy & O'Leary, 1989). This is an important finding because of the longitudinal nature of the study: Murphy and O'Leary found that, among a group of people with no prior experience of physical aggression, psychological aggression predicted first instances of physical aggression 6 and 12 months later. Moreover, they found that marital dissatisfaction alone (i.e., with no concurrent psychological aggression) did not precede physical aggression. If these findings are replicated in the workplace, there will be considerable intervention and prevention implications: Job dissatisfaction alone might not predict workplace violence. (This issue is explored in more detail later.)

The model of workplace violence that I propose draws primarily on two types of literature, as will become evident. First, I examined the literature on work stress in general and acute work stressors or workplace disasters in particular. In this respect, I assumed that the outcomes of workplace violence would bear some similarity to the consequences of acute workplace stressors or disasters. Second, I used the literature on family violence as an aid in generating hypotheses about the prediction of workplace violence and in understanding the effects of workplace violence.

Predicting Workplace Violence

Despite the enormity of the problem of workplace violence, there is still little scientific information about the causes and predictors of workplace violence. Indeed, a general reading of the literature would reveal that most of the information that is available tends to come from one of several sources: descriptive statistics from surveys or inferences drawn from post hoc investigations of violent incidents such as murders in the United States Postal Service (e.g., "A Post Office Tragedy," 1992) or in other workplaces in different countries (Cowan, 1994). There also have been attempts to construct a profile of the "typical," or average, "disgruntled worker," invariably to construct screening devices that would exclude such employees from the workplace to begin with (Slora et al., 1991). Such attempts, however, have not resulted in a validated questionnaire (Anfuso, 1994).

On the basis of these sources, together with information about the prediction of family violence, I suggest that both contextual (or workplace) factors and personal factors will predict workplace violence (see Figure 1).

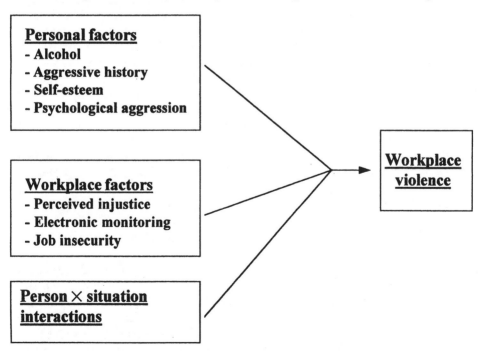

Figure 1. Predictors of workplace violence.

Workplace Factors

Previous researchers have concentrated almost exclusively on personal factors in an attempt to predict workplace violence. Consistent with social learning theory (Bandura, 1973), however, I suggest that an approach that takes into account both the person and the situation, and their interaction, will result in a more valid predictive model. Work stress in general is associated with marital violence (Barling & Rosenbaum, 1986), and three specific workplace factors that may be of considerable relevance in predicting workplace violence are employees' perceived workplace justice, the use of electronic surveillance, and feelings of job insecurity.

Organizational justice reflects employees' perceptions of fairness about procedures and policies (procedural justice) as well as organizational outcomes (i.e., distributive justice; Greenberg, 1990a). There are several reasons why perceived justice with respect to policies and procedures may affect workplace violence. At a general level, Greenberg (1990b) found that when employees perceived an inequity in the workplace (in his research, it was a short-term pay freeze), they engaged in attempts to restore their sense of justice (by employee theft). In that research, the inequity and the consequences were both financially related. By extension, if employees perceive themselves to be threatened at work, whether in terms of a physical threat or a perceived threat to the security of their work, violence may be a predictable outcome.

At an anecdotal level, several workplace murders have been attributed to workers who had been passed over for promotions or laid off, believing that the procedures used were unfair (McGarvey, 1994; Stuart, 1992). Certainly, the congressional investigation into the murders at the Royal Oaks Post Office attributed unfair management procedures and intimidating and inconsistent disciplinary procedures as one of the precipitating events ("A Post Office Tragedy," 1992). Likewise, the murder of four people at Concordia University in Montreal was preceded by one individual's fears that tenure might not be granted (Cowan, 1994). Thus, although it is not the only causal factor, perceptions of procedural injustice may predict workplace violence.

An overly close and punitive style of supervision has been characteristic of many workplaces throughout the 20th century. Although by no means a new practice, as is evident from Charlie Chaplin's movie *Modern Times*, one recent and dramatic development in the workplace involves the increased use of electronic monitoring (Schliefer, 1992). Garson (1985) noted that electronic monitoring is an invasion of privacy and that it is a management technique designed to increase the pace of work and exert greater managerial control. Electronic monitoring is associated with psychological stress and strain (Lund, 1992; Schliefer, 1992). Given both the rapid increase in the pace of work in organizations, together with the use of electronic monitoring that has pervaded organizations experiencing workplace violence such as the United States Postal Service, I predict that the experience of being monitored electronically may indeed increase the likelihood of workplace violence. In one study, Greenberg and Barling

(1995) showed that both perceived injustice and electronic surveillance were associated with workplace aggression. However, the generalizability of their findings may be restricted because only psychological aggression at work was studied.

With continued downsizing, mergers, and restructuring, job insecurity is widespread, and job insecurity may precipitate workplace violence for two reasons: First, the psychological bases of job insecurity are feelings of powerlessness and loss of control (Ashford, Lee, & Bobko, 1989), which themselves may increase the likelihood of violence being perceived as one possible means for regaining control. Second, different writers have noted that murder and incidents of less severe workplace violence sometimes occur after employees are laid off (e.g., McGarvey, 1994; Stuart, 1992; Thompson, 1994). Thus, job insecurity will predict workplace violence to the extent to which it is experienced as a direct threat.

Before discussing personal factors that predict workplace violence, it is worth noting that most of the references cited earlier linking workplace factors and employee violence (e.g., Cowan, 1994; McGarvey, 1994; "A Post Office Tragedy," 1992; Stuart, 1992; Thompson, 1994) were not based on empirical research. Future researchers ought to investigate the extent to which perceived organizational justice, electronic surveillance, and job insecurity predict workplace violence, especially because Greenberg and Barling's (1995) findings pertain only to psychological violence in the workplace. It also would be useful for future research to identify other workplace predictors.

Personal Factors

Inspection of the literature might suggest that personal factors alone contribute to workplace violence. This literature overwhelmingly has focused on the development of a profile of the "disgruntled" employee, with the implication that preselection (or more accurately, preexclusion) of such individuals could reduce dramatically incidents of workplace violence. However, this literature is limited because it is descriptive rather than predictive and it is at a level of generality that fosters neither research nor practical interventions.

Largely on the basis of the literature on family violence, I expect that four personal factors will predict workplace violence: alcohol use, past history of aggression, lack of self-esteem, and the use of psychological aggression in the workplace.

Excessive alcohol use is associated with aggressive behavior across a variety of settings, including family violence (e.g., Heyman, O'Leary, & Jouriles, 1995; Pan, Neidig, & O'Leary, 1994). Profiles of potentially violent employees emphasize their excessive alcohol consumption (Graham, 1991). From a more psychologically oriented perspective, Cox and Leather (1994) argued that alcohol abuse will increase workplace violence because it increases the likelihood of the situation being "misread" and decreases intellectual and verbal functioning. Greenberg and Barling (1995) found that binge drinking was associated with psychological aggression against coworkers and subordinates. Thus, inappropriate alcohol use will predict workplace violence.

There are several reasons why an individual's past history of aggression might predict workplace violence. First, aggression is a highly stable behavior (Huesmann, Eron, Lefkowitz, & Walder, 1984). Malone, Tyree, and O'Leary (1989) reviewed the literature on family violence and found that the use of aggression as an adolescent was associated with current marital violence. The previous use of aggression also has been documented as being one of the personal characteristics of aggressive employees in attempts to profile the potentially aggressive employee (Graham, 1991; Mantell & Albrecht, 1994). In addition, the history of aggression against peers and families while still a teenager was a substantial predictor of psychological aggression against coworkers and subordinates (Greenberg & Barling, 1995). Thus, because aggression is stable across contexts and across time, an individual's past history of aggression in general will predict violence in the workplace.

The third personal factor that predicts workplace violence is lack of self-esteem. Poor self-esteem is a characteristic of aggressive children (Lochman & Lampron, 1986) and aggressive spouses (Rosenbaum & O'Leary, 1981), and a threat to self-esteem can arouse an aggressive response (Caprara et al., 1987). Again, low self-esteem is supposedly characteristic of aggressive employees (Mantell & Albrecht, 1994). Issues of causality remain to be resolved, however. Just as it is possible that low self-esteem results in employees' resorting to workplace violence, it is equally possible that individuals who resort to physical violence in the workplace and elsewhere experience diminished self-esteem as a result. The possibility that self-esteem is implicated both as a cause and an effect should not be ignored.

Although the focus in this chapter specifically is on physical violence in the workplace, psychological aggression cannot be ignored for several reasons, as noted earlier. Perhaps the most important of these emerges from research on family violence, in which it has been shown in a longitudinal design that psychological aggression precedes marital violence but that marital dissatisfaction does not (Murphy & O'Leary, 1989). If this phenomenon is replicated in the workplace context, there would be important implications for intervention and possible prevention.

Person–Situation Interactions

Although it is possible that personal or work factors might operate separately in predicting workplace violence, a more comprehensive understanding can be gleaned from their interaction. The notion that personal and situational factors will interact in predicting workplace violence is consistent with social learning theory (Bandura, 1973). In particular, the effects of workplace factors (perceived injustice, electronic surveillance, and job insecurity) will be greatest under conditions of high alcohol consumption, a long history of past general aggression, and low self-esteem. By contrast, the influence of perceived injustice, electronic surveillance, and job insecurity will be minimized when alcohol consumption is normal, there is little history of past aggression, and self-esteem is good.

Some support has been obtained for such interaction effects (Greenberg & Barling, 1995). Specifically, high alcohol consumption exacerbated the effects of job insecurity and procedural justice on psychological aggression against subordinates and of procedural justice on psychological aggression against coworkers. This research also showed the importance of Person × Workplace interactions in predicting workplace sexual harassment (Dekker & Barling, 1995). One specific direction for future research therefore would be to examine other interactions among personal factors (e.g., a history of aggression, alcohol use, self-esteem, and current use of psychological aggression in the workplace) and workplace factors (e.g., perceptions of justice, electronic surveillance, and job insecurity).

Before concluding this section on predicting workplace violence, it is noteworthy that the target of workplace violence has been ignored. Greenberg and Barling (1995), however, found that somewhat different factors predict psychological aggression against supervisors, coworkers, and subordinates. Although the generalizability of this finding may be limited because of their concentration on psychological aggression, it does point to the need for future researchers to specify more clearly the target of physical violence in the workplace.

The Psychological Experience of Workplace Violence

In searching for models to aid in understanding the nature and consequences of workplace violence, the literature on family violence may be especially useful because of its considerable emphasis on understanding the victims. However, in considering the consequences of workplace violence, some deviation is necessary in one important respect. In the literature on family violence, the research focus primarily has been on what would be called the *primary victim* (i.e., the individual who was abused). There certainly is some research on the primary victims of workplace violence. For example, employees who were held up in bank robberies (Leymann, 1988), train drivers who hit someone who jumped onto the tracks (Farmer, Tranah, O'Donnell, & Catalan, 1992; Theorell, Leymann, Jodko, Konarski, & Norbeck, 1994), reservists engaged in grave registration duty during Operation Desert Storm (Sutker et al., 1994), and military personnel engaged in peace-keeping missions (Lamerson & Kelloway, 1995) all suffer an increased risk of developing posttraumatic stress disorder. However, an understanding of the effects of workplace violence must go further and consider the perceptions and behaviors of "secondary" victims (i.e., employees who themselves were not violated but whose perceptions, fears, and expectations are changed as a result of being vicariously exposed to the violence).

Embracing this perspective has important implications for the way in which the psychological experience of workplace violence should be studied. First, an objective approach to understanding workplace violence cannot be sufficient. An objective approach would classify individuals according to whether they have personally experienced workplace violence or dichotomously classify events as violent. A more productive approach would emphasize individuals' perceptions of workplace events, which would be consistent with a traditional work stress framework (Pratt & Barling, 1988), in which objective, quantifiable workplace events are stressors; individuals' interpretations and perceptions of these events reflect psychological stress; and it is the stress that ultimately generates psychological or physical strain. A second major implication of this framework is that the perception of the workplace event is multifaceted (with actual exposure reflecting only one of its perceived characteristics).

Subjective Experience of Workplace Violence

Understanding the subjective experience of workplace violence is important in itself and also helps in predicting how different people exposed to workplace violence might respond differently. An understanding of the subjective experience of workplace violence is complicated because individuals neither experience nor respond to workplace violence in the same way. Having said that, there is a set of core experiences that includes direct or vicarious exposure to the violence, perceived vulnerability, the "low point" (explained later), predictability, and severity that together constitute the subjective experience of workplace violence.

Exposure to the violence. As stated previously, one need not be the direct object of workplace violence to be affected. Exposure to workplace violence can occur personally or vicariously. For example, employees can witness workplace violence directly or view fellow employees being attacked, such as in a bank robbery, where there would presumably be more vicarious than direct victims. Similarly, if a former employee returns to the worksite to settle violently a perceived grievance with a specific supervisor, there would be both direct and vicarious victims. In addition, employees may view stories about workplace violence on TV or hear about workplace violence through friends or read reports in the newspapers. Such vicarious exposure presumably would be detrimental because employees may infer that they, too, might be attacked in a similar fashion in the future. Extrapolating from Bandura's (1973) social learning theory, direct exposure to workplace violence will be more harmful than vicarious exposure, which in turn will be more personally damaging than hearing or reading about the incident.

Vulnerability, or the "loss" of control. As noted earlier, the different aspects of perceived workplace violence combine to affect employees. For example, the nature of the exposure to workplace violence might well affect employees' perceived vulnerability, that is, beliefs about whether they themselves might become primary victims (Killias, 1990).

Killias (1990) suggested that three main factors are involved in vulnerability: exposure to risk (i.e., workplace violence), loss of control, and the anticipation of serious consequences. Exposure to workplace violence already has been discussed. Killias's notion of the anticipation of serious consequences is highly similar to that of the low point. What is critical here (and again shows the interactive nature of the dimensions under consideration) is that exposure to workplace violence will be associated with feelings of *loss* of personal control. Whereas employees previously believed that they exerted sufficient control over workplace events, they may now believe that they have lost the ability to control one of their most basic needs (i.e., the need for a safe and secure workplace).

The difference between the *loss* and the *lack* of control is critical for understanding the experience and consequences of workplace violence, and the literature on work stress is instructive. Workplace or technological disasters have been shown to exert more negative effects than natural disasters, presumably because they involve a loss of control: Initially, individuals had or perceived they had control, but they feel they have lost control (e.g., once they agreed to the implementation of a process or technological processes were introduced that removed decision making from them). By contrast, natural disasters (e.g., hurricanes) involve a feeling of a lack of control and individuals probably do not believe they had any control over the event in the first place (see Baum, Fleming, & Davidson, 1983). This suggests that the feelings of loss of control following exposure to workplace violence may exert substantial negative effects.

The low point of the violent episode. One critical question is when any negative effects after a violent episode in the workplace might be expected to subside. Research on disasters has identified dimensions that affect the nature and severity of the outcomes. One additional dimension that has received empirical attention is the low point, which is the point at which individuals involved personally or vicariously (a) no longer perceive any likelihood of recurrence of the violent event or (b) believe the consequences of the event have dissipated. Events that have long-lasting outcomes are typically those in which individuals are chronically concerned about recurrence, or the long-term consequences, as was the case at Three Mile Island, which involved lingering uncertainty about potential long-term effects of the event (e.g., exposure to radioactivity; Baum et al., 1983). Indeed, the actual time elapsed since a critical event bears little relation to the negative psychological and physiological consequences. The low point in the Three Mile Island disaster (which occurred more than 15 years ago) has probably still not been reached because of chronic concerns about initial exposure to radioactivity and its possible negative consequences, and the long-term effects of the disaster endure (Davidson, Fleming, & Baum, 1987). By contrast, an explosion at a dynamite factory that killed 14 people and obliterated the buildings involved but that had little likelihood of recurrence exerted no effects on organizational commitment, job satisfaction, personal well-being, or marital satisfaction after 14 days (Barling, Bluen,

& Fain, 1987), probably because the low point was reached immediately after the event.

The low point also could be extremely useful in predicting how long-lasting the negative effects of any workplace violence might endure. Because events lacking a clear low point will result in long-term strain, only when employees believe that they are no longer likely to experience workplace violence will they become free of negative symptoms (cf. Pratt & Barling, 1988; Solomon & Thompson, 1995).

Predictability. Baum et al. (1983) suggested that the lack of predictability in a natural or technological disaster contributes to the aftermath's severity. Warning of a disaster allows individuals to take precautionary measures to minimize the subsequent impact (i.e., evacuation prior to or seeking shelter during a tornado warning). This suggests that employees who can predict violence and are prepared to deal with such events may not experience negative outcomes to the same degree of severity or duration. For example, prison guards are expected to deal with violence from inmates; thus, they are constantly vigilant, receive training on how to deal with violent incidents, and are more prepared to deal with violence. On the other hand, teachers do not expect to have to manage violent behavior on the job, and they often are given no training in how to do so. Hence, the teacher who is slapped, shoved, pushed, or even threatened by a student might experience workplace violence differently than a prison guard who is threatened or assaulted by an inmate. Findings from a study by Barling (1995) provide some support for this: Although military police experienced twice the level of workplace violence as wait staff in a restaurant (they completed identical questionnaires), exposure to such violence for military police had no negative effects, whereas exposure for the wait staff was associated with negative organizational outcomes (e.g., intentions to quit the job, weaker company loyalty).

Severity. It is assumed that the severity of workplace violence will be related to the severity of the psychological and physiological outcomes. In the most literal sense, the more violent the crime, the more severe the direct physical threat to person, property, or both.

Thus, a violent event has several dimensions that would influence victims' subjective experience of workplace violence. These characteristics combine additively to determine how adverse the experience of workplace violence might be. Thus, employees who are the primary victims of extreme physical violence feel that they have lost control within the organization, believe that violence is likely to recur but that they cannot predict where or when, and are most likely to experience workplace violence the most negatively.

Outcomes of Workplace Violence

The effects of workplace violence are numerous, varied, and related to the nature of the violence. Primarily on the basis of previous research that I have conducted on work stress (Barling, 1990, 1992, 1994; Barling & MacEwen, 1992; MacEwen & Barling 1991; MacEwen, Barling, & Kelloway, 1992; Stewart & Barling, in press), unemployment experiences (Grant & Barling, 1994), retirement experiences (Higginbottom, Barling, & Kelloway, 1993), Type A behavior (MacEwen & Barling, 1993), and sexual harassment (Barling et al., in press), I have generated a mediational model predicting that workplace violence will exert direct and indirect outcomes. Direct outcomes are considered to be the first effect of the psychological experience of workplace violence (specifically, negative mood and cognitive distraction). Indirect outcomes are a consequence of the direct outcomes (e.g., emotional exhaustion, depression, psychosomatic complaints, accidents, turnover intentions). The model of how these dimensions influence personal and organizational factors is depicted in Figure 2.

Direct Outcomes

On the basis of my prior research, I expect that the direct outcomes of workplace violence will be negative mood (e.g., anger, anxiety, depressive symptoms) and cognitive distraction. However, to understand the consequences of workplace violence, fear is included as a third direct outcome because it is expected that it will be a critical direct outcome of workplace violence. In turn, these three variables would be responsible for transmitting any effects of the experience of workplace violence to psychological, psychosomatic, and organizational outcomes.

Negative mood. There is substantial empirical evidence showing that stress in general, and workplace stress as well, affect negative mood. This effect is stable across diverse settings (e.g., Solomon & Thompson, 1995), which supports the robust nature of this phenomenon. Focusing on work stress, for example, daily work stress (Barling & Kryl, 1990; Barling & MacIntyre, 1993; MacEwen et al., 1992) and chronic work stress (Barling & MacEwen, 1992; Motowidlo, Manning, & Packard, 1986; Stewart & Barling, in press) are associated with negative mood. More specific work-related stressors, such as experiencing sexual harassment (Barling et al., in press), unemployment (Grant & Barling, 1994) and Type A behavior (MacEwen & Barling, 1993), also have been associated with negative mood and depressive symptoms. These findings are consistent with McManus's (1992) observation that exposure to workplace violence leads to emotional numbing. Results of several studies also have indicated that negative mood mediates the relation between psychological stress and other negative outcomes (e.g., Barling & MacEwen, 1992; Kelloway & Barling, 1991). Thus, negative mood will mediate any negative effect of the experience of workplace violence on organizational and personal outcomes.

Cognitive distraction. Within the literature on stress there also is support for the notion that stress alters arousal and attention: When arousal

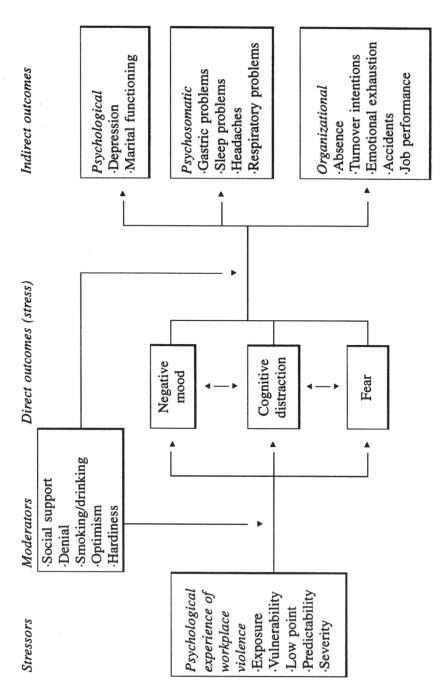

Figure 2.   Outcomes of workplace violence.

and stress are either above or below an optimal level, attention will be affected negatively. Workplace stressors produce cognitive overarousal as individuals increase their vigilance in an attempt to cope with the situation. There is some empirical support for this notion. For example, the chronic stress caused by unemployment is related to cognitive difficulties (Fryer & Warr, 1984). Likewise, chronic work stress is associated with cognitive distraction (Barling & MacEwen, 1992), as is the chronic stress associated with balancing employment and child-care demands (MacEwen & Barling, 1993) and employment and elder-care responsibilities (Barling, MacEwen, Kelloway, & Higginbottom, 1994). Again, the notion that cognitive difficulties will be a result of exposure to workplace violence is consistent with the finding that nurses who had been assaulted by patients subsequently reported difficulties concentrating on the job (Whittington & Wykes, 1989). In addition, chronic stress is associated with intrusive imagery (Baum, 1990). Consequently, exposure to workplace violence will result in cognitive difficulties, which in turn will predict negative psychological and organizational outcomes.

Fear of violence. One of the major consequences of exposure to workplace violence, whether experienced directly or vicariously, will be fear. Recent research has shown that being the primary victim of an episode of physical violence is not required for individuals to experience negative effects. Likewise, the violent crime rate was not related to perceived danger of victimization (Hall & Spector, 1991). Instead, the widespread effect and importance of the fear of being a victim of workplace violence has been demonstrated.

Perceived danger had a significant positive correlation with anxiety and illness symptoms in Hall and Spector's (1991) research. In a study of bank employees, perceived fear of workplace violence was associated with psychosomatic outcomes and thoughts about quitting the organization (Rogers & Kelloway, in press). In terms of the fear of violence, bus drivers indicated that the possibility of assault was the most prevalent source of job stress (Duffy & McGoldrick, 1990). Approximately 70% of bus drivers reported that the fear of being assaulted on the job was a regular and major problem. The third most prevalent source of stress was related closely to the fear of workplace violence, namely the risk of carrying large sums of money, which 67% of the drivers viewed as a regular major problem (Duffy & McGoldrick, 1990). This again signals the importance of studying workplace violence among both primary and secondary victims.

Note that these three mediating variables (negative mood, cognitive distraction, and fear) are interrelated. For example, fear of workplace violence probably is associated both with an inability to concentrate on the job (cognitive distraction) and anger or sadness (negative mood; see Figure 2).

Indirect Outcomes

One of the primary reasons for focusing on negative mood and cognitive distraction is that previous research has shown that they are differentially associated with indirect outcomes. For example, cognitive distraction is associated with psychological withdrawal from the situation, whereas negative mood increases the likelihood that individual tolerance levels are reduced and inappropriate attention is given to negative behaviors (MacEwen & Barling, 1993; MacEwen et al., 1992; Repetti, 1989). In addition, it is likely that fear will be associated with behavioral withdrawal. I predict that organizational functioning, psychological well-being, and psychosomatic well-being will be indirect outcomes of workplace violence, inasmuch as negative mood, cognitive distraction, and fear will be affected directly by the experience of workplace violence and will exert differential effects on the indirect outcomes.

Psychological well-being. At least two different factors are likely to be affected (viz., personal well-being and family functioning). One critical indicator of personal well-being is depression, and this serves as an exemplar for the effects of workplace violence. At an epidemiological level, crime victims are at an elevated risk of depression (Stuart, 1992). At an individual level, one occupational group in which depression has been investigated with respect to workplace violence is teaching. Teachers are interesting in this respect because of the low incidence of actual assaults (Williams, Winfree, & Clinton, 1989). Schonfeld (1991) conducted a longitudinal study of people entering the teaching profession and found that exposure to workplace violence predicted depressive symptoms. Similarly, Sutker, Davis, Uddo, and Ditta (1995) found that exposure to extreme war zone stress was associated with clinical depression. The mediational concept allows researchers to suggest that negative mood and fear resulting from workplace violence (rather than cognitive distraction) will result in depression.

Marital (or relationship) functioning and family functioning could also be indirect outcomes of workplace violence. Crime victims often report some marital problems (Stuart, 1992). On a more general level, there is substantial support for the notion that depression and negative mood predict marital and parental dysfunction. Importantly, these findings have shown specific effects of depressive symptoms on negative marital interactions and spousal violence (Grant & Barling, 1994; MacEwen & Barling, 1993), psychological aggression within the marriage (Barling & MacEwen, 1992; MacEwen & Barling, 1993), and parenting behavior (Barling, MacEwen, & Nolte, 1993; MacEwen & Barling, 1993). Recent longitudinal research has shown that it is depression that affects marital dysfunction in community samples and has ruled out the alternative hypothesis that marital dysfunction affects depressive symptoms (Higginbottom et al., 1993). Thus, marital and family dysfunction could be indirect outcomes of exposure to workplace violence, mediated largely but not exclusively through negative mood. However, cognitive distraction also will play a mediating role in the extent to which it increases the likelihood of affected family members being perceived as distant or rejecting (Barling et al., 1993; MacEwen & Barling, 1993).

Psychosomatic functioning. Although there is less empirical evidence, I predict that psychosomatic functioning (e.g., sleep problems, headaches and migraines, gastrointestinal problems, and upper respiratory tract infections) will be an indirect outcome of workplace violence for two reasons: First, after assaults by patients, nurses report sleep disturbance, fatigue, and muscle tenderness (Whittington & Wykes, 1989), and perceived danger at work is associated with illness symptoms (Hall & Spector, 1991), as is fear of workplace violence (Rogers & Kelloway, in press). Second, psychosomatic complaints are outcomes of work-related psychological stress (Barling & Boswell, 1995; Barling & Charbonneau, 1992).

Organizational functioning. The psychological experience of workplace violence will affect indirectly organizational functioning through the mediating influence of negative mood, cognitive distraction, and fear. Although there is a paucity of research on organizational functioning as outcomes of workplace violence, when violent incidents occur at work, it would be expected that workplace perceptions and behaviors will be affected. Psychological attachment to the organization (i.e., organizational commitment, absenteeism, turnover intentions), emotional exhaustion, job performance, and accidents will be affected indirectly.

The experience of workplace violence would influence employees' attachment to the organization in different ways. First, perhaps the most obvious short-term method for avoiding the possibility of workplace violence is by avoiding the workplace. Employees who are afraid might engage in withdrawal behaviors such as using more sick leave to avoid returning to the environment in which the violence occurred (Mantell & Albrecht, 1994). Certainly, there are data showing that absenteeism reflects an attempt to cope with work stress (Barling et al., 1994; Kristensen, 1992). Thus, workplace violence is expected to affect absenteeism indirectly through the mediating role of fear. Similarly, I predict that the fear of workplace violence will reduce an individual's desire to remain permanently in an organization where the violence occurred. Employees experiencing workplace violence thus will be expected to experience higher turnover intentions. In his research on teachers, Schonfeld (1991) found that the fear of workplace violence may be a sufficient cause to search for alternative employment. Rogers and Kelloway (in press) found a similar effect among bank employees who feared workplace violence.

Second, commitment to the organization in which the violence occurs could be affected. Two types of organizational commitment (i.e., affective and continuance commitment) have been identified as important correlates of job performance (Meyer, Paunonen, Gellatly, Goffin, & Jackson, 1989). Affective commitment characterizes employees who stay with an organization because they want to; continuance commitment describes individuals who stay because they need to, perhaps because of financial constraints, a lack of relevant skills, or a lack of appealing alternatives. Occupational violence is likely to reduce an individual's desire to remain at a given job. Thus, employees may remain with the organization after a violent event because of a lack of other alternatives, increasing their continuance commitment.

Direct or vicarious exposure to workplace violence and the resulting fear also would be expected to wear down employees emotionally. One examination of the predictors of emotional exhaustion in a police organization was conducted by Gaines and Jermier (1983). Although no significant correlation was found between their three-item measure of physical danger and emotional exhaustion, the questionnaire they used did not assess fear specifically or the psychological experience of workplace violence. It also is possible that individuals in occupations in which exposure to physical harm is expected might have developed some tolerance to violence or positive coping strategies (Barling, 1995; Gaines & Jermier, 1983). At a general level, there are data showing that negative mood mediates the relation between work-role stress and emotional exhaustion (Barling & MacIntyre, 1993). Thus, emotional exhaustion could be an indirect outcome of workplace violence.

An indirect link also may exist between workplace violence and workplace accidents, inasmuch as cognitive distraction (and intrusive imagery) will mediate the link between violence in the workplace and accidents. This is partially supported by Duffy and McGoldrick's (1990) finding that being physically attacked by passengers was a significant predictor of transit accidents for bus drivers. Physical attack also was often the result of having to reprimand passengers for shouting or smoking, which itself could increase cognitive distraction and therefore accidents (Guastello, 1990).

Data also show that the likelihood of performing the job satisfactorily among employees whose attention is distracted is reduced (Barling & Boswell, 1995). Presumably, cognitive distractions as a function of ruminating about workplace violence would exert similar indirect effects on job performance.

Moderators of the Workplace Violence–Outcome Relationship

Just as clearly as the study of workplace stress (and presumably workplace violence) predicts negative outcomes, it is equally clear that not all individuals respond negatively when faced with workplace stress. This makes it critical to understand the factors that moderate any negative effect of workplace violence. Although no previous research has identified specific moderators of the violence–outcome relationship, to my knowledge, predictions can be made on the basis of the literature. In general, having adequate social support or inappropriate regressive (or negative) coping strategies (e.g., alcohol consumption, smoking) may influence the subjective experience of workplace violence (see Figure 2).

Whittington and Wykes (1989) suggested that social support may be important in reducing the negative effects of exposure to workplace violence. However, the role of social support in this context may be complex: The results of their study revealed that nurses experiencing the most severe outcomes also were receiving the most support from work and other sources. At the same time, the nurses also reported dissatisfaction with the support they were receiving and were found to rely more on smoking and drinking. Thus, it is possible that the positive relationship found between support and symptomatology emerged because individuals were not receiving appropriate support and were engaging in negative coping strategies such as drinking at the same time. Thus, both the quantity and the type of social support must be considered (Pratt & Barling, 1988).

The direction of effects of social support probably will depend on its type and congruence with respect to the stressor (Ganster, Fusilier, & Mayes, 1986; House, 1981; MacEwen & Barling, 1988; Pratt & Barling, 1988). In the workplace, it is expected that support from a victim's supervisor will reduce any negative effect on organizational functioning. Similarly, support from a spouse after a violent episode at work may reduce marital dissatisfaction. Family cohesion reduces the likelihood of developing posttraumatic stress disorder after exposure to extreme war stress (Sutker et al., 1995). A variety of research has provided counterintuitive evidence that social support either does not moderate the relationship between work stress and work strain (Ganster et al., 1986) or it increases strain (e.g., Kaufmann & Beehr, 1986; MacEwen & Barling, 1988). These results may be attributable to the nature or type of the support (emotional) and suggest that other forms of support (i.e., instrumental or informational) may be more appropriate. For example, employees who are provided with training or knowledge (i.e., informational support) or preventive equipment (i.e., instrumental support) will be more likely to feel comfortable returning to work and less fearful in the future. These factors also may allow the individual to regain perceived control after the violent episode.

Although typically considered a negative coping mechanism (Wykes & Whittington, 1991), denial often is observed in victims of workplace violence and may have positive effects. Wykes and Whittington conducted a longitudinal study on nurses' coping strategies with respect to the level of psychological difficulties. Denial was significantly related to a decrease in psychological difficulty over a 3-week period. Nurses often have to continue working with the perpetrator, which might have resulted in the beneficial effect for denial in this sample.

Personality factors such as dispositional optimism may influence the relationship between workplace violence and direct outcomes (i.e., stressors and stress) because it will influence the way in which workplace events are perceived. For example, hardy individuals are less likely to develop posttraumatic stress disorder after exposure to war-related violence (Sutker et al., 1995). Thus, future researchers might investigate whether coping strategies such as social support, smoking, and alcohol use will influence the relation between the actual violent event and the subjective experience of the event and between subjective experience of the workplace violence and direct and indirect outcomes (see Figure 2).

Conclusion

Evidence that workplace violence now constitutes a major problem is over-whelming (e.g., Anfuso, 1994; Budd & Arvey, 1994), and numerous questions with important implications remain to be answered. For example, does the nature of the target influence the nature of the predictors of workplace violence (Greenberg & Barling, 1995)? Likewise, if research shows that psychological aggression (but not job dissatisfaction) precedes physical violence in the workplace (cf. Murphy & O'Leary, 1989), important diagnostic and preventive implications would be apparent. Given the enormity of the problem of workplace violence, both in terms of its incidence and consequences, it is encouraging that basic research has now begun that will help to assess the model presented.

The model presented in this chapter goes beyond previous speculation by explicating the psychological experience of workplace violence and by integrating the prediction, experience, and direct and indirect effects of workplace violence. However, many of the links in the model are based on knowledge from other areas, primarily knowledge on work stress and on family violence, and the model invites empirical scrutiny. At the same time, as such basic research continues, researchers should not lose sight of the fact that research is needed to focus on factors that would help in reducing or preventing the likelihood of workplace violence and on helping the direct and indirect victims of incidents of workplace violence.

References

Anfuso, D. (1994). Workplace violence. *Personnel Journal, 73,* 66–77.

Ashford, S. J., Lee, C., & Bobko, P. (1989). Content, causes and consequences of job insecurity: A theory-based measure and substantive test. *Academy of Management Journal, 32,* 803–829.

Bandura, A. (1973). *Social learning theory.* Englewood Cliffs, NJ: Prentice Hall.

Barling, J. (1990). *Employment, stress and family functioning.* New York: Wiley.

Barling, J. (1992). Work and family: In search of the missing links. *Journal of Employee Assistance Research, 1,* 271–285.

Barling, J. (1994). Work and family: In search of more effective interventions. In C. L. Cooper & D. M. Rousseau (Eds.), *Trends in organizational behavior* (Vol. 1, pp. 63–73). New York: Wiley.

Barling, J. (1995). *Some correlates of workplace violence.* Manuscript submitted for publication.

Barling, J., Bluen, S. D., & Fain, R. (1987). Psychological functioning following an acute disaster. *Journal of Applied Psychology, 72,* 683–690.

Barling, J., & Boswell, R. (1995). Work performance and the achievement-strivings and impatience-irritability dimensions of Type A behavior. *Applied Psychology: An International Journal, 44,* 143–153.

Barling, J., & Charbonneau, D. (1992). Disentangling the relationship between the achievement striving and impatience-irritability dimensions of Type A behavior, performance and health. *Journal of Organizational Behavior, 13,* 369–377.

Barling, J., Dekker, I., Loughlin, C. A., Kelloway, E. K., Fullagar, C., & Johnson, D. (in press). Prediction and replication of the outcomes of workplace sexual harassment. *Journal of Managerial Psychology.*

Barling, J., & Kryl, I. P. (1990). Moderators of the relationship between daily work stress and mood. *Work and Stress, 4,* 319–329.

Barling, J., & MacEwen, K. E. (1992). Linking work experiences to facets of marital functioning. *Journal of Organizational Behavior, 13*, 573–582.

Barling, J., MacEwen, K. E., Kelloway, E. K., & Higginbottom, S. F. (1994). Predictors and outcomes of elder-care-based interrole conflict. *Psychology and Aging, 9*, 391–397.

Barling, J., MacEwen, K. E., & Nolte, M. L. (1993). Homemaker role experiences influence toddler behaviors via maternal well-being and parenting behavior. *Journal of Abnormal Child Psychology, 21*, 213–229.

Barling, J., & MacIntyre, A. (1993). Daily work role stressors, mood and emotional exhaustion. *Work and Stress, 7*, 315–325.

Barling, J., & Rosenbaum, A. (1986). Work stressors and wife abuse. *Journal of Applied Psychology, 71*, 346–348.

Baum, A. (1990). Stress, intrusive imagery, and chronic disease. *Health Psychology, 9*, 653–675.

Baum, A., Fleming, R., & Davidson, L. M. (1983). Natural disaster and technological catastrophe. *Environment and Behavior, 15*, 333–354.

Budd, J. W., & Arvey, R. D. (1994). *The correlates and consequences of workplace violence.* Unpublished manuscript, University of Minnesota, Industrial Relations Center, Minneapolis, MN.

Caprara, G. V., Gargaro, T., Pastorelli, C., Prezza, M., Renzi, P., & Zelli, A. (1987). Individual differences and measures of aggression in laboratory studies. *Personality and Individual Differences, 8*, 885–893.

Cowan, J. S. (1994). *Lessons from the Fabrikant file: A report to the Board of Governors of Concordia University.* Unpublished manuscript, Concordia University, Montreal, Quebec, Canada.

Cox, T., & Leather, P. (1994). The prevention of violence at work: Application of a cognitive behavioral theory. *International Review of Industrial and Organizational Psychology, 9*, 213–246.

Davidson, L. M., Fleming, R., & Baum, A. (1987). Chronic stress, catecholamines, and sleep disturbance at Three Mile Island. *Journal of Human Stress, 13*, 75–83.

Dekker, I., & Barling, J. (1995). *Personal and organizational predictors of men's workplace sexual harassment.* Manuscript submitted for publication.

Duffy, C. A., & McGoldrick, A. E. (1990). Stress and the bus driver in the UK transport industry. *Work and Stress, 4*, 17–27.

Farmer, R., Tranah, R., O'Donnell, I., & Catalan, J. (1992). Railway suicide: The psychological effects on drivers. *Psychological Medicine, 22*, 407–414.

Fryer, D., & Warr, P. (1984). Unemployment and cognitive difficulties. *British Journal of Clinical Psychology, 23*, 67–68.

Gaines, J., & Jermier, J. J. (1983). Emotional exhaustion in a high stress organization. *Academy of Management Journal, 26*, 567–586.

Ganster, D. C., Fusilier, M. R., & Mayes, B. T. (1986). Role of social support in the experience of stress at work. *Journal of Applied Psychology, 71*, 102–110.

Garson, B. (1985). *The electronic sweatshop.* New York: Penguin Books.

Graham, J. P. (1991). Disgruntled employees: Ticking time bombs? *Security Management, 36*, 83, 85.

Grant, S., & Barling, J. (1994). Linking unemployment experiences with marital functioning: A mediational model. In G. Keita & J. Hurrell (Eds.), *Job stress in a changing workforce: Investigating gender, diversity and family* (pp. 311–327). Washington, DC: American Psychological Association.

Greenberg, J. (1990a). Organizational justice: Yesterday, today, and tomorrow. *Journal of Management, 16*, 399–432.

Greenberg, J. (1990b). Employee theft as a reaction to underpayment inequity: The hidden costs of pay cuts. *Journal of Applied Psychology, 75*, 561–568.

Greenberg, L., & Barling, J. (1995). *Predicting employee aggression: Roles of person behaviors and workplace factors.* Manuscript in preparation.

Guastello, S. J. (1990). Psychological variables related to transit safety: The application of catastrophe theory. *Work and Stress, 5*, 17–28.

Hall, J. K., and Spector, P. E. (1991). Relationships of work stress measures for employees with the same job. *Work and Stress, 5*, 29–35.

Heyman, R., O'Leary, K. D., & Jouriles, E. N. (1995). Alcohol and aggressive personality styles: Potentiators of serious physical aggression against wives? *Journal of Family Psychology, 9,* 44–57.

Higginbottom, S. F., Barling, J., & Kelloway, E. K. (1993). Linking retirement experiences and marital satisfaction: A mediational model. *Psychology and Aging, 8,* 508–516.

Hill, C. (1988). Protecting employees from attack. *Personnel Management, 20,* 34–39.

House, J. S. (1981). *Work stress and social support.* Reading, MA: Addison-Wesley.

Huesmann, L. R., Eron, L. D., Lefkowitz, M. M., & Walder, L. O. (1984). Stability of aggression over time and generations. *Developmental Psychology, 20,* 1120–1134.

Kaufmann, G. M., & Beehr, T. A. (1986). Interactions between job stressors and social support: Some counterintuitive findings. *Journal of Applied Psychology, 71,* 522–526.

Kelloway, E. K., & Barling, J. (1991). Job characteristics, role stressors and mental health. *Journal of Occupational Psychology, 64,* 291–304.

Killias, M. (1990). Vulnerability: Towards a better understanding of a key variable in the genesis of fear of crime. *Violence and Victims, 5,* 97–108.

Kristensen, T. S. (1992). Sickness absence and work strain among Danish slaughterhouse workers: An analysis of absence from work regarded as coping behavior. *Social Science and Medicine, 27,* 15–28.

Lamerson, C. D., & Kelloway, E. K. (1995). *Peacekeeping stress: Testing a model of organizational and personal outcomes.* Manuscript in preparation.

Lanza, M. L., Kayne, H. L., Hicks, C., & Milner, J. (1991). Nursing staff characteristics related to patient assault. *Issues in Mental Health Nursing, 12,* 253–265.

Leather, P. J., Cox, T., & Farnsworth, M. G. (1990). Violence at work: An issue for the 1990s. *Work and Stress, 4,* 3–5.

Leymann, H. L. (1988). Stress reactions after bank robberies: Psychological and psychosomatic reaction patterns. *Work and Stress, 2,* 123–132.

Lochman, J. E., & Lampron, L. B. (1986). Situational social problem-solving skills and self esteem of aggressive and non-aggressive boys. *Journal of Abnormal Child Psychology, 14,* 605–617.

Lion, J. R., Snyder, W., & Merrill, G. L. (1981). Underreporting of assaults on staff in a state hospital. *Hospital and Community Psychiatry, 32,* 497–498.

Lund, J. (1992). Electronic performance monitoring: A review of research issues. *Applied Ergonomics, 23,* 54–58.

MacEwen, K. E., & Barling, J. (1988). Interrole conflict, family support and marital adjustment of employed mothers: A short-term longitudinal study. *Journal of Organizational Behavior, 9,* 241–250.

MacEwen, K. E., & Barling, J. (1991). Maternal employment experiences affect children's behavior via mood, cognitive difficulties and parenting behavior. *Journal of Marriage and the Family, 53,* 635–644.

MacEwen, K. E., & Barling, J. (1993). Type A behavior and marital satisfaction: Differential effects of achievement striving and impatience/irritability. *Journal of Marriage and the Family, 55,* 1001–1010.

MacEwen, K. E., Barling, J., & Kelloway, E. K. (1992). Effects of short-term role overload on marital interactions. *Work and Stress, 6,* 117–126.

Malone, J., Tyree, A., & O'Leary, K. D. (1989). Generalization and containment: Different effects of past aggression for wives and husbands. *Journal of Marriage and the Family, 51,* 687–697.

Mantell, M. R., & Albrecht, S. (1994). *Ticking bombs: Defusing violence in the workplace.* Homewood, IL: Irwin.

McGarvey, R. (1994, January). Loose cannons. *Entrepreneur, 22,* pp. 242, 244–246, 248.

McLean Parks, J., & Kidder, D. L. (1994). "Till death us do part . . .": Changing work relationships in the 1990's. In C. L. Cooper & D. M. Rousseau (Eds.), *Trends in organizational behavior* (pp. 112–136). New York: Wiley.

McManus, M. (1992, November). *Disaster work: A model of stress and mental health interventions.* Paper presented at the Second American Psychological Association–National Institute for Occupational Safety and Health Conference on Occupational Stress, Washington, DC.

Meyer, J. P., Paunonen, S. V., Gellatly, I. R., Goffin, R. D., & Jackson, D. N. (1989). Organizational commitment and job performance: It's the nature of the commitment that counts. *Journal of Applied Psychology, 74*, 152–156.

Motowidlo, S. J., Manning, J. S., & Packard, M. R. (1986). Occupational stress: Its causes and consequences for job performance. *Journal of Applied Psychology, 71*, 618–629.

Murphy, C. M., & O'Leary, K. D. (1989). Psychological aggression predicts physical aggression in early marriage. *Journal of Consulting and Clinical Psychology, 57*, 579–582.

Pan, H. S., Neidig, P. H., & O'Leary, K. D. (1994). Predicting mild and severe husband-to-wife physical aggression. *Journal of Consulting and Clinical Psychology, 62*, 975–981.

A post office tragedy: The shooting at Royal Oak. (1992). Report of the Committee on Post Office and Civil Services, House of Representatives. Washington, DC: U.S. Government Printing Office.

Pratt, L. I., & Barling, J. (1988). Differentiating between daily hassles, acute and chronic stressors: A framework and its implications. In J. R. Hurrell, L. R. Murphy, S. L. Sauter, & C. L. Cooper (Eds.), *Occupational stress: Issues and developments in research* (pp. 41–53). London: Taylor & Francis.

Repetti, R. L. (1989). Effects of daily workload on subsequent behavior during marital interaction: The roles of social withdrawal and spouse support. *Journal of Personality and Social Psychology, 57*, 651–659.

Rogers, K. A., & Kelloway, E. K. (in press). Violence at work: Personal and organizational outcomes. *Journal of Occupational Health Psychology*.

Rosenbaum, A., & O'Leary, K. D. (1981). Marital violence: Characteristics of abusive couples. *Journal of Consulting and Clinical Psychology, 49*, 63–71.

Schliefer, L. M. (1992). Electronic performance monitoring. *Applied Ergonomics, 23*, 4–5.

Schonfeld, I. S. (1991, August). *A longitudinal study of occupational stressors and depressive symptoms in first year female teachers*. Paper presented at the 99th Annual Convention of the American Psychological Association, Washington, DC.

Schwarz, E. D., & Kowalski, J. M. (1993). Malignant memories: Effect of a shooting in the workplace on school personnel's attitudes. *Journal of Interpersonal Violence, 8*, 468–485.

Slora, K. B., Joy, D. S., & Terris, W. (1991). Personnel selection to control employee violence. *Journal of Psychology and Business, 5*, 417–426.

Solomon, M. J., & Thompson, J. (1995). Anger and blame in technological disasters. *Stress Medicine, 11*, 199–206.

Stewart, W., & Barling, J. (in press). Father's work experiences affect children's behavior via work-related affect and parenting behaviors. *Journal of Organizational Behavior*.

Stuart, P. (1992). Murder on the job. *Personnel Journal, 71*, 72–84.

Sutker, P. B., Davis, J. M., Uddo, M., & Ditta, S. R. (1995). War zone stress, personal resources and PTSD in Persian Gulf war returnees. *Journal of Abnormal Psychology, 104*, 444–452.

Sutker, P. B., Uddo, M., Brailey, K., Vasterling, J. J., & Errera, P. (1994). Psychopathology in war-zone deployed and nondeployed Operation Desert Storm troops assigned grave registration duties. *Journal of Abnormal Psychology, 103*, 383–390.

Theorell, T., Leymann, H., Jodko, M., Konarski, K., & Norbeck, H. E. (1994). "Person under train" incident from the subway driver's point of view: A prospective 1-year follow-up study. The design, and medical and psychiatric data. *Social Science and Medicine, 38*, 471–475.

Thompson, M. (1994, May 23). The living room war. *Time*, pp. 36–37.

Toufexis, A. (1994, April 25). Murder-on-the-job mayhem. *Time*, pp. 35–36, 39.

Whittington, R., & Wykes, T. (1989). Invisible injury. *Nursing times, 84*(42), 30–32.

Williams, L. E., Winfree, L. T., & Clinton, L. (1989). Trouble in the schoolhouse: New views on victimization, fear of crime and teacher perceptions of the workplace. *Violence and Victims, 4*, 27–44.

Wykes, T., & Whittington, R. (1991). Coping strategies used by staff following assault by a patient: An exploratory study. *Work and Stress, 5*, 37–48.

3

Violence and Hostility at Work: A Model of Reactions to Perceived Injustice

Robert Folger and Robert A. Baron

Corpus Christi, Texas—A former employee opened fire Monday at a refinery inspection company, killing the owner, his wife, and three workers before fatally shooting himself.... "When we arrived, we learned preliminarily that a disgruntled employee walked in and started shooting..." said Assistant Police Chief Ken Bung. (Associated Press, 1995a, p. B1)

Evendale, Ohio—A fired truck driver who was going after "the one that screwed me over" walked into his former employer's office Friday and shot three people to death, then calmly waited to be arrested, police said. (Associated Press, 1995b, p. A12)

Portland, Oregon—A man accused of shooting two people and taking four others hostage in an office tower appeared in court Friday.... James Rincker, 24, ... a gunman dressed in military camouflage and a black beret held, ... hostages for 4 1/2 hours Thursday at the Charles Schwab stock brokerage.... Police initially said Rincker intended to shoot female office workers for having him fired from his job as a package deliveryman. But investigators said Friday that Rincker had problems with authority in general. (Associated Press, 1996, p. A6)

Shocking incidents such as these recently have drawn a tremendous amount of media attention. Some disturbing statistics suggest that this attention appears to be fully justified. Consider the following facts:

- Each week, an average of 15 people are murdered at work in the United States alone, a total of more than 7,600 during the past 10 years (National Institute for Occupational Safety and Health, 1993).
- During 1992, the last year for which complete data are available, the Bureau of Labor Statistics reported that 1,004 employees were murdered on the job—a rate more than one third higher than the annual average during the 1980s. Among these victims, 177 were

in managerial professional occupations, 335 were in sales, 225 were in the service sector, and 202 were drivers or factory workers (Rigdon, 1994).

At face value, these statistics seem to suggest that current public concern with workplace violence is fully appropriate. As we suggest later in this chapter, however, closer examination of the data suggests that these dramatic and tragic episodes actually constitute only a small part of a larger problem: growing workplace aggression. We define the term *workplace aggression* as any form of behavior by individuals that is intended to harm current or previous coworkers or their organization (cf. Baron & Neuman, 1996). Thus, our definition includes instances of *workplace violence* but also encompasses many other forms of aggression, everything from spreading negative rumors about target individuals or their protégés, through withholding information or resources needed by targets or even purposely failing to return phone calls from them (Baron & Neuman, 1996). We believe that changes occurring in organizations in recent years have "set the stage" for an increase in the incidence of many forms of workplace aggression, including workplace violence; several of these changes are reviewed.

The major purpose of this chapter, however, is somewhat different. We suggest potential links between two important bodies of knowledge: the findings of basic research on the causes and nature of human aggression and the causes and effects of felt injustice. Our thesis is that feelings of injustice, and closely related phenomena, play an important role in many forms of workplace aggression, especially in the dramatic and damaging forms known as workplace violence.

To accomplish this goal, we review some basic information about the causes of human aggression, with special attention given to the role of frustration (cf. Baron & Richardson, 1994). Next, we point out links between some of these antecedents and the literature on felt injustice, emphasizing the potential role of injustice in the occurrence of workplace violence. This is followed by presentation of a model of workplace violence that emphasizes the roles of both the characteristics of individuals and various features of workplace environments. We conclude with efforts to extend this model to other forms of workplace aggression and with some discussion of potential techniques for preventing or reducing workplace violence.

Antecedents of Human Aggression

Research on the nature and causes of human aggression has continued unabated for several decades. As a result, there is a rich body of scientific data on the nature and roots of aggression (e.g., Baron & Richardson, 1994; Huesmann, 1994). This literature suggests that aggression stems from a host of factors and conditions. Many of these, however, seem to fall into several basic categories: (a) *biological causes of aggression*—sex hormones, drugs, nervous system structures; (b) *cognitive causes of aggression*—interpretations of a given situation, memories, associations, strongly held attitudes; (c) *individual causes of aggression*—the stable characteristics of individuals (i.e., specific personality traits); (d) *situational and environmental causes*—external causes of increased arousal such as aspects of the physical environment (e.g., temperature, noise, crowding, etc.); and (e) *social causes of aggression*—the words or deeds of other people, the norms and expectations of a given society or group. Table 1 is an overview of some of the factors in each of these categories that have been found to play an important role in human aggression.

Detailed discussion of the many factors listed in Table 1 is beyond the scope of this chapter. However, we comment briefly on two factors that, we believe, may be particularly important with respect to the occurrence of workplace violence.

The Role of Frustration in Human Aggression

The first of these, which can be construed primarily as a social cause of aggression, is frustration—interference with ongoing, goal-directed behavior (e.g., Berkowitz, 1989). Frustration involves events that prevent individuals from attaining their goals (i.e., what they want). Research shows that frustration is certainly not the only determinant of aggression, nor perhaps always the most important, but it does seem to be related to aggression under certain conditions. Specifically, frustration leads to increased aggression when individuals perceive that such thwarting has been produced by the purposeful actions of others and that it seems somewhat unfair, illegitimate, or unwarranted (e.g., Berkowitz, 1989).

Why does illegitimate or unexpected frustration serve as a stronger determinant of aggression than frustration that is viewed as legitimate or that is expected? One possible answer was provided by Berkowitz (1989), who suggested that frustration is an aversive, unpleasant experience and that it leads to aggression because of this. In short, frustration sometimes produces aggression because of a basic relationship between negative affect and aggressive behavior, a relationship that has been confirmed in many different studies (e.g., Pahlavan, Duda, & Bonnet, 1994).

In the light of this suggestion, it is possible that illegitimate or unexpected frustration generates greater amounts of negative affect than frustration that is expected or viewed as legitimate, which might partly explain the especially strong effects of such frustration on subsequent aggression. Whatever the precise mechanism or mechanisms involved, however, it is clear that frustration does often play an important role in many instances of human aggression. As we note soon, it also may play a key role in workplace violence and workplace aggression. We return to this topic in more detail.

Table 1. Factors Influencing Human Aggression

Biological	Individual	Cognitive	Situational and environmental	Social
Sex hormones	Type A behavior pattern	Attributions concerning causes of provocative actions	Environmental variables (e.g., temperature, noise, crowding)	Arbitrary or unjustified frustration
Nervous system structures (e.g., limbic)	Hostile attribution bias	Personal standards and values	Aggression-related cues (e.g., weapons)	Verbal or physical provocation
Physical disorders	Irritability and emotional sensitivity	Memory for various means of aggressing	External sources of increased arousal	Instigation from others (e.g., direct orders, audience encouraging aggression)
Characteristic level of arousal	Gender	Cognitive evaluation of appropriateness of acts of aggression	External sources of increased self-awareness (e.g., presence of a mirror, audience)	Presence of or exposure to aggressive models
Drugs (e.g., alcohol)	Locus of control	Errors or biases in social cognition (e.g., self-serving bias, reduced ability to process information in the presence of intense emotions)	Almost any external cause of annoyance or negative affect	Target characteristics

Hostile Attributional Bias and Human Aggression

The second factor to note is a personality cause of aggression, a trait that renders specific individuals especially "ready" to aggress against others. Although many personal factors have been linked to aggression (e.g., the Type A behavior pattern; Berman, Gladue, & Taylor, 1993), perhaps the most intriguing, and potentially important, of these is the *hostile attributional bias* (Dodge, Price, Bachorowski, & Newman, 1990).

Hostile attributional bias is the tendency to perceive hostile intentions or motives in others' actions even when these are ambiguous. In other words, individuals high in hostile attributional bias rarely give others the benefit of the doubt: They simply *assume* that any provocative actions from others are intentional and react accordingly—with strong retaliation (Dodge et al., 1990).

The results of many studies offer support for the potential impact of this factor on human aggression. For example, in one revealing experiment, Dodge et al. (1990) examined the relationship between hostile attributional bias and aggression among a group of male adolescents confined to a maximum security prison for juvenile offenders. These young men had been convicted of a wide range of violent crimes, including murder, sexual assault, kidnapping, and armed robbery. The researchers hypothesized that hostile attributional bias among the adolescents would be related to the number of violent crimes they had committed and to trained observers' ratings of the prisoners' tendencies to engage in aggression in response to provocation from others. Results offered support for both predictions. In summary, it appears that the tendency to perceive malice in the actions of others, even when it does not really exist, is one personal characteristic closely related to high levels of aggression against others.

The Multiple Roots of Human Aggression

Before concluding this section and discussing links between basic research on human aggression and workplace violence, we emphasize the following point: Aggression, like other forms of complex behavior, is multidetermined. It stems from the interplay of a wide range of biological, individual, cognitive, social, situational, and environmental factors (Baron & Richardson, 1994; Geen, 1991). Thus, although we focus on the role of frustration and personal characteristics in workplace violence in the remainder of this chapter, many other variables and conditions should not be overlooked. Indeed, all modern theories of human aggression (e.g., Anderson, Deuser, & DeNeve, 1995) take this account. Moreover, these theories appear to offer invaluable insights into the nature and causes of workplace violence. For example, consider how such theories could be applied to the following incident:

Pedro, a clerk at a credit union, became angry with one of his fellow employees, a college student working there as a summer fill-in. He informed the student that he knew "he was out to get him," was spreading false rumors about him, and was trying to sabotage his career. When the student strongly denied these charges, Pedro became verbally abusive, cursing him loudly in front of other employees and accusing him of receiving special treatment because he was related to a high official at the credit union. A supervisor stepped in and ended this episode, but the next day, Pedro loudly accused the student and a female employee, who had previously rebuffed Pedro's romantic overtures, of "making fun of him" as they conversed. They vigorously denied this accusation, stating that they were talking about a totally unrelated topic, but Pedro refused to believe them and threatened to "make them pay" for their actions. The situation reached a climax about a week later on a suffocatingly hot day when the credit union's air conditioning failed. During that steamy afternoon, Pedro informed the student that this was the day on which he would get his revenge and "teach him that he could not treat people from his country this way." That evening, Pedro followed the student home on public transportation, muttering curses and grimacing all the way. He kept fingering his pocket, and the student was certain that Pedro was carrying a weapon. Fortunately, the student had arranged for several friends to meet him, and they were standing on the train station when he got off. When Pedro saw them, he shook his fist but retreated. That night, he was arrested for assaulting and seriously wounding a neighbor. He never returned to the credit union.

What factors contributed to Pedro's threatening and potentially dangerous behavior? Modern theories of aggression would point to several that probably played a role: (a) aspects of Pedro's personality, such as a strong tendency to attribute others' actions to hostile motives, the hostile attributional bias to which we referred earlier (e.g., Dodge et al., 1990); (b) the high levels of physical discomfort he experienced when the air conditioning broke down during a heat wave (e.g., Baron, 1994); (c) jealousy over the female employee's friendliness toward the college student; (d) Pedro's belief that the student was getting special, favored treatment because he was related to one of the credit union officials; and (e) Pedro's conviction that the student was mistreating him because of prejudice against people of Hispanic descent.

In short, modern perspectives on human aggression would suggest that this employee's behavior stemmed from a complex interplay among many personal, social, cognitive, and situational factors. We believe that efforts to understand the nature and roots of workplace violence must adopt a similar, sophisticated perspective. Moreover, we suggest that these efforts should rest, as much as possible, on the large scientific literature on human aggression (cf. Baron & Richardson, 1994; Huesmann, 1994). Failure to do so would be inefficient and, from a scientific point of view, inexcusable.

The Role of Felt Injustice in Workplace Violence

Having considered some basic antecedents of human aggression, we now attempt to link these to workplace aggression and violence. We contend that because of the context in which such events occur, they are influenced powerfully by an issue to which we have already alluded: fairness (cf. Folger & Cropanzano, in press; Greenberg, 1990b; Tyler, 1994). Succinctly put, individuals want to feel that they are being treated fairly by others, and, in the workplace context, that they are being treated fairly not only by coworkers and supervisors but also by their organization. We contend that feeling treated unfairly, especially in certain ways, may play a powerful role in the occurrence of many forms of workplace aggression, including workplace violence. Consider the following brief accounts of actual instances of workplace violence (Stuart, 1992): (a) an employee, upset with his supervisor and wanting a transfer, shot and killed his supervisor; (b) a former employee who had feuded with the owner then killed him; (c) a former employee who was upset about a workers' compensation claim that had been denied returned to his former workplace and wounded the owner with a handgun; and (d) an employee killed his supervisor, with whom he had been involved in a job dispute for more than a year.

These and many other events suggest that the individuals who engaged in workplace violence often expressed strong feelings of anger and resentment toward the individuals they attacked. In other words, they engaged in extreme acts of aggression because, at least in part, they felt that they had been treated unfairly by the target individuals. Such conclusions on the part of the perpetrators of workplace violence then led to feelings of anger and resentment toward the perceived sources of this injustice, resulting ultimately in the murderous acts just described. What are the causes of such feelings? And what is the nature of perceived injustice? We consider these issues and then discuss a theory that helps to link injustice to frustration, intense resentment, and the desire for vengeance (Folger, 1986, 1987, 1993), and ensuing violence.

Perceived Fairness: A Basic Framework

Several decades of research on the nature and effects of perceived fairness suggests that individuals do make several kinds of judgments concerning this issue. All, however, may be important with respect to workplace violence.

Distributive fairness. Perhaps the most basic kind of judgment individuals make with respect to fairness concerns *outcomes*. Have they received a fair share of available rewards given their relative contributions to any social exchange (Adams, 1965)? In general, people expect their outcomes and inputs to be proportional; the more they have contributed, the larger the share of available rewards they anticipate. Thus, if someone who makes a large contribution to a group receives the lion's share of the rewards, whereas someone who makes a small contribution receives a much smaller share, everything is fine. Contributions and outcomes are in balance, and perceived distributive fairness, or equity, exists. By contrast, if individuals perceive that they are receiving a smaller share of the available rewards than they deserve (relative to others or to various standards for fair returns), strong feelings of inequity or unfairness may occur (Adams, 1965).

Such judgments, though, are in the eye of the beholder: Individuals do the comparing and decide whether their share of available rewards are fair relative to their inputs. Their perceptions of fairness then affect their subsequent behavior.

Procedural and interpersonal justice: It is not just what one gets. How one got it matters too. Distributive justice plays a key role in shaping perceptions of fairness, but it is not the entire story when such judgments are made. In addition to concern over how much they receive (relative to others or some other criterion), individuals also look at the broader context. In particular, our discussion focuses on the (a) procedures followed in dividing available rewards, or *procedural justice*, and (b) considerateness and courtesy shown to them by the parties responsible for dividing the available rewards, or *interpersonal justice* (Folger & Bies, 1989). In other words, in reaching conclusions about whether they have been treated fairly, people do not focus solely on their actual outcomes; they also care about how the decisions to distribute rewards in a specific way were reached (the procedures followed) and how they were treated throughout the process, especially when being informed about their share (interpersonal factors).

What factors influence judgments concerning the fairness of procedures? Research findings point to several that are important (Lind & Tyler, 1988). First, individuals view procedures as being fair to the extent that they are consistent (i.e., applied in the same manner across all the individuals involved). Second, they tend to view procedures as being fair when they are based on accurate information about how much each person contributed. Third, procedures are viewed as being fair when the interests of all concerned parties are represented. Additional determinants of procedural justice include opportunities to correct errors in distributions and the extent to which they are based on widely accepted moral and ethical standards (Brockner et al., 1994; Leventhal, Karuza, & Fry, 1980). To the extent that these conditions exist, individuals perceive their treatment by a group or other people as being fair: After all, correct, reasonable procedures have been used and who can argue with these?

What about *interpersonal justice*? What factors play a role with respect to this type of fairness? Research on this topic is recent, but already two important factors have been identified. The first is the extent to which individuals feel that they were given clear and rational reasons for the division of rewards that was adopted (Bies, Shapiro, & Cummings, 1988). In other words, people want to understand why they received what they did and will perceive they have been treated fairly to the extent such information is provided.

A second factor that influences perceptions of interpersonal justice involves the courtesy and sensitivity with which reward allocations are presented. Have they been treated with the respect they deserve? Or have the people in charge of distributing rewards acted in a high-handed and insensitive manner? These are the types of questions people ask themselves in deciding whether they have been treated in an interpersonally fair manner.

Evidence for the important role of both these factors—clear explanations for the reasons behind reward distributions and sensitive treatment of group members—has been obtained in several recent studies (e.g., Brockner et al., 1994; Greenberg, 1994; Shapiro, Buttner, & Barry, 1995). Taken together, then, recent research on perceived fairness in groups, whether at work or in other contexts, indicates that such judgments are indeed influenced by many different factors. Distributive justice (i.e., how much one receives relative to others) is important, but it is not the entire story. In addition, judgments of fairness are influenced by factors relating to procedures and to what might be described as the "style" in which information about reward allocations is communicated. Perceived fairness is indeed in the eye of the beholder, but, as is true with all aspects of social perception, many factors shape people's conclusions about others' behavior.

Perceived Fairness and Frustration: Are They Linked?

Now we come to a crucial aspect of our proposals: the contention that a close link exists between frustration—especially frustration perceived as being illegitimate—and perceived unfairness. We are not the first to propose such a link. Writing more than 20 years ago, Brown and Herrnstein (1975) carefully reviewed related evidence from animal and human studies and concluded the following:

> Frustration correctly conceived *may not be fundamentally different from injustice, inequity, and relative deprivation* [italics added]. All may conceivably be considered variations on a single kind of instigator. (p. 271)

> The basic notion is that all these instigating circumstances may be placed under the rubric of "the disappointment by illegitimate means of legitimate expectations." (p. 274)

> Legitimacy implies operating according to norms, prescriptions for the way people in groups ought to think or act, which when violated lead to reproach, anger, even violence. (p. 285).

Note the connections that these authors saw among frustration, injustice, and violence. We, too, believe that these connections make sense, although we do not believe that the links are necessarily simple or direct.

Rather, we contend that whether perceived unfairness leads to extreme reactions such as workplace aggression and violence can be understood best in the context of referent cognitions theory (e.g., Folger, 1987, 1993).

Referent Cognitions Theory

According to referent cognitions theory (RCT), when people contemplate the treatment they have received from others, they evaluate it in relation to standards of comparison (referent outcomes) drawn from any of several potential sources, including their own past outcomes, the outcomes of others, and ideal conceptions about entitlements and rewards. Note that these referent outcomes, which shape a person's reactions, do not have to come from expectations that are based on the person's past experiences. They also do not have to come from observing other people's outcomes. As noted by norm theory (Kahneman & Miller, 1986), "postcomputed" standards can grow out of an experience itself, producing an after-the-fact standard applied retrospectively to evaluate the experience.

In fact, a given situation might call attention to any of several context-specific standards. Consider the experience of anticipating a 4% raise based on previous raises one has received from the same supervisor. Suppose this percentage compares favorably not only with one's past experience but also with the 3% raises that one knew had been given to comparable employees. Despite those prior grounds for a positive reaction from expectations and social comparison, one's reaction might still be negative if one discovers that the 4% raise was granted at the same time as an announcement of 18% annual inflation.

Referent comparisons, which indicate any discrepancy between the outcome received and the referent outcome used for evaluating it (e.g., 4% vs. 18%), determine the degree of dissatisfaction with a given outcome. Note that this dissatisfaction refers to affect about the relative unfavorability of the outcome, such as dissatisfaction with the amount of money in a pay raise (compared with what it might have been if only it had been the same amount as the referent outcome). Dissatisfaction, defined as negative affect about outcome unfavorability, is not the same psychological phenomenon as the emotion of resentment, which has a social target and is directed at someone else as a target. For example, employees might resent a top management team that is perceived as being responsible for not generating enough corporate profits so that employees' salaries could keep pace with inflation. Socially targeted resentment occurs when someone else is considered blameworthy. The resentful, aggrieved party holds another party accountable for the dissatisfying experience, such as when people believe that they would have obtained better outcomes if a decision maker had used other procedures that should have been implemented (e.g., had used sounder judgment and obtained more reliable information). In short, RCT indicates how some dissatisfying occurrence can be transformed into outwardly directed resentment, which then can result in anger, hostility, or even moral outrage and righteous indignation.

The distinction drawn by RCT between mere dissatisfaction and re-sentment is related to the distinction drawn earlier between mere frus-tration and arbitrary or illegitimate frustration (e.g., Pastore, 1950). Dis-satisfying outcomes are only one component of RCT. Perceived illegitimate conduct by a social agent (person or institution) is a second component of RCT: Frustrating, dissatisfying outcomes can seem arbitrary or unjustified on the basis of how someone else has acted, namely without just cause, in a manner deemed unreasonable because it violates accepted norms for appropriate conduct. Once one recognizes that another person's conduct can transform mere dissatisfaction into resentful hostility (anger directed against another person), then the connection to aggression makes sense. Aggression, after all, also involves a particular form of orientation toward another person rather than merely toward an object. In the sense of every-day language, and also as defined by many researchers (e.g., Baron & Richardson, 1994; Geen, 1991), people do not commit acts of aggression toward inanimate objects.

RCT thus helps explain why, how, and when feelings of unfairness translate into something more intense and potentially explosive than a mere sense of dissatisfaction or simple frustration. Under appropriate con-ditions, RCT contends, unfairness may lead to strong feelings of anger, resentment, and an accompanying desire for revenge. As noted recently by Greenberg and Scott (1996), such motives may find expression in many forms of behavior, including theft and vandalism, which we would include within our working definition of workplace aggression. In extreme cases, such feelings may be powerful enough, or the individuals involved may be sufficiently prone to aggression (i.e., high in hostile attributional bias), that the result is something even more damaging: workplace violence.

In summary, we contend that under certain conditions, individuals perceive that they have been treated unfairly. When other circumstances also prevail (e.g., when individuals have certain personal characteristics that predispose them to attribute malevolence to others, when they believe that the treatment they have received violates widely accepted norms of fairness or "fair play," and when they readily can imagine much better outcomes for themselves that are consistent with such principles), these feelings may translate into strong resentment and a powerful desire for revenge. We now look more closely at this suggestion of a complex inter-play among personal characteristics and existing situational conditions as determinants of workplace violence.

Person–Situation Interactions and Workplace Violence: A "Popcorn" Model

As noted earlier, modern theories of aggression view violence as resulting from a complex interplay between many different variables and conditions (e.g., Anderson et al., 1995; Zillmann, 1994). By the same token, under-standing why certain individuals engage in workplace violence requires considering both their personal characteristics and many aspects of the environments in which they work. To illustrate these interactions, we refer to our approach, colloquially, as the "popcorn model" (cf. Folger & Skarlicki, 1995). The employee who explodes violently and shoots his or her supervisor is akin to the first kernel of popcorn to explode. Obviously, an observer might focus on trying to explain why this particular kernel exploded before all the others. Although the popped kernels look similar to each other, a microscopic view or chemical assay might help reveal the extent to which each kernel is unique. Similarly, careful study of the individuals in a given workplace would reveal important differences with respect to various personal characteristics previously found to be related to aggression, such as the hostile attributional bias (Dodge et al., 1990), the Type A behavior pattern (Berman et al., 1993), and certain aspects of the "Big Five" dimensions of personality (e.g., Caprara, Barbaranelli, Pastorelli, & Perugini, 1994).

At the same time, the current environment (i.e., the various conditions existing in the workplace itself) may play a role, just as the oil does with respect to popping kernels. These conditions together might be considered as being analogous to the temperature of the oil: The hotter it becomes, the more kernels (employees) are likely to pop (engage in overt acts of aggression). In terms of this metaphor, we believe that the "heat" definitely has been turned up at work these days. Many of the changes occurring in modern organizations—downsizing, layoffs, freezes or actual cutbacks in wages and benefits, increased use of outsourcing, and increasing diversity—all may be contributing to an environment in which the emotional heat on employees has been intensified greatly. Indeed, growing evidence suggests that employees do respond to such changes with strong anger and resentment. In one recent study on this topic (Baron & Neuman, 1996), several hundred employees of a number of different companies were asked to rate the frequency of various forms of aggression in their organizations and to report the frequency with which they had experienced the changes just listed (downsizing, layoffs, etc.). Results were clear: There was a substantial correlation between reported aggression and the magnitude of such changes. In other words, the more participants reported having experienced these unsettling changes, the more aggression they reported both witnessing and experiencing in their organizations.

Additional research indicates that individuals fired as a result of downsizing, as well as those who remain on the job, report increased feelings of anger, frustration, and anxiety after such changes in their organizations (e.g., Brockner et al., 1994; Konovsky & Brockner, 1993). Other changes appear to produce corresponding reactions of heightened stress and anxiety (Boje & Winsor, 1993). Perceptions of mistrust and feelings of unfairness seem to be running higher than ever.

Moreover, evidence also suggests that one response by top management in such situations involves a hunker-down, threat-rigidity mentality (cf. Staw, Sandelands, & Dutton, 1981) and a "kick 'em when they're down" style of treating laid-off employees. For example, Smeltzer and Zener (1992) reported one company that merely "sent the same one-page announcement to the media and employees" when announcing layoffs. Numerous additional horror stories concerning insensitive handling of layoffs by management also exist (e.g., Brockner, 1992; Cameron, 1994; D. C. Feldman & Leana, 1989; Sutton, Eisenhardt, & Jucker, 1986). These reports depict a previously unresearched managerial phenomenon associated with layoff situations: that managers often engage in distancing behavior rather than being interpersonally sensitive to a victim's plight.

In reviewing the causes of interpersonal distancing by top management and impersonal, insensitive treatment of laid-off employees, Folger and Buttram (1995) drew attention to remarks made by Winston Churchill. The day after the bombing of Pearl Harbor, Churchill sent the Japanese ambassador a very proper British letter indicating England's declaration of war. The public reacted with outrage to the genteel tone of the letter, whose closing said "I have the honor, sir, to be your humble servant, Winston S. Churchill." Responding to the public's criticism, Churchill (1950) commented that "if you have to kill a man, it costs you nothing to be polite" (p. 611).

The "Churchill effect" refers to the paradox that, precisely when politeness and interpersonal sensitivity is most needed (e.g., in layoff situations), managers often tend to distance themselves from layoff victims. Respondents in layoff research have described anything but politeness by management when layoffs are implemented; instead, abusive and insensitive treatment adds insult to injury, pouring salt into laid-off employees' wounds by treating them with a lack of dignity and respect. This abusive treatment creates a toxic work environment ripe with the potential for violent backlash. Therefore, in focusing on that situational context as the "hot oil" of the popcorn metaphor, we draw on the literature on organizational justice for the theoretical grounding of our approach to vengeance-seeking employees and the occurrence of workplace violence.

Perpetrators of Workplace Violence: Are They Resentful?

Descriptions of the individuals who commit workplace violence often describe them as "disgruntled" and frequently mention resentment, the central focus of RCT. Consider, for example, the following: "the vengeful worker is typically a middle-aged white male who faces termination in a worsening economy. . . . He feels entitled to a well-paying, meaningful job. . . . He resents that his birthright has been snatched from him" (Fox & Levin, 1994, p. 166). At middle age, "youthful enthusiasm has been shattered and replaced by . . . a growing sense of resentment" (Fox & Levin, 1994, p. 167). Various sources of "job frustration" involving threats to careers, such as the worker displacements from repeated waves of downsizing, create "enough resentment to be translated into extreme violence" because "vengeful workers . . . feel that they have been treated unfairly" (Fox & Levin, 1994, p. 168). This portrait of revenge after job loss, which portrays downsizing as a prime situational instigator of resentment about unfair treatment, also fits the summary by Bensimon (1994) concerning factors that cause violence toward employers: "They include the pressures of widespread job losses, layoffs, mergers, downsizings, and working in 'lean and mean' companies" (Fox & Levin, 1994, p. 28).

Neither layoffs nor dismissals nor disciplinary actions, however, provoke violence in and of themselves. Rather, a strong desire for vengeance is spawned by the wounded pride and loss of face that occurs when such actions are conducted in a demeaning manner. In short, they occur when outcome losses are accompanied by violations of two forms of justice we described previously: procedural and interactional justice.

Again, we note that such effects are much more likely to occur for some individuals than others. In particular, those who tend to attribute others' actions to malevolent intentions (e.g., those high in hostile attributional bias) and who have "short fuses" because of high irritability (cf. Caprara et al., 1994) are the most likely to explode. Such explosions will occur, however, only when feelings of having been treated unfairly are fanned into resentment and the desire for vengeance. Unfortunately, growing evidence suggests that many organizations' policies and practices foster precisely this deadly combination. Consider, for example, additional findings in the literature on the impact of layoffs.

The literature on layoffs suggests that instead of adopting a sensitive and polite approach to the victims of downsizing, management often demonstrates aloofness and abusiveness likely to heighten resentment. For example, Schweiger, Ivancevich, and Power (1987) claimed that most displaced employees did not complain about the decisions that were made by human resource managers; "rather, they complained about *how they were made*" (italics added; p. 130). Most employees realized the need for layoffs, job changes, and so on. However, the main complaint "was how management handled these decisions and the time they took to make and communicate them" (Schweiger et al., 1987, p. 130). Schweiger et al. (1987) noted that it was "not the terminations per se that created . . . bitterness, but the manner in which the terminations were handled" (p. 130). Management puts itself in the position of making a bad situation worse, for "not only did employees have to deal with the loss of attachment, but also the harsh way in which terminations were often carried out" (Schweiger et al., 1987, p. 130).

Unfortunately, a recently reported profile of the workplace killer included characteristics such as "has been 'let go' in an insensitive manner" as a key element (Bensimon, 1994, p. 30). The same article attributed to James Fox (whose work on violence includes Fox & Levin, 1994) the following statement: "It's a matter of changing the way things are done in the company. You can't just grease the squeaky wheel. You've got to grease the whole machine" (Bensimon, 1994, p. 30). Although the metaphor is different, clearly the sentiment is the same as that expressed by the popcorn model. Bensimon's (1994) conclusion is explicit: "Time and time again, disgruntled workers who have become violent have said that what impelled them was not the fact that they were demoted or fired or laid off, but the dehumanizing way the action was carried out" (p. 30).

Other reports have emphasized that "the typical workplace murderer will blame others" (Stuart, 1992, p. 74) in a manner that externalizes the source of problems. Certainly, as we have noted, large individual differences exist with respect to this tendency toward such externalization of blame (cf. Dodge et al., 1990). A workplace environment in which many people share the view that management treats workers unfairly, however, will only exacerbate any such tendency in a given blame-prone individual. Moreover, a common workplace practice—inflated performance appraisals—does seem to put management in a potentially blameworthy position when firings and layoffs occur. Stuart (1992) pointed out, for example, that although the vengeful worker "may have . . . an unstable work history," the same employee "often gets a satisfactory performance appraisal because he intimidates supervisors" (p. 74). Notably, such circumstances lead the employee "to believe his behavior is justified" (Stuart, 1992, p. 74), consistent with the RCT emphasis on process justification.

Although anecdotal evidence can be only suggestive, some reports clearly zero-in on management practices as a source of potential problems. Consider, for example, the case of the laid-off employee (cited earlier) who killed the vice president and general manager of the plant where he had been employed, along with the regional sales manager. This employee had worked as a production test technician. In an interview afterward, the senior lead technician in the production test department emphasized "the need for middle management to respect the workers" (Stuart, 1992, p. 81) and that "there was a gap between the supervisors and the people. There was a perception that management didn't care, that they were only concerned with profits" (Stuart, 1992, p. 81). Such comments add a chilling footnote to the results from a survey conducted among certain public service employees in the early 1990s, in which "only a quarter of the 500,000 workers who responded said they were being 'treated with respect and dignity'" by management (Bensimon, 1994, p. 29).

In summary, existing evidence from several different sources suggests that the popcorn model may be a useful metaphor for understanding the roots of workplace aggression and, especially, the extreme forms labeled *workplace violence*. This model contends that researchers must focus both on the characteristics of individuals and concurrent conditions existing in organizations to understand when the frustration of feeling treated unfairly leads to anger and resentment and when such feelings translate into overt acts of violence. The model itself certainly does not provide the answers to this complex puzzle, but it does at least tell researchers where to look for the answers.

Extending the Model: The Many Forms of Aggression in the Workplace

We have concentrated primarily on the root causes of violence at work, with specific attention given to violence perpetrated by disgruntled current and former employees. We also have emphasized the situational causes that involve grounds for people to become disgruntled (e.g., resentment toward supervisors and the organization), that is, on company policies and supervisory practices as one potential source for perceptions that the workplace situation is heating up with management–labor conflicts. For convenience, conceptually we have subsumed all such workplace violence triggers under a reformulated concept of frustration borrowed from the frustration–aggression hypothesis. Our modified description of frustration, incorporating the "illegitimate violation of legitimate expectations" and the Outcome × Process interaction of RCT, represents one way to conceptualize antecedents of violence in situational terms, a key category of independent variables.

What about violence itself—the dependent variable? Scientific evidence on vengeful workplace killers is difficult to find. As a low-base-rate phenomenon, the rarity of violent workplace homicides directed against employers makes a meaningful test of antecedents difficult to conduct. Here, Organ's (1990) insights about rethinking the satisfaction–performance relationship can help in rethinking the dependent variable in the frustration–aggression relationship.

Organ (1990) suggested that, rather than using ordinary indicators of performance (often influenced by factors beyond workers' control), researchers might well consider behaviors over which workers have control. In essence, his logic noted that useful information would be rare and hard to uncover when conceptualizing the dependent variable in the normal manner: The conceptualization itself made the phenomenon a low-base-rate behavior. This prompted the reconceptualization of performance measurement by turning to citizenship behaviors (i.e., positive forms of behavior under discretionary motivational control spawned by a high degree of loyalty, commitment, and esprit de corps within a company's labor force).

The popcorn model suggests that researchers should adopt a similar strategy with respect to workplace violence. Recall that the popcorn analogy not only points to hot oil as a factor causing the explosion of the first kernel, but it also brings to mind what happened to those kernels that did not pop. Homans (1974) proposed that when an individual feels unfairly treated by a more powerful source (e.g., the person's supervisor or the corporation), attempts to restore justice largely will be indirect. Therefore, before resorting to direct and visible forms of violence, disgruntled employees may engage in more covert forms of retaliation. Thus, when violence from a vengeful employee does occur, that incident might represent merely the "tip of the iceberg"; in other words, more subtle and covert forms of aggression might have been occurring all along that were prompted by the situational toxicity of an unfair climate.

As a useful step toward understanding workplace violence and hostility, we suggest that researchers also investigate organizational retaliation behaviors (ORBs) initiated by disgruntled current or former employees, a term that is intentionally contrasted with organizational citizenship behaviors (OCBs). ORBs retain the OCB feature of involving behavior that has an intentional, discretionary motivational character. Many such behaviors already have been identified as potential reactions to inequity. Withholding effort, for example, retaliates against the employer by reducing the corporation's profits. The RCT perspective, however, modifies the equity theory predictions by also incorporating effects from process-related variables. Hence, existing organizational justice analyses of topics such as sabotage and vandalism (e.g., DeMore, Fisher, & Baron, 1988), professional deviance (Raelin, 1994), or employee theft (e.g., Greenberg & Scott, 1996) help illustrate examples of ORBs.

Although we can use many such investigations to illustrate a link from the sense of injustice to retaliatory actions by employees aimed against employers, the scattered array of findings lacks coherence. These findings need integration that provides a conceptual road map for locating points on the retaliatory landscape and the relationships among them. In the following section we sketch a direction that such efforts might take that is drawn from previous discussions by Baron and his colleagues (e.g., Neuman & Baron, in press). Baron used the term *workplace aggression* rather than *workplace violence*. Given the low-base-rate problem mentioned earlier, however, we think the best route to further progress can come from extending the dependent variable beyond an exclusive focus on violent homicides. Moreover, the definition of aggression we have adopted in this chapter emphasizes the component of intention. This emphasis parallels the element of discretionary motivation common to OCBs and ORBs. Therefore, we present an analysis of workplace aggression as the broader dependent variable of interest.

Forms of Aggression: 1. The Buss Framework as a Foundation

Aggressive actions appear in many guises. We find Buss's (1961) framework useful for categorizing these forms of aggression. His taxonomy (see Table 2) differentiates among the sometimes subtle, but often important, nuances in behavioral manifestations of hostile feelings. Buss categorized forms of aggression (behavioral expressions of hostility) along three dimensions: physical and verbal, active and passive, and direct and indirect. Combinations of these dimensions identify forms of aggression and how harm is delivered to the target.

Consider, for example, the category *physical forms*. These include actions such as attack with a weapon, physical restraint, unwanted touching, pushing, hitting, or punching. The *verbal forms* label anchors the opposite endpoint of this first dimension. People inflict this form of aggression through words rather than deeds. Instances of verbal aggression can include threats, insults, sarcasm, and language that is offensive to the target.

Consider the active–passive dimension. *Active* forms of aggression inflict harm through the performance of some behavior. By contrast, people inflict *passive* aggression by withholding some action. Note the usefulness of this distinction when combined with either pole of the physical–verbal dimension described earlier. Insults, for example, illustrate the active–verbal combination. The passive–verbal combination, on the other hand, includes forms of aggression such as failing to provide the target with needed information (e.g., withholding communication).

Table 2. Examples of Eight Types of Workplace Aggression Categorized
According to Buss's (1961) Typology

Direct aggression	Indirect aggression
Physical	
Active (cell 1)	Active (cell 2)
Homicide	Theft
Assault	Sabotage
Sexual assault	Defacing property
Dirty looks	Consuming needed resources
Interrupting others	Hiding needed resources
Obscene gestures	Removing needed resources
Passive (cell 3)	Passive (cell 4)
Intentional work slowdowns	Showing up late for meetings
Refusal to provide needed resources	Delaying work, making target look bad
Leaving area when target enters	Failure to protect target's welfare
Preventing target from expressing self	Causing others to delay action
Verbal	
Active (cell 5)	Active (cell 6)
Threats	Spreading rumors
Yelling	Whistle-blowing
Sexual harassment	Talking behind target's back
Insults and sarcasm	Belittling opinions
Flaunting status	Attacking protégé
Unfair performance evaluation	Transmitting damaging information
Passive (cell 7)	Passive (cell 8)
Failure to return phone calls	Failure to transmit information
Giving target the silent treatment	Failure to deny false rumors
Damning with faint praise	Failure to defend target
Refusing target's request	Failure to warn of impending danger

The final dimension contrasts direct versus indirect forms of aggression. The term *direct* aggression refers to harm aimed expressly (directly) at the intended target. On the other hand, *indirect* aggression involves harm caused through an intermediary or by attacking something that the target values. Again, examining combinations of dimensional end points illustrates the usefulness of this taxonomy. For example, the direct–verbal combination would include actions such as insulting the target to his or her face. Actions such as spreading false rumors behind the target's back instead would fall under the indirect–verbal heading.

Table 2 includes these and other examples of the eight forms of aggression that fit into the categories of Buss's (1961) framework. We start with this framework as a reference point because of its classic status within the aggression literature and because we think it combines generality (comprehensiveness) with specificity (useful distinctions) in a heuristically useful manner. We consider Buss's framework to be sufficiently general to cover a wide variety of behaviors associated with intentional harm, the kinds of actions that often represent ways of "getting even" and retaliating (in line with motives such as revenge and punishment for wrongdoing). On the other hand, the literature contains several other notable treatments addressing forms of aggression in the workplace. Those interested in workplace aggression and violence can certainly benefit from examining those other accounts in detail (e.g., Baron, 1993; Cox & Leather, 1994; Robinson & Bennett, 1995). In the following section, we review them only briefly. We do not attempt to correlate their categories with specific categories in Buss's framework, although much overlap is evident.

Forms of Aggression: 2. Other Treatments of Workplace Aggression and Related Behaviors

First, we note briefly a typology of deviant workplace behavior proposed by Robinson and Bennett (1995). Buss's (1961) framework in Table 2 focuses on interpersonal forms of aggression (i.e., actions designed to inflict harm on the target person or organization). On the other hand, in Robinson and Bennett's (1995) typology of deviant behavior, not all of the categories require intentions to harm others or the organization.

Although many deviant actions do indeed inflict harm, such actions might stem from many motives other than, or in addition to, the motive to inflict harm. For instance, wasting resources, one of several forms of *production deviance* identified by Robinson and Bennett (1995), might stem from carelessness rather than from an intentional desire to harm the organization or its representatives in positions of authority. Similarly, blaming coworkers, an action that would fit into Robinson and Bennett's category of *political deviance*, might involve efforts to protect one's own reputation and image rather than intentions to harm rivals. In short, although Buss's (1961) and Robinson and Bennett's (1995) frameworks have considerable overlap, the latter conceivably might include behaviors that do not reflect aggression according to the definition we have adopted in this chapter.

The organizational literature on frustration–aggression also has included various measures of aggression as dependent variables. Of note are measures used by Spector and his colleagues (e.g., Chen & Spector, 1992; Spector, 1975, 1978; Storms & Spector, 1987), with labels such as hostility and complaining, aggression, and sabotage. For example, Spector (1975) administered both a predictor questionnaire of organizational frustration and a criterion questionnaire containing measures of those responses to frustration. He computed correlations between each response factor and the total score on the Organizational Frustration Questionnaire. The results showed the highest correlation (.70) between the Organizational Frustration total score and the Hostility and Complaining scale. The latter included items such as "Told people outside the job what a lousy place you work at" and "Said something derogatory about your boss to other people"; the former included statements such as "Policies at work are not fair" (Spector, 1975, p. 636). In a similar study, Mangione and Quinn (1975) investigated frequencies of the following behaviors (negatively correlated with job satisfaction): spread rumors or gossip to cause trouble at work; did work badly or incorrectly on purpose; stole merchandise or equipment from employer; and purposely damaged employer's property, equipment, or product.

More recently, authors also have begun to explore the negative pole of a continuum anchored on the positive end by OCB (on the logic of examining constructive vs. destructive motivational approaches among employees; see Cropanzano & Folger, 1996). Among those labeled "anticitizenship behaviors" by Ball, Trevino, and Sims (1994) were the following: lying in order to get the boss into trouble, finding fault with what the organization is doing, and talking back to supervisors. Similarly, Lehman and Simpson (1992) reported using measures of antagonistic work behaviors that included filing formal complaints and disobeying a supervisor's instructions.

Workplace Aggression: The Need for Systematic Research

Returning to Buss's (1961) framework, we now note the following two points that Table 2 helps to highlight: (a) Aggressive behavior manifests itself in a variety of ways. Despite this apparent diversity of forms, all such actions share a common element—the desire to inflict harm on some target person or entity. (b) Many behaviors represented in Table 2 have received little or no attention in systematic research. Examples of these underresearched and often wholly neglected actions include belittling others' opinions, delaying work to make others look bad, removing or needlessly consuming required resources, flaunting status, and intentionally showing up late for meetings. Rather than investigating such topics, some workplace aggression research concentrates on physical forms of assault of an active and direct nature (cell 1 in Table 2). Such assaults have the flavor of high drama, but they do not adequately represent the full gamut of workplace aggression. Clearly, additional research should address other forms of aggression, such as the passive and indirect variety.

We think Table 2 also points to the following additional questions: (a) Why has the literature on aggression overlooked these potentially important, and often damaging and costly, forms of aggressive behavior? (b) Why has the research—at least that prevalent in the organizational literature—failed to view these behaviors as aggressive?

Regarding the first question, some forms of aggression might go unacknowledged because, in general, most research on human aggression has focused on relatively direct, active forms: physical and verbal assaults (see, e.g., Baron & Richardson, 1994; Huesmann, 1994). By contrast, we purposely emphasize that aggression in workplaces can, and generally does, take many different forms. Also, much research has tended to focus on affective (hostile), as opposed to instrumental, aggression (Geen, 1991). Clearly, much aggression in organizational settings is instrumental in nature. Our definition of aggression as intentional harm-doing behavior is consistent with the views held by many aggression researchers (cf. Berkowitz, 1974, 1981; Feshbach, 1970). Our definition delimits the aggressive behaviors of interest but also adopts a broad enough scope so that potentially significant forms are not overlooked.

Another reason for some lacunae in aggression research may involve what comes to mind when aggressive behavior is considered as a topic. We suspect that acts of physical violence or direct verbal assaults (e.g., threats, taunts, insults) have the greatest salience. Accordingly, most aggression research has tended to focus on issues related to such actions.

Regarding the question of why organizational researchers have not typically viewed many of the behaviors listed in Table 2 as being aggressive in nature, we think the answer involves several points. First, because much behavior in organizations is goal directed (e.g., aimed at obtaining status, power, or material or financial gain), research in this setting tends to focus on self-serving interests rather than hostile motives. Therefore, many behaviors listed in cells 3, 4, 7, and 8 of Table 2 have been studied within the context of organizational politics (cf. Drory & Romm, 1990; S. P. Feldman, 1988; Ferris & Kacmar, 1992; Ferris & King, 1991; Velasques, Moberg, & Cavanaugh, 1983) rather than as instances of workplace aggression. Second, many of the Table 2 actions may not be recognized as being aggressive. Because hostile intentions are concealed easily, these behaviors may go completely unnoticed or be perceived as inadvertent or coincidental. Finally, these behaviors are not always motivated by aggressive intent: People do show up late for meetings or fail to return phone calls for reasons completely unrelated to aggression. This, too, makes it less likely that organizational researchers will identify such actions as instances of workplace aggression.

Having categorized various behaviors with respect to their role as forms of workplace aggression, we now turn to the question of how such actions might be prevented. In the following section on prevention, however, the scope is not broad. Instead, we focus on those aspects of prevention that are relatively unique to our perspective on perceived injustice as a motive behind some acts of workplace violence.

Prevention Activities: Implications of the Fairness Analysis

Not all workplace violence stems from attempted retaliation for perceived injustice. In fact, the vast majority of homicides in the workplace occur in connection with other illegal activities, such as robberies. By the same token, many programs for the prevention of workplace violence involve measures for increased security. These should help prevent violence regardless of the motive, whether committed in connection with some other crime or committed as an act of revenge.

Aggression and violence associated with perceived injustice, however, also call for special measures. First, because the motive for retaliation can come from an "insider" (i.e., someone still employed who has ready access to the workplace), measures directed at protection against outside intruders might be inadequate. Second, the roots of revenge in perceived unfair treatment actually create special opportunities for the prevention of workplace violence, opportunities that require serious review of any grounds employees might have for feeling unfairly treated. Finally, hostility toward the organization by employees need not lead to violence (e.g., homicide) to have dysfunctional consequences. As our review in the previous section indicated, workplace aggression by employees can take many forms. Programs designed only to prevent episodes of violence would not necessarily address these other, more broad-ranging forms of aggression, nor would they necessarily be likely to treat the underlying causes of perceived unfair treatment.

We next review three categories of fairness—distributive, procedural, and interpersonal injustice—and discuss the role that each can play as part of efforts at preventing aggression and violence in the workplace. However, our discussion focuses only on actions that the management of an organization can take. We do not mean to imply that perceived unfairness occurs only when management acts unfairly. By the same token, we do not mean to absolve an employee of responsibility for aggressive or violent actions.

We illustrate preventive actions by management in two categories: layoffs and performance appraisals. These certainly do not exhaust the areas for preventive actions to improve perceived fairness. They do, however, reflect typical dissatisfying outcomes for employees (e.g., being fired, failing to receive a promotion, having a grievance settled disadvantageously, not receiving a requested work assignment). RCT indicates that any such sources of dissatisfying outcomes can become grounds for resentment depending on whether management impropriety seems to have been involved. Therefore, in the following sections, we address three general forms of perceived impropriety and their determinants (see Exhibit 1).

Preventing Perceptions of Distributive Injustice

Consider job loss due to a layoff. This dissatisfying outcome obviously can cause substantial frustration, as well as even more intense emotional reactions. Recall, however, the RCT principle that negative feelings about outcomes generate resentment toward individuals or institutions only when the latter's actions constitute wrongdoing (i.e., the institution or its agents seem blameworthy). Nonetheless, if a sufficiently extreme discrepancy exists between outcome–input payoffs and fair rates of return, this discrepancy itself might be perceived as evidence for assumed wrongdoing of some kind.

Layoffs involve an outcome—job loss—so extreme that it might constitute a wrongful inequity in which punishment (job loss) occurs despite innocent behavior (the employee's faithful service to the employer). As long as the employee's service has met all requirements for remaining hired, the employee probably feels "innocent" and hence "unjustly punished" by the loss of a job. Note that employees also grant to management a certain amount of discretionary authority (i.e., agreeing to do what managers ask, within reason). The broader implications of this agreement constitute an unwritten "psychological" contract (cf. Rousseau, 1995): Employees agree

Exhibit 1. Distributive, Procedural, and Interpersonal Justice Actions to Prevent Workplace Aggression

Distributive justice

Layoffs and firings
  Do not raise chief executive officer's pay when downsizing
  Try other financial alternatives to layoffs
  If firing by performance ratings, check their validity
Performance appraisal
  Use job-related, relevant criteria
  Develop criteria based on job analysis

Procedural justice

Layoffs and firings
  Use employee voice or input where possible
    Details on severance, and so on
    Suggestions on avoiding bias
    Consistently applied guidelines
    Timeliness of feedback
    Adequate explanations
Performance appraisal
  Clarify in advance standards and expectations
  Solicit employee's own opinion about performance (e.g., self-appraisal)
  Explain and discuss ratings (explore discrepancies)

Interpersonal justice

Layoffs and firings
  Notify in a timely manner
  Explain sincerely and with sincere concern
  Express sincere remorse
  Avoid distancing and aloofness
  Treat with dignity and respect
Performance appraisal
  Same as for layoffs and firings

to abide by discretionary authority partly because a certain degree of employment security also is considered part of the bargain.

Layoffs can violate an implied psychological contract unless employees perceive that holding a job, as an outcome, is not only attributable to the inputs of labor and discretion granted to management but also is based on an organization's ability to pay wages (i.e., enough profits). A dire economic necessity presumably might represent the type of emergency that sets aside the normal provisions of standard contracts, including implied contracts of the psychological variety (e.g., job security in return for loyal service as an employee). A company presumably "restructures" its labor force via downsizing and the use of layoffs because a reasonable analysis of the business's financial picture calls for such action; the action might be warranted by the business conditions the firm faces. In essence, layoffs represent an alteration to the original psychological contract (e.g., "You can work here as long as you remain loyal and productive") based on a change in the firm's financial circumstances.

An employee's belief that the old outcome–input contract no longer holds, however, requires answers to questions such as the following: Which conditions changed in the first place? Was it indeed necessary to reduce labor costs and, if so, why? Given the necessity of reducing labor costs, on what grounds does a layoff constitute the only (or the best) way to achieve that result? What other actions were considered, and why were they not chosen as an alternative to a layoff? We argue that until management has persuasive answers to such questions, it runs the risk of perceived distributive unfairness from having violated the original implied contract. As Wilhelm (1993) put it, "downsizing violates . . . the desire for justice. . . . The fairness evaporates when a company is going through a downsizing campaign, in order to save costs, while CEO salary remains very high" (p. 478).

Other distributive questions would apply when employees lose their jobs individually rather than through layoffs: With a firing "for cause," distributively just causes would entail employee inputs below a satisfactory level for retention (e.g., incompetent performance, embezzlement, or other forms of unacceptable misconduct).

Performance appraisals also deliver outcomes (e.g., performance ratings and sometimes accompanying differences in pay) that should indicate a fair match with actual performance inputs (e.g., quality and quantity of materials produced). An employee can question whether that fair match of outcomes to inputs exists. For example, the courts have often ruled against organizations—such as those sued on employment discrimination grounds—when the criteria for selection are not job related. Criteria for performance also must be job related and relevant in order to reflect legitimate grounds for assessment. A company that does not use legitimate criteria (e.g., based on a job analysis of required knowledge, skills, and abilities as inputs) can thus subject itself to charges of distributive injustice.

Preventing Perceptions of Procedural Injustice

Imagine that drastic action was required to keep an organization afloat in light of changed government regulations over which it had no control or advance warning and that all other possible means were explored thoroughly before resorting to layoffs. Would such circumstances imply no further responsibilities for fair treatment of employees?

The existence of procedural justice criteria suggests that companies "legitimately entitled" to conduct layoffs can still violate employees' sense of procedural fairness. What would procedurally improper layoffs look like? Actually, there are two sets of answers to this question that correspond to the distinction between the topic of procedural justice in this section and the topic of interpersonal justice that we address in our third and final section on fairness criteria. The distinction becomes clearer by restricting attention in this section to formal procedures such as those used to make decisions or to resolve disputes. Organizational behavior, social and industrial/organizational psychology, and other disciplines have generated much theory and research that sheds light on acceptable criteria for the fairness of such procedures. Here, we review these criteria only briefly. (For more extensive treatment, see Folger & Bies, 1989; Lind & Tyler, 1988; Tyler & Bies, 1990.)

Although norms of procedural justice can vary from context to context and from one culture to the next, the following are worth noting. First, procedural legitimacy is hard to defend unless some mechanism exists for taking affected parties' viewpoints into account. Second, fair procedures also need mechanisms for reducing the extent to which a decision maker's own personal prejudices and biases can influence the decision. Third, decision-making criteria should be applied consistently. Fourth, parties affected by the results of the decision-making process should be notified quickly. Finally, those affected are owed an explanation about the criteria used and the methods of decision making.

How would such criteria apply to layoffs? Considering employees' viewpoints might seem difficult to do when top-level financial decisions have to be made with the strategic direction of the firm in mind. That is, the basis for downsizing or restructuring would seem to be dictated by factors more familiar to top-level executives (e.g., information about global competitors). On the other hand, certain aspects of the procedure might benefit from employee input. A task force of employees could be formed, for instance, to address matters such as severance pay (e.g., how to make sure that employees understand their options).

Applications of the other procedural fairness criteria also could be found by exercising sufficient ingenuity. In fact, the principles of considering employee viewpoints and suppressing personal biases could be combined by using an employee task force to make recommendations about how to prevent both the practice and the appearance of prejudice. The same is true for recommendations about the remaining criteria: Advice from employees might be useful about how to apply decision-making criteria consistently, how to provide timely feedback, and how to provide explanations. Although not in the realm of downsizing, applications of these principles to the introduction of a wage freeze and the introduction of a no-smoking policy have been illustrated by Greenberg (1990a, 1994).

How would such criteria apply to performance appraisals? To illustrate, we highlight features from two recent works on "due process" and performance appraisal (Folger, Konovsky, & Cropanzano, 1992; Taylor, Tracy, Renard, Harrison, & Carroll, 1995).

Folger et al. (1992) proposed due process as a metaphor applicable to procedures for making performance appraisal decisions. They noted that legal authorities typically identify three defining features of due process. The first is adequate notice, meaning that laws must be a matter of public record and defendants must be informed in a timely manner about charges brought against them. The second feature is a fair hearing, one in which relevant evidence is presented and each party has a chance to respond.

The third feature is that the final judgment itself should be well reasoned (and reasonable); in other words, it should not show signs of biased influence such as corruption or coercion from external pressures.

Taylor et al. (1995) tested the Folger et al. (1992) due process model by implementing a new performance appraisal system for a government agency. Matched employees were assigned randomly to the existing system or to the newly designed, due process system. Employees reacted much more favorably to the due process system on each of the following dimensions: fairness of appraisal, accuracy, satisfaction with the appraisal system, satisfaction with the appraisal rating, and a six-item scale on which each employee evaluated his or her manager.

What were the differences between the two systems that caused these reactions? In the area of adequate notice, for example, the due process system's unique features included a preliminary meeting between manager and employee to discuss performance expectations for the upcoming review period. The due process system also included a special feedback session given midway through that period. The fairness of the final appraisal session as a "hearing" was enhanced by having due process participants complete a self-appraisal rating form. When a manager indicated his or her rating of an employee, this additional feature of the review session allowed employees "to challenge this assessment and to provide their own commentary" (Taylor et al., 1995, p. 496). Finally, the case for a reasoned judgment, based on evidence, was strengthened by training and a manual designed for the due process system. These helped managers to explain ratings to employees as grounds for discussion.

Another aspect of the results from this field experiment helps underscore the importance of procedural fairness. Notably, the old appraisal system—historically criticized because it seemed to produce rating inflation—again yielded higher ratings. In other words, employees perceived the due process system more positively even though it resulted in lower overall ratings. We argue that in the absence of the perceived fairness of the due process system, these lower ratings would have instead been more likely to generate resentment.

Preventing Perceptions of Interpersonal Injustice

The organizational literature commonly distinguishes among distributive, procedural, and interactional justice; we use the term *interpersonal* as an alternative label for the last of these. This label is consistent with recent findings (e.g., Greenberg, 1993a, 1994) that emphasize the importance of interpersonal sensitivity as conduct relevant to perceptions of fair treatment. Essentially, this form of conduct helps ensure that people feel they have been treated with dignity, respect, and the politeness of common courtesy. Interpersonal justice refers not to formal procedures but to the actions of people who implement those procedures and how those people conduct themselves. Do they, for example, act in a manner that is attentive, considerate, and respectful toward those affected by decisions?

What would ensure that layoffs are conducted with interpersonal sensitivity for those who lose their jobs? Strange as it might seem, layoffs often are implemented in a demeaning fashion. Managers conducting layoffs easily can fall prey to being distant and aloof about communicating bad news (cf. Brockner, 1992). Therefore, observing some simple courtesies toward employees who are laid off would go a long way toward easing the pain of job loss, or at least not increasing the painfulness by "adding insult to injury."

First, employees should receive the news of a layoff as much in advance as possible. Far too often, any indication of an impending layoff remains hidden until the arrival of a security guard who asks laid-off employees to clear out their desks and leave the organization's premises that very day. The need for withholding information about a company's financial picture and the need for adequate security certainly must receive consideration, but not to the point of total disregard for an employee's self-respect.

Second, announcing a layoff should include providing a thorough explanation. Research indicates that explanations enhance perceived fairness if they are adequate and sincere (Bies, 1987a). Sincerity relates to interpersonal demeanor. We think employees are quick to detect insincere attempts to make them feel good. Using explanations to deflect blame in a Machiavellian manner usually backfires, primarily because manipulative attempts at persuasion almost inevitably reveal a lack of genuine concern and caring.

Similarly, sincere concern for the well-being of employees who are laid off cannot be manufactured artificially by simply hiring an outplacement service, extending severance benefits, and in other ways attending only to employees' needs for financial security and for enhanced prospects of a new job. Trying to soothe the pain of job loss by easing the financial burden might reduce some of the guilt that can be experienced when harming another person, and certainly it is better than ignoring the laid-off employee's needs altogether. There is a danger, however, that a focus on the employee's economic well-being will become a substitute for attending to emotional needs as well.

Dealing with the emotional side of loss sometimes calls for making an apology, an act known to reduce hostility (cf. Baron, 1988, 1990). The willingness to apologize and express remorse, for example, also conveys that someone has benevolent intentions and can be trusted to act fairly (cf. Bies, 1987b). Saying "I'm sorry," however, might be taken as admission of having made a mistake, something representatives of top management might be reluctant to do and that the executive team might be reluctant to approve.

Dealing adequately with painful emotions cannot be done by sending a memorandum, by hiring an outplacement service, and by extending severance benefits to laid-off employees. Ultimately, management of the grieving process requires sympathy and compassion as conveyed in face-to-face conversations with employees. A private meeting of a supervisor and a laid-off employee, for example, should allow the employee opportunities to raise questions about process fairness and to articulate reactions. Denying the opportunity of expression can seem unfair and can cause resentment.

Many of the same principles apply to the performance appraisal context, even if a low performance rating pales by comparison to the loss of being laid off. The supervisor who communicates the bad news of a low rating must not be cold, aloof, and distancing, the coping mechanisms people use to avoid experiencing the vicarious pain of someone else's suffering. The same tendency causes the person giving negative feedback to do so as quickly as possible. Perhaps for that reason, the folklore of human resources management refers jokingly to the "invisible appraisal": Supervisors will swear that they conducted an appraisal session, whereas employees cannot recall that event having ever occurred; the bad news of a poor rating is given in an offhand manner and glossed over so quickly that the employee either cannot remember the topic having come up or cannot recall what was said.

Treating employees with dignity during negative feedback accomplishes many worthwhile purposes, including the prevention of anger and aggressive actions, which appear to be quite common in this context (e.g., Geddes & Baron, 1996), and increasing the sense of interpersonal fairness. First, employees who receive negative feedback should have a chance to indicate their opinion about its validity. Second, a manager who actually invites comments, and shows an interest in hearing how an employee feels about bad news, sends a signal about empathy and compassion. He or she also conveys a sense of respect for the employee's feelings. Suppose that the manager instead tries to tell the employee how to feel (e.g., "You should be glad to get this kind of constructive advice") or prevents the employee from expressing opinions. Such approaches actually represent an affront to the employee's dignity. Ironically, that very action creates an additional sense of outcome loss, namely a loss of face by the employee.

We would be remiss not to mention that managers obviously also risk losing face by taking the kinds of actions we recommend for the delivery of bad news. The irony of Churchill's (1950) statement about how it "costs nothing to be polite" is that even simple acts of common courtesy can require emotional and psychological sacrifice. Perhaps only in the context of preventing something so abhorrent as a workplace homicide can managers be asked to make such sacrifices. Giving up emotional detachment often is difficult. Just as people resist change because it makes them uncomfortable, managers can become uncomfortable when told about the need to show compassion, caring, consideration, and empathy. Such stuff lacks the legitimation of "keeping an eye on the bottom line" and acting in accord with facts, figures, financials, and the logic of economic rationality.

We therefore conclude with brief comments on the analogy between seeking organizational change and seeking to implement interpersonal fairness. If being interpersonally sensitive can constitute a "high-cost" activity, then it may engage many of the same sources of resistance that are marshaled against organizational change. Telling managers to treat employees with dignity and respect is not enough; in terms of the organizational development metaphor of a force-field analysis, delivering that type of message deals only with the forces for change and ignores the forces of resistance.

To deal with potential resistance, consider the analogy of system overload. When demands on a system threaten to overwhelm it, one method of adaptation aims to reduce those demands, whereas another aims to increase the system's capacity for coping with them. Similarly, when managers are asked to convey emotional sensitivity and to treat employees with dignity and respect, the demands of that task should not exceed the managers' capacity to enact them. That is, efforts must be made to provide managers with the emotional and psychological resources they need to enhance their capacity for dealing with the trauma of employees' losses. The modeling of sincerity and honesty by top management must play a part in supplying this resource base; just as employees tend to treat customers the way they are treated by their supervisors, supervisors tend to treat their subordinates in a manner consistent with upper-level management's treatment of those supervisors.

Top management also can make it easier to be sympathetic, show common courtesy, and treat employees with dignity and respect. The harder it is to justify top management's own actions, the harder it is to face employees who are adversely affected by those actions. As indicated in our discussion of layoffs from the standpoint of distributive justice criteria, the basis for a layoff affects the perception of its fairness. Layoffs conducted for inexcusable reasons, just as performance reviews that assign a rating arbitrarily and capriciously, will not make it easy for a supervisor to "face the music" of discussing the impact of these decisions with affected employees. Making a decision requires not only being fair but also being perceived as fair (cf. Greenberg, 1990b). However, just as important, it can be difficult to create the perception of being fair in a vacuum, totally divorced from the reality of any actual fairness, or at least an honest, sincere attempt to be as fair as can reasonably be expected. Good-faith intentions go a long way. The lack of interpersonal sensitivity, on the other hand, often is perceived to be a signal about the lack of such intentions.

Additional Prevention Activities

Although prevention activities based on our justice analysis point mainly toward influences on perceived unfairness, we briefly summarize other prevention activities for two reasons. First, many of these come from research on aggression yet are frequently neglected in writings on workplace violence. Second, these activities can be effective at reducing hostile impulses that stem from perceived unfairness, even though the activities themselves do not directly address those perceptions (for a review, see Baron & Richardson, 1994).

Conflict often can be reduced, for example, by inducing emotional states incompatible with anger in potential aggressors, such as by introducing humor or otherwise altering mood in ways that make it more positive (cf. Baron, 1984). Nonaggressive models also prove effective; we cited the value in the example set by top management earlier, but the same idea extends to all levels of management in modeling how to resolve disputes constructively and graciously (hence the value of training in conflict resolution, communication effectiveness, and related social skills). Finally, research on aggression also shows that a variety of cognitively based approaches can successfully reduce hostile impulses. We touched on these when mentioning the value of explaining the causes of negative outcomes, but they are worth making explicit. For example, warning people in advance about a future event that might otherwise provoke their anger often helps to prevent such anger (Zillmann, 1994). Similarly, explaining why someone acted in an otherwise anger-provoking way can defuse at least part of the anger not only when the explanation is given in advance, but even if given after the fact (provided that not too much time elapses between event and explanation).

Conclusion

Our analysis of workplace violence and aggression has focused only on the hostile, retaliatory motive portrayed in expressions such as "disgruntled employee." Before summarizing, we first note some things we have neglected or inevitably underemphasized. We presented a Person × Situation analysis but focused mostly on the situation because other accounts already emphasize the characteristics of the violent perpetrator (e.g., efforts at profiling and screening). Relatedly, we focused on how managers might prevent some of the sources of workplace aggression by acting fairly and acting so that their intentions are perceived to be fair-minded. On the other hand, some violent perpetrators apparently externalize blame to an excessive degree, perhaps so much that no efforts to be fair might ever prevent the "chip-on-the-shoulder" mentality entirely.

We tried to gain depth of analysis by sacrificing breadth. Not all workplace aggression represents a motive to retaliate and get even with the corporation. For those acts that do reflect a retaliation, however, we tried to increase the depth of analysis in two respects. First, we took a closer look at the motive itself. Second, we provided a broader, more detailed examination of various hostile behaviors that can result from such a motive.

In this two-part approach we used the frustration–aggression hypothesis as a starting point to describe a situational instigator (frustration) and a behavioral reaction (aggression). However, the term *frustration*, we argued, is too nonspecific for the situational context and the corresponding emotion. We argued that feelings of injustice constitute a more specific and accurate characterization. The terms *injustice* and *unfairness* (used interchangeably in this chapter) serve as shorthand for related phrases such as the "illegitimate frustration of legitimate expectations." We also argued from the RCT perspective that such phrases combine outcome and process: A loss or sense of relative deprivation on an outcome dimension by itself focuses only on the outcome as an object of attention; emotions such as frustration or dissatisfaction refer only to feelings about outcomes, not attitudes toward people (e.g., hostility). Such emotions in themselves do not tell the whole story about sources of aggression. The process also matters.

The process can shape inferences about people who control outcomes, such as inferences about their intentions. Outcomes result from procedures (e.g., for decision making). People institute and implement procedures. Moreover, two people who adopt the same broad procedural guidelines do not necessarily govern all the details of related actions by the same codes of conduct (e.g., details about how a decision is announced and how opportunities to discuss the result are handled). For that reason, employees do not respond simply to layoffs or negative performance reviews as outcomes. *What* they experience can produce dissatisfaction and frustration, but *how* the management of that experience is conducted by those in charge—procedurally and interpersonally—determines whether frustration about an outcome turns into resentment of unjust treatment. Resentment, in turn, is the emotional base from which retaliatory actions are launched.

In the other half of this chapter, we went beyond violence per se (e.g., homicide) and considered other types of retaliatory actions by disgruntled employees (i.e., those who feel unfairly treated). In the case of the frustration side of the frustration–aggression formula, we expanded beyond frustration because it was too nonspecific as the instigating state. In the case of aggression, we expanded beyond acts of violence because they are too specific a form of retaliation. Table 2 illustrates this effort.

We also discussed ways to prevent retaliatory workplace aggression by targeting specific forms of injustice with specific forms of management practice, illustrating these as practices for conducting layoffs and performance appraisals. To anchor any such advice more firmly and to ground it in sound, informed analysis, however, a great deal of work obviously remains to be done. Our final comments therefore indicate only briefly how much remains unknown.

For example, not nearly enough evidence exists to estimate the degree of association between indications of the motive for retaliation on the one hand and acts of workplace aggression on the other. At an even more problematic level, more information is needed about the development of resentment over time, so that the transition to retaliation from resentment held in check becomes more understandable. Resentment at a single point in time does not exist in a vacuum. It can be reinforced by additional perceived injustices and built over time. It also can be reinforced by others' resentments. Finally, the level of violence in society as a whole can play a part both in instigating aggressive behaviors and in shaping the specifics of action (e.g., by modeling the use of weapons).

Although many unanswered questions remain, we think that much progress already has been made. We hope that this chapter has not only chronicled some of the progress but that it also will help to contribute some ideas toward sustaining and accelerating such advances.

References

Adams, J. S. (1965). Inequity in social exchange. *Advances in Experimental Social Psychology, 2*, 267–299.

Anderson, C. A., Deuser, W. E., & DeNeve, K. M. (1995). Hot temperatures, hostile affect, hostile cognition, and arousal: Tests of a general model of affective aggression. *Personality and Social Psychology Bulletin, 21*, 434–448.

Associated Press. (1995a, July 12). Employee kills five at Texas firm. *Albany Times*, B1.

Associated Press. (1995b, December 16). 3 die in shooting spree. *The Times Picayune*, A12.

Associated Press. (1996, January 6). Charges filed in office attack. *The Times Picayune*, A6.

Ball, G. A., Trevino, L. K., & Sims, H. P. (1994). Just and unjust punishment: Influences on subordinate performance and citizenship. *Academy of Management Journal, 37*, 299–322.

Baron, R. A. (1984). Reducing organizational conflict: An incompatible response approach. *Journal of Applied Psychology, 69*, 272–279.

Baron, R. A. (1988). Negative effects of destructive criticism: Impact on conflict, self-efficacy, and task performance. *Journal of Applied Psychology, 73*, 199–207.

Baron, R. A. (1990). Countering the effects of destructive criticism: The relative efficacy of four potential interventions. *Journal of Applied Psychology, 75*, 235–245.

Baron, R. A. (1994). The physical environment of work settings: Effects on task performance, interpersonal relations, and job satisfaction. *Research in Organizational Behavior, 16*, 1–46.

Baron, R. A., & Neuman, J. H. (1996). Workplace violence and workplace aggression: Evidence on their relative frequency and potential causes. *Aggressive Behavior, 22*, 161–173.

Baron, R. A., & Richardson, D. R. (1994). *Human aggression* (2nd ed.). New York: Plenum.

Baron, S. A. (1993). Violence in the workplace: A prevention and management guide for businesses. Ventura, CA: Pathfinders Publishing Co.

Bensimon, H. F. (1994). Crisis and disaster management: Violence in the workplace. *Training and Development, 28*, 27–32.

Berkowitz, L. (1974). Some determinants of impulsive aggression: The role of mediated associations with reinforcements for aggression. *Psychological Review, 81*, 165–176.

Berkowitz, L. (1981). The concept of aggression. In P. F. Brain & D. Benton (Eds.), *Multidisciplinary approaches to aggression research* (pp. 3–15). Amsterdam: Elsevier/North Holland Biomedical Press.

Berkowitz, L. (1989). Frustration–aggression hypothesis: Examination and reformulation. *Psychological Bulletin, 106*, 59–73.

Berman, M., Gladue, B., & Taylor, S. (1993). The effects of hormones, Type A behavior pattern and provocation on aggression in men. *Motivation & Emotion, 17*, 125–137.

Bies, R. J. (1987a). Beyond "voice": The influence of decision-maker justification and sincerity on procedural fairness judgments. *Representative Research in Social Psychology, 17*, 3–14.

Bies, R. J. (1987b). The predicament of injustice: The management of moral outrage. *Research in Organizational Behavior, 9*, 289–319.

Bies, R. J., Shapiro, D. L., & Cummings, L. L. (1988). Voice and justification: Their influence on procedural fairness judgments. *Academy of Management Journal, 31*, 676–685.

Boje, D. M., & Winsor, R. D. (1993). The resurrection of Taylorism: Total quality management's hidden agenda. *Journal of Organizational Change Management, 6*, 57–70.

Brockner, J. (1992). Managing the effects of layoffs on survivors. *California Management Review, 34*, 9–28.

Brockner, J., Grover, S., Reed, T., & Dewitt, R. L. (1992). Layoffs, job insecurity, and survivors' work effort: Evidence of an inverted-U relationship. *Academy of Management Journal, 35*, 413–425.

Brockner, J., Konovsky, M., Cooper-Schneider, R., Folger, R., Martin, C., & Bies, R. J. (1994). Interactive effects of procedural justice and outcome negativity on victims and survivors of job loss. *Academy of Management Journal, 37*, 397–409.

Brown, R., & Herrnstein, R. J. (1975). *Psychology*. Boston: Little, Brown.

Bureau of Labor Statistics. (1992). *Census of fatal occupational injuries* (Report no. 891). Washington, DC: Author.

Buss, A. H. (1961). *The psychology of aggression*. New York: Wiley.

Cameron, K. S. (1994). Strategies for successful organizational downsizing. *Human Resource Management, 33*, 189–211.

Caprara, G. V., Barbaranelli, C., Pastorelli, C., & Perugini, M. (1994). Individual differences in the study of human aggression. *Aggressive Behavior, 20*, 291–303.

Chen, P. Y., & Spector, P. E. (1992). Relationships of work stressors with aggression, withdrawal, theft, and substance abuse: An exploratory study. *Journal of Occupational and Organizational Psychology, 65*, 177–184.

Churchill, W. S. (1950). *The grand alliance*. Boston: Houghton Mifflin.

Cox, T., & Leather, P. (1994). The prevention of violence at work: Application of cognitive behavioural theory. *International Review of Industrial and Organizational Psychology, 9*, 213–243.

Cropanzano, R., & Folger, R. (1996). Procedural justice and worker motivation. In R. M. Steers, L. W. Porter, & G. A. Bigley (Eds.), *Motivation and leadership at work* (6th ed., pp. 72–83). New York: McGraw-Hill.

DeMore, S. W., Fisher, J. D., & Baron, R. M. (1988). The equity control model as a predictor of vandalism among college students. *Journal of Applied Psychology, 18*, 80–91.

Dodge, K. A., Price, J. M., Bachorowski, J. A., & Newman, J. P. (1990). Hostile attributional biases in severely aggressive adolescents. *Journal of Abnormal Psychology, 99*, 385–392.

Drory, A., & Romm, T. (1990). The definition of organizational politics: A review. *Human Relations, 43*, 1133–1154.

Feldman, D. C., & Leana, C. R. (1989). Managing layoffs: Experiences at the *Challenger* disaster site and the Pittsburgh steel mills. *Organizational Dynamics, 18*, 52–64.

Feldman, S. P. (1988). Secrecy, information, and politics: An essay in organizational decision making. *Human Relations, 41*, 73–90.

Ferris, G. R., & Kacmar, K. M. (1992). Perceptions of organizational politics. *Journal of Management, 18*, 93–116.

Ferris, G. R., & King, T. R. (1991). Politics in human resources decisions: A walk on the dark side. *Organizational Dynamics, 20*, 59–71.

Feshbach, S. (1970). Aggression. In P. H. Mussen (Ed.), *Carmichael's manual of child psychology* (pp. 159–259). New York: Wiley.

Folger, R. (1986). Rethinking equity theory: A referent cognitions model. In H. W. Bierhoff, R. C. Cohen, & J. Greenberg (Eds.), *Justice in social relations* (pp. 145–162). New York: Plenum.

Folger, R. (1987). Reformulating the preconditions of resentment: A referent cognitions model. In J. C. Masters & W. P. Smith (Eds.), *Social comparison, justice, and relative deprivation: Theoretical, empirical, and policy perspectives* (pp. 183–215). Hillsdale, NJ: Erlbaum.

Folger, R. (1993). Reactions to mistreatment at work. In K. Murningham (Ed.), *Social psychology in organizations: Advances in theory and research* (pp. 161–183). Englewood Cliffs, NJ: Prentice Hall.

Folger, R., & Bies, R. J. (1989). Managerial responsibilities and procedural justice. *Employee Responsibilities and Rights Journal, 2*, 79–90.

Folger, R., & Buttram, R. (1995). *The Churchill paradox in managing hard times: Kicking employees when they're down and out*. Unpublished manuscript.

Folger, R., & Cropanzano, R. (in press). *Organizational justice and human resources management*. Thousand Oaks, CA: Sage.

Folger, R., Konovsky, M. A., & Cropanzano, R. (1992). A due process metaphor of performance appraisal. In B. M. Staw & L. L. Cummings (Eds.), *Research in Organizational Behavior* (pp. 129–177). Greenwich, CT: JAI Press.

Folger, R., & Skarlicki, D. (1995, August). *A popcorn model of workplace violence*. Paper presented at the annual meeting of the Academy of Management, Vancouver, British Columbia, Canada.

Fox, J. A., & Levin, J. (1994). *Overkill*. New York: Plenum.

Geddes, D. H., & Baron, R. A. (1996). Workplace aggression as a consequence of negative performance feedback. Unpublished manuscript, Temple University, under review.

Geen, R. G. (1991). *Human aggression*. Pacific Grove, CA: Brooks/Cole.

Greenberg, J. (1990a). Employee theft as a reaction to underpayment inequity: The hidden costs of pay cuts. *Journal of Applied Psychology, 75,* 561–568.

Greenberg, J. (1990b). Looking fair vs. being fair: Managing impressions of organizational justice. *Research in Organizational Behavior, 12,* 111–157.

Greenberg, J. (1993a). Stealing in the name of justice: Informational and interpersonal moderators of theft reactions to underpayment inequity. *Organizational Behavior and Human Decision Processes, 54,* 31–103.

Greenberg, J. (1993b). The social side of fairness: Interpersonal and informational classes of organizational justice. In R. Cropanzano (Ed.), *Justice in the workplace* (pp. 79–103). Hillsdale, NJ: Erlbaum.

Greenberg, J. (1994). Using socially fair treatment to promote acceptance of a work site smoking ban. *Journal of Applied Psychology, 79,* 288–297.

Greenberg, J., & Scott, K. S. (1996). Why do workers bite the hand that feeds them? Employee theft as a social exchange process. In B. M. Staw & L. L. Cummings (Eds.), *Research in Organizational Behavior* (Vol. 18, pp. 111–156). Greenwich, CT: JAI Press.

Homans, G. C. (1974). *Social behavior: Its elementary forms* (rev. ed.). New York: Harcourt, Brace & Jovanovich.

Huesmann, L. R. (Ed.). (1994). *Aggressive behavior: Current perspectives*. New York: Plenum.

Kahneman, D., & Miller, D. T. (1986). Norm theory: Comparing reality to its alternatives. *Psychological Review, 93,* 136–153.

Konovsky, M. A., & Brockner, J. (1993). Managing victim and survivor layoff reactions: A procedural justice perspective. In R. Cropanzano (Ed.), *Justice in the workplace* (pp. 133–153). Hillsdale, NJ: Erlbaum.

Lehman, W. E. K., & Simpson, D. D. (1992). Employee substance abuse and on-the-job behaviors. *Journal of Applied Psychology, 77,* 309–321.

Leventhal, G. S., Karuza, J., & Fry, W. R. (1980). Beyond fairness: A theory of allocation preferences. In G. Mikula (Ed.), *Justice and social interaction* (pp. 167–218). New York: Springer-Verlag.

Lind, E. A., & Tyler, T. R. (1988). *The social psychology of procedural justice*. New York: Plenum.

Mangione, T. W., & Quinn, R. P. (1975). Job satisfaction, counterproductive behavior, and drug use at work. *Journal of Applied Psychology, 59,* 114–116.

National Institute for Occupational Safety and Health. (1993). *Homicide in the workplace*. (Document No. 705003). Washington, DC: U.S. Government Printing Office.

Neuman, J. H., & Baron, R. A. (in press). Aggression in the workplace. In R. A. Giacalone & J. Greenberg (Eds.), *Anti-social behavior in organizations*. Thousand Oaks, CA: Sage.

Organ, D. W. (1990). The motivational basis of organizational citizenship behavior. *Research in Organizational Behavior, 12,* 43–72.

Pahlavan, J. G., Duda, D., & Bonnet, P. (1994). Evidence for a motor mechanism of pain-induced aggression instigation in humans. *Aggressive Behavior, 20,* 1–7.

Pastore, N. (1950). A neglected factor in the frustration-aggression hypothesis: A comment. *Journal of Psychology, 29,* 271–279.

Raelin, J. A. (1994). Three scales of professional deviance within organizations. *Journal of Organizational Behavior, 15,* 483–501.

Rigdon, J. E. (1994, April 12). Companies see more workplace violence. *Wall Street Journal,* pp. B1, B9.

Robinson, S. L., & Bennett, R. J. (1995). A typology of deviant workplace behaviors: A multidimensional scaling study. *Academy of Management Journal, 38,* 555–572.

Rousseau, D. M. (1995). *Psychological contracts in organizations*. Thousand Oaks, CA: Sage.

Schweiger, D. M., Ivancevich, J. M., & Power, F. R. (1987). Executive actions for managing human resources before and after acquisition. *Academy of Management Executive, 2,* 127–138.

Shapiro, D. L., Buttner, E. H., & Barry, B. (1995). Explanations: What factors enhance their perceived adequacy? *Organizational Behavior and Human Decision Processes, 58,* 346–368.

Smeltzer, L. R., & Zener, M. F. (1992). Development of a model for announcing major layoffs. *Group and Organization Management, 17,* 446–472.

Spector, P. E. (1975). Relationships of organizational frustration with reported behavioral reactions of employees. *Journal of Applied Psychology, 60,* 635–637.

Spector, P. E. (1978). Organizational frustration: A model and review of the literature. *Personnel Psychology, 31,* 815–829.

Staw, B. M., Sandelands, L. E., & Dutton, J. E. (1981). Threat-rigidity effects in organizational behavior: A multilevel analysis. *Administrative Science Quarterly, 26,* 501–524.

Storms, P. L., & Spector, P. E. (1987). Relationships of organizational frustration with reported behavioral reactions: The moderating effect of locus of control. *Journal of Occupational Psychology, 60,* 227–234.

Stuart, P. (1992). Murder on the job. *Personnel Journal, 71,* 72–83.

Sutton, R., Eisenhardt, K., & Jucker, J. (1986). Managing organizational decline: Lessons from Atari. *Organizational Dynamics, 14,* 17–29.

Taylor, M. S., Tracy, K. B., Renard, M. K., Harrison, J. K., & Carroll, S. J. (1995). Due process in performance appraisal: A quasi-experiment in procedural justice. *Administrative Science Quarterly, 40,* 495–523.

Tyler, T. R. (1994). Psychological models of the justice motive: Antecedents of distributive and procedural justice. *Journal of Personality and Social Psychology, 67,* 850–863.

Tyler, T. R., & Bies, R. J. (1990). Beyond formal procedures: The interpersonal context of procedural justice. In J. Carroll (Ed.), *Applied social psychology and organizational settings* (pp. 77–98). Hillsdale, NJ: Erlbaum.

Velasques, M., Moberg, D. J., & Cavanaugh, G. F. (1983). Organizational statesmanship and dirty politics: Ethical guidelines for the organizational politician. *Organizational Dynamics, 11,* 65–79.

Wilhelm, P. G. (1993). Application of distributive justice theory to the CEO pay problem: Recommendations for reform. *Journal of Business Ethics, 12,* 469–482.

Zillmann, D. (1994). Cognition-excitation interdependencies in the escalation of anger and angry aggression. In M. Potegal & J. F. Knutson (Eds.), *The dynamics of aggression: Biological and social process* (pp. 45–75). Hillsdale, NJ: Erlbaum.

4

Research, Practice, and Legal Issues Regarding Workplace Violence: A Note of Caution

Thomas W. White

Every day Americans are reminded that they live in a turbulent society in which fear of falling victim to violence casts an ominous shadow over their daily activities. Contributing to these concerns are the growing number of violent incidents reported in the workplace, a setting that was once thought to be relatively safe from violence.

The fact that homicide is frequently cited as a leading cause of death on the job has added to that concern and is reinforced by the accounts of mass murder that attract national press attention. One of many such accounts appearing in *U.S. News & World Report* (Sloan, 1993) has fed this perception. This report indicated that 18 postal workers or former workers had killed a total of 34 coworkers and 4 civilians and injured 34 others in the years since 1980. Stories such as this appear in the printed media regularly and heighten people's sense of generalized fear and insecurity. Perhaps more important, these accounts also fuel the popular perception that coworker homicide is reaching epidemic proportions and has become a serious threat to people's safety on the job. However, despite what might first appear to be overwhelming consensus about the need to combat this growing social problem, a closer examination of the data suggests that a far different and more cautious approach may be warranted.

In this chapter I review the literature on workplace violence, focusing specifically on the issue of coworker-initiated violence. I discuss the standard procedures used to collect and report workplace violence data, review several pertinent research articles, and propose an explanation of why the public has developed a number of misconceptions about the extent of coworker violence. In addition, I explore the need for a more focused definition of workplace violence and assessment issues related to identifying potentially violent employees. Finally, several legal, ethical, and practice problems are discussed for clinicians involved in providing professional

---

The opinions or assertions contained herein are my private views and should not be construed as official or as reflecting the views of the Department of Justice or the Federal Bureau of Prisons.

services in the area of violence assessment, risk management, and violence-related employee assistance.

By critically evaluating the existing data, one can see a much different picture about workplace violence than media-driven perceptions would suggest. Moreover, the picture raises serious questions about why, where, and how psychological resources should be used to deal with the problem of workplace violence.

Research Literature

Despite the recent attention being devoted to the topic of workplace homicide, there are only a few sources of factual information available on the subject. In fact, finding reliable data about workplace violence of any type can be difficult. With only a few exceptions, data about workplace violence must be gleaned from statistics gathered on the broader topic of occupational health and safety.

Statistical information about the nature of workplace injuries and fatalities is routinely collected by several federal agencies such as the National Institute for Occupational Safety and Health, the Occupational Safety and Health Administration (OSHA), the Federal Bureau of Investigation, the Bureau of Justice Statistics using the National Crime Victimization Survey (NCVS), and the U.S. Bureau of Labor Statistics. In addition, a wide range of information pertaining to workplace fatalities also is collected by many state agencies and private organizations. However, the information collected by these agencies varies considerably depending on the agency's emphasis or mission.

Because there are no standardized statistics collected by all agencies and no central repository of any such data, it may be necessary to search through the figures of several agencies to locate particular pieces of information, and, after doing so, it may still be difficult to cross-reference the information with the data from other agencies. Moreover, although there is usually general agreement about most of the basic figures, even these numbers can vary somewhat across different sources. In addition, because the data are collected primarily by government agencies for specific statistical reporting requirements, using the information for other purposes is sometimes difficult and marginally effective.

Aside from problems with information access and reliability, there are far more serious concerns about how these narrowly focused data have shaped public perception about the phenomena of workplace homicide. For example, government statistics (National Institute for Occupational Safety and Health [NIOSH], 1993) clearly show that homicide is the third leading cause of death in the workplace, with more than 1,000 people killed annually. This is a sobering statistic that is frequently quoted by experts and the media who warn against the rising tide of crime and violence in corporate America.

These statistics also are frequently cited while reporting sensational stories involving workplace violence. These accounts are more often than not accompanied by descriptions of employees who have killed coworkers. By intermingling fears about rising crime rates, workplace homicide rates, and coworker murders, the public has come to view workplace violence as being synonymous with the picture of a violent, potentially murderous coworker. This image is reinforced further when the rate for all types of workplace homicides (i.e., robberies, criminal assault, etc.) is not clearly separated from the homicide rate for coworker deaths or from nonlethal acts of violence.

Unfortunately, being forced to rely on limited information is not confined to the general public. In most cases, researchers also must rely on a narrow range of statistical data gathered by government agencies. These data are typically descriptive in nature, making it impossible to draw valid inferences about causal relationships. Also, because large-scale, national research efforts are both costly and time-consuming, the number of privately funded studies examining workplace violence issues is limited. Consequently, professional publications and the popular media have relied on a small number of research articles to draw their conclusions about the nature and cause of workplace violence.

Because there are so few studies citing statistics about workplace violence, it is relatively common to encounter the same data being reported over and over again in professional articles. The practice of repeating the same statistics in numerous forums, both public and professional, gives the perception that there is general agreement among professionals about the topic that may not in fact exist. Unquestionably, the limited amount of empirical research has shaped significantly what is being reported. This situation speaks to the need for a broad-based research effort to identify and clarify some of the most basic issues in the field of workplace violence.

Incidence Rate

Despite the current interest in the subject, data about coworker homicide were not even collected on all 50 states before the 1992 reporting year. In the 1992–1994 reporting years, coworker homicide accounted for approximately 4% (Castillo, 1994), 6% (Cole, 1995), and 5% (Baker, 1995), respectively, of all workplace homicides. A further analysis of these data indicates that the vast majority of workplace homicide (70–80%) is, and always has been, perpetrated during the commission of robberies and other miscellaneous retail and service-industry criminal activities.

These facts have been well-known within the field of occupational health for many years and clearly are not new information (NIOSH, 1993). These data show unequivocally that the number of coworker homicides are rare and do not pose the significant threat to life that might be concluded from media reports. To put these numbers into better perspective, calculations show that the average worker has a far better chance of being struck by lightning than being murdered by a coworker (Thompson, 1995). Similarly, on the basis of my calculations obtained from news reports I would estimate that approximately 8–10 times as many people die from

E. coli bacteria caused by undercooked hamburger than from coworker homicides.

The data on coworker homicide seem clear, are highly consistent, and are difficult to be misinterpreted: Coworker homicide is a unique and infrequent phenomenon that accounts for a small number of occupational homicides each year. American workers who do face an increased potential to be killed at work are those working in traditional high-risk occupations that always have been subject to high crime rates. Although any homicide is a personal and human tragedy, focusing on these relatively infrequent events serves only to obscure the issues and diverts resources from the much larger and much more significant occupational health problem posed by crime-related homicides.

Current Trends

The topic of coworker homicide has generated interest in a variety of other workplace violence issues. The most fruitful of these endeavors is the study of nonfatal incidents of violence. One of the rare national studies on the subject of nonfatal violence was conducted in July 1993 by the Northwestern National Life Insurance Company (see Appendix A, this volume). This investigation was the first comprehensive assessment of the effects of violence in the workplace funded by nongovernmental sources, and its results have received wide acceptance and national recognition.

In the Northwestern Life study 600 full-time civilian workers in a variety of occupations were surveyed. Among the survey's many findings was that 25% of all workers said that they had been attacked, threatened, or harassed on the job between July 1992 and July 1993. This is becoming perhaps the most frequently referenced statistics in recent articles written about workplace violence. Extrapolating from these data, the survey estimated that 2.2 million American workers were victims of physical attacks, 6 million were threatened, and 16 million were harassed. In addition to questions pertaining to assaults between July 1992 and July 1993, respondents also were asked about physical assaults during their lifetime. Of the 89 respondents who had been assaulted at some time in their lives, 30% said that they had been attacked by coworkers or former employees.

On the basis of the frequency of its appearance in the literature, the data from the Northwestern Life survey (see the Appendix) might be considered a "milestone" study. More important, it has been extremely influential in shifting the spotlight from coworker homicide to a wider range of nonfatal acts of violence such as threats and assaults. The results have been cited in the popular press as powerful evidence for the pervasiveness of workplace violence in America as well as the need for more effective intervention strategies for reducing violence (Braverman, 1993; Lawlor, 1993). Both these conclusions may be true, and this study certainly opens the door for further discussion of that topic. However, although the data have considerable value as the foundation for future research efforts, Castillo (1994) pointed out a number of meaningful methodological considerations that warrant cautious interpretation of the results. Most of Castillo's concerns pertained to the representativeness of the subject sample and the limited respondent responses to some questions. For example, the sample size of 600 was relatively small, it excluded self-employed individuals, and it overrepresented managers and underrepresented service workers.

Possibly the most important note of caution comes from the study's most significant finding: that a large number of workers experience physical assaults while on the job. As noted earlier, the Northwestern National Life survey data estimated that 2.2 million workers were subject to physical attacks during the year of the survey. This statistic is quoted widely and acknowledged as one of the strongest pieces of evidence to support the existence of a growing, and still unaddressed, workplace violence problem. However, it is rarely noted that these figures are extrapolations from only 3% (18 cases) of the respondents in the survey.

Given the concerns expressed by Castillo (1994), the findings may be more representative of potential subject bias than the pervasiveness of workplace assaults. Without minimizing the value of this preliminary effort, the methodological issues raise serious questions about the generalizability of the data. In view of the widespread acceptance of these findings, the need to replicate the results using a larger, more representative population sample seems critical before definitive conclusions can be drawn from these data.

Findings from the NCVS (Bureau of Justice Statistics, 1994) and other Justice Department publications also have been quoted on numerous occasions to support the claim of increased incidents of nonfatal violence at work. The NCVS collects survey data annually from more than 100,000 respondents from a representative sample of U.S. homes to determine incidence rates of nonfatal violence. The research is focused primarily on crime data such as theft, rape, robbery, and aggravated assault, but there also is a question about where these crimes had occurred. On the basis of these responses, it was estimated that during 1992, more than 600,000 people were victims of violent crimes while at work (Bureau of Justice Statistics, 1994). However, because of the way in which the responses are categorized, it is impossible to determine what proportion of these workers were subjected to assaults from coworkers and which workers were victims of criminal activities. Nevertheless, these data, like those from the Northwestern National Life survey (see Appendix A), have been valuable in reinforcing the general perception that nonfatal violence at work is a serious and growing problem.

A point must be made about using crime statistics for purposes of estimating workplace violence. Because of the attention being given to the topic of workplace violence, many behaviors previously categorized as criminal acts are being redefined as acts of workplace violence. The most conspicuous examples of this are the recent bombings at the World Trade Center and the government building in Oklahoma City. However, changing the name of a violent act does not make it a new phenomenon, nor does it mean that the event was not adequately addressed through the criminal justice system before being redefined.

Violence, whether at work or in the community, is still violence and falls under the legitimate domain of law enforcement. In other words, reclassifying an assault that occurs at work as an act of workplace violence does not necessarily change the nature, quality, or ultimate disposition of the act. It simply gives the appearance that something new has occurred when, in fact, an old behavior has been renamed. To some extent, it inflates the perception of violent events that occur by including them in the crime statistics and then repeating them again in the context of violence at work.

Redefining the Issue

The initial public interest in workplace homicide, despite its relatively low incident rate, was instrumental in focusing public attention on the topic of workplace violence. However, over the years the topic has been expanded and redefined. Today, workplace violence means more than co-worker homicide. It encompasses a wide range of behaviors, including physical attacks, threats of violence, and, in some cases, verbal harassment and intimidation.

Indeed, considerable justification for using an expanded definition of workplace violence that includes nonlethal behavior was made easier by the findings of the NCVS (Bureau of Justice Statistics, 1994), discussed earlier, reporting more than 600,000 victims of violence at work. The most important impetus, however, came from the findings of the Northwestern National Life study (see Appendix A), which concluded that as many as 24 million workers had experienced threats, assaults, or harassment while on the job.

Despite the cautious inferences this single, unreplicated study should have suggested, these figures have been embraced enthusiastically with little regard to the limitations imposed by its methodological shortcomings, and, consequently, they have had a powerful impact on public perceptions about the nature and magnitude of violence in the workplace. By drawing broad inferences from a pool of limited, narrowly focused research studies, the public and professionals have expanded greatly the range of behaviors now being defined as workplace violence. Moreover, broadening the definition also significantly magnifies the extent of the problem. Using the Northwestern National Life Insurance data as a baseline, expanding the definition of workplace violence beyond physical attacks increases the incidence rate 10-fold, from 2.2 to 24.2 million. After hearing these statistics, it is easy to understand why the topic of workplace violence strikes at the heart of people's sense of personal security and well-being.

Future Concerns

Expanding the definition of workplace violence in this way seems to have a number of important implications for the future. First, it obviously will call attention to many events in the workplace that may have been ignored in the past. Most important of these, aside from acts of physical assault, are the feelings of intimidation, fear, and emotional discomfort that result from the potential of being assaulted. Including these behaviors in the larger domain of workplace violence will force employers to take these actions more seriously and serve to create a less tolerant atmosphere for threatening or violent acts. All these consequences have the clear potential to positively shape the workplace in the future. They may not only reduce the incidence of violent behavior, but they also may reduce the ambient levels of anxiety and fear that violence inevitably creates.

Yet, this course is not without problems. The danger inherent in expanding the definition of workplace violence beyond actual acts of violence or serious threats of physical attack is that it actually blurs rather than sharpens the focus on the violence reduction target. In fact, using a definition of violence that includes harassment and intimidation may so broaden the topic that it could be meaningful only to the victim. It is easy to see how this could quickly degenerate into a legal morass, creating endless debate about what constitutes violent rhetoric, emotional intimidation, or hostile environments.

At its extreme, this could diminish the public's interest in serious acts of coworker violence because it could become lost in the background noise of verbal confrontation and controversy. Should this happen, it could actually serve to trivialize all but the most egregious acts of workplace violence and significantly limit the effectiveness of meaningful intervention efforts. Thus, it appears that there may be a fine line between focusing on an important and meaningful workplace issue and creating a situation in which researchers' zeal to highlight a problem works to their disadvantage.

Employment Law and Liability

As might be expected in this litigious society, the public attention surrounding workplace violence already has led to a proliferation of lawsuits filed against employers for a number of occupation-related violence issues. Although the OSHA does not have specific regulations concerning workplace violence, its General Duty Requirement Sec. 5(a)(1) sets forth an employer's duty to keep the workplace free from hazards that may cause death or serious physical harm.

Driven by these federal OSHA regulations and by more specific state OSHA regulations, there is a growing tendency to expect businesses and supervisors to identify violent employees, develop proactive measures for dealing with work-related episodes of violence, and, more important, to be held accountable when they do not. Although the state of employment law in this area is rapidly undergoing minute-by-minute change, employers are increasingly fearful of the prospect of defending themselves from lawsuits if an employee is injured or killed by a fellow employee. For regardless of the cost in purely human terms, many businesses fear that when viewed with the benefit of 20/20 hindsight, their policies and procedures for dealing with violent situations will be judged critically and they will be found negligent despite their best efforts.

Most of these cases have been civil tort actions seeking compensation for negligence by the employer for not adequately protecting the employee from violent coworkers. Awards vary considerably depending on the particular facts in each case, but with the potential for multimillion dollar settlements, it is clear that employers have much to lose if they are found negligent in even one case. Under these conditions, it is not surprising that employers feel vulnerable, fearing that any action they take may result in substantial liability. The best degree of legal protection against these claims can be obtained by developing policies, procedures, and practices that deal with the most broadly defined employee behaviors. Businesses are turning with increasing frequency to psychological consultants to help them assess their company's potential for violence and develop effective policies and treatment programs.

Liability concerns also are important for psychologists involved in assessing an employee's potential for dangerousness or violence during preemployment interviews or after an employee has engaged in some act of violence involving a coworker. This role appears to be suitable for psychologists with the requisite skills and experience, but, although it clearly holds great potential, it also offers the possibility for significant malpractice problems. Employers seeking protection from growing litigation will understandably seek to use the recommendations of psychologists to justify their decisions about the termination or retention of potentially violent employees. Consequently, psychologists who recommend the nonhiring or termination of employees for being violent may find themselves sued for misdiagnosing the presence of violence, and employees attacked by coworkers found not violent also will sue for misdiagnosing the absence of violence. One has only to look to the rising number of malpractice lawsuits for the misdiagnosis of suicide and hospital releases to see the potential proportions of this problem.

The extent to which psychologists who are involved in violence assessment, risk management, and treatment programs for violent employees may be held legally and financially liable for unsatisfactory outcomes is still unclear. However, until the courts make decisions on many of these issues, the prudent practitioner should proceed with extreme caution.

Theory and Consultation

In providing both clinical and consulting services, many psychologists appear to be focusing on work stress to explain the increase in violence being reported (Braverman, 1993; Lawlor, 1993). Identifying stress-related variables as a major impediment to worker well-being as well as corporate prosperity is neither new or controversial. They have been studied extensively for years with only moderate success in accounting for a variety of workplace maladies (Book of Abstracts, 1995). Because negative emotional factors such as stress and anxiety probably will never be eliminated from the workplace, it always will be possible to find them where violence has occurred. However, their presence does not establish a causal link. To my knowledge, there are no empirical investigations showing that increases in environmental stressors are related directly to increases in violent workplace incidents.

The absence of a direct link between working conditions and violence has not deterred experts from using the proposed connection as the basis for supervisor training, policy development, and employee risk assessment. However, although it is hard to argue against the value of reducing stressful working conditions in any setting, proposing remedies for violence on the basis of ameliorating these conditions without adequate research support seems to be questionable. In fact, given the minimal success of past efforts to explain other workplace problems using these conditions, pointing to them again to account for violence appears to be little more than putting old wine in new bottles.

It seems safe to say that, given the current state of the art, it is difficult to determine how work-related stressful conditions affect workplace violence. At this point, it is an empirical question that needs urgent and critical study.

Characteristics of Violent Employees

Because violence toward coworkers occurs rarely even in poor work environments, it can be inferred that the primary triggers for violence lie within the worker, not within the negative environment. As such, it can be concluded that perpetrators represent a unique subset of the workforce that can and should be identified. Most of the information concerning perpetrators of violence has been obtained from a small number of employees who murder coworkers, thereby limiting the generalizability of the data to nonfatal acts of violence.

One study, however, has attempted to examine directly the relationships among personality types, psychopathology, and workplace violence. Feldmann and Johnson (1994) analyzed data from 60 workplace violence incidents from across the United States and Canada. Their data were collected initially from media sources and supplemented by telephone contacts with law enforcement agencies, victims, witnesses, and family members. Individual interviews were attempted with perpetrators whenever possible. Their database revealed some interesting and heretofore undiscovered relationships. For example, the authors found that 68% ($n = 41$) of the perpetrators of violent acts evidenced some type of preincident psychiatric diagnosis. However, more detailed examination revealed that relatively few of these respondents demonstrated psychotic features that would cause them to immediately stand out from other members of the workforce. The specific breakdown of individual diagnostic categories provides further insight into this population. Thirty-four percent were diagnosed as having depression, whereas slightly more than 50% of the remaining respondents were diagnosed as having borderline or narcissistic disorder, antisocial personality, drug or alcohol abuse, or bipolar disorder. On the basis of the relative frequencies of these diagnostic categories, a large portion of perpetrators had diagnoses clustered in the personality disorders. In fact, the authors concluded that most of their respondents evidenced unstable personality disorders that made them respond poorly to stress, have conflicted relationships, and react with anger to perceived threats to their sense of self-esteem. These features, as well as suicidal ideation expressed by the depressed respondents, were representative of the majority of respondents who committed acts of workplace violence. The link between suicide and workplace violence is important because reports suggest that 25–50% of coworker homicides end in suicide.

Mental Illness, Dangerousness, and Assessment Guidelines

No discussion of violence, within or outside the workplace, would be complete without mentioning the research on the assessment and prediction of dangerousness. One major difficulty with this material as it relates to workplace violence is that it is largely derived from studies of populations with mental illness (Meloy, 1987; Monahan & Steadman, 1994). This suggests caution when applying these data to less disturbed individuals.

Much of the published research on dangerousness has emphasized the difficulty in developing reliable violence predictors. Monahan (1981) argued convincingly that no single psychological test or scale is a highly reliable predictor of future violence, suggesting the need for a multifaceted assessment process. Several authors have provided some direction for developing guidelines for workplace violence assessments. Meloy (1987, 1994), for instance, developed a model for assessing and predicting violence that blends personal, situational, and intrapsychic correlates of violent behavior. These individual pieces of information are compared with normative or base-rate data for those committing acts of violence. A major point emphasized in this model is the need to be data driven and to tie one's predictions, as much as possible, to directly relevant data.

Monahan (1981, 1984) suggested that violence may be predicted under certain circumstances as long as the clinician considers an adequate range of variables during the evaluation. Given that standardized clinical assessment instruments are inadequate predictors of future violence, the results of these studies suggest that a comprehensive assessment should include relevant demographic correlates of violence, a history of past violence, background investigations, predispositions for coping with stress by violent means, and other measures directly related to acts of violence. Taken together, the conclusions of Meloy (1987) and Monahan (1981) emphasize the need for a comprehensive, data-based, holistic approach to adequately assess dangerousness. In this perspective, behavior results from a combination of interacting psychological, environmental, and physiological factors that must be examined relative to each other to obtain a complete picture of the individual.

The data from Feldmann and Johnson's (1994) study, combined with the material from the literature on dangerousness, provide some insight into identifying and assessing the characteristics of those committing acts of workplace violence. First, they show that most perpetrators of workplace violence, although diagnosable, are not judged to be mentally ill enough to evidence severe or psychotic disturbances. Second, although much of the literature on dangerousness focuses on more clinically disturbed populations, it still has some relevance because portions of the populations overlap, particularly those with depression, suicidal tendencies, and mental illness. Third, given the general personality disturbances described by Feldmann and Johnson, it seems that most individuals who commit acts of workplace violence may have characteristics that more closely resemble criminal populations than those who have serious mental illness. This clearly suggests the relevance of strong forensic and clinical backgrounds for psychologists entering into the assessment of potentially violent employees. Finally, because the typical media profile of perpetrators of workplace violence does not generalize easily to many who commit these acts, the need seems critical to use a multifaceted assessment approach similar to that proposed by Meloy (1987) for predicting dangerousness.

Conclusion

In recent years, the topic of workplace violence has gained considerable attention in the popular media and has become one of the premier topics in the field of occupational health and safety. The growing interest in reducing workplace violence offers many opportunities for psychologists with the appropriate background and training. However, before these opportunities can be fully realized, there are several scientific, practice, and legal concerns that must be explored adequately and resolved.

The first of these concerns is accurately defining the nature and scope of the problem. A majority of Americans view workplace violence as a rapidly growing problem and associate it with the image of a disgruntled employee who enters the workplace and murders coworkers. Much to the contrary, coworker-initiated violence occurs rarely and accounts for only a small percentage of all workplace homicides. The discrepancies between reality and perception exist because data about workplace fatalities are limited, narrowly focused, and imprudently presented, particularly in the popular media. In addition, the few research investigations that have been published are subject to methodological criticism, poor reliability, and easy misinterpretation by the general public. Before psychologists can begin to address adequately the complex topic of workplace violence, a more accurate picture of the problem first must be developed using the results of empirical research investigations. However, to date, this topic has received little attention by the academic research community.

Some of the public confusion is caused by the subtle redefinition of workplace violence to include a number of behaviors such as threats, harassment, and intimidation in addition to actual physical violence. Expanding the definition has had both positive and negative consequences. A more inclusive definition may call attention to many previously unidentified problems affecting American workers and ultimately produce a greatly reduced ambient level of fear and anxiety in the workplace. On the other hand, it may so greatly expand the domain of behavior under investigation that it diverts public attention from serious cases of physical violence. It would seem that psychologists, using the scientist–practitioner model, are in a unique position to assess the breadth of the problem and develop targeted treatment and intervention strategies that are effective and efficient.

For those involved in management consulting, it seems important to test and validate empirically the theoretical assumptions that form the foundations of their intervention programs. It is hard to argue that anxiety, frustration, stress, and a myriad of other factors do not impact negatively on a host of behaviors affecting the workplace. Similarly, most people also would agree that, if possible, it would be beneficial for any organization to reduce their corrosive effects. However, it seems necessary to appeal to more than common sense to prove this point when it comes to violence. Given the relatively limited amount of violence that occurs, even in poor work environments, it may be more reasonable to focus on identifying individuals who act out violently under adverse conditions rather than attempt to initiate large-scale environmental change. For those who remain committed to the environmental impact perspective, it is important to demonstrate objectively a clear nexus between these variables and rates of violence and then develop intervention programs targeted directly at specific causative factors.

Perhaps the greatest professional risks for individual psychologists pertain to assessment practices and standards of care for identifying and managing potentially violent individuals. Assessments of potential violence should be grounded, as much as possible, in the integrative, data-driven approach that allows a rational and legally defensible interpretation of the findings. Clinicians should be familiar with the available data on violent employee protocols, the interface between the dangerousness literature and workplace violence, and the inadequacy of standardized assessment instruments in predicting dangerousness. Those providing treatment services should closely link treatment interventions with the objective data obtained during assessments and be prepared to take responsibility for unsuccessful outcomes. Like dangerousness prediction, forensic assessments, and other clinical–legal activities, practitioners must acknowledge and appreciate the specialized nature of these activities and be prepared for the inevitable legal challenges that will ensue.

In closing, these comments are not intended to be critical but cautionary. I aim to open a dialogue about the actual nature of workplace violence as well as psychology's role in dealing with this problem. Of primary concern for psychology at this point appears to be the need to acknowledge the limitations of the current research base and embark on a more empirically derived, data-based approach to examining the topic of workplace violence. With a narrow range of research data to draw on and with no established standards of care for guidance, there are a number of important practice–legal issues that cannot be addressed adequately yet.

However, many psychologists are currently involved in providing services in violence assessment, risk management, and violence-related employee assistance. Without satisfactory resolution of these issues, these practitioners often must rely on a mixture of generic psychological theory, common sense, and a large measure of good fortune when providing their expertise. Under those conditions, it must be recognized that the potential for misdiagnosing acts of workplace violence seems high and that the legal consequences for being wrong seem substantial, particularly as the state of unemployment law in this area becomes more focused. This should encourage the prudent practitioner to ensure comprehensiveness in providing assessment, management, or treatment services and should strongly mitigate against exceeding one's level of expertise.

References

Baker, D. L. (1995, September). *Preventing and mitigating workplace violence: Practical approaches, model programs.* Paper presented at Work, Stress and Health 95: Creating Healthier Workplaces conference, Washington, DC.

Book of abstracts. (1995, September). Book provided at Work, Stress and Health 95: Creating Healthier Workplaces, Washington, DC.

Braverman, M. (1993, December 12). Violence: The newest worry on the job. *The New York Times,* p. 11.

Bureau of Justice Statistics. (1994). *Criminal victimization in the United States, 1992: A national crime victimization survey report (NCJ-145125).* Washington, DC: U.S. Department of Justice.

Castillo, D. N. (1994, June). *Nonfatal violence in the workplace: Directions for future research.* Paper presented at the Third Annual Workshop of the Homicide Research Working Group, Atlanta, GA.

Cole, L. L. (1995, September). *Predictors of non-fatal workplace violence.* Paper presented at Work, Stress and Health 95: Creating Healthier Workplaces conference, Washington, DC.

Feldmann, T. B., & Johnson, P. W. (1994, August). *Violence in the workplace: A preliminary report on workplace violence database.* Paper presented at the annual meeting of the American Bar Association, New Orleans, LA.

Lawlor, J. (1993, October 10). Survey: Homicides at work on the rise. *USA Today,* pp. 10, 18.

Meloy, J. R. (1987). The prediction of violence in outpatient psychotherapy. *American Journal of Psychotherapy, 41,* 38–45.

Meloy, J. R. (1994, December). *Assessment of violence potential.* Workshop sponsored by Specialized Training Services, Minneapolis, MN.

Monahan, J. (1981). *The clinical prediction of violent behavior.* Washington, DC: U.S. Government Printing Office.

Monahan, J. (1984). The prediction of violent behavior: Toward a second generation of theory and policy. *American Journal of Psychiatry, 141,* 10–15.

Monahan, J., & Steadman, H. (1994). *Violence and mental disorder: Developments in risk assessment*. Chicago: University of Chicago Press.

National Institute for Occupational Safety and Health. (1993). *Fatal injuries to workers in the United States, 1980–1989: A decade of surveillance. National profile*. Washington, DC: U.S. Department of Health and Human Services.

Sloan, M. (1993, December). Outlook: Workplace violence. *U.S. News & World Report*, *115*(23), 12.

Thompson, J. D. (1995, March). *Psychiatric disorders, workplace violence and the Americans with Disabilities Act*. Paper presented at the 18th Annual Symposium on Mental Health and the Law, Richmond, VA.

Part II

Patterns and Correlates of Workplace Violence

Introduction

As the preceding chapters have made clear, workplace violence results from an interplay between personal and contextual factors. Some of these factors receive closer examination in the next three chapters).

Bennett and Lehman begin with the relationship observed in many previous studies between alcohol and aggression and investigates the relevance of this relationship for the workplace. The general literature points to several factors that make violence more likely to accompany alcohol use: the presence of escalating interpersonal conflict, support for drinking in the work culture, and the presence of such exacerbating factors as pain and stress. Bennett and Lehman test the importance of such factors with a sample of municipal employees. They find that drinking climates at work, in fact, place employees at greater risk of witnessing violence. The presence of more alienating than socially integrative factors also contributes to risk. Employee antagonism is higher, and violence therefore more likely, when employees experience low workgroup cohesion.

Possible effects of domestic violence on the workplace have received relatively little research attention so far. These effects could be important. Domestic abuse has significant implications for employability and productivity at work; workers who have trouble getting to work on time or are frequently absent may be undetected victims of domestic violence, which affects an estimated 14% of all American women. These effects of abuse could cost U.S. businesses $3–5 billion each year in lost productivity and health-care expenses. Friedman et al. examine the impact of domestic violence on the workplace. They consider employers' awareness of the problem to be too limited and argue for greater employer responsibility to prevent and to respond to employee victimization outside work. Among policies and programs they review are providing guidelines for individual and family safety strategies, temporary leave and voluntary transfer policies for victims, enhanced safety measures against domestic violence, legal assistance, training for management in responding to employee victimization, and domestic violence counseling and referral services. The authors prioritize among such measures in a comprehensive list of possible strategies for employers.

Hurrell, Driscoll, and Worthington examine job characteristics, particularly different job stressors, as they affect the occurrence of on-the-job physical assaults among approximately 7,000 state government employees. They identify 9% of the females and 17% of the males in their sample as having been physically assaulted on the job within the past year. The victims were younger than those not assaulted. The largest groups of female victims were mental health workers, clerks, human service workers, and nursing personnel. The largest group of male victims were state police personnel, mental health workers, guards, or clerks. These categories are not surprising, but the researchers call attention to the high risk these workers experienced: one of every two mental health workers and over half of male state police personnel had been assaulted. These jobs were rated for 11 types of stress. Four of the 11 stressor variables were associated with assaults for both sexes: limited job control, a high level of responsibility for people, limited opportunity for alternative employment, and skill underutilization. Two other stressors were significantly associated with assault among females: role conflict and low mental demands. Client contact increased the risk of physical assault for both men and women, and verbal threats also appeared to be associated with assault. The consequences of workplace assaults for the victims included higher than normal levels of depression and lower levels of job satisfaction. Workplace assaults also damaged self-esteem among males but not among females.

5

Alcohol, Antagonism, and Witnessing Violence in the Workplace: Drinking Climates and Social Alienation–Integration

Joel B. Bennett and Wayne E. K. Lehman

> In many respects, the topic of violence in the workplace follows the same sort of business time line as drug and alcohol abuse on the job did at the start of the 1980s. And, at least from a statistical standpoint, drug and alcohol abuse was also underreported or poorly classified in terms of its impact on the labor force. The government could offer reams of reports for drug abuse on the streets, but—like violence on the job—the numbers were not as easily applied to the workplace. (Mantell, 1994, p. 15)

The relationship between alcohol use and aggressive or violent behavior is perhaps the most investigated biobehavioral linkage in the empirical literature (Martin, 1993; Pihl & Ross, 1987). Studies in epidemiology, ethnography, criminal behavior, animal behavior, psychopharmacology, and personality and social psychology have all established an associative, if not always causal, link between alcohol and aggression. Although the job-related consequences of substance use have been studied in the work environment, researchers have yet to examine alcohol's role in work violence. As the quote by Mantell implies, there is a growing interest in both job-related substance use and job-related violence. Given the large amount of research on the alcohol–aggression link, it is surprising that these research interests have overlapped so little.

Previous research that is relevant to an understanding of alcohol and job-related aggression can be divided into two broad domains: (a) studies assessing the association between alcohol and either violence or aggression, and (b) studies on specific workplace or situational factors that may be common moderators of aggression and alcohol use. Within each of these

Preparation of this work was supported by the National Institute on Drug Abuse (NIDA) Grant DA04390 to Wayne E. K. Lehman and D. Dwayne Simpson. The interpretations and conclusions, however, do not necessarily represent the position of NIDA or the U.S. Department of Human Services.

domains the literature can be categorized according to three separate and somewhat overlapping areas. Studies of alcohol and aggression have been focused on (a) violent crime and victimization; (b) the cognitive association between alcohol and aggression at both the broad cultural and experimental level of analysis; and (c) an additive, social psychological model of alcohol in combination with situational and personal factors. Research relevant to workplace or situational influences on alcohol use has examined (a) the role of self-awareness as a factor in alcohol-mediated aggression, (b) worker alienation and associated stressors, and (c) workplace drinking norms or climates that promote coworker use of alcohol.

This chapter is divided into two main sections. The first section reviews the different areas of research just outlined and provides general background knowledge about the alcohol–aggression relationship and workplace factors that may be relevant to this relationship. The focus is more on individual alcohol use and subsequent aggression. The second section reports an empirical study that directly examines alcohol use within the work setting. The focus is more on the perceptions of drinking climates or drinking norms at work. Thus, the chapter considers alcohol from two perspectives: It discusses alcohol as it affects the individual aggression of employees who drink and it studies the impact of coworker drinking as it affects employee risk for witnessing violence.

The following review suggests that when alcohol is added either to employee frustrations or criminal activity, the potential for aggression is increased. The majority of workplace homicides are associated with robberies and miscellaneous crimes among retail and other provider services (U.S. Department of Labor, 1994). A large proportion of workplace violence is not associated with overt or planned criminal activity. The Society for Human Resource Management (1993) surveyed 479 human resource professionals and found that 33% of the respondents reported at least one incident of violence in the years between 1989 and 1993. Importantly, only 10% of the respondents indicated that the violence was linked to drug or alcohol abuse. Substance abuse ranked third behind personality conflict (38%) and family or marital problems (15%) as a perceived cause of violence. It is not clear from this survey whether the respondents used personnel files, memory of direct experience, hearsay, or some other data to arrive at their answers.

The lack of importance attributed to alcohol as a cause of violence contrasts with a 1993 survey of 600 civilian workers conducted by the Northwestern National Life Insurance Company (see Appendix A, this volume). Among the findings, 59% of the respondents said that alcohol and other drug abuse was the leading social issue contributing to workplace violence. The disparate findings from this and the human resource survey are reminiscent of an issue discussed in the alcohol–aggression literature. Namely, the broadly construed cultural belief that substance use leads to aggression may be more a function of socialization than an accurate perception of cooccurrence (Lang & Sibrel, 1989; Pernanen, 1981). Those responsible for keeping careful records—such as human resource professionals—may provide more accurate estimates of work aggression, whereas an opinion poll of employees may be subject to cultural stereotypes of the alcohol–aggression link (cf. "conjunctive error," Fiske & Taylor, 1991).

One alternative to asking for either estimates or opinions is to frame survey questions that ask about employees' direct experience with violence. The results of such a survey are provided in the second half of this chapter. After sketching the two domains of research discussed above, the chapter focuses on the role of workplace social contexts and drinking climates as moderators of the alcohol–aggression link. A conceptual model is next presented that blends previous research and examines the impact of personal factors, work alienation versus social integration, and stress on workplace violence. This synthesis and supportive findings indicate that employees may be more likely to encounter violent behavior and themselves act in an antagonistic manner if they work within drinking climates that lack social integration.

Review of Alcohol–Aggression Literature

The following review offers a sketch of previous research and highlights the importance of the setting surrounding violent incidents. It should be noted that the studies in the research literature occur across a variety of contexts (experimental, epidemiological, and interviews) and levels of analysis (cultural, situational, and personal). One could argue that the observed relationship between alcohol and aggression in the extreme situation of homicide may not generalize to less violent aggression in work contexts; however, data from both criminal investigations and experimental research point to the importance of context (pharmacological-ocial-cultural-situational) when understanding the alcohol–aggression link (Martin, 1993; Moss & Tarter, 1993; Parker, 1993).

Violence and Victimization

There is notable consistency across epidemiological analyses linking about 50% of homicides with alcohol (British Medical Association, 1995; Masi, 1994; Ravenholt, 1984; U.S. Department of Justice [USDOJ], 1985). Moreover, other studies show that alcohol is regularly used by serious offenders (McBride, 1981), and criminals have higher rates of alcoholism than the general population when comparable measures are used (Greenberg, 1981; Roizen & Schneberk, 1977).

Alcohol often leads to both hostility and extreme violence through interpersonal conflict (Collins, 1981). Many studies have found that a majority of alcohol-related homicides involve situations of escalating conflict, arguments, and disputes (Collins, 1988; Greenberg, 1981; Lindquist, 1991; Murdoch, Pihl, & Ross, 1990; Spunt, Goldstein, Brownstein, Fendrich, & Langley, 1994). Despite these findings, some claim that alcohol is rarely a direct cause of violence (Martin, 1993) and that situations of conflict often mediate the alcohol–aggression relationship. Moreover, others are convinced that there is no evidence of alcohol leading to aggression at all, but only that alcohol "may increase the risk of aggression and violence in a minority of high risk individuals" (British Medical Association, 1995; p. 1). Whereas epidemiological research links alcohol with criminal violence, there is little multivariate evidence showing alcohol's independent contributions beyond multiple health, economic, and social problems (Roizen, 1993).

Still, there are inconsistencies across the literature. Pernanen (1991), in his review of alcohol and violence, claimed that

> a more general *sequential* view is needed of the process whereby violence develops from conflict incitement or frustration through arousal and overt aggression to the use of physical force, and finally ends in some form of resolution of the violence episode. (p. 199)

A sizable body of research in experimental psychology leads to a nearly identical conclusion. Taylor and Chermack (1993) organized findings from over a dozen studies and viewed interpersonal altercations progressing across three stages: preescalation, escalation, and postescalation. They found that subjects under the influence of alcohol behave more aggressively during conflict escalation.

Workplace implications. To the degree that workplace violence involves crime, general knowledge about the role of alcohol in crime may be relevant. Although the most sensationalized reports of workplace violence involve a disgruntled or laid-off worker who commits violence as revenge, workplace homicides against women are most commonly committed by criminal assailants who do not know the employee (Younger, 1995). Also, alcohol-induced violent behavior is often a result of escalating conflict between parties who know each other, rather than an aberrant and abrupt event. The majority of violent incidents also involve less severe aggression in the form of fights and threats. When alcohol enters into evolving situations of disharmony, the potential for aggression increases. Interestingly, one recent survey found that perceived lack of coworker harmony is one of the most significant predictors of fear of violence at work (Cole, Grubb, Sauter, & Swanson, 1995).

To the extent that alcohol enters into situations of disharmony or conflict, the potential for violence may increase. Employee alcohol use without conflict may not be problematic, but alcohol use could be a warning sign of potential workplace violence (Dunkel, 1994; Johnson, 1995; Mantell, 1994). In a more general vein, some believe "red flags that warn of violence do not always exist" (Thornburg, 1993, p. 42), whereas others feel that "violence doesn't just happen—it's frequently preceded by warning signs" ("Preventing Drug-Related Violence With Training," 1995, p. 4). Temporally sensitive research is needed to distinguish spontaneous aggression from aggression mediated by preexisting, cumulative, or escalating workplace factors (Kelly & McGrath, 1988). The preceding review suggests that alcohol use in conflict situations may be one of these preexisting factors.

Culture and Individual Expectancy: The Cognitive Association Between Alcohol and Aggression

Culture. Anthropologists view cultural beliefs as significant mediators of alcohol's effects on behavior (MacAndrew & Edgerton, 1969). Learned social definitions of alcohol as a cause of events often guide a drinker's behavior (Roizen & Schneberk, 1977). Although alcohol has pharmacological effects that may involve aggression (Buydens-Branchey & Branchey, 1992; Pihl, 1993; Pihl, Peterson, & Lau, 1993), people also learn that alcohol can be an excuse for aggression in certain social contexts (Pernanen, 1991).

One widespread belief about alcohol is in its role as causing individuals to lose control of their behavior. Levine (1978, 1981, 1983) traced the evolution of this belief in American culture. In particular, the Temperance movement promoted the view of alcohol as a "disinhibitor" of moral restraint, an idea consistent with the Puritan emphasis on self-control and a Protestant work ethic that viewed alcohol as interfering with achievement. In the 1990s, television and the mass media vividly convey the association between alcohol and corruption. One analysis of television characters found alcohol or drug users more likely to be portrayed as both perpetrators and victims than nonusers (Gerbner, cited in Prevention Pipeline, 1995).

Surveys of alcohol and aggression support analyses of cultural beliefs (Christiansen & Teahan, 1987; Goldman, 1987; Lindman & Lang, 1994). For example, students from the United States report among the highest alcohol–aggression expectancies and the highest frequencies of alcohol-related aggression (Lindman & Lang, 1994; also see Wechsler, Davenport, Dowdall, Moeykens, & Castillo, 1994). Analysis of stories and myths also capture cultural beliefs about drinking. For example, folktales from cultures where drinking was either heavy or light were analyzed to show that drinking offers a sense of magical potency, particularly for males in (hunting) societies teaching achievement and self-reliance (McClelland, Davis, Kalin, & Wanner, 1972). The link between drinking and aggression seems more prevalent in societies that emphasize personal over a more socialized power.

Individual expectancy. Broad societal analyses, like those mentioned above, presume a homogeneity of belief about the alcohol–aggression link and underemphasize individual differences (Blum, 1981). Most people are inclined to expect that alcohol produces more aggression in others than themselves (Lang & Sibrel, 1989). Reviews and meta-analyses of both correlational and experimental studies suggest a heterogeneity of belief (Hull & Bond, 1986). Moreover, only when individual expectations are combined with alcohol's pharmacological effects does aggression increase (Bushman

& Cooper, 1990; Hull & Bond, 1986; Lang & Sibrel, 1989; Moss & Tarter, 1993; Steele & Southwick, 1985; Taylor & Chermack, 1993).

One meta-analysis of 30 experiments on alcohol and aggression indicated that, by itself, the belief in drinking alcohol (e.g., as an excuse for aggression) is not a sufficient cause of aggression; both the pharmacological and psychological expectancy effects of alcohol appear necessary (Bushman & Cooper, 1990). Alcohol-related aggression is greater for individuals distracted from focusing on internal cues when drinking (i.e., lessened self-awareness), who have no alternative but to aggress, and whose confederate partner has the option of retaliating. Taylor and Chermack (1993) also pointed to the importance of inhibitory cues in situations of escalating conflict. Intoxicated individuals are more responsive to instigation, they aggress during the escalation phase of a conflict, and they are influenced by mood, aggressive predisposition, and escalating provocation. Their conclusions are congruent with Bushman and Cooper's meta-analysis and the model of self-awareness (Hull, 1981) discussed below.

Workplace implications. Workplace implications of culture and the cognitive association between alcohol and aggression may come through an understanding of organizational culture (Furnham & Gunter, 1993; Trice & Beyer, 1993). In fact, organizations provide their own cultural meanings, which may or may not sanction drinking (Ames, Delaney, & Janes, 1992; Walsh, Rudd, Biener, & Mangione, 1993). For some occupations, alcohol can be an important means of socializing (Cosper, 1979; Cosper & Hughes, 1982), and alcohol and drug policy also conveys the meaning of alcohol use to employees (Cavanaugh & Prasad, 1994; Thompson, Riccucci, & Ban, 1991).

The history of workplace policy on alcohol also parallels the wider culture (Ames, 1989). After the Prohibition and the Depression, industrial workers became angry when attempts to regulate drinking interfered with their social relations at work. Ames (Ames, 1989; Ames & Janes, 1992) has argued that current workplace policy overemphasizes control of the *individual* propensity to drink and pays less attention to the influence of history, culture, and drinking climates at work. Drinking climates and substance use policies do influence the situations faced by workers who have alcohol problems (Ames et al., 1992; Beattie et al., 1993) and, perhaps, an aggressive disposition (Blum, 1981; Boyatzis, 1975). Mantell (1994) differentiated between work cultures that are "toxic" versus "nourishing" and employees who are high and low on maturity. He argued that the combination of toxic environments and immature employees results in workplace violence. Research shows employees have fewer feelings of personal hostility, cynicism, and mistrust if they perceive greater collegiality at work (McCann, Russo, & Benjamin, 1995). A nourishing work culture may provide the strong norms necessary for individuals with either alcohol problems or an aggressive predisposition to curb their behavior.

An Additive Model: The Social Psychology of Aggression

A large body of research in social psychology has explored both situational and dispositional causes of aggression. They include evidence that aggressiveness (a) may be an inborn and stable personality trait (Olweus, 1979); (b) is stimulated by frustration and exposure to aversive environments (Berkowitz, 1978); (c) is facilitated by transfer of arousal from other situations (Zillman, 1971); (d) is learned from social models and the mass media (Bandura, 1965; Geen, 1983); (e) is exacerbated by a certain amount of social anonymity, deindividuation (Prentice-Dunn & Rogers, 1982), or lack of social self-consciousness (Hull, 1981); and (f) is stimulated by current aggressive cues in the environment (Krebs & Miller, 1985; Lippa, 1990; Sabini, 1992). If any of these factors are simultaneously present, alcohol increases the likelihood of aggression. Frustration is more likely to lead to aggression if individuals are intoxicated (Gustafson, 1984, 1991, 1993). Alcohol use is tied to antisocial personality disorder and associated traits (hyperactivity, impulsivity, a disinhibitory motivational state, and deviant temperament; Moss & Tarter, 1993). Subjects with an aggressive disposition are particularly likely to retaliate to provocation when intoxicated (Bailey & Taylor, 1991). In other studies, alcohol subjects are more aggressive if exposed to aversive stimuli such as noise or pain (Jeavons & Taylor, 1985; Zeichner, Pihl, Niaura, & Zacchia, 1982).

Workplace implications. The potential for alcohol use to result in aggressive behaviors likely depends upon a number of person and situation factors operating simultaneously. Because work environments are complex they may contain many elements that are frustrating for individuals. For example, the theme of power or empowerment may be particularly important for understanding job-related violence. Allcorn (1994) lists a variety of power-related factors that may cause anger among employees. These include the negative effects of an overly hierarchical organization (rigidity and depersonalization, deskilling, promotion of dependency, top-down power versus participation), negative leadership traits (perfectionism, arrogance, narcissism), and alienation. Others have commented on the frustrating effects of downsizing on drug-induced violence ("Preventing Drug-Related Violence With Training," 1995), and aversive environmental factors such as heat, exposure to noxious fumes, continuous time pressures, shift work, and financial transaction with the public (Yandrick, 1993). Each of these factors may be the real-world analogues for frustration and provocation that lead to alcohol-induced aggression in experimental research.

Alcohol use may occur as only one element in an array of traits that make up an employee. Prevention programs that focus on screening out individuals because of aggressiveness or substance use may be narrowly focused. A more systemic approach that involves many components of the work environment would be helpful in workplace harm reduction (Braverman, 1995). A similar approach has been suggested for the use of Employee Assistance Programs (EAP) in reducing alcohol problems among employees (Roman, 1990b). Given legal, human resource, and general work policy mandates for both substance use and violence prevention (Daw, 1994; Engel, 1987; Johnson, 1994; Kinney, 1995; Mathiason, 1995; Overman, 1993), it would be helpful to know if a program that integrates EAP, harm reduction, or other elements (health promotion, stress reduction, work safety; O'Donnell & Harris, 1994) would be more effective than separate training programs.

Workplace Factors as Common Moderators of Both Alcohol and Aggression

The foregoing review points to a complex array of interacting factors that precede alcohol-related aggression. Of such factors, which might be the most important for understanding the role of alcohol in job-related violence? To what degree do workplace factors operate to simultaneously increase both alcohol use and aggression or facilitate an association between the two? These questions can help to select variables for investigation. A related question pertains to the direction of the alcohol–aggression relationship. The previously cited literature often assumes that alcohol precedes violence. But, is it possible that work violence can lead to substance use or that the two cooccur in an inextricable pattern? Galvin (1995) describes alcohol use as a response to posttraumatic stress for those who witness violence. Alternatively, employees may use alcohol to inhibit personal tendencies toward violence. Alcohol can cloud judgment, cause irritability, and facilitate an employee becoming either a victim or a perpetrator.

It may help to borrow from the extensive literature on job-related alcohol use to gain further focus with these questions (Czajkoski, 1995; Normand, Lempert, & O'Brien, 1994; Roman, 1990a; Wright & Wright, 1993) and find areas of overlap with findings from the alcohol–aggression literature. Comparison of these bodies of research suggest that three interrelated processes underlie alcohol-related aggression within the work setting. These are (a) the relative strength or weakness of work group norms as these guide the individual self-regulation of deviant behavior, (b) the effects of alienation as a force countervailing the integrative effects of social cohesion at work, and (c) the relative pervasiveness of alcohol use as part of the drinking climate within work groups. These social mechanisms focus on coworker relationships as the common denominator of both alcohol and aggression. Previous conjectures about work violence point to the importance of stressors and strains such as layoffs, job insecurity, poor working conditions, and inadequate rewards. Given the effects of positive work group climate as a buffer against stress (Cohen & Wills, 1985; Greller, Parsons, & Mitchell, 1992) and hostility (McCann et al., 1995), it seems plausible that work relationships also buffer against factors that lead to alcohol-related violence.

Group Norms and Self-Regulation

Hull (1981) has developed a self-awareness model of the causes and effects of alcohol consumption that applies to aggressive behavior (see also Banaji & Steele, 1989; Frankenstein & Wilson, 1984; Gaines, 1981; Hull & Reilly, 1983; Hull, Young, & Jouriles, 1986; Wilson, 1983). Essentially, alcohol decreases self-awareness and, as a result, it reduces adherence to personal standards of behavior. Because the lack of self-awareness or deindividuation is associated with socially prescribed aggression (Carver, 1974; Scheier, Fenigstein, & Buss, 1974), Hull posited that alcohol leads to "decreased responsivity to situational norms of appropriate conduct" (p. 592).

If led to believe others would behave nonaggressively in the same situation or if given the opportunity to reflect on their own behaviors, intoxicated individuals do not behave any more aggressively than nonintoxicated individuals. Conversely, social norms that prescribe aggression will promote such behavior in intoxicated individuals (Bailey, Leonard, Cranston, & Taylor, 1983; Jeavons & Taylor, 1985; Steele & Southwick, 1985; Zeichner & Pihl, 1979). Hull and his colleagues have also found that alcohol may be used to reduce self-awareness among individuals experiencing negative life events or failures (Hull et al., 1986). People drink as a way of escaping self-reflection on negative experiences.

Such research has implications for the work setting, particularly if considering those workplace mechanisms that fail to communicate explicit social norms or otherwise decrease self-awareness. Work that is monotonous—lacking in complexity or social interaction—gives individuals less opportunity to reflect on their social behavior than more complex and social work (Kohn, 1976). The concept of alienation, reviewed below, speaks to associated feelings of meaninglessness and normlessness (Seeman, 1959). Similarly, work cultures that do not emphasize healthful living, but instead support addictive or codependent norms, may promote careless use of alcohol (McMillan & Northern, 1995; Schaef & Fassel, 1988).

Another mechanism for reduced self-awareness may lie within one's work group (Hackman, 1992). Allcorn (1994) described how social groups at work meet significant belonging and attachment needs that, if not fulfilled, can lead to the anxiety and anger that precedes violence. Employees can feel abandoned, neglected, shunned, and isolated if members of their work group are unavailable, remote, or indifferent. The lack of positive group cohesion can set the stage for the development of aggression along several lines: (a) through failing to provide explicit norms for individual behavior (cf. "anomie"; Roman, 1981); (b) through increasing social anxiety and anger, which may lead to alcohol use as a way of reducing awareness of these negative states; and (c) through interaction effects, with the lack of norms combined with alcohol eliciting aggression in isolated or hostile employees.

Alcohol may be introduced into a negative work setting as a method of creating the belonging that employees may not otherwise feel. At the individual level, alcohol use may be a personal response to feelings of alienation (Seeman, 1959). At the group level, alcohol may provide a source of solidarity against stress and anxiety (Ames & Janes, 1990). As pointed out by Gaines (1981), "much drinking is the result of social stimulation that channels attention to the self" (p. 147) and so it can replace negative feelings about a social situation with positive feelings. Thus, alcohol might provide a conformity mechanism while simultaneously reducing self-awareness and personal control over behavior (Cosper, 1979; Cosper & Hughes, 1982).

Alienation

Alienation has been mentioned in news reports of work violence, and its effects on alcohol use have been systematically analyzed in empirical studies. Many researchers discuss alienation as a multidimensional construct (Seeman, 1959) but often focus on a generalized sense of powerlessness as measured by Rotter's I-E scale (Rotter, 1966). Many studies have found that powerlessness is associated with alcohol abuse (Janes & Ames, 1989; Seeman & Anderson, 1983; Seeman, Seeman, & Budros, 1988); these effects may be moderated by work and social factors. Still, it is worth noting that other "alienations" exist: meaninglessness, normlessness, social isolation, and self-estrangement.

Seeman and colleagues (Seeman & Anderson, 1983; Seeman et al., 1988) define alienation as both personal feelings of powerlessness and lack of integration within one's community. From their surveys of employed males, a nonwork feeling of powerlessness was the most consistent predictor of drinking problems, and social networks away from work can pull the powerless worker into heavy drinking patterns. Moreover, those who drink with others (versus alone) show more drinking problems, more powerlessness, and more estrangement from their social network. Some of the highest drinking scores were for those with less intrinsically satisfying work, less network support, and more powerlessness. This research echoes findings that drinking may be a way of feeling powerful among men who are not socially integrated (McClelland et al., 1972).

Parker and Farmer (1990) extended Seeman's work to examine powerlessness and self-estrangement as psychological alienations. These are distinct from social structural alienation (Kohn, 1976), and are assessed in less substantively complex work (i.e., work requiring less thought or independent judgment and more routine, heavy, and dirty labor). The authors found less complex work was associated with an inability to control one's drinking. Problematic and impaired-control drinking was also high for employees who felt *less* powerlessness, but who were in undemanding jobs that apparently led to self-estrangement, boredom, or disinterest. The authors argued for distinctions between burned-out, underchallenged, and alienated employees.

A more recent analysis defined alienating work as low job autonomy, low use of work capacities, and low involvement in workplace decision making (Greenberg & Grunberg, 1995). The authors concluded that alienating work did not directly increase problem drinking, although it did have a negative impact on job satisfaction, which, in turn, affected beliefs and justifications for using alcohol as a coping mechanism. Drinking to cope had a strong positive influence upon both heavy and problem drinking. The authors also compared different types of units (work mills), according to their degree of worker involvement in participatory decision making, and found that such participation was associated with less alcohol problems. This finding suggests that positive group norms, at the organizational level, may inhibit alcohol use.

Drinking Climates

A number of other studies point to the influence of work relations on drinking and the emergence of work group drinking norms. Employees may drink to conform (Cosper, 1979; Cosper & Hughes, 1982) and work-group alcohol use may evolve in stressful occupations as a leisure-coping mechanism (Ames & Janes, 1992). Moreover, alcoholics may be "enabled" by drinking coworkers who deny or normalize their performance problems (Roman, Blum, & Martin, 1992). Beattie et al. (1993) found that workplace support for alcohol involvement was associated with other work support for subjective distress. Alcoholics in treatment were interviewed about a number of social–work factors that comprised the workplace support measure. These included peer modeling (coworkers drinking on and off the job) and support (talking about drinking during work hours, expecting the patient to drink at work, and lending money to drink). The results implicate drinking climate as a social support mechanism for buffering against stress.

Fillmore (1990), in a national survey of workers, discovered less job-related drinking among occupations requiring more teamwork. Fennell, Rodin, and Kantor (1981) found that lack of coworker and supervisor support had high probabilities of being associated with drinking alcohol. Delaney and Ames (1995) concluded from their analyses that "whether one views work teams as reducing job strain or increasing social integration, our data show that . . . participating in, and receiving support from a team . . . may naturally rule out behaviors like drinking" (p. 285). Each of these studies point to the importance of work relationships as a moderator of alcohol use.

Alcohol-Related Violence and Workplace Integration–Alienation: A Conceptual Model and Research Survey

It is reasonable to assume that much, if not most, employee aggression occurs in verbal or indirect ways. Thus, it would be helpful to know how much drinking climates and work group norms are related to more benign behavioral forms of hostility as compared with overt physical violence. Our initial investigation explored employee self-reports of behaviors that, when taken together, could be construed as signs of antagonism. Essentially, we hypothesized that employees who report low group cohesion in their primary work groups and who also report drinking norms will also report a greater frequency of antagonistic behaviors. This pattern—low cohesion and drinking climates—should also predict greater exposure to violence.

The following study primarily focused on employee potential to witness violent events. In order to predict such potential, we developed a conceptual model that integrates much of the research reviewed in the first half of this chapter. The model emphasizes the importance of the work setting as moderating the relationship between alcohol and aggression. Based on the previous review, there appear to be two specific work factors—operating either within the organizational culture, the immediate work situation, or through individual attitudes—that would serve as common moderators for both alcohol use and aggression. These factors— here labeled as integrative and alienating—may also influence alcohol use and violence through personal factors as well as external stressors. A general overview of the proposed model is depicted in Figure 1 and brief descriptions of each factor are given below.

Social Integration

Work social norms influence the regulation of deviant or unhealthy behavior at work (Allen & Bellingham, 1994; Schein, 1969; Trice & Beyer, 1993). At the cultural level, integrative work norms include a communicated policy on wellness or healthiness about work (Rosen, 1991); at the situational level, integrative norms are those of team orientation, group cohesion, and role clarity (Campion & Medsker, 1993; Thomas, 1992); and at the individual level, such norms are embodied as job commitment, job satisfaction, and faith in management (Lawler, 1973). Individuals who work within cultures and situations that convey social integration or who feel positive about their workplace are likely to experience less hostility, have less problems with alcohol, and have less opportunity to encounter violent coworkers. These different integrative factors probably interact in an additive way. For example, those who work in a healthy organization and who experience both positive situational norms and positive job feelings are less likely to encounter drinking climates and violence than, say, employees who have positive job feelings but who lack a positive sense of culture or their work situation.

Social Alienation

Operating in opposition to integrative factors are socially alienating factors in the work setting (Katz & Kahn, 1966/1978). At the cultural level, these include the communicated norms of perfectionism, work addiction, and avoidant communication (McMillan & Northern, 1995). These norms might be diagnostic of an addictive organization where employees feel

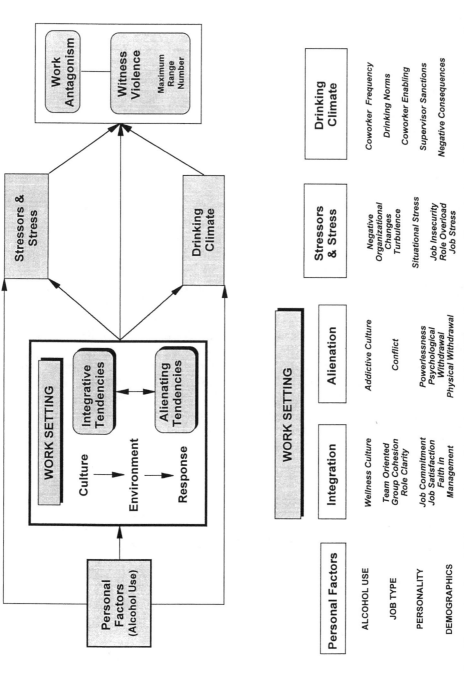

Figure 1.   Conceptual model: Integration–alienation and drinking climate as predictors of workplace antagonism and witnessing violence.

pressured to overwork and avoid any conflicts that may arise (Fassel, 1990; Schaef & Fassel, 1988). At the situational level, alienating factors may be expressed as interpersonal conflict between coworkers or with supervisors (Zaleznik, 1970; Zaleznik & Kets de Vries, 1975). Powerlessness and physical and psychological withdrawal may be adaptive responses to job dissatisfaction or alienation (Hulin, 1991). In the model proposed here, powerlessness is defined as perceptions of lack of control over one's job and is distinguished from a more generalized lack of personal efficacy (Bandura & Schunk, 1981). This distinction is important because other studies of alienation and alcohol use often use either measure, but not both (Greenberg & Grunberg, 1995).

Integrative Versus Alienating Tendencies

Theoretically, the integrative and alienating factors may oppose each other so that the presence of one logically intends the other's absence. Thus, it is unlikely that the same individual who feels powerless on the job also feels satisfied and committed to it or that those who work in a cohesive group experience much alienation. Another way of viewing these factors is to frame them as tendencies that exist within and across any work culture, situation, or individual. As theorized by others, tendencies toward health in any given organization may or may not be balanced with tendencies toward dysfunction (Allcorn, 1992; Diamond, 1993; Kets de Vries, 1991). This idea of tendencies may be replicated across different levels of an organization so that in cultures that tend toward healthiness, work groups will tend toward cohesion, and individuals will tend toward commitment. Conversely, addictive cultures may replicate as conflict-avoidant groups and psychologically withdrawn employees. Overall, if tendencies toward alienation outweigh tendencies toward integration, the chances for alcohol use and violence increase.

Personal Factors

The work setting, whether it tends toward integration or alienation, is not a social vacuum, and is composed of personal elements that each employee brings to the job. As we have seen from the earlier review of social psychology, some of these factors are personal and some are situational. Employees who are depressed or who have general negative attitudes may be more likely to be victims than those who have high self-esteem (Brockner, 1988) or a sense of personal self-efficacy (Paulhus, 1983). Employees who work in risk-sensitive jobs of heavy labor or who have more chances of interacting with customers or other employees are also more likely to be exposed to dangerous or violent situations. Other factors such as gender, age, race, and educational level might play a role. Finally, individuals may bring personal problems with alcohol use to the work setting, independently of work risk factors (Trice & Sonnenstuhl, 1990).

Stressors and stress. Both individuals and occupational settings are subject to ongoing stress (Beehr & Bhagat, 1985; Kahn & Byosiere, 1992; Osipow & Spokane, 1984). At the individual level, a variety of personal stresses have been identified that include role overload and general feelings of job stress. Another individual stressor that has been identified as a potential precursor of violence are feelings of job insecurity (Ashford, Lee, & Bobko, 1989; Brockner, Grover, Reed, & DeWitt, 1992). At the organizational level, a major stressor is organizational change and turbulence (Huber & Glick, 1993). Many organizational changes, such as through downsizing, or other structural modifications, can lead to employee feelings of stress. In addition, employees may experience more immediate situational stress from the layoff or firing of coworkers, increases in responsibility, or some other change in working conditions. If either individual or organizational stresses are added to alienating factors, personal alcohol use, or risk-prone personal factors, the probability of drinking climates and violence may also increase.

Drinking climate. The concept of drinking climate or the effect of organizational culture on drinking has been discussed at length by others (Ames & Delaney, 1992; Fine, Akabas, & Bellinger, 1982; Roman et al., 1992; Walsh et al., 1993). As conceptualized in the current model, drinking climates were composed of five interrelated factors that employees perceive about their work group. These included the frequency of coworker drinking, coworker behaviors associated with drinking, supervisory enabling of workplace drinking, coworker enabling (e.g., ignoring employees with drinking or drug problems), and negative consequences due to coworkers with substance abuse problems. Individuals who report working in such settings—whether or not these reports are related to other work setting, personal, or stress factors identified in the model—should be more likely to experience violence just by virtue of being around those who drink.

Antagonism and Witnessing Violence

The proposed theoretical model views employee violence as the result of escalating conflict within the work culture (see Baron, 1990; Katz & Kahn, 1966/1978, chapter 18). As such, it focuses on aggressive events of greater probability than extreme violence or homicide. These are employee antagonism and employee witnessing of violence. Individuals may reflect coworker conflict through antagonistic behaviors such as filing complaints, or being counterproductive, critical, and argumentative with coworkers. Initial research with a measure of job antagonism suggests it is a distinct individual difference variable of work behavior (Lehman & Simpson, 1992). Based on previous estimates, individuals are four times as likely to be a witness to violence than to be a victim themselves, and are also more likely to report witnessing than to report their own perpetration (Pernanen, 1991).

The primary dependent variable in the current model focuses on actual exposure to violent events during the workday or while at work. Employee reports of violence include the severity of violence (e.g., from making threats to causing injury), the range across different types of violence, and the number of incidents of exposure.

Primary Hypotheses

The major research questions to be tested in this model are listed below:

1. Does drinking climate add to the prediction of violence over and above other personal, work setting, or stressor variables? (The personal and work use of alcohol are here included as part of personal variables.)
2. To what degree do alienating versus integrative tendencies within the work setting interact with alcohol variables as predictors of violence?

These two research questions guided five specific hypotheses of the study.

1. Employees working in drinking climates (high drinking norms) that lack social cohesion will be the most likely to show signs of antagonism. This hypothesis was tested across three samples.
2. Employees working in drinking climates (high drinking norms) that lack social cohesion will be the most likely to witness violence at work. This and the following hypotheses were tested in one sample.
3. Alienating tendencies will show a positive relationship to employee antagonism and exposure to violence, whereas integrative tendencies will show a negative relationship with these outcomes.
4. Employees experiencing relatively more alienating factors will also experience more violence than employees experiencing relatively more integrative factors.
5. Drinking climates will have both an independent relationship with employee antagonism and witnessing of violence and will be moderated by the relative degree of alienation–integration. Specifically, employees reporting more alienating conditions will be more adversely affected by drinking climates than those who report drinking climates along with integrative conditions.

Sample Description

The samples, which included municipal workers randomly selected from the total city workforce of three cities in the southwestern United States (excluding uniformed fire and police officers), were to complete a paper-and-pencil questionnaire titled "Employee Health and Performance in the

Workplace." The three cities and corresponding municipal workforces differed in size and racial composition.

City 1 was the largest with approximately 5,500 employees. A total of 1,068 questionnaires were returned by employees from 65 different work groups for a completion rate of 87%. This city was distinguished by a relatively large Hispanic population (70%). The municipal workforce of City 2 consisted of approximately 3,000 employees in 178 work groups. These workers were assessed once in 1992 and again in 1995 as part of a larger study on organizational change. In the 1992 survey, 1,081 employees from 114 work groups completed usable questionnaires, resulting in a participation rate of 95%. In the 1995 survey, 909 employees from 87 work groups completed usable surveys, for a response rate of 97%. The municipal workforce was more ethnically balanced than City 1, with roughly 55% White, 25% African American, and 20% Mexican American. City 3 was the smallest with roughly 800 employees. A total of 335 questionnaires were completed for an 84% rate of participation. The majority of employees were White (75%), with 12% African American, and 13% Mexican American.

The cities were otherwise similar in terms of important demographic features. In all samples, approximately 80% of surveyed employees were over 30 years old, between 55% and 65% were male, between 30% and 40% had completed some college. Twenty-five percent of each sample had a college degree. The majority of each sample (from 54% to 67%) had worked for their respective city for at least 6 years, and many had held their current position for at least three years (all over 65%).

Questionnaire Administration

Research staff administered questionnaires to small employee groups during working hours on city property. All questionnaires were anonymous and confidential. No names were collected, and no original data were given to city officials. Participation was completely voluntary and employees could choose to withdraw their participation at any time.

The questionnaire included six sections that covered the following areas: (a) demographic and personal background, (b) job background and work environment, (c) job performance, (d) perceptions of substance use at work, (e) self-report drug and alcohol use both on and off the job, and (f) a questionnaire evaluation. Employees returned the completed forms directly to the research staff, who then sent the forms directly to research offices.

Variables

Each of the composite survey scales are listed in Table 1 along with representative items and, where appropriate, internal reliability estimates (Cronbach's alpha). These scales were all administered in the 1995 survey to City 2 employees. Eight *personal factors* were assessed that included

Table 1. Scales and Representative Items Used in the Current Study

Scale, factor, or measure	Number of items; alpha	Description or representative item(s)
Alcohol use	12 items used to derive 4 point scale	Drinks, gets drunk (or 5 in a row): None (= 1), light drinker (less than once/month = 2), heavy drinker (weekly = 3), Problem drinker (e.g., morning drinking, blackouts, treatment, arrests = 4)
Use at work[a]	6 items used to derive 5 point scale	Drinking on the job or coming to work high on alcohol: None = 1; less than once/month = 2, monthly = 3, using other drugs at or just before work = 4, missing work due to alcohol or drug use, selling drugs at work = 5
Risk-sensitive jobs	3 items	Daily use of light and heavy machinery or equipment, or working near toxic substances
Social exposure jobs	2 items	Daily communication with public or coworker and group interaction as part of job
Self-esteem	4 items; .73	Happy with friends and self; self-pride
Personal efficacy	4 items; .62 (Paulhus, 1983)	My accomplishments are entirely due to hard work. I can learn almost anything if I set my mind to it.
Depression	5 items; .73	Lack of interest in life, tired, lonely, sad, worried
Negative affectivity	6 items; .75 (Stokes & Levin, 1990)	Expecting the worst, pessimistic (Whenever someone criticizes me I think about it for days. Happy endings only occur in the movies and in fairly tales.)

Integrative Tendencies

Wellness culture	5 items; .65	Sense of vitality in coworkers; health a priority in department; flexible family/schedule policies; appreciation of culture/lifestyle differences; wellness classes offered
Team orientation (from Campion & Medsker, 1993)	6 items; .71	Team potency: My group can take on nearly any task. Team spirit: My work group has a lot of team spirit. Interdependence of feedback; management support
Group cohesion	5 items; .75	When I face a difficult job, my coworkers can be counted on to help out. (cooperation, trust, fairness)
Role clarity	6 items; .72	My job responsibilities are clearly defined. (kept informed, new employees trained well, clear authority)

Table 1. (*Continued*)

Scale, factor, or measure	Number of items; alpha	Description or representative item(s)
Job commitment	6 items; .69	Willing to stay on job even if city has problems; proud of work; feels part of the city workforce
Job satisfaction	6 items; .91	Satisfaction with job autonomy, worthwhile accomplishments, decision making, responsibility
Faith in management	3 items; .75	Supervisors don't take advantage; meet workers views.
Alienating Tendencies		
Addictive culture (see McMillan & Northern, 1995)	8 items; .57	Perfectionism: supervisor is picky, work group reworks until done perfectly; conflict avoidance: better to keep ideas to self, employees rarely speak their minds; workaholism: rush to deadlines, can't forget job pressures after work, uneven work pace
Conflict	3 items, count of dichotomous	Trouble with boss; increased arguments with coworkers; interunit communication worsened
Powerlessness	7 items; .70	Lack of control over work, management overcontrolling, cannot work independent of supervisor.
Psychological withdrawal	7 items (Lehman & Simpson, 1992); .80	Daydreams, thoughts of leaving work, loafs, excessive chatting, works on personal matters
Physical withdrawal	6 items (Lehman & Simpson, 1992); .57	Lateness, falls asleep at work, misses meetings, takes long breaks and lunches
Stressors / Stress		
Negative organizational changes	9 items; .86	Rating negative changes in job conditions (workload, technology, empowerment, pay, group commitment)
Turbulence	2 items; .62	Increased complexity and change in work process
Situational stress	3 items, count of dichotomous	Coworker layoffs, new responsibility, environment
Job insecurity	Four subscales (Ashford, Lee, & Bobko, 1989); .62 to .92	Perceived importance of job features, perceived threat of loss of these features, felt lack of ability to counteract these threats
Role overload	5 items; .67	Heavy pressure, lack of personnel, unqualified
Job stress (Kahn, Wolfe, Quinn, Snoek, & Rosenthal, 1964)	3 items; .83	Do you feel stress as a result of your job?

(table continues)

Table 1. (*Continued*)

Scale, factor, or measure	Number of items; alpha	Description or representative item(s)
	Drinking Climate	
Coworker frequency	3 items; .83	Frequency of coworker drinking and signs of use
Drinking norms	5 items; .81	Frequency coworkers socialize with alcohol
Coworker enabling[a]	4 items; .67	Likelihood that employees ignore coworkers with drinking problems
Supervisor enabling[a] (from Ames & Janes, 1992)	2 items; .56	Likelihood that supervisor would do anything to curb alcohol use
Negative consequences	6 items; .95	Frequency of work problems due to coworker substance use

[a]These scales included reference to substance use in general or to both alcohol and drug use.

two composite measures of alcohol use at and away from work, two measures of job characteristics, and four personality scales (e.g., self-esteem and personal efficacy).

Seven *integrative tendencies* were assessed: one measure of culture (wellness culture), two measures of situational integration (team orientation and group cohesion), and four positive work-orientation measures (e.g., job satisfaction). Five *alienating tendencies* were assessed: one measure of culture (addictive culture), one measure of situational alienation (conflict), and three negative work measures (e.g., psychological withdrawal).

Six scales assessed *stress*. Two scales assessed organizational stress—perceived negative organizational change and turbulence. One scale assessed situational stress and three assessed personal stress (job insecurity, role overload, and job stress).

Five scales assessed some feature of drinking climates. These scales primarily asked for employee perceptions of their coworkers' attitudes and behaviors surrounding both alcohol and drug use. The measure of drinking norms was utilized in the three cities and showed adequate internal reliability as measured by Cronbach's alpha (City 1, $\alpha = .63$; City 2 − 1992, $\alpha = .81$; City 3, $\alpha = .62$). The scale was partly adapted from work by Beattie (Beattie et al., 1993) and included items asking how often one or more coworkers drank alcohol either while on the job or just before going to work, coworkers drank together off the job, joined coworkers on these occasions, talked at work about drinking, and felt pressured to drink with coworkers. Description of other drinking climate scales are provided in Table 1.

Criterion Variables

Antagonism. Eight statements (derived from Lehman & Simpson, 1992) represented employee antagonism. Employees indicated how often

Table 2. Items From the Measure of Job Antagonism: Distribution of
Employee Responses Answering From Three Combined Municipal Samples

	% responding		
	None	Once or twice	Three or more
During the last 12 months, how many times have you:			
1) Criticized the work of your coworkers?	46	31	22
2) Argued with coworkers	48	35	16
3) Reported a coworker or supervisor to another supervisor for doing something that went against the rules or policies?	68	24	8
4) Gone against your supervisor's instructions?	77	17	6
5) Not completed tasks or jobs you were assigned?[a]	79	17	4
6) Filed a formal complaint about a problem at work?	87	11	3
7) Purposely spread rumors or gossip about coworkers?	90	7	3
8) Intentionally done your job wrong or poorly knowing the result would be incorrect?[a]	92	7	1

Note. Based on a total of 2,445 employees. *N*s vary due to missing cases on some items.
[a]These items were not used in City 3; *n* for these items was 2,106.

in the past year they showed these behaviors with responses ranging from
1 (*none*) to 5 (*6 or more times*). The items and the combined frequency of
response across the three samples are displayed in Table 2. Only six items
were used in City 3 due to other survey goals in that municipality. Alphas
were adequate (.68, .68, and .55). Employee average response to the combined items was consistent across the three samples (City 1: $M = 1.4$, SD
$= .47$; Cities 2 and 3: $M = 1.6$, $SD = .54$).

Witnessing violence. In City 2 (1995), employees were asked, "In the
past three years, have you ever *personally experienced* or *directly witnessed* any of the following dangerous incidents during your work day?"
and responded (*no/yes*) to four types of incidents: (a) someone throws objects dangerously, breaks or destroys objects, or smashes windows; (b)
someone makes a serious verbal threat or makes a threatening gesture
with a dangerous object (something sharp or a weapon); (c) someone
strikes, kicks, pushes, or pulls hair without causing injury; and (d) someone assaults or attacks, causing physical injury. These items were combined into both a *range of violence* score (mean of a, b, c, d) and a *maximum
violence* or *severity index* in which a 4-point ordinal scale was constructed
on the basis of the most severe violence witnessed: 0 (*none*), 1 (*breaks
objects or threatens*), 2 (*hit, no injury*), and 3 (*attack, with injury*). Following these responses, researchers also asked employees to write down the

overall number of such events witnessed. For a measure of *violent inci-dence*, this last item was recoded for 0 (*none*), 1 (*one*), and 2 (*two or more*).

Employees also indicated (*no/yes*) if the violence was due to or related to any of the following: (a) alcohol or substance use, (b) relationship, mar-ital, or family problems, (c) personality conflicts, and (d) job-related stress. Finally, they wrote in how many of the violent incidents witnessed had occurred (a) between two coworkers, (b) between a coworker and a super-visor, and (c) between a coworker and a citizen (not a City employee). This item was recoded for 0 (*none*), 1 (*one*), and 2 (*two or more*).

Analytic Plan

Analysis of variance. We used ANOVA to test the hypothesis that em-ployees who reported different levels of drinking norms and group cohe-sion would also report different levels of personal antagonism and violent witnessing. Employees were classified into one of three groups represent-ing low, medium, and high drinking norms and one of two groups repre-senting low and high cohesion. Employees in City 1 and 3 were considered to be *low* on coworker alcohol use if they scored at the 35th percentile or lower ($n = 378, 115$), *medium* if they scored between the 35th and 65th percentile ($n = 344, 90$), and *high* if they scored above the 65th percentile ($n = 323, 120$). A different measure of coworker use was adapted in City 2 (1992), where 63% provided the lowest score on that scale ($n = 678$). Scores between the 63rd and 84th percentile were *medium* ($n = 226$) and above the 84th percentile were *high* ($n = 169$). Employees were assigned to *low* ($n = 505, 578, 147$) versus *high* ($n = 540, 495, 178$) cohesion groups, based on scoring below or above the median within the city sample. In City 2 (1995), 67% provided the lowest score on the coworker scale ($n = 577$). Scores between the 67th and 84th percentile were *medium* ($n = 146$) and above the 84th percentile were *high* ($n = 134$). Low cohesion ($n = 437$) and high cohesion ($n = 417$) groups were formed using a median split on the cohesiveness measure.

Regressions. We have formulated a general model of workplace vio-lence that portrays exposure to violence as being a function of demographic and personal characteristics, work climate variables organized into alien-ating and integrative factors, work-related stress and stressors, and drink-ing climate. The research staff conducted a series of multiple regressions in which three workplace violence variables (antagonistic behaviors, level of workplace violence, and range of violence) were regressed on domains of variables representing the areas listed above. First, we regressed the three violence criteria on each of the variable domains separately. Next, the three violence criteria were regressed on the combined set of variables from all of the domains except for drinking climate. Finally, we added the drinking climate variables to the regression equations in order to assess whether drinking climate was able to uniquely account for variance in the violence criteria. We evaluated the resulting change in R^2 (ΔR^2) to determine the amount of variance in the violence variables that drinking climate was able to uniquely account for after statistically controlling for the personal and other work-related variables.

We also regressed the violence criteria on the combined set of alienating and integrative factors to determine if both domains better predicted violence than either domain alone. ΔR^2 was computed for alienating and integrative factors separately by subtracting the R^2 without the specific domain from the R^2 for the combined set of alienating and integrative variables.

Results

Frequency of Witnessed Violence

Witnessing of violent events were coded in two ways: maximum responses to four items specifying type of violence (i.e., objects thrown, threats, hitting without injury, and assault with injury) followed by an open-ended item asking how many of these or other violent events were witnessed. The percent of employees responding to the violence items is reported in Table 3. As the first column of the table indicates, 38% ($n = 335$) of those responding to the four types of violence items ($n = 888$), reported witnessing violence within the past 3 years at work. The first row of the table

Table 3. Frequency and Level of Violence Witnessed at Work: Associated Relationships and Causes

	N	Not classified	Break objects/ serious threats	Hit, no injury	Assault, with injury
			Level of violence (% of those witnessing)		
Witnessed any violence	335 (38%)		195 (58%)	76 (23%)	64 (19%)
Incident occurred between coworker and:					
Coworker	224	18%	43%	21%	18%
Supervisor	162	22%	39%	18%	20%
Citizen	122	30%	35%	14%	20%
Cause:					
Personality conflicts	282	23%	40%	21%	15%
Job stress	242	21%	40%	21%	18%
Relationships	118	25%	37%	19%	19%
Substance use	77	24%	36%	17%	24%

Note. Total of 889 responded to violence questions. Ns vary due to missing cases. Percentages are based on the row totals.

indicates 22% of the full sample—or 58% of those witnessing violence—experienced someone throwing or breaking objects or making serious threats at work. Another 16% experienced maximum violence as either hitting or attacks by others.

Slightly fewer employees specified the number of incidents witnessed, with 12% (110) reporting one and 21% (184) reporting two or more (not reported in table). Among these were 65 employees who wrote in a number for witnessing violence who had not responded to the four prompts. If these employees are included (added to the 335), the total estimate for the entire sample becomes 45%. A number of employees responded to only several of the items in this portion of the survey. This was largely due to those individuals not witnessing any of the four types of violence and leaving the remainder of the items blank.

Relationship. Table 3 presents employee perceptions of both the relationship involved and the cause of the violence. As noted earlier, a number of employees did not respond to these items once they indicated they had not experienced any violence. Conversely, there were also employees who did report their perceptions of relationships and causes even though they did not report witnessing violence. It seemed the latter group was willing to provide estimates or opinions of these factors. The second column of Table 3 shows the percentage of employees who could not be classified according to the maximum level of violence because they did not respond to those four items.

Of those indicating the relationship of the witnessed violence, 26% (224) specified between coworkers, 20% between a coworker and supervisor, and 15% between a coworker and (nonemployee) citizen. Because many employees reported more than one incident, they also indicated more than one type of relationship. For those employees specifying only one type of relationship ($n = 138$), 51% (or 71) reported between coworkers, 19% between a coworker and supervisor, and 30% between a coworker and citizen. Table 3 also shows employees had a somewhat equal chance of experiencing more severe levels of violence regardless of the type -of relationship experienced. For example, 18% of coworker–coworker violence consisted of attack or assault with injury, followed by 20% of coworker–supervisor, and 20% of coworker–citizen violence. There was a tendency for greater hitting (no injury) between coworkers (21%) than between coworkers and citizens (14%).

Attributed cause. The most attributed cause of violence was personality conflicts (32% of the full sample or 84% of those witnessing violence), followed by job-related stress, relationship problems, and substance use. Importantly, only 9% ($n = 77$) of the entire sample (23% of witnessing sample) attributed violence to substance use. Employees often gave multiple causes for violent events, even in those instances where only one incident was experienced. As Table 4 shows, it was rare for employees to specify any of the four possibilities as the sole cause of violence. The most common combination of causes was personality conflicts and job-related

Table 4. Percentage of Subjects Attributing Their Experience of Violent Incidents to Four Different Causes (Sole and Combined Attributions)

Violence due to:	Total	Sole attributed cause	Job-related stress	Family/marital relationship problems	Substance abuse
			Attributed cause in combination with		
Personality conflicts	282 (32%)	60 (7%)	193 (22%)	90 (10%)	56 (6%)
Job-related stress	242 (27%)	32 (4%)		87 (10%)	47 (5%)
Family/marital relationship problems	118 (13%)	10 (1%)			50 (6%)
Substance use	77 (9%)	9 (1%)			

Note. Percentages are based on the total of 888 who responded to violence questions.

stress (n = 193), accounting for 22% of all employees, followed by personality conflicts in combination with relationship problems (10%).

Demographics and job characteristics. Employees were classified according to several demographic and job characteristics. As Table 5 shows, younger (less than 30 years of age) male employees who worked with machinery or near toxic chemicals (risk sensitive jobs) were those most likely to experience violent behaviors. Compared with females, males reported almost twice as many incidents (26%) involving objects breaking or serious threats, but only slightly more incidents involving hitting and assaults. Males also reported a higher frequency of violent incidents than females, 38% in comparison to 29%. Although more of the older (23%) than younger (16%) employees witnessed less severe violence, younger employees were twice as likely (25%) to experience more severe violence than older employees (13%). There was also a tendency for Anglo American employees to experience more incidents of violence than other racial groups.

Employees were classified as supervisors if they were responsible for hiring, overseeing, and evaluating a work group of more than two employees. These employees were more likely to experience violent incidents (42%) than nonsupervisory personnel (32%). Employees were also grouped according to their EEOC job classification. Those in clerical positions reported lower frequencies of violence than other classifications. In contrast, those who held skilled or technical positions were the most likely to witness violence.

Table 5. Percentage of Employees Experiencing Different Levels and Frequencies of Violence, Classified by Demographic and Job Characteristics

	Total %	Gender %		Age %		Race %			Education %	
		Male	Female	<30	>30	Anglo	African	Hispanic	High-school	College
Maximum violence		***		**						
Object breaking/serious threats	22	26	14	16	23	24	18	19	22	22
Hit, no injury	8	9	7	14	7	9	10	13	7	9
Assault, with injury	7	8	6	11	6	7	8	8	9	6
Total n	888	590	289	176	712	489	204	145	327	561
Incidents witnessed		*					*			
Once	13	13	12	13	13	12	15	10	11	14
Two or more	25	25	17	24	21	25	15	21	20	23
Total n	847	553	286	163	684	468	194	140	302	545

	Supervisor %		Job class %				Risk sensitive %	
	No	Yes	Official/ profess.	Skilled/ tech.	Paraprof./ service	Clerical	No	Yes
Maximum violence			***				***	
Object breaking/serious threats	21	26	18	26	25	10	20	24
Hit, no injury	8	11	9	10	5	4	7	10
Assault, with injury	8	4	6	8	10	5	5	11
Total n	726	162	199	451	79	129	508	380
Incidents witnessed	*		**					
One	12	19	15	11	13	13	13	13
Two or more	21	23	20	27	18	11	20	24
Total n	692	155	192	422	78	128	490	357

Note: Asterisks indicate that observed values in the subtable immediately below (e.g., Gender × Maximum violence, or Race × Incidents witnessed) are significantly different from expected values at a particular probability level. $*p < .05$; $**p < .01$; $***p < .001$.

Results of ANOVAS: *Drinking Norms and Group Cohesion*

The first two hypotheses stated that employees working in drinking climates (high drinking norms) that lack group cohesion will be the most likely to show signs of antagonism and to witness violence.

Antagonism. The frequency of response for each item of the antagonism scale is shown in Table 2. Although over 50% of employees admit to criticizing or arguing with coworkers, fewer report coworkers for doing something wrong (32%), go against supervisor instructions (23%), or file complaints (14%). The results of ANOVA (Drinking Norms × Cohesion) revealed main significant effects for each city (at .001) on both category variables (all $ps < .001$). No interactions were significant. The antagonism means for each of the groups are plotted in Figure 2 and clearly show that employees who report high drinking norms are more antagonistic than those reporting low drinking norms and those with low group cohesion are more antagonistic than those with high group cohesion. Moreover, employees experiencing drinking norms in low cohesion groups are the most antagonistic, whereas those reporting low coworker alcohol use and high cohesion are the least antagonistic.

Violence. The results of ANOVA (Drinking Norms × Cohesion) revealed significant main effects for each of the three violence scores on both variables (all $ps < .001$). For average violence, the interaction approached significance, $F(2, 851) = 2.83$; $p = .06$. The means for each of the violence scores—average, range, and number of incidents—are plotted in Figure 3. Similar to results on antagonism, employees who report high drinking norms or low cohesion witness more violence than other groups. The re-

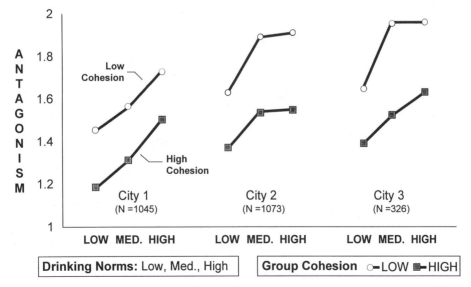

Figure 2. Antagonism: Main effects of drinking norms and group cohesion (three cities).

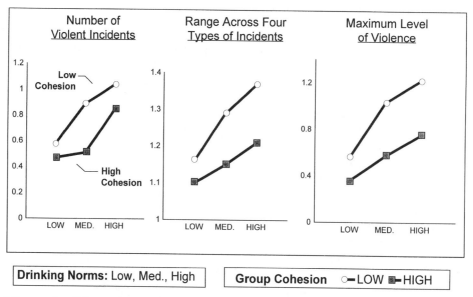

Figure 3. Witnessing violence: Main effects of drinking norms and group cohesion (three measures of violence).

lationship between antagonism and the violence measures was positive and significant at .001: for maximum level, $r = .27$; for range of violence, $r = .30$; and for number of incidents, $r = .30$.

Results of Regression Analyses

The primary purpose of the regression analyses was to assess the conceptual model and related hypotheses described above (see Figure 1). This model includes six sets of predictor variables (demographic and personal factors, work setting [alienation and integration], stress and stressors, and drinking climate) and both antagonism and the criterion measures of violence. Results for the regression analyses are presented in Table 6. The table shows the zero-order correlations between each predictor variable and the three violence criteria, the beta weights for the full regression models with all variable domains (including drinking climate), the R^2 for regressions for each domain separately as well as for the full regression models with and without drinking climate, and the R^2 for the combined integration and alienation domains. Also shown in the table are the ΔR^2 when drinking climate is added to the regression model after all other domains, when the integration domain is added to the model with the alienation domain, and when the alienation domain is added to the model with the integrative domain. ΔR^2 indicates the proportion of variance that is uniquely associated with that domain of variables after controlling for all other variables in the model.

Antagonistic behaviors. Overall, the set of variables from all domains not including drinking climate accounted for 51.9% of the variance in antagonistic behaviors; adding drinking climate variables to the regression equation increased the variance accounted for to 54.4%. Thus, drinking climate added significantly to the prediction of antagonistic behaviors after controlling for all the other personal and work climate variables, although the amount of added prediction by drinking climate was not very large.

Of the different variable domains, alienating factors had an R^2 of .413 with antagonistic behaviors, drinking climate had an R^2 of .226, and integrative factors had an R^2 of .210. As predicted by the third hypothesis, the alienating scales had a positive relationship with antagonism, whereas the integrative scales had a negative relationship. The combined set of integrative and alienating factors accounted for 45.2% of the variance in antagonistic behaviors. Of that, more than half (24.2%) was uniquely accounted for by alienating factors compared to a ΔR^2 of 3.9% for integrative factors. However, the large influence of alienating factors on antagonistic behaviors may be due to the inclusion in this domain of psychological and physical withdrawal measures, which are conceptually and methodologically similar to antagonistic behaviors.

Examination of the significant β weights indicates that employees who report higher levels of antagonistic behaviors are more likely to report higher alcohol use and drug use at work; lower group cohesion, lower faith in management, and higher job insecurity; and higher role overload, stress, coworker alcohol use, and consequences of coworker use.

Number of violent incidents. The prediction of violent incidents was not nearly as strong as that for antagonistic behaviors. The R^2 for all variable domains except for drinking climate was .158, and adding drinking climate to the regression equation increased the R^2 to .199, for an increase of .041. Thus, more than 20% of the total variance predicted in the number of violent incidents was uniquely associated with drinking climates. Drinking climate also had the largest R^2 (.117) of all of the variable domains when each was tested separately. R^2 for each of the other domains ranged from .036 for demographic factors to .078 for alienating factors.

The combined set of integrative and alienating factors had an R^2 of .096. Alienating factors were the stronger predictors, with an independent R^2 of .078 compared with .059 for integrative factors. However, the unique variance associated with alienating factors was .037 and for integrative factors an insignificant .018.

An employee who reports witnessing more incidents of violence, based on the β weights, is more likely than employees who report fewer incidents of violence to be female, have lower negative affectivity, have more physical withdrawal behaviors, report more recent turbulence in their work environment, and report greater consequences of coworker substance use.

Range of violence. The results for the range of violence variable were similar overall to those for number of violent incidents, although predic-

Table 6. Zero-Order Correlations and Regressions for Violence Variables

	Antagonistic behaviors			# of violent incidents			Range of violence		
	r	β	R^2	r	β	R^2	r	β	R^2
Demographic			.057***			.036***			.038***
Age	-.19***	-.02		-.08*	.00		-.11**	.02	
Gender (male)	-.08*	.00		-.13***	-.10*		-.14***	-.08	
Education	-.08*	-.01		-.04	.00		-.10**	-.01	
White	.04	.07		.08*	.07		.01	.02	
Black	.01	.07		-.07	.01		-.02	.02	
Personal			.169***			.048***			.081***
Alcohol use	.23***	.08*		.13**	.03		.13**	.01	
Drug use at work	.29***	.09**		.12**	.00		.20***	.07	
Risky job	.17***	.07		.10*	-.03		.16***	.01	
Social exposure	.06	.04		.06	.04		.04	.02	
Personal efficacy	-.07	-.02		.02	.01		-.03	-.01	
Negative affectivity	.13**	-.03		.00	-.13**		.06	-.06	
Depression	.18***	-.04		.08*	.08		.12**	.08	
Self-esteem	-.19***	-.02		-.05	.02		-.10*	.00	
Integration			.210***			.059***			.071***
Wellness culture	-.33***	.01		-.21***	-.09		-.23***	-.07	
Teamwork	-.30***	.01		-.13**	.02		-.15***	-.03	
Group cohesion	-.41***	-.16***		-.19***	-.01		-.21***	-.04	
Role clarity	-.32***	-.01		-.17***	.02		-.20***	-.06	
Organizational commitment	-.30***	.06		-.13***	.02		-.16***	-.02	
Job satisfaction	-.30***	-.06		-.16***	-.05		-.14***	.05	
Faith in management	-.36***	-.13**		-.18***	-.01		-.19***	-.04	
Alienation			.413***			.078***			.109***
Addictive culture	.34***	-.03		.20***	-.01		.21***	.00	
Increased conflict	.42***	.18***		.15***	.05		.19***	.09	
Powerlessness	.16***	-.03		.10*	.03		.10*	.03	

	β	β	R²	β	β	R²	β	β	R²
Psychological withdrawal	.40***	.04		.12**	−.07		.12**	−.11*	
Physical withdrawal	.53***	.33***		.21***	.13**		.26***	.13**	
Stressors			.176***			.070***			.065***
Negative changes	.30***	−.04		.11**	−.10		.10*	−.15**	
Turbulence	.25***	−.02		.22***	.13**		.15***	.03	
Situational stress	.21***	.01		.16***	.04		.21***	.08	
Job insecurity	.17***	−.07*		.14***	.01		.13**	.03	
Role overload	.32***	.08*		.20***	.07		.18***	.05	
Stress	.33***	.13***		.14***	−.02		.13**	−.01	
Drinking Climate			.226***			.117***			.143***
Freq. of coworker alcohol use	.40***	.08*		.27***	.08		.28***	.09	
Drinking norms	.31***	.03		.23***	.06		.31***	.15***	
Coworker enabling	.24***	−.05		.19***	.02		.19***	.00	
Supervisor enabling	.18***	.03		.12**	.00		.13**	.00	
Consequences of coworker use	.40***	.12**		.30***	.15**		.32***	.10	
All variables			.544***			.199***			.234***
All variables except Drinking Climate			.519***			.158***			.184***
ΔR^2 for Drinking Climate			.025***			.041***			.050***
Combined Integration and Alienation			.452***			.096***			.128***
ΔR^2 for Integration[a]			.039***			.018			.019
ΔR^2 for Alienation[b]			.242***			.037***			.057***

Note: R^2 is given for regressions using each set of predictors separately. *$p < .05$, **$p < .01$, ***$p < .001$.
[a]ΔR^2 for Integration is equal to the R^2 for Integration and Alienation combined minus the R^2 for Alienation alone.
[b]ΔR^2 for Alienation is equal to the R^2 for Integration and Alienation combined minus the R^2 for Integration alone.

tion was generally stronger for range of violence. The full set of predictor variables excluding drinking climate had an R^2 of .184; adding drinking climate to the regression equation increased the R^2 to .234, for an increase of .050. Similar to the results for violent incidents, drinking climate uniquely accounted for more than 20% of the total variance. Drinking climate also had the largest R^2 (.143) when testing each domain separately. The R^2 for the other domains ranged from .038 for demographic variables to .109 for alienating factors.

The combined set of integrative and alienating factors gave an R^2 of .128. Taken separately, alienating factors were better predictors of range of violence with an R^2 of .109 compared to .071 for integrative factors. The variance uniquely accounted for by alienating factors was .057, as compared with only 1.9% for integrative factors. Again, each of the alienating scales showed positive relationships with the criterion, in contrast to the negative relationships seen with integration.

An employee who is likely to report a wider range of types of violent actions was one with lower psychological but higher physical withdrawal, fewer recent changes in the workplace, and more favorable drinking norms in the work group.

Comparing Employees Reporting Greater Tendencies Toward Either Integration or Alienation

Regression analyses showed that the scales assessing alienation and the scales assessing integration each explained separate parts of the variance in witnessing work violence. The combined variance explained by the two sets of scales was also significant. A measure that assesses the relative degree of alienation versus integration might further elucidate some of the regression findings. Secondary analyses showed the five scales assessing alienating factors were interrelated and had adequate internal consistency ($\alpha = .61$). These scales were averaged and treated as a single measure of alienation at work ($M = 2.09$, $SD = .37$; $Mdn = 2.10$). The seven integrative factor scales showed even stronger internal consistency ($\alpha = .89$). These scales were also averaged and treated as a single measure of social integration at work ($M = 3.32$, $SD = .60$; $Mdn = 3.38$).

As expected, the two composites were highly and inversely related ($r = -.72$). For the following analyses, employees were classified into two groups according to their scores on these two composite measures: (a) *Alienated*: included employees ($n = 353$) who scored above the median on the alienation composite and below the median on the integration composite; (b) *Integrated*: included employees ($n = 344$) who scored above the

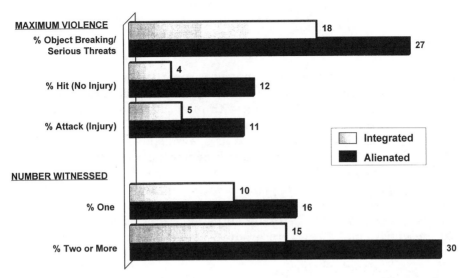

Figure 4. Witnessing violence: Percent of alienated versus integrated employees.

median on the integration composite and below the median on the alienation composite.[1]

Reported Violence for Those in Integrative Versus Alienating Environments

The fourth hypothesis stated that employees experiencing relatively more alienating factors will also experience more violence than employees experiencing relatively more integrative factors. Figure 4 displays the percentage of employees reporting violence within the two different groups. It is clear that employees who scored high on alienating factors are much more likely to witness violence than employees scoring high on integrative factors (in each chi-square analysis, $p < .001$). Fifty percent of alienated employees experienced some form of violence and 23% reported as the most severe form hitting or attacks or assaults. In comparison, 27% of integrated employees reported some form of violence and only 9% were in the maximum form of hitting or attacks or assaults. Alienated employees were almost twice as likely to witness some form of violence as integrated employees. Results with the write-in responses were similar, with alienated employees (46%) being almost twice as likely to report some incident as integrated employees (25%).

---

[1]Individuals ($n = 212$) who scored either above or below the median for both measures ere excluded from the analyses for ease of presentation. Similar results were obtained when this middle group was retained. Each of the following analyses was done using both the integrative and alienating composites as separate measures. Results were most consistent and striking when the combined groups were used.

Effects of Both Alienation–Integration and Drinking Climate on Violence

The fifth hypothesis stated that employees reporting more alienating conditions will be more adversely affected by drinking climates than those who report drinking climates along with integrative conditions. To examine this hypothesis, a series of two-way ANOVAS were conducted with the alienation–integration variable used as one independent factor, and each of the drinking climate variables (drinking norms, coworker drinking frequency, coworker enabling, negative consequences, and supervisor enabling) used as the second independent factor. Respondents were classified into low or high groups on each of the climate scales using median splits, with the exception of the drinking norms and supervisor enabling variables, in which employees were grouped as low, medium, or high due to skewed distributions on these variables. The three violence measures were used as dependent variables.

For all three measures of violence, the ANOVAS revealed significant main effects ($p < .002$) for the Alienation–Integration variable and each of the climate variables except supervisor enabling. Several interactions were also significant for the maximum level of violence and range of violence variables. For maximum level of violence there were significant interactions for Alienation–Integration and Drinking norms, $F(2, 668) = 5.61$, $p < .004$; Coworker enabling, $F(1, 692) = 4.6$, $p < .05$; and Negative Consequence of coworker use, $F(1, 657) = 7.09$, $p < .008$. For range of violence, there were significant interactions for Alienation–Integration and Drinking Norms, $F(2, 669) = 3.96$, $p < .004$; and Negative Consequence of Coworker Use, $F(1, 658) = 9.28$, $p < .003$. The interaction for Coworker Enabling approached significance, $F(1, 694) = 3.63$, $p < .06$.

The interaction effects for maximum level of violence are plotted in

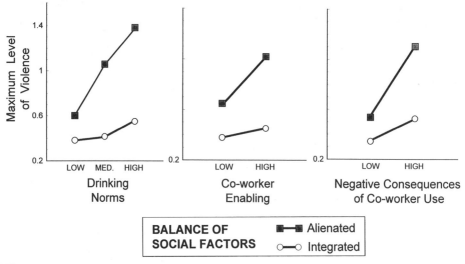

Figure 5. Maximum level of violence: Interaction effects of alienation–integration and drinking climate variables.

Figure 5. These are between Alienation–Integration and Drinking norms, Coworker enabling, and Negative consequences of coworker use. A similar pattern of effects was obtained with interactions on range of violence. The interactions show a consistent amplifier pattern in which exposure to violence is higher among alienated than integrated employees, increases for both groups as they are exposed to drinking climates, but increase more for alienated employees with such exposure. Thus, the group with the highest reported level of witnessing violence is alienated employees experiencing high drinking norms. Moreover, the greatest differences in witnessing violence between alienated and integrated employees occur among those exposed to high drinking norms, high coworker enabling, and more negative consequences of coworker use.

Summary and Discussion

The primary purpose of the current study was to assess the relationship between alcohol use—perceived as part of drinking climates at work— and both job antagonism and witnessing of violence. The current methodology did not assess actual violent perpetration or victimization, but instead identified factors that put employees at risk for either witnessing violence or behaving in an antagonistic manner at work. To this end, we presented a conceptual model synthesizing past research literature and tested five distinct hypotheses. The conceptual model suggested that individuals will be more likely to encounter violence if they are exposed to drinking climates and if they experience greater social alienation and less integration within their work setting.

The two major findings of the current investigation followed from the two questions guiding our hypotheses:

1. Does drinking climate add to the prediction of violence over and above other variables?
2. To what degree do alienating versus integrative tendencies within the work setting interact with alcohol variables as predictors of violence?

Results showed that drinking climates accounted for significant variance in antagonism and violence over and above variance accounted for by demographic, personal, work setting, and stress factors. Moreover, there were several significant interactions between work factors and drinking climates as predictors of exposure to violence. Specifically, employees reporting more alienating (than socially integrative) factors were more adversely affected by drinking climates than those who reported drinking climates along with integrative factors. The results confirm the other hypotheses and offer partial support for the model. The following is a brief summary and comment on each hypothesis and the related implications, strengths, and weaknesses of the findings.

(Hypotheses 1 and 2) *Employees who experienced strong drinking norms among their coworkers as well as those who reported low cohesiveness in their work groups were more likely to exhibit antagonistic behaviors at work and witness violence.*

These findings were consistent across three distinct samples of employees. Previous empirical models point to drinking norms as a work risk factor for alcohol, performance, and health problems (Trice & Sonnenstuhl, 1990; Walsh et al., 1993). The current findings add to these models by showing that such norms—as well as a lack of social bonding at work—also represent a risk for antagonistic work behaviors and exposure to violence.

Other research indicates that group cohesiveness is a multidimensional construct—consisting of both instrumental/cooperation and group pride dimensions (Mullen & Copper, 1994). Most items on our cohesiveness measure suggest it assesses cooperative task orientation. Evaluation of harm reduction programs should explore this distinction. It would be helpful to know whether prevention activities should target individual or group alcohol use and focus on team building or cooperation skills as potential buffers against antagonism and violence.

(Hypothesis 3) *Alienating factors showed a positive relationship to employee antagonism and exposure to violence, whereas integrative factors showed a negative relationship to these outcomes.*

According to simple correlation analyses, and in order of their strength, these alienating factors were each positively related to antagonism and exposure to violence: physical withdrawal, increased conflict, addictive culture, psychological withdrawal, and powerlessness. Contrasting negative correlations were obtained for these integrative factors: group cohesion, faith in management, wellness culture, and role clarity. Moreover, these internal aspects of the work setting—in comparison to employee demographics or external stressors—seemed to play a significant role in predicting antagonism or violent exposure.

These findings also extend past research literature on substance use and alienation to include violence as a potential consequence of alienation (Greenberg & Grunberg, 1995; Parker & Farmer, 1990; Seeman et al., 1988). Parker and Farmer make the distinction between psychological and structural alienation; the latter refers to job characteristics such as lack of complex work. The current alienation index adds to the psychological dimension by including reliable measures of job withdrawal, and to the structural dimension by including measures of conflict and addictive culture (perfectionism, work addiction, conflict avoidance). These measures were more closely associated with antagonism and violence than was powerlessness, which is the most common operationalization of alienation (Greenberg & Grunberg, 1995).

If the alienated and integrative factors are compared, the alienating factors (especially job withdrawal or isolation) tended to be better predictors of antagonism and violence. One implication of these findings pertains to recent discussions about healthy companies and wellness cultures (Rosen, 1991). Efforts at preventing workplace violence may benefit by addressing alienation as well as building health. Wellness, stress reduction, or employee empowerment programs may be helpful for employees, but those who lack a positive social orientation to work might particularly benefit from team building or social health strategies to strengthen work groups (Gottlieb & McLeroy, 1994). Future research will benefit from more careful analysis of the psychological–structural distinction than was attempted here. Of most importance will be applied studies that examine the impact of violence prevention programs in cultures that tend to be more addictive or alienated than healthy or cohesive.

(Hypothesis 4) *Employees reporting relatively more alienating factors witnessed more violence than employees reporting relatively more integrative factors.*

To arrive at this finding, we used a composite of all alienating and integrative factors. The finding makes the assumption that workplaces contain various tendencies toward either social isolation and alienation or toward social cohesion and integration. This is the first time this measure has been used and it should be subject to further tests of its psychometric qualities. Still, it proved useful in distinguishing employees with varying potential for witnessing violence; roughly 50% of alienated employees, in comparison to 25% of integrated employees, witnessed some form of violence within the past 3 years at work. For comparison purposes, 38% of the full sample reported witnessing violence, and the demographic characteristic most predictive of witnessing violence was gender (43% of males versus 27% of females).

We deliberately avoided labeling alienation and integration as organizational culture or climate variables. The current composite may be construed as a measure of *psychological* climate rather than of *aggregate, collective,* or *organizational* climate (Rousseau, 1988). The measure uses unaggregated individual perceptions of personal attitude, job events, culture, and social interactions rather than group consensus or coworker summaries of the work environment. Future research should aggregate individual measures at the work group and department level to better assess the alienation–integration distinction at the organizational level (Danserau & Alutto, 1990; Rousseau, 1990). It is also not clear whether alienation–integration represents two separate categories or a single dimension (Furnham & Gunter, 1993). For conceptual clarity, the present measure is best viewed as assessing the relative balance between integrative and alienating tendencies rather than as climates or a dimension of organizations. In contrast, the drinking climate variables each assessed perceptions of their coworker environment and may more accurately be labeled a climate measure.

(Hypothesis 5) *Drinking climate variables had both an independent relationship with employee antagonism and witnessing of violence and a further relationship moderated by the relative degree of alienation–integration. Specifically, employees reporting more alienating conditions were more adversely affected by drinking climates than those who reported drinking climates along with integrative conditions.*

This is a key finding of the current study and extends the results on group cohesion and drinking norms (Hypotheses 1 and 2 above). The conceptual model views work setting as having a particular impact on coworker violence for employees who also experience drinking climates. In predicting exposure to violence, there were five significant interactions between the alienation–integration groupings and employee perceptions of three drinking climate variables (drinking norms, coworker enabling, and negative consequences of substance use). The probability of violence increased significantly for alienated employees as they were exposed to stronger drinking climates. In contrast, employees who felt relatively more social integration at work—such as through group cohesion, job commitment, or a wellness culture—gave reports of violence that did not vary according to different levels of drinking climate.

These interaction effects are consistent with previous research highlighting the role of self-awareness and group norms as an inhibitor of the alcohol–aggression relationship (Bushman & Cooper, 1990; Hull, 1981; Taylor & Chermack, 1993). Although drinking norms might develop at work, they may not necessarily result in negative behaviors if employees feel they are part of cohesive work groups. If alcohol use does occur in the workplace, the presence of positive social norms—here represented as group cohesion—may help curb its facilitative effects on violence.

Occupational drinking customs do not always imply deviance, and drinking subcultures may involve only moderate versus heavy or pathological drinking patterns (Ames & Janes, 1990; Cosper, 1979). The current set of significant interactions suggest that drinking norms in low cohesive settings may become more pathological than similar norms in high cohesive settings. Future research should better distinguish between these patterns and assess whether drinking norms might serve a positive socialization function for some socially cohesive groups. We should point out that two of the climate measures—enabling and consequences—referred to both alcohol and drugs and it is possible that some employees were referring to drug use and not alcohol use among their fellow workers. Still, the nteraction between drinking norms and alienation–integration was significant for two of the violence measures.

Others have argued that health is as much socially as individually produced (Gottlieb & McLeroy, 1994; Walsh et al., 1993). Understanding social norms around substance use should help tailor health promotion programs within the workplace. The current results strongly argue for a similar approach in workplace violence programs. There appear to be social risk factors at work that significantly affect the probability of witnessing violence. Employees who experience more social alienation than integration at work, who know of coworker substance use, are adversely affected by it, and somehow enable it, may be especially vulnerable to witnessing violence.

Additional Major Findings

As noted above, drinking climate factors moderated the relationship between alienation–integration and violence. The findings also show that the relationship between alcohol and aggression is significantly moderated by the situational context. Interestingly, the most consistent single predictor for both antagonism and witnessing violence was physical withdrawal from work (i.e., lateness, falling asleep on the job, taking extra long breaks, missing meetings, or leaving). This finding has several interpretations. Either employees who socially isolate do so as a result of having witnessed violence, or social isolation leaves them vulnerable to violent witnessing because they lack the protective social attachment of a group (Allcorn, 1994). These findings are also consistent with Hull's self-awareness model in which individuals may use alcohol to withdraw from painful situations (Hull, 1981). Unfortunately, correlational analyses of survey data cannot determine cause–effect relationships.

The data also support a distinction between employee antagonism and the potential to witness violence. The relationship between antagonism and the violence measures was positive although not remarkably strong ($r = .30$), implying that some employees who witness violence are not experiencing it as a function of their own hostility. More importantly, predictor variables in the regression model accounted for 54% of the variance in antagonism and 20% to 23% of the variance in violent witnessing. There are both methodological and theoretical explanations for these differences.

Methodologically, items from the antagonism measure used the same format and are interspersed within the survey along with items from two of the alienating factor scales—psychological and physical withdrawal. These measures assess employees' typical and personal behaviors on the job and they had among the highest correlations with antagonism. In contrast, the violence measures were separated in the survey from antagonism and asked for employees to recall less typical (and perhaps maximal) experiences of *others'* behavior over a 3-year period. Thus the stronger relationship seen between alienation and antagonism may be due to common method variance between the three job behavior scales. To assess the relative contribution of the withdrawal measures additional regression analyses were conducted. When the two withdrawal measures were removed from analysis, the prediction of the remaining alienating variables was still significant for both antagonism and the violence measures. Thus, it is possible to predict both antagonism and violence if just addictive climate, conflict, and powerlessness are considered as alienating factors.

Theoretically, the stronger relationship seen between antagonism and the withdrawal measures may be due to actual tendencies within individuals to withdraw from situations as a function of their own antagonism. Seeman (1959) originally described two aspects of alienation: social isolation and self-estrangement. Isolation refers to feelings of loneliness, rejection, and exclusion from valued groups. Self-estrangement refers to the feeling that one is acting in ways that are somehow not true to self and one's own needs. It is possible that coworkers avoid antagonistic employees and the latter come to isolate themselves from their fellow workers. It is also possible that employees who feel self-estranged act out their feelings through withdrawal and antagonism. In contrast, isolation may lead to greater potential witnessing of violence and violence may lead to a need to isolate from violent coworkers. Future research should also explore different definitions of antagonism. In this regard, interested readers may wish to consult Unterberg (1993) for his differentiation of overreactive, aggressive, litigious, divisive, demanding, and passive–aggressive employees.

Additional Limitations

The foregoing review and empirical study should be viewed as a preliminary attempt to investigate the alcohol–aggression relationship within the workplace. Although the findings are consistent with previous literature on alcohol and aggression, there are limitations to the study that should be considered in any interpretation of the results. First and foremost, our measures of alcohol and aggression are unique in focusing more on the perception of others than on the perception of self. This departs from previous literature on alcohol and aggression, which most often analyzes individual use and subsequent individual violence. In particular, we operationalized alcohol and substance use at the level of the organization (i.e., coworkers and norms) rather than at the individual level, and we operationalized violence in terms of having been a past witness to some form of violence.

These operationalizations have several drawbacks. The alcohol measure fails to assess whether employees have independently observed coworker use or whether they are personal users who join in with their fellows. The violence measure fails to assess whether those who observed violence were actually the perpetrators or victims of violence. Because we did not assess self-reports of personal violence toward coworkers, the current survey neglects the phenomena that previous literature focuses on: that is, the relationship between personal alcohol use and subsequent violent behavior.

The current survey also framed items for respondents as observers, rather than participants, of both violence and alcohol use. This could cause inflated correlations due to the personal or cultural belief that alcohol causes violence. It would be helpful to explore employee beliefs about "drunken comportment" or whether employees have stereotypes in which violence is a natural consequence of alcohol use (MacAndrew & Edgerton, 1969; Pernanen, 1991; Roizen & Schneberk, 1977). It is possible that drinking climates become part of a "self-fulfilling prophecy" in which employees use alcohol as an excuse for aggression (Darley & Fazio, 1980; Fagan, 1993). Future research should utilize more objective and behavioral data—such as personnel files and drug-test results—that examine relationships between recorded incidents of violence (e.g., compensation claims) and actual substance use (e.g., drug-test results) as these occur within work units or work groups.

Another limitation involves potential bias in self-reports. Individuals tend to underreport their use of alcohol (Embree & Whitehead, 1993), just as they may be reluctant to report coworkers under the influence of alcohol or drugs (Hood & Duphorne, 1995). There is also the possibility of over-reporting. Our definition of antagonism includes being overly critical, griping, spreading rumors, and whistle-blowing. Because they like to complain, antagonistic individuals may have overreported negative instances of coworker use. Because of their aggressiveness, they may also over-report some acts as instigative or violent.

Antagonistic employees may be vulnerable to a negative halo effect: having any exposure to a negative incident at work could cause them to view the entire work setting as negative. In fact, negative consequences of coworker substance use was one of the strongest predictors of both antagonism and violence. An employee who had only one experience with coworker use might generalize and also infer drinking norms and enabling. We hasten to add that the measure of negative affectivity—which, more precisely, assesses a dispositional tendency toward pessimism and negativity—was not significantly related to the violence or antagonism measures once the withdrawal variables were accounted for. Job antagonism appears to be more job specific rather than reflective of an overriding tendency toward viewing others in a negative manner.

In summary, the relationship between alcohol use and aggression—studied in many other contexts—appears to occur within the workplace. This finding supports and extends Fagan's (1993) analysis of the role of social setting in alcohol-related violence:

> The variation in intoxicated behaviors within social contexts suggests that the context itself exerts a powerful influence on the violence outcomes of drinking situations, one that is far greater than the effects of the substance itself. Thus, if drinkers bring sources of situational arousal to a setting, their interpretation of cues may be guided in the direction of finding a blameworthy target for their grievances. If a locale is dominated by people with such grievances, the social controls within the scene are hard pressed to avoid an escalation into violence. (pp. 184–185)

Although the current results cannot be used to infer employee alcohol use as a cause of violence, they do suggest that drinking climates at work, along with social alienation versus integration, may put employees at risk for both showing antagonism and reporting violent events while at work. A replication of these results, confirming of the predictive value of drinking climates, should have significant implications for prevention of workplace violence. Administrators of harm reduction programs might pay attention to biases and tendencies toward viewing either workplace violence or substance use wholly as an individual problem. It is apparent that employee relationships and social norms at work significantly contribute to these problems. Future research should address the aforementioned limitations of the current measures and definitions of violence and substance use. Such efforts should give a better understanding of the role of organizational climate as predictors of violence over and above individual substance use.

References

Allcorn, S. (1992). *Codependency in the workplace*. Westport, CT: Quorum.

Allcorn, S. (1994). *Anger in the workplace: Understanding the causes of aggression and violence*. Westport, CT: Quorum.

Allen, J., & Bellingham, R. (1994). Building supportive cultural environments. In M. P. O'Donnell & J. S. Harris (Eds.), *Health promotion in the workplace* (2nd ed., pp. 204–214). Albany, NY: Delmar.

Ames, G. M. (1989). Alcohol-related movements and their effects on drinking policies in the American workplace: An historical review. *Journal of Drug Issues, 19*(4), 489–510.

Ames, G., & Delaney, W. (1992). Minimization of workplace alcohol problems: The supervisor's role. *Alcoholism: Clinical and Experimental Research, 16*(2), 180–189.

Ames, G., Delaney, W., & Janes, C. (1992). Obstacles to effective alcohol policy in the workplace: A case study. *British Journal of Addiction, 87*, 1055–1069.

Ames, G., & Janes, C. (1990). Drinking, social networks, and the workplace: Results of an environmentally focused study. In P. M. Roman (Ed.), *Alcohol problem intervention in the workplace: Employee assistance programs and strategic alternatives* (pp. 95–111). Westport, CT: Quorum.

Ames, G. M., & Janes, C. (1992). Obstacles to effective alcohol policy in the workplace: A case study. *British Journal of Addiction, 87*, 1055–1069.

Ashford, S. J., Lee, C., & Bobko, P. (1989). Content, causes, and consequences of job insecurity: A theory based measure and substantive test. *Academy of Management Journal, 32*, 803–829.

Bailey, D. S., Leonard, K. E., Cranston, J. W., & Taylor, S. P. (1983). Effects of alcohol and self awareness on human physical aggression. *Personality and Social Psychology Bulletin, 9*(2), 289–295.

Bailey, D. S., & Taylor, S. P. (1991). Effects of alcohol and aggressive disposition on human physical aggression. *Journal of Research Personality, 25*, 334–342.

Banaji, M. R., & Steele, C. M. (1989). Alcohol and self-evaluation: Is a social cognition approach beneficial? *Social-Cognition, 7*(2), 137–151.

Bandura, A. (1965). Influence of model's reinforcement contingencies on the acquisition of imitative responses. *Journal of Personality and Social Psychology, 1*, 589–595.

Bandura, A., & Schunk, D. H. (1981). Cultivating competence, self-efficacy, and intrinsic interest through proximal self-motivation. *Journal of Personality and Social Psychology, 41*, 586–598.

Baron, R. A. (1990). Conflict in organizations. In K. R. Murphy & F. E. Saal (Eds.), *Psychology in organizations: Integrating science and practice* (pp. 197–216). Hillsdale, NJ: Erlbaum.

Beattie, M. C., Longabaugh, R., Elliott, G., Stout, R. L., Fava, J., & Noel, N. E. (1993). Effect of the social environment on alcohol involvement and subjective well-being prior to alcoholism treatment. *Journal of Studies on Alcohol, 54*, 283–296.

Beehr, T. A., & Bhagat, R. S. (1985). *Human stress and cognition in organizations: An integrated perspective*. New York: Wiley.

Berkowitz, L. (1978). Whatever happened to the frustration-aggression hypotheses? *American Behavioral Scientist, 21*, 691–708.

Blum, R. (1981). Violence, alcohol, and setting: An unexplored nexus. In J. J. Collins (Ed.), *Drinking and Crime* (pp. 110–142). New York: Guilford Press.

Boyatzis, R. E. (1975). The effect of alcohol consumption on the aggressive behavior of men. *Quarterly Journal of Studies on Alcohol, 35*, 959–972.

Braverman, M. (1995, September). *Beyond profiling: An integrated, multidisciplinary approach to preventing workplace violence*. Paper presented at the conference on Work, Stress and Health '95: Creating Healthier Workplaces, Washington, DC.

British Medical Association. (1995, September). MP's and Portman group clash on alcohol and crime. *UK Alcohol Alert: Incorporating Alliance News* (Series No. 12). London: Institute of Alcohol Studies.

Brockner, J. (1988). *Self-esteem at work: Research, theory, and practice.* Lexington, MA: Lexington Books.

Brockner, J., Grover, S., Reed, T. F., & DeWitt, R. L. (1992). Layoffs, job insecurity, and survivors' work effort: Evidence of an inverted-U relationship. *Academy of Management Journal, 35,* 413–425.

Bushman, B. J., & Cooper, H. M. (1990). Effects of alcohol on aggression: An integrative research review. *Psychological Bulletin, 107,* 341–354.

Buydens-Branchey, L., & Branchey, M. H. (1992). Cortisol in alcoholics with a disordered aggression control. *Psychoneuroendocrinology, 71*(1), 45–54.

Campion, M. A., & Medsker, G. J. (1993). Relations between work group characteristics and effectiveness: Implications for designing effective work groups. *Personnel Psychology, 46,* 823–850.

Carver, C. S. (1974). The facilitation of aggression as a function of objective self-awareness and attitudes towards punishment. *Journal of Experimental Social Psychology, 10,* 365–370.

Cavanaugh, J. M., & Prasad, P. (1994). Drug testing as symbolic managerial action: In response to "a case against workplace drug testing." *Organization Science, 5*(2), 190–198.

Christiansen, B. A., & Teahan, J. E. (1987). Cross-cultural comparisons of Irish and American adolescent drinking practices and beliefs. *Journal of Studies on Alcohol, 48,* 558–652.

Cohen, S., & Wills, T. A. (1985). Stress, social support, and the buffering hypothesis. *Psychological Bulletin, 9,* 310–357.

Cole, L. L., Grubb, P. L., Sauter, S. L., & Swanson, N. G. (1995, September). *Predictors of non-fatal workplace violence.* Paper presented at the conference on Work, Stress and Health '95: Creating Healthier Workplaces, Washington, DC.

Collins, J. J. (1981). *Drinking and Crime: Perspectives on the relationships between alcohol consumption and criminal behavior.* New York: Guilford Press.

Collins, J. (1988). Suggested explanatory frameworks to clarify the alcohol use/violence relationship. *Contemporary Drug Problems, 15,* 107–121.

Cosper, R. (1979). Drinking as conformity: A critique of sociological literature on occupational differences in drinking. *Journal of Studies on Alcohol, 40*(9), 868–891.

Cosper, R., & Hughes, F. (1982). So-called heavy drinking occupations: Two empirical tests. *Journal of Studies on Alcohol, 43*(1), 110–118.

Czajkoski, E. H. (Ed.). (1995, Spring). Drugs in the Workplace. Special Issue. *Journal of Drug Issues, 25*(2).

Danserau, F., & Alutto, J. A. (1990). Level-of-analysis issues in climate and culture research. In B. Schneider (Ed.), *Organizational Climate and Culture.* San Francisco: Jossey-Bass.

Darley, J. M., & Fazio, R. H. (1980). Expectancy confirmation processes arising in the social interaction sequence. *American Psychologist, 35,* 867–881.

Daw, J. (1994, August). Violence is invading the workplace: How can MFT's help? *Family Therapy News,* pp. 17–18.

Delaney, W. P., & Ames, G. (1995). Work team attitudes, drinking norms, and workplace drinking. *Journal of Drug Issues, 25*(2), 275–290.

Diamond, M. A. (Ed.). (1993). *The unconscious life of organizations: Interpreting organizational identity.* Westport, CT: Quorum.

Dunkel, T. (1994, August). Danger zone: Your office. *Working Woman,* pp. 39–41, 70–73.

Embree, B., & Whitehead, P. (1993, May). Validity and reliability of self-reported drinking behavior: Dealing with the problem of response bias. *Journal of Studies of Alcohol, 54*(3), 334–344.

Engel, F. (1987). Violence, crime, and trauma at work: An overlooked problem. *EAP Digest,* p. 29.

Fagan, J. (1993). Set and setting revisited: Influences of alcohol and illicit drugs on the social context of violent events. In S. Martin (Ed.), *Alcohol and interpersonal violence: Fostering multidisciplinary perspectives* (National Institute on Alcohol Abuse and Alcoholism: Research Monograph J. 24; NIH Publication No. 93-3496; pp. 161–192). Rockville, MD: U.S. Department of Health and Human Services.

Fassel, D. (1990). *Working ourselves to death: The high cost of workaholism, the rewards of recovery.* New York: Harper Collins.

Fennell, M. L., Rodin, M. B., & Kantor, G. K. (1981). Problems in the work setting, drinking, and reasons for drinking. *Social Forces, 60*(1), 115–132.

Fillmore, K. M. (1990). Occupational drinking subcultures: An exploratory epidemiological study. In P. M. Roman (Ed.), *Alcohol problem intervention in the workplace: Employee assistance programs and strategic alternatives* (pp. 77–94). Westport, CT: Quorum.

Fine, M., Akabas, S., & Bellinger, S. (1982). Cultures of drinking: A workplace perspective. *Journal of the National Association of Social Workers, 27*(5), 436–440.

Fiske, S. T., & Taylor, S. E. (1991). *Social cognition* (2nd ed.). New York: McGraw-Hill.

Frankenstein, W., & Wilson, G. T. (1984). Alcohol's effects on self-awareness. *Journal of Addictive Behaviors, 9*(4), 323–328.

Furnham, A., & Gunter, B. (1993). Corporate assessment: Auditing a company's personality. London: Routledge & Kegan Paul.

Gaines, L. S. (1981). Cognition and the environment: Implications for a self-awareness theory of drinking. In *Social drinking contexts* (Research Monograph 7, DHHS Publication No. 1097, ADM 81-0, Center for Substance Abuse, pp. 138–154). Rockville, MD: National Institute on Alcohol Abuse and Alcoholism.

Galvin, D. M. (1995 July/August). Preventing AOD-related violence: An internet challenge. *Prevention Pipeline,* pp. 14–18.

Geen, R. G. (1983). Aggression and television violence. In R. G. Geen & E. I. Donnerstein (Eds.), *Aggression: Theoretical and empirical reviews* (Vol. 2, pp. 103–125). New York: Academic Press.

Goldman, M. (1987). Expectancy theory: Thinking about drinking. In H. Lane & K. Leonard (Eds.), *Psychological theories of drinking and alcoholism* (pp. 181–226). New York: Guilford Press.

Gottlieb, N. H., & McLeroy, K. R. (1994). Social health. In M. P. O'Donnell & J. S. Harris (Ed.), *Health promotion in the workplace* (Chap. 17, pp. 459–493). Albany, NY: Delmar Publications.

Greenberg, E., & Grunberg, L. (1995, March). Work alienation and problem alcohol behavior. *Journal of Health and Social Behavior, 36,* 83–102.

Greenberg, S. (1981). Alcohol and crime: A methodological critique of the literature. In J. J. Collins (Ed.), *Drinking and crime* (pp. 70–109). New York: Guilford Press.

Greller, M. M., Parsons, C. K., & Mitchell, D. R. D. (1992). Additive effects and beyond: Occupational stressors and social buffers in a police organization. In J. C. Quick, L. R. Murphy, & J. J. Hurrell, Jr. (Eds.), *Stress and well-being at work* (pp. 33–47). Washington, DC: American Psychological Association.

Gustafson, R. (1984). Alcohol, frustration, and direct physical aggression: A methodological point of view. *Psychological Reports, 55,* 959–966.

Gustafson, R. (1991). Male physical aggression as a function of alcohol, frustration, and subjective mood. *International Journal of the Addictions, 26*(3), 255–266.

Gustafson, R. (1993). What do experimental paradigms tell us about alcohol-related aggressive responding? *Journal of Studies on Alcohol: Alcohol and Aggression* (Suppl. 11), pp. 20–29.

Hackman, J. R. (1992). Group influences on individuals in organizations. In M. D. Dunnette & L. M. Hough (Eds.), *Handbook of industrial and organizational psychology* (pp. 199–268). Palo Alto, CA: Consulting Psychologists Press.

Hood, J. C., & Duphorne, P. L. (1995). To report or not to report: Nurses' attitudes toward reporting co-workers suspected of substance abuse. *Journal of Drug Issues, 25*(2), 313–340.

Huber, G. P., & Glick, W. H. (1993). *Organizational change and redesign.* New York: Oxford University Press.

Hulin, C. L. (1991). Adaptation, persistence, and commitment in organizations. In M. D. Dunnette & L. M. Hough (Eds.), *Handbook of industrial and organizational psychology* (pp. 445–506). Palo Alto, CA: Consulting Psychologists Press.

Hull, J. G. (1981). A self-awareness model of the causes and effects of alcohol consumption. *Journal of Abnormal Psychology, 90*(6), 586–600.

Hull, J. G., & Bond, C. F. (1986). Social and behavioral consequences of alcohol consumption and expectancy: A meta-analysis. *Psychological Bulletin, 99*(3), 347–360.

Hull, J. G., & Reilly, N. P. (1983). Self-awareness, self-regulation, and alcohol consumption: A reply to Wilson. *Journal of Abnormal Psychology, 92*(4), 514–519.

Hull, J. G., Young, R., & Jouriles, E. N. (1986). Applications of the self-awareness model of alcohol consumption: Predicting patterns of use and abuse. *Journal of Personality and Social Psychology, 5*(4), 790–796.

Janes, C., & Ames, G. (1989). Men, blue collar work, and drinking: Alcohol use and misuse in an industrial subculture. *Culture, Medicine and Psychiatry, 13*, 245–274.

Jeavons, C. M., & Taylor, S. P. (1985). The control of alcohol-related aggression: Redirecting the inebriate's attention to socially appropriate conduct. *Aggressive Behavior, 11*, 93–101.

Johnson, D. L. (1994, March/April). Workplace violence: Why it happens and what to do about it. *EAP Digest*, pp. 18–22.

Johnson, D. L. (1995, September). *Workplace violence: Practical strategies involving EAPs and mental health professionals*. Paper presented at the conference on Work, Stress and Health '95: Creating Healthier Workplaces, Washington, DC.

Kahn, R. L., & Byosiere, P. (1992). Stress in organizations. In M. D. Dunnette & L. M. Hough (Eds.), *Handbook of industrial and organizational psychology* (pp. 571–650). Palo Alto, CA: Consulting Psychologists Press.

Kahn, R. L., Wolfe, D. M., Quinn, R. P., Snoek, J. D., & Rosenthal, R. A. (1964). *Organizational stress: Studies in role conflict and ambiguity*. New York: Wiley.

Katz, D., & Kahn, R. L. (1978). *The social psychology of organizations* (2nd ed.). New York: Wiley. (Original work published 1966)

Kelly, J. R., & McGrath, J. E. (1988). *On time and method*. Newbury Park, CA: Sage.

Kets de Vries, M. F. R. (1991). *Organization on the couch: Clinical perspectives on organizational behavior and change*. San Francisco: Jossey-Bass.

Kinney, J. A. (1995). *Violence at work: How to make your company safer for employees and customers*. Englewood Cliffs, NJ: Prentice Hall.

Kohn, M. L. (1976). Occupational structure and alienation. *American Journal of Sociology, 82*, 111–130.

Krebs, D. L., & Miller, D. T. (1985). Altruism and aggression. In G. Lindzey & E. Aronson (Eds.), *Handbook of social psychology* (3rd ed., pp. 1–72). New York: Random House.

Lang, A., & Sibrel, P. (1989). Psychological perspectives on alcohol consumption and interpersonal aggression: The potential role of individual differences in alcohol-related criminal violence. *Criminal Justice and Behavior, 16*(3), 299–324.

Lawler, E. E. (1973). *Motivation in work organizations*. Monterey, CA: Brooks/Cole.

Lehman, W. E. K., & Simpson, D. D. (1992). Employee substance use and on-the-job behaviors. *Journal of Applied Psychology, 77*(3), 309–321.

Levine, H. (1978). The discovery of addiction: Changing conceptions of habitual drunkenness in America. *Journal of Studies on Alcohol, 39*, 143–174.

Levine, H. (1981). The good creature of God and the demon rum: Colonial American and 19th century ideas about alcohol, crime, and accidents. In R. Room & G. Collins (Eds.), *Alcohol and disinhibition: Nature and meaning of the link* (NIAAA Research Monograph 12). Rockville, MD: National Institute on Drug Abuse.

Levine, H. (1983). The committee of fifty and the origins of alcohol control. *Journal of Drug Issues, 13*(1), 95–116.

Lindman, R., & Lang, A. (1994). The alcohol-aggression stereotype: A cross-cultural comparison of beliefs. *International Journal of the Addictions, 29*(1), 1–13.

Lindquist, P. (1991). Homicides committed by abusers of alcohol and illicit drugs. *British Journal of Addiction, 86*, 321–326.

Lippa, R. A. (1990). *Introduction to social psychology*. Belmont, CA: Wadsworth.

MacAndrew, C., & Edgerton, R. B. (1969). *Drunken comportment: A social explanation*. Chicago: Aldine.

Mantell, M. (1994). *Ticking bombs: Defusing violence in the workplace*. New York: Irwin.

Martin, S. (Ed.). (1993). *Alcohol and interpersonal violence: Fostering multidisciplinary perspectives* (National Institute on Alcohol Abuse and Alcoholism: Research Monograph No. 24; NIH Publication No. 93-3496). Rockville, MD: U.S. Department of Health and Human Services.

Masi, D. A. (1994, March/April). Violence in the workplace: The EAP perspective. *EAP Digest, 14*(1), 23–24.

Mathiason, G. G. (1995). Terror and violence in the workplace. *The 1993 National Employer* (2nd ed., pp. 137–173). San Francisco, CA: Littler, Mendelson, Fastiff, Tichy, & Mathiason.

McBride, D. (1981). Drugs and violence. In J. A. Inciardi (Ed.), *The drugs-crime connection* (pp. 105–123). Beverly Hills, CA: Sage.

McCann, B. S., Russo, J., & Benjamin, G. A. H. (1995, September). *Hostile people at work: Implications for health effects of job strain*. Paper presented at the conference on Work, Stress, and Health '95: Creating Healthier Workplaces, Washington, DC.

McClelland, D. C., Davis, W. N., Kalin, R., & Wanner, E. (1972). *The drinking man*. New York: The Free Press.

McMillan, J. J., & Northern, N. A. (1995). Organizational codependency: The creation and maintenance of closed systems. *Management Communication Quarterly, 9*(1), 6–45.

Moss, H. B., & Tarter, R. (1993). Substance abuse, aggression, and violence: What are the connections? *American Journal on Addictions, 2*(2), 149–160.

Mullen, B., & Copper, C. (1994). The relation between group cohesiveness and performance: An integration. *Psychological Bulletin, 115*, 210–227.

Murdoch, D., Pihl, R., & Ross, D. (1990). Alcohol and crimes of violence: Present issues. *International Journal of the Addictions, 25*(9), 1065–1081.

Normand, J., Lempert, R. O., & O'Brien, P. O. (1994). *Under the influence? Drugs and the American work force*. Washington, DC: National Academy Press.

O'Donnell, M. P., & Harris, J. S. (1994). Health promotion in the workplace (2nd ed.). Albany, NY: Delmar.

Olweus, D. (1979). Stability of aggressive reaction patterns in males: A review. *Psychological Bulletin, 86*, 852–875.

Osipow, S. H., & Spokane, A. R. (1984). Measuring occupational stress, strain, and coping. In S. Oskamp (Ed.), *Applied social psychology annual: Applications in organizational settings* (pp. 67–86). Beverly Hills, CA: Sage.

Overman, S. (1993, July). Be prepared should be your motto. *HR Magazine*, pp. 46–49.

Parker, D. A., & Farmer, G. C. (1990). Employed adults at risk for diminished self-control over alcohol use: The alienated, the burned out, and the unchallenged. In P. M. Roman (Ed.), *Alcohol problem intervention in the workplace: Employee assistance programs and strategic alternatives* (pp. 27–43). Westport, CT: Quorum.

Parker, R. N. (1993). The effects of context on alcohol and violence: Alcohol, aggression, and injury [Special issue]. *Alcohol Health and Research World, 17*(2), 117–122.

Paulhus, D. (1983). Sphere-specific measures of perceived control. *Journal of Personality and Social Psychology, 44*, 1253–1265.

Pernanen, K. (1981). Theoretical aspects of the relationship between alcohol use and crime. In J. J. Collins (Ed.), *Drinking and crime* (pp. 1–69). New York: Guilford Press.

Pernanen, K. (1991). *Alcohol in human violence*. New York: Guilford Press.

Pihl, R. O. (1993). Alcohol, serotonin, and aggression. *Alcohol Health and Research World, 17*(2), 113–116.

Pihl, R. O., Peterson, J. B., & Lau, M. A. (1993). A biosocial model of the alcohol–aggression relationship. *Journal of Studies on Alcohol, 11*(Sept. Suppl.), 128–139.

Pihl, R. O., & Ross, D. (1987). Research on alcohol related aggression: A review and implications for understanding aggression. *Drugs and Society, 1*(4), 105–126.

Prentice-Dunn, S., & Rogers, R. W. (1982). Effects of public and private self-awareness on deindividuation and aggression. *Journal of Personality and Social Psychology, 43*, 503–513.

Preventing drug-related violence with training. (1995, November). *Drugs in the Workplace*, *10*(11), 1.

Prevention Pipeline. (1995, July/August). A cultural environment approach to prevention. *Prevention Pipeline: Violence and AOD use* (pp. 9–12). Rockville, MD: Center for Substance Use Prevention.

Ravenholt, R. T. (1984). Addiction mortality in the United States, 1980: Tobacco, alcohol, and other substances. *Population and Development Review, 10,* 697–724.

Roizen, J. (1993). Issues in the epidemiology of alcohol and violence. In S. Martin (Ed.), *Alcohol and interpersonal violence: Fostering multidisciplinary perspectives* (National Institute on Alcohol Abuse and Alcoholism: Research Monograph J. 24; NIH Publication No. 93-3496; pp. 3–36). Rockville, MD: U.S. Department of Health and Human Services.

Roizen, J., & Schneberk, D. (1977). Alcohol and crime. In M. Aarens, T. Cameron, J. Roizen, R. Roizen, R. Room, D. Schneberk, & D. Wingard (Eds.), *Alcohol, casualties and crime.* Berkeley, CA: Social Research Group.

Roman, P. (1981). Situational factors in the relationship between alcohol and crime. In J. J. Collins (Ed.), *Drinking and Crime* (pp. 143–151). New York: Guilford Press.

Roman, P. M. (Ed.). (1990a). *Alcohol problem intervention in the workplace: Employee assistance programs and strategic alternatives.* New York: Quorum.

Roman, P. M. (1990b). Strategic considerations in designing interventions to deal with alcohol problems in the workplace. In *Alcohol problem intervention in the workplace: Employee assistance programs and strategic alternatives* (pp. 371–406). New York: Quorum.

Roman, P. M., Blum, T. C., & Martin, J. K. (1992). "Enabling" of male problem drinkers in work groups. *British Journal of Addiction, 87,* 275–289.

Rosen, R. H. (1991). *The healthy company: Eight strategies to develop people, productivity, and profits.* Los Angeles, CA: Jeremy P. Tarcher.

Rotter, J. B. (1966). Generalized expectancies for internal versus external control of reinforcement. *Psychological Monographs, 80*(1, Whole No. 609).

Rousseau, D. (1988). The construction of climate in organizational research. In L. C. Cooper and I. Roberson (Eds.), *International Review of Industrial and Organizational Psychology* (pp. 139–158). Chichester: Wiley.

Rousseau, D. M. (1990). Assessing organizational culture: The case for multiple methods. In B. Schneider (Ed.), *Organizational climate and culture* (pp. 153–192). San Francisco: Jossey-Bass.

Sabini, J. (1992). *Social psychology.* New York: Norton.

Schaef, A. W., & Fassel, D. (1988). *The addictive organization.* New York: Harper & Row.

Scheier, M. F., Fenigstein, A., & Buss, A. H. (1974). Self-awareness and physical aggression. *Journal of Experimental Social Psychology, 10,* 264–273.

Schein, E. H. (1969). *Process consultation: Its role in organization development.* Reading, MA: Addison-Wesley.

Seeman, M. (1959). On the meaning of alienation. *American Sociological Review, 24,* 783–791.

Seeman, M., & Anderson, C. (1983). Alienation and alcohol: The role of work, mastery, and community in drinking behavior. *American Sociological Review, 48,* 60–77.

Seeman, M., Seeman, A., & Budros, A. (1988). Powerlessness, work, and community: A longitudinal study of alienation and alcohol use. *Journal of Health and Social Behavior, 29*(3), 185–198.

Society for Human Resource Management. (1993, December). *Violence in the workplace survey results.* Alexandria, VA: Author.

Spunt, B., Goldstein, P., Brownstein, H., Fendrich, M., & Langley, S. (1994). Alcohol and homicide: Interviews with prison inmates. *Journal of Drug Issues, 24*(1), 143–163.

Steele, C. M., & Southwick, L. (1985). Alcohol and social behavior. I: The psychology of drunken excess. *Journal of Personality and Social Psychology, 48,* 18–34.

Stokes, J. P., & Levin, I. M. (1990). The development and validation of a measure of negative affectivity. *Journal of Social Behavior and Personality, 5,* 173–186.

Taylor, S. P., & Chermack, S. T. (1993). Alcohol, drugs and human physical aggression. *Journal of Studies on Alcohol,* [Suppl. 11], pp. 78–88.

Thomas, K. W. (1992). Conflict and negotiation processes in organizations. In M. D. Dunnette & L. M. Hough (Eds.), *Handbook of industrial and organizational psychology* (pp. 651–718). Palo Alto, CA: Consulting Psychologists Press.

Thompson, F. J., Riccucci, N. M., & Ban, C. (1991). Drug testing in the federal workplace: An instrumental and symbolic assessment. *Public Administration Review, 51*(6), 515–525.

Thornburg, L. (1993, July). When violence hits business. *HR Magazine*, pp. 40–45.

Trice, H. M., & Beyer, J. M. (1993). *The cultures of work organizations.* Englewood Cliffs, NJ: Prentice Hall.

Trice, H., & Sonnenstuhl, W. (1990). On the construction of drinking norms in working organizations. *Journal of Studies on Alcohol, 31*(3), 201–220.

Unterberg, M. P. (1993). Personalities, personal style, and trouble getting along. In J. P. Kahn (Ed.), *Mental health in the workplace: A practical psychiatric guide* (pp. 318–345). New York: Van Nostrand Reinhold.

U.S. Department of Labor, Bureau of Labor Statistics. (1994). *Violence in the workplace comes under closer scrutiny* (Issues in Labor Statistics, Summary No. 94-10). Washington, DC: U.S. Government Printing Office.

U.S. Department of Justice, Bureau of Justice Statistics. (1985, November). Jail inmates 1983. *Bureau of Justice Statistics Bulletin.* Washington, DC: U.S. Department of Justice.

Walsh, D. C., Rudd, R. E., Biener, L., & Mangione, T. (1993). Researching and preventing alcohol problems at work: Toward an integrative model. *American Journal of Health Promotion, 7*(4), 289–295.

Wechsler, H., Davenport, A., Dowdall, G., Moeykens, B., & Castillo, S. (1994). Health and behavioral consequences of binge drinking in college: A national survey of students at 140 campuses. *Journal of American Medical Association, 272*(21), 1672–1677.

Wilson, G. (1983). Self-awareness, self-regulation, and alcohol consumption: An analysis of J. Hull's Model. *Journal of Abnormal Psychology, 92*(4), 505–513.

Wright, R. S., & Wright, D. G. (1993). *Creating and maintaining the drug-free workforce.* New York: McGraw-Hill.

Yandrick, R. (1993, September). When employees make good on bad intentions. *EAPA Exchange*, pp. 14–16.

Younger, B. (1995, May). Women at risk: Crucial violence prevention concerns for female employees. *EAPA Exchange*, pp. 10–12.

Zaleznik, A. (1970). Power and politics in organizational life. *Harvard Business Review, 48,* 47–60.

Zaleznik, A., & Kets de Vries, M. F. R. (1975). *Power and the corporate mind.* Boston: Houghton Mifflin.

Zeichner, A., & Pihl, R. O. (1979). Effects of alcohol and behavior contingencies on human aggression. *Journal of Abnormal Psychology, 88,* 153–160.

Zeichner, A., Pihl, R. O., Niaura, R., & Zacchia, C. (1982). Attentional processes in alcohol-mediated aggression. *Journal of Studies on Alcohol, 43,* 714–724.

Zillmann, D. (1971). Excitation transfer in communication mediated aggressive behavior. *Journal of Experimental Social Psychology, 7,* 417–434.

6

The Impact of Domestic Violence on the Workplace

Lucy N. Friedman, Susan Brown Tucker, Peter R. Neville, and Maria Imperial

Domestic violence has serious consequences for the workplace, but in discussions of workplace violence it is rarely acknowledged. Many so-called "problem employees" who have difficulties getting to work on time or focusing on their tasks, or who are frequently absent from work, may in fact be victims of domestic violence. These effects of abuse can cost corporations resources, in terms of both lost productivity and additional management needed to address (often incorrectly) the employee's problems.

Violence does not have to occur inside the walls of offices or factories to affect a victim's ability to work. The battered woman who receives threatening calls or visits by her abuser at work, or who is suffering from the mental and physical bruises of the night before, is likely to have difficulty fulfilling her employer's expectations. Reduced productivity, higher staff turnover, and increased health care costs are among the effects felt by the employer.

The woman who misses hours or days from work because of court dates or doctor appointments, or because she is hiding from the batterer, risks losing her job. Battered women who lose their jobs because of abuse often find themselves more tightly bound to the batterer for support, making it even more difficult to leave.

Although the epidemic of domestic violence is receiving increasing attention, there has been relatively little focus on the site where many battered women spend a third of their lives: the workplace. As a society, we have yet to fully acknowledge the impact of domestic violence on the workplace, both for the victim and the employer. According to Isaac (cited in Pereira, 1995), corporate awareness of domestic violence today is about where it was with substance abuse 20 years ago. Because of this, researchers are not taking advantage of the opportunities for intervention that the workplace offers.

Recently, a small number of corporations (e.g., Polaroid, Liz Claiborne, The Body Shop, and others) have begun to test strategies to identify employees who are victims of abuse, get them the services they need, and help them keep their jobs. These corporate-based domestic violence interventions need to be evaluated to determine whether they are effective in terms of saving lives and costs, and, if so, they must be replicated and expanded.

Drawing on both research and practical experience, we examine the current knowledge about the effect of domestic violence on employment. We then provide an initial overview of the emergence of corporate interest and action, including barriers and promising strategies for creating supportive work environments for battered women.

The Nature of the Problem

Domestic violence is becoming recognized as a serious public epidemic, not a private issue hidden at home. Approximately 14% of women from all walks of life in the United States have been abused violently by their husbands or boyfriends (EDK Associates, 1993). Figures on the impact of abuse on women's health and well-being underscore the seriousness of the problem. Between 22% and 35% of women visiting hospital emergency rooms do so for injuries sustained from ongoing abuse (Randall, 1990). Rosenberg, Stark, and Zahn (1986) found that domestic violence is associated with 50% of all cases of alcoholism among women and 26% of suicide attempts by women (and 50% of suicide attempts by African American women). According to the Federal Bureau of Investigation (1993), 29% of the women murdered in 1992 were killed by a husband or boyfriend. Additional research on the effect of abuse on women's physical and mental health, their children's well-being, and the housing, social service, and criminal justice systems has demonstrated the prevalence of domestic violence and its devastating effect on women and society (Institute for Women's Policy Research, 1996).

However, only a handful of investigators have examined how domestic violence harms the workplace. Although few in number, their findings suggest that the impact is enormous. Data from the Bureau of Justice Statistics show that women are five times more likely than men to be attacked at work by an intimate partner (Bachman, 1994), accounting for approximately 13,000 violent attacks against women each year (Center for Women in Government, 1995). From a strictly economic perspective, the Bureau of National Affairs (1990) has estimated that domestic violence costs employers $3–5 billion each year in reduced productivity, staff turnover, and increased health costs.

A 1987 study by Victim Services, with the support of the American Insurance Association, surveyed 50 women who had both worked and been battered within the previous year (Friedman & Couper, 1987). The study identified a broad range of barriers to employment for battered women, including the insidious ways that batterers actively prevent women from working. Almost two thirds reported that they were late to work because of the abuse; specific reasons included being too exhausted after violent incidents occurring late the night before, needing extra time to cover up bruises, and waiting for pain killers to take effect. Twenty percent said that they were late for work because their partners, who were opposed to their employment or were jealous, tried to sabotage their jobs by turning off the alarm clock, keeping them up all night, or refusing to babysit at the last minute. Three quarters of the women had been harassed by the batterer at work, either by phone or in person. Fifty-four percent had missed an average of 3 days of work per month because of debilitating injuries, embarrassment, depression, or keeping appointments with lawyers and doctors. Job loss was a common occurrence for these women, with 56% reporting that they had lost at least one job as a direct result of the violence; reasons included missing time from work, batterers disrupting the workplace, depression, and an inability to concentrate (Friedman & Couper, 1987).

Similar results were reported by Stanley (1992) in a study at Domestic Violence Intervention Services of Tulsa, Oklahoma, which surveyed 118 battered female clients. Nineteen percent of those not employed had been prevented from working by the batterer. Of the 82 who were employed at the time of abuse, 96% reported some kind of problem in the workplace as a result of the abuse. Seventy percent were too distracted by the violence to perform well at work. Sixty percent were reprimanded by their employers for problems caused by the abuse. More than 70% were telephoned excessively at work by their abuser, and more than 50% missed days of work. Thirty percent reported that the abuse had caused them to lose a job (Stanley, 1992).

In addition to causing problems in the workplace, domestic violence can lead to welfare dependency and prevent women from attempting to enter or reenter the workplace. Initial findings by Lloyd at Northwestern University indicated that nearly half of the welfare recipients surveyed said domestic violence had played a factor in their need for public assistance (cited in Ehrenreich, 1995). Once battered women go on welfare, domestic violence often perpetuates their dependency. The Taylor Institute (Raphael, 1995) issued a report on what staff from welfare-to-work programs observed about the impact of domestic violence on their students' chances for success. The report identified a consistent theme across job training programs: Batterers' control over women often extends to sabotaging their participation in job training programs and undermining other efforts to increase women's economic stability and independence.

Businesses' Responses to Domestic Violence

Unlike other social ills that employers have addressed to ensure a strong workforce (e.g., substance abuse and inadequate schooling), domestic violence largely has gone unacknowledged and unaddressed by businesses. In 1987, the Philadelphia Coalition on Domestic Violence ran a print advertisement targeted at the local business community with the headline, "Do You Want a Solution to a $5 Billion Problem?" The advertisement ran in metropolitan Philadelphia newspapers, suburban newspapers, and local business publications and emphasized that domestic violence is a social and labor crisis that businesses need to address. It offered free assistance and literature to businesses. The coalition did not receive a single inquiry (Penney, 1992).

Since then, however, some employers have made progress toward creating an employer response to battering. A Liz Claiborne study conducted in 1994 by Roper Starch Worldwide identified a growing concern about domestic violence among corporate leaders. Fifty-seven percent felt it was a major social problem, and 40% were aware of employees in their own companies who were victims of abuse. Two thirds also believed that it hurt their companies' bottom lines—affecting productivity, attendance, and health care costs—and that taking steps to address the problem among their employees would improve their financial performance (Family Violence Prevention Fund, 1994). The author of a recent *Wall Street Journal* article suggested that a concern to "keep talent, reduce absenteeism and avoid liability" (Pereira, 1995, p. B-1) is beginning to translate into action by corporations, ranging from holding seminars for employees to posting guards at abused victims' homes.

Although still limited in number, corporate domestic violence initiatives are creating innovative ways to help reduce the risk of violence for employees while maintaining their employment. One of the leading corporations in this area, the Polaroid Corporation, has developed a set of companywide personnel and management policies and support services for both victims and batterers (Polaroid Corporation, n.d.). A specially trained employee assistance program (EAP) provides counseling and referrals for employees from violent families and holds lunchtime seminars on topics such as mandatory arrest for batterers, the cycle of violence, and safety plans for victims. To help victimized employees who need time off to go to court, arrange housing, or escape abuse, Polaroid offers flexible work hours, short-term paid leaves of absence, and extended leave with guaranteed jobs on return. In addition, recognizing that many of their own employees have used local shelters to escape abuse, Polaroid gives financial support to those shelters and has successfully recruited 50 other corporations to get involved in similar partnerships with shelters throughout Massachusetts. In large part, the extent and success of Polaroid's initiative is attributable to the interest and full support of the president and chief executive officer (CEO) of the company and the commitment and energy of James Hardeman, manager of Polaroid's EAP.

CoreStates Financial Corporation offers an array of domestic violence services to its 13,000 employees. Its commitment grew from responses to an employee survey that demonstrated the prevalence of abuse and need for services, and it has since expanded beyond EAP counseling to human resources consultants available around the clock to help employees seek shelter, police protection, financial aid, and child care. CoreStates also has initiated legal action for restraining orders on behalf of employees and encourages managers to offer flexible work hours, job guarantees after extended leaves, and site transfers to escape from the batterer (Penney, 1992).

At Liz Claiborne, the Women's Work initiative demonstrates this company's commitment to helping victims of abuse by holding regular seminars on domestic violence for employees—on company time—and through contributions to local domestic violence services. Similarly, The Body Shop recently trained its managers to help abused employees and launched a fundraising and media awareness campaign to support domestic violence services (Newell & McIlwraith, 1995).

Unions also have begun to take an interest in domestic violence issues. District Council 37, representing 130,000 public employees in New York, has been providing legal services to battered women for more than 20 years (Mann, personal communication, December 14, 1995). Starting with Supreme Court matrimonial cases, its Municipal Employees Legal Services Program became significantly involved in legal representation for battered women in 1981, when it started handling family court cases, including petitions for orders of protection. Since then, it has added a social work staff to handle the nonlegal needs of battered women, such as worksite transfers, temporary income support if a battered woman needs to leave her job, and counseling for women and their children.

In Canada, the British Columbia Federation of Labour held a conference on violence against women in 1991 and issued a report profiling steps that unions are taking and can take to address domestic violence (Prieur & Rowles, 1992). Linking the subordinate position of women in the labor force to their position in society, the federation argued that "the pervasiveness of violence against women makes a mockery of more than a century of struggle by the labour movement to secure social and economic equality and dignity for working people" (Prieur & Rowles, 1992, p. 7). Among the initiatives profiled in the report are the Canadian Teachers' Federation's distribution of a curriculum kit to 19,000 schools on violence, date rape, and working with children exposed to domestic violence, and the Labour Community Services of Toronto's success in convincing the city government to institute a 3-hour training program, on the employer's time, for city employees. The report also suggested other strategies for unions: negotiating employer-paid legal assistance for battered women into contracts, training union stewards to help victimized union members, publishing articles on domestic violence in union newspapers, and using the lobbying force of the union to fight for expanded battered women's services and shelters.

Overall, however, positive examples such as these remain isolated exceptions to the rule. The Tulsa study cited earlier indicated that only 20% of the women had been offered any assistance by their employer. In most cases, the assistance consisted of simplistic advice such as "Why don't you just leave him?" In a focus group of corporate human resource representatives held in 1996 by Victim Services in New York, we learned that employers are generally unaware of domestic violence as a workplace problem, or even that it is present among their staff, and that employers need to be educated regarding the myths of domestic violence (e.g., that all staff levels, from executive to mailroom, can experience domestic violence).

Expanding Employer Action

In reviewing the positive examples of workplace interventions in domestic violence, there is the question of how to translate those successes into more widespread concern and action throughout the business world. One step is to demonstrate to corporate leaders that domestic violence is lurking within their workforce and that it reduces their profitability. Corporate leaders need to see evidence that identifying victimized employees and enabling them to maintain their employment and levels of productivity are in the company's best interest, if for no other reason than that it makes good business sense. As shown earlier, a limited amount of data already exists suggesting the prevalence and financial impact of abuse, but more are needed to stimulate broad-based action.

Toward this end, Victim Services, together with the Institute for Women's Policy Research and the Domestic Violence Training Program in New Haven, and with the support of the Rockefeller Foundation, are developing a research agenda to document the costs of domestic violence to society and the cost-effectiveness of interventions. One of the agenda components is the employment-related costs of abuse, including wages lost to missed time from work, reduced productivity, and so forth. More extensive data on these costs and on the cost-effectiveness of corporate interventions would create a more compelling argument for action. In addition, Victim Services is engaged in a project with the New York City Department of Personnel to assess the prevalence of domestic violence among city employees and its impact on the workplace. The data from this study should help demonstrate that, although often hidden, domestic abuse affects a significant enough number of people in the workforce for it to be a major issue of concern for employers.

Not all corporate leaders will require such extensive documentation of the prevalence and cost impact of domestic violence to reach out to victimized employees. Simply hearing the statistics mentioned earlier may be argument enough. Some CEOs may be motivated by the victimization of a family member, whereas others may see that taking a high-profile, proactive approach to a social problem is a good marketing strategy. For others, such as Patrice Tanaka & Co., who recognize that employees' personal and professional lives often overlap (Tanaka, 1995), the overall well-being of victimized employees will be a company priority.

There are many steps employers can take depending on a company's level of commitment, available resources, and size. Possible steps might include the following.

1. *Specialized EAPs.* Although there are more than 10,000 EAPs nationwide providing counseling, referrals, and other services in both public and private sectors, few are trained to deal with victims of domestic abuse (Magee & Hampton, 1993). To increase their capacity to work with victimized and victimizing employees, EAPs can bring in local domestic violence specialists to train counselors. They can create new services such as individual counseling and support groups for battered women, education and prevention seminars and information campaigns for all employees, coun-

seling for batterers, and referral networks with local battered women's shelters and services. Isaac (1994), at the Harvard School of Public Health, is studying EAPs to assess their degree of activity on domestic violence and to identify productive strategies for addressing this problem.

2. *Domestic violence personnel policies.* To minimize the risk of losing their employees, corporations can institute personnel policies that accommodate the needs of battered women. Paid time off, flexible working hours, and guarantees of employment after long-term leaves of absence allow women to deal with demands on their time created by the abuse, such as medical and legal appointments, ensuring safe shelter, or recovering from violent incidents. In cases in which the batterers harass or attack victims at work, voluntary relocation to a new worksite can provide an additional layer of safety without forcing women to leave their jobs. Procedures that allow employees to disclose their abuse confidentially and guidelines for managers and employees that define their respective roles and responsibilities in working with victimized workers further enhance the victim sensitivity of the workplace. The development and implementation of model personnel policies incorporating these components could help demonstrate the effectiveness of this strategy to others in the corporate sector.

3. *Training for managers and supervisors.* Because managers may be among the first to see the signs of abuse, training them to know what to look for and how to help victimized employees is a critical element of a corporate domestic violence strategy. Such a program might cover issues of employee confidentiality, the dynamics of domestic abuse, appropriate and inappropriate ways to approach a victim, available resources (including EAPs, medical services, and programs in the community), and flexible management practices to accommodate victims' needs (e.g., flextime, leaves of absence, worksite protection from the batterer).

4. *Corporate orders of protection.* In some states, including California and Massachusetts, employers can apply for orders of protection on behalf of victimized employees, thereby protecting the well-being of the workplace and the employee, who in some cases might risk enraging the batterer if she initiates legal action herself.

5. *General education and prevention programs.* Because of the tradition of secrecy and silence, domestic violence remains for many a taboo subject. Breaking down this wall of isolation and shame is a key component of helping victimized employees. Seminars describing the nature and prevalence of domestic violence and options for getting help can let women know that they are not to blame and that there are alternatives to being a victim. Holding seminars on company time demonstrates concretely that the company is committed to helping and ensures a greater level of participation; discussions about domestic violence can be incorporated into seminars on other subjects, such as health, insurance benefits, and office safety. Education programs also can be conducted through brochures, posters, videos, and other media because some victims may feel more comfortable learning about their options in a private than in a group setting.

6. *Financial and volunteer support for community programs.* Similar to corporate support of schools and education programs to ensure a strong future workforce, support for domestic abuse services and violence prevention programs helps enhance the employment pool by removing barriers to battered women's productivity and enabling them to perform at the highest level possible. Direct financial support and encouraging employees to volunteer in local services are two ways corporations can help reduce levels of violence in the community.

7. *Job training and employment opportunities for battered women.* Women who leave an abuser often need assistance in getting jobs and becoming self-sufficient. By offering training and employment to battered women, employers can help them create a bulwark of independence against abusive relationships. For the past 3 years, Victim Services' Project Opportunity has provided such training for battered women and has placed a large portion of them in jobs within the agency (Tate, 1995).

Conclusion

Domestic violence does not stay at home; it follows victims and their families into all areas of their lives, including the workplace. Society as a whole has become more concerned about domestic violence and more willing to take action, but for too long the personal–professional barrier has obscured the impact of domestic violence on employment. Some employers are beginning to take notice. However, broad-based corporate action is unlikely without expanded research and education efforts to raise employers' recognition of the impact of abuse on the well-being of their employees and their companies.

References

Bachman, R. (1994, July). *Violence and theft in the workplace* (Crime Data Brief No. NCJ-148199). Washington, DC: U.S. Department of Justice.

Bureau of National Affairs. (1990). *Violence and stress: The work / family connection* (Special Rep. No. 32). Washington, DC: Author.

Center for Women in Government. (1995, Fall). Hidden violence against women at work. *Women in Public Service*, 5.

EDK Associates. (1993). *Men beating women: Ending domestic violence. A qualitative and quantitative study of public attitudes on violence against women.* New York: Author.

Ehrenreich, B. (1995, April 3). Battered welfare syndrome. *Time*, p. 82.

Family Violence Prevention Fund. (1994, Fall/Winter). You bet your bottom dollar. *News From the Homefront*, pp. 1–2, 6.

Federal Bureau of Investigation. (1993). *Uniform crime reports for the United States* (Report No. 027–001–00066–1). Washington, DC: Author.

Friedman, L., & Couper, S. (1987). *The cost of domestic violence: A preliminary investigation of the financial cost of domestic violence.* New York: Victim Services.

Institute for Women's Policy Research. (1996). *Measuring the costs of domestic violence and the cost-effectiveness of interventions: An initial assessment of the state of the art and proposals for further research.* Washington, DC: Author.

Isaac, N. (1994). *Corporate sector response to domestic violence: Project abstract.* Cambridge, MA: Harvard School of Public Health, Injury Control Center.

Magee, R., & Hampton, S. (1993). Family violence and the workplace: The role of employee assistance programs. *Family Violence & Sexual Assault Bulletin, 9*(1), 19.

Newell, P., & McIlwraith, A. (1995). *Blow the whistle on violence against women.* Wake Forest, NC: The Body Shop.

Penney, L. (1992, August 1). The corporate cost of domestic violence. *Focus,* pp. 30–31, 33–34, 60.

Pereira, J. (1995, March 2). Employers confront domestic abuse. *Wall Street Journal,* p. B-1.

Polaroid Corporation. (n.d.). *Polaroid Corporation and the domestic violence issue.* Cambridge, MA: Author.

Prieur, D., & Rowles, M. (1992). *Taking action: A union guide to ending violence against women.* Burnaby, British Columbia, Canada: B.C. Federation of Labour.

Randall, T. (1990). Domestic violence intervention calls for more than treating injuries. *Journal of the American Medical Association, 264,* 939–940.

Raphael, J. (1995). *Domestic violence: Telling the untold welfare-to-work story.* Chicago: Taylor Institute.

Rosenberg, M. L., Stark, E., & Zahn, M. A. (1986). Interpersonal violence: Homicide and spouse abuse. In J. M. Last (Ed.), *Maxcy-Rosenau public health and prevention medicine* (12th ed., pp. 1399–1426). New York: Appleton-Century-Crofts.

Stanley, C. (1992). *Workplace efficiency: The effect of family violence on work performance.* Tulsa, OK: Domestic Violence Intervention Services.

Tanaka, P. (1995). *It's all about soul.* (Available from Patrice Tanaka & Co., 320 West 13th Street, 7th Floor, New York, NY 10014).

Tate, G. (1995). *The connection between welfare-to-work transition and domestic violence: An exploratory study.* Unpublished manuscript, Victim Services, New York.

7

Job Stress, Gender, and Workplace Violence: Analysis of Assault Experiences of State Employees

Joseph J. Hurrell, Jr., Karen A. Worthington, and Richard J. Driscoll

Between 1980 and 1989, nearly 7,600 U.S. workers were murdered in their workplace (Jenkins, Layne, & Kisner, 1992), and during 1992 alone nearly 1,004 Americans were murdered on the job (Rigdon, 1994). Although extreme, homicide is only one of many growing forms of workplace violence that can encompass a wide spectrum of behaviors ranging from verbally aggressive acts to physical assaults resulting in injury and death. A recent survey conducted by the Northwestern National Life Insurance Company (see Appendix A, this volume) indicated that between July 1992 and July 1993, nearly 1 of 4 full-time workers in America had been harassed, threatened, or attacked on the job. Likewise, a recent American Management Association survey of 311 organizations showed that almost 25% indicated that at least one employee had been attacked or killed on the job since 1990 (Rigdon, 1994), whereas a report about workplace violence (National Safe Workplace Institute, 1992) indicated that during 1992, there were 111,000 physically violent workplace incidents costing employers $4.2 billion.

Results of the Northwestern National Life study (see Appendix A) suggest that stressful job conditions may contribute to the potential for workplace violence. Workers who reported that they were highly stressed, for example, experienced twice the rate of violence and harassment as less stressed employees. Although it is widely believed that stressful job conditions may contribute to, or be associated with, violent outcomes in the workplace, there have been few empirical attempts to examine relationships between specific job stress factors (or job stressors) and violence or to develop theories regarding linkages between stressful job conditions and violent behavior. Job stressors suspected of contributing to the potential for workplace violence include ambiguous and conflicting role expectations, excessive workload, poor organizational communications, lack of job security, and poor cooperation among employees (Chen & Spector, 1992; Spector, 1975; Tetrick, 1994; also see Appendix A). In the current study, we examined relationships between the occurrence of on-the-job physical

Exhibit 1.   Stressor Variables Used as Predictors in Regression Analyses

Role ambiguity
Role conflict
Intergroup conflict
Intragroup conflict
Job control
Workload
Variance in workload
Responsibility for people
Skill underutilization
Mental demands
Opportunities for alternative employment

assaults and 11 different job stressors in a large sample of state government employees.

Method

Data used in this analysis were collected as part of a comprehensive cross-sectional job stress survey of public service employees in a northeastern state in the spring of 1989. The survey was designed by a joint labor management committee with the help of the first author. The NIOSH Generic Job Stress Questionnaire (Hurrell & McLaney, 1988) was administered statewide by representatives of the State Bureau of Employee Health to all active state employees (approximately 7,000 individuals). The NIOSH questionnaire contains a variety of multi-item scales measuring psychological job stressors and their attendant physical and psychological consequences. Questionnaires were distributed by supervisors and union officials who had been trained to distribute the questionnaires and tallied response rates. Completed questionnaires were returned to a contact person at the State Bureau of Employee Health, who then coded and compiled responses. Participation in the survey was voluntary and anonymous, and the overall response rate was nearly 70%. One hundred fifty different occupations were represented in the survey.

The 11 stressor variables from the NIOSH questionnaire included in the current analysis (see Exhibit 1) were composed of scales with internal consistency (alpha) coefficients, computed in the current study, ranging from .80 to .91. A single item in the questionnaire, which asked respondents whether they had been physically assaulted on the job within the past year, served as a measure of workplace assault. Bivariate analyses of the data were conducted by gender to determine the association of the 11 stressor variables with the incidence of on-the-job assaults in the year prior to the survey. Multivariate analysis, using unconditional logistical regression and a backward elimination procedure, then was used to examine the effects of each stressor variable found to be significant in the bivariate analysis. Age was included in each of the regression models as a covariate.

Table 1. Demographic Characteristics of Respondents by Gender and Assault Status

	Women		Men	
Variable	Assaulted ($n = 233$)	Unassaulted ($n = 2,292$)	Assaulted ($n = 389$)	Unassaulted ($n = 1,935$)
Age	35.91*	38.31	36.58**	40.87
Years employed	5.92*	6.88	8.32	9.14
Years at present job	4.07	3.96	5.64	5.11

*$p < .05$.   **$p < .005$.

Table 2. Leading Job Categories for Assault by Gender

Job category	Workers in category	% assaulted in category	% of assaults within gender
Women			
Mental health workers	121	48	29
Clerks	497	4	8
Human service case workers	174	18	7
Nursing personnel	32	17	4
Men			
State police personnel	157	51	21
Mental health workers	63	65	11
Guards	57	35	8
Clerks	274	11	8

Additionally, scores on measures of depression (Radloff, 1977), self-esteem (Rosenberg, 1965), and job satisfaction (Quinn & Shepard, 1974) among assaulted and unassaulted workers were compared to assess the possible consequences of on-the-job assault. These measures, also included in the NIOSH questionnaire, had internal consistency (alpha) coefficients, computed in the current study, of .91, .80, and .93, respectively.

Results

Two thousand five hundred twenty-five women and 2,324 men participated in the survey. Nine percent (233 employees) of the women and 17% (398 employees) of the men reported that they had been physically assaulted on the job within the past year. Demographic information by gender and assault category are presented in Table 1. Both men and women who reported an assault were younger than their unassaulted counterparts and women who reported an assault tended to have less job tenure (see Table 1).

Among women who had been assaulted (see Table 2), the greatest percentage of assaults occurred among mental health workers (29%), fol-

Table 3. Final Regression Model Predicting Assaults

Stressor	Odds ratio	95% CI
Women		
Low mental demands	3.00	1.99–4.51
Low job control	2.68	1.76–4.07
Responsibility for people	2.63	2.38–2.87
Role conflict	1.63	1.42–1.85
Skill underutilization	1.38	1.08–1.58
Limited job opportunities	1.28	1.02–1.60
Men		
Low job control	2.33	1.73–3.12
Responsibility for people	1.77	1.60–1.95
Limited job opportunities	1.41	1.19–1.67
Skill underutilization	1.37	1.22–1.41
Age	1.05	1.03–1.06

CI = confidence interval.

lowed by clerks (8%), human services case workers (7%), and nursing personnel (4%). Within these job categories, nearly half of all mental health workers and a fifth of nurses and case workers reported being assaulted on the job during the past year. For men, the leading job categories for assault included state police personnel (21%), mental health workers (11%), and guards and clerks (both 8%). More than half of all male mental health workers and state police personnel, along with one third of all male guards, reported an assault during the previous year.

Results of the final regression models for assaults for men and women are presented in Table 3. On-the-job assaults for women were significantly associated with six stressors. Women who had been assaulted were three times more likely than unassaulted women to have jobs with low mental demands (odds ratio [OR] = 3.00, 95% confidence interval [CI] = 1.99–4.51) and more than twice as likely to have jobs with low decision control (OR = 2.68, 95% CI = 1.76–4.07). Furthermore, assaulted women were more likely than unassaulted women to experience role conflict (OR = 1.68, 95% CI = 1.42–1.85), skill underutilization (OR = 1.38, 95% CI = 1.08–1.58), and limited alternative job opportunities (OR = 1.28, 95% CI = 1.02–1.60).

Assaulted men were more likely than unassaulted men (see Table 3) to report low job decision control (OR = 2.33, 95% CI = 1.73–3.12) and supervisory responsibility (OR = 1.77, 95% CI = 1.60–1.95). In addition, assaulted men were more likely to describe limited alternative job opportunities (OR = 1.41, 95% CI = 1.19–1.67) and to have jobs that failed to fully use their training and experience (OR = 1.37, 95% CI = 1.22–1.41).

Two additional variables—working with clients and exposure to verbal threats—were examined for their relationship to workplace assaults. After controlling for gender, workers who had contact with clients were 2.6 times more likely to be assaulted than those who had no client contact (OR = 2.63, 95% CI = 2.08–3.34). However, this relationship was not statistically significant in the presence of the stressor variables or when stratified by occupational category. Additionally, exposure to verbal threats was

Table 4. Mean Depression, Self-Esteem, and Job Satisfaction Scores by Gender and Assault Status

Score	Women		Men	
	Assaulted	Unassaulted	Assaulted	Unassaulted
Depression	7.55	6.24*	7.32	5.07*
Self-esteem	4.08	4.08	4.05	4.17*
Job satisfaction	2.41	2.57*	2.60	2.39*

*$p < .0001$.

found to be significantly associated with workplace physical assault. Workers who experienced verbal threats within the previous year were 2.7 times more likely to report an assault than those who had not been threatened (OR = 2.76, 95% CI = 2.53–3.00).

Table 4 shows a comparison of mean depression, self-esteem, and job satisfaction scores for assaulted and unassaulted workers by gender. Women who had been assaulted reported higher symptom scores for depression and less job satisfaction than women who had not been assaulted ($p < .001$). Men who had been assaulted showed significantly higher symptoms scores for depression, lower self-esteem, and less job satisfaction than did unassaulted men ($p < .001$).

Discussion

Although 9% of the women and 17% of the men in the sample reported being physically assaulted within the past year, it was not possible to compare these seemingly high rates with those of other work settings because of the lack of comparative data. However, workplace violence appears to be particularly prevalent in government organizations. Although government employees make up approximately 18% of the total U.S. workforce, 30% of the victims of violence at work between 1987 and 1992 were federal, state, or local government employees (Bureau of Justice Statistics, 1994). This overrepresentation may be explained by a potentially high risk of violence for particular government occupations such as public safety personnel. However, Bensimon (1994) suggested that assaults within government agencies, such as the U.S. Postal Service, where assaults among employees seem exceptionally high (see Kurland, 1993), may be a result of a culture that exists within the organization that fosters aggression. Clearly, more research aimed at the analysis of organizational cultures that may serve to promote violence is needed.

Although the leading job categories of assaulted workers (see Table 2) provide few surprises, the percentages of workers who had been assaulted within these categories are alarming. One of every two mental health workers and more than half of the male state police personnel had been assaulted in the previous year. These results for mental health workers are consistent with those described by Madden, Lion, and Penna (1976) and Poster and Ryan (1989), who have reported that among staff members in mental health facilities, 42–73% are assaulted at least once in their career. The assaults by occupations listed in Table 2 represent a major share of the assault burden within this workforce and suggest that intervention efforts aimed at reducing the risk and incidence of assault among the five different job titles could ultimately affect half of all assaults reported by the study population.

With respect to the job stressors–assault relationship, 4 of the 11 stressor variables examined were found to be associated with assaults among both men and women. Limited job control, high levels of responsibility for people, limited opportunities for alternative employment, and skill underutilization all were found to be significant predictors associated with assault in the models for both sexes. This consistency may suggest that these job conditions are associated with increased frequency of assault. Although the mechanisms linking these particular stressors to physical assaults are unclear, it seems possible that the stressors may be causally associated with individual-strain variables that serve as antecedents to violence. Spector and his colleagues (Chen & Spector, 1992; Spector, 1975; Storms & Spector, 1987), for example, found evidence linking a sense of "organizational frustration" and violence. However, alternative explanations of the data are possible. Because the workers have been assaulted, for example, they may now perceive that they have lost control over major components of their job, report concerns about their relationship with their supervisor or supervisees, and question whether the job fully uses their skills and training.

Among women, two additional stressors, role conflict and low mental demands, were found to be significantly associated with assault. What remains to be determined is whether women in unchallenging jobs and in jobs with conflicting expectations are at increased risk for assault or whether women who have been assaulted now question the conflicting roles and the mental demands of the job that have put them at risk for assault.

Workers who have client contact appeared to be at increased risk of physical assault, regardless of the worker's gender. This is not surprising and is consistent with studies (e.g., Northwestern National Life Insurance Company, see Appendix A) that have shown that the greatest risk of physical assault for workers comes not from coworkers (so called *iternecine violence*), but from individuals outside the organization (e.g., customers, clients, and patients).

Verbal threats also appear to be associated with physical assault. Although we were unable to establish the temporal association between when threats occurred and when the assault occurred, it is reasonable to acknowledge the strong association between the two and, thus, any verbal threats within a work setting should be a potent warning and taken seriously.

The results of this study also suggest that employees who experience workplace assaults may suffer from higher levels of depression, and experience lower levels of job satisfaction, than colleagues who are not assaulted. Furthermore, the data also indicate that workplace assaults may damage self-esteem levels of men but not women.

As can be expected when dealing with a cross-sectional study design, causal inferences are not possible. It was not possible to determine whether the differences in perceptions of job conditions reported by assaulted and nonassaulted employees were a function of real differences in job conditions or the result of changes in the perceptions of job conditions that occurred after the assault. The causal relationship of these variables are more appropriately evaluated in a longitudinal study design. Moreover, we used self-reported predictors (stressor scales) and self-reported outcomes, which are subject to recall bias. On the positive side, however, we controlled for many organizational factors that would confound other studies (i.e., there was only one personnel system for all employees, economic conditions were all the same), and the results present an interesting view of job conditions that may be associated with an increased frequency of assault.

Although we focused on only one type of workplace violence (physical assaults), it seems clear that there is a need for greater attention to a variety of difficult conceptual and measurement issues. A seemingly important endeavor involves arriving at an agreement among researchers on a definition of violence (Roberts, Mock, & Johnstone, 1981). Large-scale studies of workplace violence (e.g., Bureau of Justice Statistics, 1994) are only beginning to point out markedly different circumstances surrounding nonfatal violent incidents as opposed to work-related homicides. Thus, there seems to be a need to develop taxonomies to classify more precisely the broad spectrum of violent behaviors in the workplace and to take into account characteristics of the assailant (e.g., fellow employee, supervisor, stranger).

The results of this study are consistent with those of the Northwestern National Life Insurance Company survey (see Appendix A), which suggest that assaults may occur more frequently among highly stressed workers than those experiencing less stress. However, the purpose of this study was to examine the complex relationship between organizational stressors and the risk of physical assault within a workforce rather than to evaluate the relationship between characteristics of the worker (e.g., negative affect, tolerance for stress and ambiguity, coping, etc.) and assault. Thus, the results are not suited for constructing a profile of "assault-prone" workers (which essentially blames the worker for the assault and thus blames the victim). Rather, the results of this study are more suited for developing organizationally focused interventions that target organizationally related risk factors for workplace violence.

References

Bensimon, H. F. (1994, January). Violence in the workplace. *Training and Development Journal*, pp. 27–32.

Bureau of Justice Statistics. (1994). *Violence and theft in the workplace* (Publication No. NCJ-148199). Washington, DC: U.S. Department of Justice.

Chen, P. Y., & Spector, P. E. (1992). Relationships of work stressors with aggression, withdrawal, theft and substance use: An exploratory study. *Journal of Occupational and Organizational Psychology, 65,* 177–184.

Hurrell, J. J., Jr., & McLaney, M. A. (1988). Exposure to job stress: A new psychometric instrument. *Scandinavian Journal of Work Environment Health, 14,* 27–28.

Jenkins, E. L., Layne, L. A., & Kisner, S. M. (1992). Homicide in the workplace: The U.S. experience, 1980–1988. *Journal of the American Association of Occupational Health Nurses, 40,* 215–218.

Kurland, O. M. (1993). Workplace violence. *Risk Management, 40,* 76–77.

Madden, D. J., Lion, J. R., & Penna, M. W. (1976). Assaults on psychiatrists by patients. *American Journal of Psychiatry, 133,* 422–425.

National Safe Workplace Institute. (1992). *Breaking point.* Chicago: Author.

Poster, E. C., & Ryan, J. A. (1989). Nurses' attitudes toward physical assaults by patients. *Archives of Psychiatric Nursing, 3,* 315–322.

Quinn, R. P., & Shepard, L. J. (1974). *The 1972-1973 Quality of Life Employment Survey: Descriptive statistics with comparisons from the 1969-1970 survey of working conditions.* Ann Arbor, MI: Survey Research Center.

Radloff, L. S. (1977). The CES-D: A self-report depression scale for research in the general population. *Journal of Applied Psychological Measurement, 1,* 385–410.

Rigdon, J. E. (1994, April 12). Companies see more workplace violence. *Wall Street Journal,* p. B1.

Roberts, T. K., Mock, L. T., & Johnstone, E. E. (1981). Psychological aspects of the etiology of violence. In J. R. Hays, T. K. Roberts, & L. S. Solway (Eds.), *Violence and the violent individual* (pp. 9–33). New York: Spectrum.

Rosenberg, M. (1965). *Society and the adolescent self-image.* Princeton, NJ: Princeton University Press.

Spector, P. E. (1975). Relationships of organizational frustration with reported behavioral reactions of employees. *Journal of Applied Psychology, 60,* 635–637.

Storms, P. L., & Spector, P. E. (1987). Relationships of organizational frustration with reported behavioural reactions: The moderating effects of locus of control. *Journal of Occupational Psychology, 60,* 227–234.

Tetrick, L. E. (1994, August). *Conflict management tactics and violence in the workplace.* Paper presented at the 102nd Annual Convention of the American Psychological Association Convention, Los Angeles.

Part III

High-Risk Occupations

Introduction

Of the occupations at highest risk of workplace violence, several are considered in the following chapters: corrections staff, police, and traffic agents; nurses and social workers; construction workers; and federal workers. Particular characteristics of each occupation increase its risk and may make consequences more severe, and efforts to manage risk need to focus on these specific factors.

Exposure to violence is a significant aspect of correctional work. Safran and Tartaglini investigate exposure to workplace violence in a clinical sample of 807 correction officers in an urban jail and consider whether violence can be predicted from demographic, employment, psychodiagnostic, and incident-related variables. Male officers were much more directly exposed to injury-producing violence than female officers; interestingly, when there was a greater proportion of female officers, the males were less exposed to violence.

Research on workplace violence focuses often on homicide and seldom on suicide. Violanti discusses suicide among police officers, an occupational group at particularly high risk. NIOSH in fact considers any police fatality on or off workplace premises as a "workplace fatality." Police suicide has been linked to workplace stress, traumatic work incidents, and limited coping ability. Violanti's analysis of 26 police suicides leads him to elaborate on three possible factors. First, the violent nature of police work and the accouterments associated with protection from that violence have a continuous battering effect on the psyche of police officers. Second, firearms are readily and immediately available. Third, the rigid nature of police organizations and the need to adhere strictly to the police role reduce personal flexibility and lead to constrictive thinking. Violanti suggests a model program to prevent police suicides.

A related occupation, generally part of the police force but involving its own distinctive stresses, is that of traffic agents, who issue summonses for parking and vehicular violations. Brondolo et al. report over 400 incidents per year of physical confrontation involving traffic agents and motorists in New York City. The frequency of these confrontations is significantly associated with burnout and job dissatisfaction. Brondolo et al. find no differences between male and female agents in frequency of confrontations, nor in the styles male and female agents use to resolve conflicts with the public. What does increase risk of confrontation is productivity: The more summonses agents issue, the more interpersonal conflicts they are likely to experience, putting productive agents in a bind about whether to perform well or to emphasize safety.

Nurses are vulnerable to assaults by patients, and this is becoming a concern for professional organizations of health-care workers. Lanza reviews the problem, noting especially that assaults are generally underreported. Nurses who have been assaulted by patients develop short- and long-term emotional, social, biophysiological, and cognitive reactions. They experience conflict between their roles as professionals and as victims, being required by their professional ethic to continue to put the patient's needs first, but also having to pay attention to their own safety and emotional security. Coworkers who witness violent incidents are also affected psychologically, experiencing heightened fear, anxiety, increased vulnerability, irritability, and guilt about the victim's plight. Lanza endorses particular interventions, such as multidisciplinary victim assault support teams, to help nursing staff cope with role problems and recover their psychological balance.

Social workers are exposed to somewhat similar risks, as Guterman, Jayaratne, and Bargal detail from a binational survey in the U.S. and Israel. Approximately half of the social workers studied in each country reported some form of victimization in the preceding year, either physical threat, physical assault, threat of a lawsuit, an actual lawsuit, verbal abuse, or sexual harassment. In both countries, physical threats from clients were reported by about one in five workers; actual physical assaults, however, were less frequent than in earlier nonrandom studies. High rates of verbal abuse from clients were reported for both countries. Israeli social workers reported threats of physical harm somewhat more frequently than American social workers, whereas American social workers reported more incidents of sexual harassment. Younger workers and those employed by public agencies appeared to be at greater risk in both countries.

An illustration of workers often ignoring the problems of workplace violence is provided by McCann, who discusses a survey among members of the Laborers' International Union of North America (LIUNA). The majority of survey respondents were construction laborers (the union also includes industrial workers and service workers). More than one third of the respondents had personally witnessed assaults, violence, or harassing behavior, but the majority of the sample nevertheless viewed their workplace as "safe." Most violence was between coworkers, and fewer than one-half of the incidents were reported to management or to persons in authority. Management did tend to take disciplinary action, or at least warned against repetition, in most cases that came to their attention.

Federal workers are at risk of violence just like other workers. Their experience can be tracked, to some degree, through workers' compensation claims filed with the Office of Workers' Compensation Programs (OWCP) of the Department of Labor. Freeman et al. review 2 years of these claims, covering both fatal and nonfatal cases in 30 federal agencies. The highest rates of violence occur among workers with jobs known to involve higher risk, such as nurses and correction officers. Agencies with the highest rates of injury are the Departments of Veterans' Affairs, Justice, and Transportation.

8

Workplace Violence and Victimization Experienced by Social Workers: A Cross-National Study of Americans and Israelis

Neil B. Guterman, Srinika Jayaratne, and David Bargal

Workers in human services are increasingly called on to work with clients for whom interpersonal violence is a presenting concern (cf. Foster, 1990; U.S. Department of Health and Human Services, 1995). Recent anecdotal reports suggest that such concerns may be spilling over into direct work with clients, heightening the risk of worker victimization by the clients themselves (e.g., Carvajal, 1995; Hill & Jennings, 1991; Hillen, 1991; Loomis & Halseth, 1993; "Man Kills Child," 1994; McCarthy, 1991; Sweeney, 1993). Although the problem of workplace violence by clients has been reported by various types of human services workers (e.g., psychiatrists, psychologists, counselors, technicians), it has been asserted that social workers in particular may face special risks (Newhill, 1995). Social workers frequently service multiproblem clients who have scarce resources and supports, often in settings that are uncontrolled (e.g., in clients' homes or neighborhoods) or in those that exercise a social control function (e.g., prisons, residential treatment settings). Furthermore, the service fields in which social workers traditionally perform their duties frequently intersect with human problems associated with violence, such as child abuse and neglect, domestic violence, substance abuse, or life in crime-ridden settings. It is not surprising, then, that many of the recent media reports of violence against human services professionals have involved social workers.

Despite the increasing frequency of anecdotal reports, the actual extent of the problem for human services workers in general and for social workers in particular, remains unclear. Several small-scale preliminary

An earlier version of this chapter was presented at a conference sponsored by the American Psychological Association and the National Institute on Occupational Health and Safety in Washington, DC, in September 1995. We dedicate this chapter to the memory of Yitzhak Rabin, who, in his role as a public servant, fell victim to work-related violence.

studies have documented what appears to be a high proportion of human services workers in selected locations who have been victimized by clients. For example, Whitman, Armao, and Dent's (1976) study of 101 psychiatrists, psychologists, and social workers in Cincinnati, Ohio, showed that 43% of the respondents reported at least one incident in which they felt threatened by a client and that 24% were actually assaulted during the year. Bernstein's (1981) study of licensed psychologists, clinical social workers, and marriage, family, and child counselors in San Diego County indicated that 14.2% reported being assaulted at least once and that 35.6% were threatened by a client at least once. Using a different method, Carmel and Hunter (1989) reviewed reports of staff injury caused by patients in a state psychiatric institution. Their study, which included psychiatrists, psychologists, social workers, and rehabilitation therapists, recorded a rate of 1.9 injuries per 100 professional staff over a 1-year period.

Initial studies focused on social work professionals paint a similarly dark picture. Several of the most in-depth studies derive from the United Kingdom. For example, Rowett's (1986) survey of 450 social workers in Shire County conducted over a 6-year period, indicated that 1 in 4 workers were assaulted by a client. Leadbetter's (1993) study, conducted over a 3-year period in Scotland, reported that from 1987/1988 to 1989/1990 physical assault rates increased from 1 in 118 workers to 1 in 52 workers. Consistent with assertions about social workers in the United States, figures from studies in the United Kingdom suggest that social workers face higher assault risks than other human services professionals, including police, health services workers, and teachers (Leadbetter, 1993). Results of two small-scale studies conducted in the United States suggest the possibility of even higher rates of violence against social workers than in the United Kingdom. For example, Schultz's (1987) survey of 150 social services workers in one state (an unspecified proportion of whom were trained as social workers) showed that 83 respondents indicated some violence, 44 indicated none, and 23 indicated that the agency had closed. Tully, Kropf, and Price's (1993) study of 121 social work students and 96 social work field instructors examined violence from clients as well as others, including colleagues. Tully et al. found that 26% of the students reported directly experiencing some form of violence, including verbal abuse and sexual harassment, as part of their field practicum experience. Of the field instructors, 62% reported verbal abuse from clients, 42% reported being threatened by a client, and 24% reported a physical attack from a client.

Altogether, the data suggest the significance of the problem for human services professionals in general and for social workers in particular in the United States and elsewhere. Given the array of local nonrepresentative studies documenting the problem, it is important to establish national incidence rates in both an absolute and a comparative cross-national sense. Although it has been asserted that rates of client violence against social workers and other mental health professionals appear to be higher in the United States than in other countries (Davis, 1991), different methods used in studies in the United States and United Kingdom preclude sound cross-national comparisons.

Given this context, we conducted a cross-national survey using representative samples of social workers in the United States and Israel in order to discern incidence rates of workplace violence and victimization. Although survey data from the United States alone can shed light on the absolute level of violence and victimization, cross-national comparison data can provide key information about the relative level of violence and victimization and provide clues about culturally based risk factors. We chose Israel as a particularly appropriate comparison nation because, although also highly industrialized and westernized, it supports a less residualistic human services system than the United States, one that is largely supported and controlled by public auspices. Furthermore, Israelis are not unfamiliar with political violence and are currently experiencing an expansion of human services programs to address problems associated with interpersonal violence (Rosenfeld, Schon, & Sykes, 1995). As in the United States, several recent dramatic incidents involving the murder of social workers and a psychologist have heightened national awareness of the risks of human services work in Israel (e.g., Levnon, 1992; Siegel, 1992).

Method

Sampling and Measurement Procedures

In the spring of 1993, questionnaires and follow-up reminder letters were mailed to simple random samples of 1,200 members of the National Association of Social Workers in the United States and 1,497 members of the Israeli Association of Social Workers. Questionnaires were returned by 743 American social workers (a 62.4% response rate) and 899 Israeli social workers (a 60.1% response rate). Because we were interested in assessing violence and victimization experienced only by social workers who worked directly with clients (rather than those who managed agencies, set policies, or did not work directly with clients), we excluded questionnaires if workers did not work directly with clients. Questionnaires also were excluded if workers were not presently working in social work or if the questionnaires were incomplete. Usable questionnaires were returned by 535 American and 591 Israeli social workers. Statistical comparisons of the demographic characteristics of each sample were made with the demographics of the complete memberships of each national organization; they were found to closely mirror each organization in composition (Bargal & Guterman, 1994; Jayaratne, Vinokur-Kaplan, Nagda, & Chess, in press).

Table 1 shows sample differences between the American and Israeli social workers on key demographic and professional variables. Across both samples, the typical respondent was a married woman near 40 years old with approximately a decade of practice since receiving her last degree. However, Table 1 indicates that the American sample had proportionally more men, was slightly older, and was less likely to be married. The most

Table 1. Sample Differences Between Social Workers in the United States and Israel

Variable	Americans (n = 535)	Israelis (n = 591)	t or χ^2
Gender (%)			
Female	82.7	89.8	13.07*
Male	17.3	10.2	
Mean age (years)	42.5	39.5	5.12**
Marital status (%)			
Married	62.5	74.4	24.30**
Divorced	12.6	6.5	
Widowed	1.9	2.7	
Living alone	14.3	10.9	
Living together	8.8	5.5	
Highest earned degree (%)			
BA or BSW	9.4	76.7	498.96**
MSW	88.7	22.3	
Doctorate	1.9	0.9	
Mean years since received highest degree	10.7	10.2	0.93
Agency aegis (%)			
Public	31.6	91.6	417.01**
Private	68.4	8.4	
Field of practice (%)			
Children and families	24.2	34.6	138.91**
Substance abuse	3.3	2.6	
Mental health	26.4	7.6	
Health care	16.2	8.4	
Aging	4.8	13.8	
Other	25.0	33.0	

*p < .01.   **p < .001.

pronounced differences across the samples emerged along professional variables. For example, the large majority of American social workers held a master's degree, and approximately 77% of the Israeli social workers held a bachelor's degree. These data reflect conventional differences in professional training and the accepted terminal degrees for practicing social workers in each nation. Reflecting differences in funding streams for social work services cross-nationally, Table 1 shows that approximately two thirds of the American social workers held positions in privately funded settings (e.g., private nonprofit or private independent practice settings), whereas more than 90% of the Israeli social workers held positions in public agency settings. Finally, the American sample was composed of proportionately fewer social workers in settings serving children, families, and the elderly, and proportionately more social workers in mental health and health care settings.

The questionnaire used in this study was 10 pages long and was originally developed in English. It contained items on job characteristics and stress, including items on violence and victimization from clients. To capture a more precise picture of the nature of social worker victimization, six questions asked workers to indicate whether they had directly experienced each of six forms of violence and victimization from their clients over the previous year: physical threats, physical assaults, threats of a lawsuit, actually sued, verbal abuse, and sexual harassment. Respondents were asked to simply check a yes or no box next to each victimization form. For use in Israel, questionnaires were translated into Hebrew by a bilingual team consisting of two of us and an Israeli social worker with professional training and experience in both the United States and Israel. Translated questionnaires then were pilot tested on Israeli social workers to revise questionable items.

Data Analysis

A two-stage, data-analytic strategy was chosen to examine different patterns of incidence cross-nationally. First, overall incidence rates were examined for differences cross-nationally using chi-square tests of significance. Second, selected worker characteristics and agency variables were entered into logistic regression analyses to examine predictive pattern differences cross-nationally among the six types of violence and forms of victimization. Logistic regression was chosen because all dependent variables were dichotomously measured (experienced or not experienced over the previous year) and it allowed for an examination of the unique contribution to victimization rates of key nominal and interval-level predictor variables independent of one another. Absolute percentages also are reported in the text of the results section in cases in which significant categorical predictor variables were found. All variables were entered simultaneously and were chosen on the basis of earlier exploratory cross-tabulation and chi-square analyses. The following four predictor variables were chosen: (a) worker experience (as measured by the number of years since workers had received their highest professional degree); (b) worker gender; (c) the agency aegis (public vs. private); and (d) the field of social work practice in which social workers provided services (coded using dummy variables). Worker age was excluded from analyses because a high correlation was found with worker experience ($r = .61$, $p < .0001$) and the attendant likelihood of introducing problems of multicolinearity among variables.

Results

Table 2 shows cross-national differences on the overall incidence rates of violence and victimization. Across all types of victimization reported, 48.8% of Americans and 47.4% of Israelis reported at least one victimization experience over the previous year. Verbal abuse was the most frequently reported form of victimization from clients, with 44.8% of Americans and 46.3% of Israelis reporting having experienced it in the previous year. Physical threats from clients was the next most frequently reported form of victimization, with 17.9% of American and 22.9% of Israeli social

Table 2. Percentages Reporting Direct Experience With Client Violence and Victimization in the Past Year: Americans and Israelis

Victimization type	Direct experience (%)		χ^2
	Americans	Israelis	
Physically threatened	17.9	22.9	4.07*
Physically assaulted	3.2	4.0	0.44
Threatened with a lawsuit	13.9	13.6	0.02
Sued	0.8	1.1	0.32
Verbally abused	44.8	46.3	0.22
Sexually harassed	5.9	0.7	22.9**
Any type of victimization reported	48.8	47.4	2.61

*$p < .05$.   **$p < .001$.

workers reporting having experienced threats over the previous year. As Table 2 indicates, a significantly higher proportion of Israelis than Americans reported having experienced physical threats, and a significantly higher proportion of Americans than Israelis reported having experienced sexual harassment (5.9% of Americans vs. 0.7% of Israelis).

Tables 3–5 summarize the results of the logistic regression analyses, examining significant predictors of violence and victimization from clients cross-nationally. Unstandardized estimated coefficients (Bs), partial correlations (rs), and p values are reported for each predictor variable. Chi-square results represent the significance of all the entered predictor variables intranationally. Partial correlations have been included to provide comparison indexes between nations.

As Table 3 shows, worker experience and gender significantly predicted both physical threats and physical assaults among workers in the United States. Less experienced workers reported a higher likelihood of receiving physical threats and assaults than more experienced workers. Similarly, American male workers were more likely to report threats and assaults from clients, with 26.7% reporting threats and 5.6% reporting assaults. By contrast, among American female workers, 16.2% reported physical threats and 2.8% reported assaults. Among female Israeli workers, work experience and gender did not appear to significantly predict the likelihood of client assault or physical threats. Israeli social workers in child and family service settings, however, did report an increased likelihood of receiving physical threats from clients (35.4% of whom reported receiving threats from clients in the past year).

Table 4 shows that among both Americans and Israelis, working in child and family service settings significantly predicted a higher likelihood of receiving a threat of a lawsuit, with 21.7% of American and 20.0% of Israeli social workers in these settings reporting experiencing it over the past year. Similarly, Israelis working with elderly clients also showed a significantly higher likelihood of receiving a threat of lawsuit from a client, with 19.7% of Israelis in these settings reporting experiencing it over the past year. No variable appeared to predict actual lawsuits against American workers, and only worker experience significantly predicted the like-

Table 3. Logistical Regression Analyses of Worker and Agency Characteristics on Physical Threats and Assaults: Americans and Israelis

Predictor variable	Americans			Israelis		
	B	r	p	B	r	p
	Physical threats					
Worker experience	0.07	.17	.0001	0.01	.00	
Gender	0.92	.12	.001	0.53	.03	
Public or private aegis	0.09	.00		0.76	.00	
Field of practice						
Aging	0.36	.00		0.28	.00	
Children and families	0.10	.00		0.95	.14	.001
Health care	0.19	.00		0.57	.00	
Mental health	0.71	.06		0.03	.00	
Substance abuse	0.05	.00		0.89	.02	
χ^2	31.42		.001	35.74		.001
	Physical assaults					
Worker experience	0.09	.12	.05	0.01	.00	
Gender	1.33	.14	.05	0.90	.00	
Public or private aegis	1.38	.09		0.63	.00	
Field of practice						
Aging	1.41	.00		0.56	.00	
Children and families	1.08	.00		0.63	.00	
Health care	0.26	.00		6.84	.00	
Mental health	1.87	.08		0.43	.00	
Substance abuse	5.32	.00		0.95	.00	
χ^2	19.48		.05	8.31		

Note: r stands for partial correlation coefficients.

lihood of a lawsuit against Israeli workers, with younger workers reporting higher incidence.

Table 5 shows logistic regression results for verbal abuse and sexual harassment. Among Americans, worker experience significantly predicted reports of verbal abuse from clients, with younger workers more likely to have reported abuse over the previous year. Again, worker experience among Israelis did not appear to predict verbal abuse. Instead, Israeli social workers in public agencies reported a significantly greater likelihood of experiencing verbal abuse, with 48.6% of those in public agencies reporting such an experience in the previous year compared with 23.9% of those in private agencies. Again, among Israeli social workers, those working in child and family service settings were more likely to experience verbal abuse from clients in the previous year, with 57.9% of these workers reporting that they had been the recipient of this form of victimization over the previous year.

Less experienced American workers were significantly more likely to have reported sexual harassment from clients over the previous year. No other predictor variables were found to significantly predict sexual harassment among American workers. Among Israelis, no variable was

Table 4. Logistical Regression Analyses of Effects of Worker and Agency Characteristics on Threats of a Lawsuit and Lawsuits: Americans and Israelis

Predictor variable	Americans			Israelis		
	B	r	p	B	r	p
Threats of a lawsuit						
Worker experience	0.01	.00		0.01	.00	
Gender	0.42	.00		0.50	.00	
Public or private aegis	0.28	.00		0.39	.00	
Field of practice						
Aging	0.18	.00		0.86	.07	.05
Children and families	1.05	.10	.05	0.80	.10	.05
Health care	0.50	.00		0.19	.00	
Mental health	0.57	.00		1.45	.00	
Substance abuse	1.01	.00		0.07	.00	
χ^2	13.75			19.30		.05
Lawsuits						
Worker experience	0.02	.00		0.09	.20	.05
Gender	0.61	.00		7.13	.00	
Public or private aegis	0.58	.00		6.89	.00	
Field of practice						
Aging	0.02	.00		6.94	.00	
Children and families	7.75	.00		0.81	.00	
Health care	8.72	.00		7.34	.00	
Mental health	7.43	.00		1.36	.00	
Substance abuse	0.19	.00		6.33	.00	
χ^2	5.07			9.04		

Note: r stands for partial correlation coefficients.

found to significantly predict the likelihood of sexual harassment from clients.

Discussion

Several important patterns emerged from a cross-national examination of incidence data on workplace violence and victimization against social workers. First, despite a number of sociodemographic and professional differences among practicing social workers in the two nations, the absolute rates of reported worker victimization were remarkably similar. Such findings underscore that social workers in the United States do not appear to face unique or inordinate dangers from their clients and instead suggest that victimization from clients crosses national boundaries in similar ways. Such similarities extend across a number of victimization types, including physical assaults, lawsuits, threats of lawsuits, and verbal abuse. Cross-national findings on physical assaults and threats contrast with earlier assertions that American social workers, compared with workers in other nations, appear to face disproportionate risks of physical vi-

Table 5. Logistical Regression Analyses of Effects of Worker and Agency Characteristics on Verbal Abuse and Sexual Harassment: Americans and Israelis

Predictor variable	Americans			Israelis		
	B	r	p	B	r	p
Verbal abuse						
Worker experience	0.03	.07	.05	0.02	.00	
Gender	0.37	.01		0.14	.00	
Public or private aegis	0.37	.04		0.87	.07	.05
Field of practice						
Aging	0.06	.00		0.19	.00	
Children and families	0.22	.00		0.52	.07	.05
Health care	0.11	.00		0.61	.04	
Mental health	0.27	.00		0.53	.00	
Substance abuse	0.44	.00		0.37	.00	
χ^2	16.08		.05	29.72		.001
Sexual harassment						
Worker experience	0.08	.14	.05	0.08	.00	
Gender	1.65	.05		7.39	.00	
Public or private aegis	0.65	.04		1.64	.00	
Field of practice						
Aging	0.37	.00		1.04	.00	
Children and families	0.50	.00		0.85	.00	
Health care	0.42	.00		7.00	.00	
Mental health	0.11	.00		6.97	.00	
Substance abuse	5.79	.00		6.47	.00	
χ^2	19.33		.05	5.27		

Note: r stands for partial correlation coefficients.

olence from clients (e.g., Davis, 1991). Furthermore, the similar proportions found cross-nationally in physical threats (approximately 1 in 5 workers) and assaults (approximately 3 or 4 out of 100) contradict findings from previous nonrepresentative American and British studies of human services professionals reporting higher physical victimization rates (e.g., Bernstein, 1981; Hillen, 1991; Madden, Lion, & Penna, 1976; Schultz, 1987; Whitman et al., 1976).

Some of the discrepancy may be attributable to methodological differences between our study and earlier ones. For example, earlier studies that used instruments focused on workplace violence alone (unlike in the current study, in which victimization questions were embedded in a larger questionnaire on workplace conditions) may have heightened self-selection biases by encouraging responses from those interested in "telling war stories," thereby artificially inflating the incidence rates of violence reported. Likewise, in several earlier studies, a time frame in which respondents should recall incidents was not specified, precluding calculation of annual rates and summing across unspecified time frames (e.g., Bernstein, 1981; Schultz, 1987). The current study's sampling procedures and comparisons with the broader membership bases from which samples were drawn (cf.

Bargal & Guterman, 1994; Jayaratne et al., in press) afforded us greater confidence in generalizing to the national level across countries. Furthermore, the assessment of varying forms of victimization and the use of a delimited time span (1 year) presented a more precise picture of incidence than several earlier studies.

Despite the lower rates of physical threats and actual assaults found in our study, however, the overall reported rates of client victimization in the United States and Israel are alarming. Overall, approximately one half of the workers in each nation reported at least one form of victimization in the past year alone, and 1 in 5 workers received at least one threat of physical harm, depicting a difficult work climate for social workers.

The results of the logistic regression analyses show several important cross-national patterns. First, worker inexperience appeared to be associated with a higher risk for several forms of client victimization among American social workers, but does not appear to play a role for Israeli social workers (except for lawsuits from clients). Findings on social workers from the United States are consistent with earlier studies in this area (e.g., Bernstein, 1981; Carmel & Hunter, 1989) and suggest that worker experience may "season" the professional in learning how to ward off victimization before it happens (Carmel & Hunter, 1989). However, findings on the social workers from Israel do not appear to support this interpretation because one would expect such "seasoning" in working with potentially dangerous clients to develop across cultures. The differences found in the role of worker experience cross-nationally prompted us to consider the role of work cultures and organizations as they intersect with worker experience. Evidence from earlier studies suggests that Israeli social services settings are hierarchically "flatter" than American social services settings and that they bestow comparatively fewer benefits to workers the longer they work (Guterman, Jayaratne, & Bargal, 1995). It may be that as American social workers acquire greater work experience, they also acquire greater leverage to improve their working conditions, including an increased ability to control the clientele with whom they work. In Israel, by contrast, it may be that additional work experience is not accompanied by improved work conditions or leverage to select less dangerous clientele. Further study is warranted, as it suggests that work experience from a cross-cultural perspective should be conceptualized not merely as an intrapersonal event but as one that involves the worker and his or her environment in a mutually evolving dynamic.

Similar considerations are necessary with respect to the role that gender plays in victimization risk from clients. Consistent with selected earlier studies conducted in the United States (Bernstein, 1981; Carmel & Hunter, 1989), American male social workers were found to be at higher risk for physical threats and assaults than were American female social workers. However, among Israeli social workers, gender did not appear to play the same role in predicting physical threat or assault risk. Again, the data here do not shed direct light on the possible reasons for these cross-national differences, but they do suggest the importance of considering other variables interacting with worker gender in the genesis of client violence, such as cultural norms and client-based characteristics (Hatti, Dubin, & Weiss, 1982; Madden et al., 1976). For example, it is plausible that the gender composition of clientele in the United States is different from that in Israel and that expectations of men in helping roles differ cross-nationally, thereby altering the likelihood of client victimization against helpers.

Among Israeli workers, those working in child and family services settings were at higher risk for three of the six forms of victimization from clients: physical threats, threats of lawsuits, and verbal abuse. The data also indicate that American social workers in these settings reported only a higher risk of lawsuit threats. Again, the data here provide only descriptive differences cross-nationally and do not explain why child and family service work in Israel but not the United States may heighten risk. One possible reason for the cross-national differences may lie in the historical development of services addressing the problem of interpersonal violence (e.g., child abuse and neglect and domestic abuse), which continues to develop later in Israel than in the United States. Intervention into family affairs, particularly in violent families, is notoriously difficult and may provoke victimization from clients who had not expected any intervention. Although it is now widely recognized in the United States that outside intervention is common and not unexpected in cases of family violence, this may not have been the case in Israel at the time of this survey. Regardless of the explanation, such findings underscore a more general need to differentially consider violence and victimization risk across service settings, clientele, and cultures. Such trends must be viewed as preliminary and suggest the need for more detailed studies on the precursory events, characteristics of clients, and their concerns at the time of the reported victimization.

Finally, Americans overall reported a rate of sexual harassment from clients more than eight times higher than Israelis. Both methodological and theoretical reasons may explain this difference. No word or phrase in Hebrew directly translates to the English term *sexual harassment* and all its attendant connotations. It may be that the Hebrew translation, *pagah b'ofen meenee* (literally, *insulted in a sexual manner*), was understood to be a more serious violation than what is intended in the English usage of the term. If so, comparison data reflect this linguistic bias. However, it also is important to examine the underlying cultural context in which the terms are embedded. At present, the issue of sexual harassment has not been addressed publically in Israel to the same degree as it has in the United States (e.g., the recent Clarence Thomas hearings, the film *Disclosure*, and the inroads made by the feminist movement in the United States more broadly). Accordingly, the lack of a linguistic equivalent in Hebrew for the term *sexual harassment* may reflect a deeper cultural difference, in which the salience and even the definition of the problem is more articulated in the minds of American workers than Israeli workers.

The complexity of cross-national studies such as this one perhaps poses as many questions as it answers. Apart from the linguistic difficulties attendant with questionnaire translation, a number of critical variables may differ cross-nationally that require alternative methodological approaches. For example, we did not examine how the behavioral manifestations of victimization types differ cross-nationally or how organizational factors as shaped by the larger culture of each respective country contribute to the development of worker–client relationships, both functional and dysfunctional ones. Alternative approaches may consider developing descriptive and behavioral measures of violence and victimization intranationally before comparisons are made. Similarly, attempts to account for organizational-level variables may reveal more directly critical mediating or moderating factors because culture appears to influence worker victimization. Indeed, alternative data-analytic strategies (e.g., moderated regression analyses, path analyses) may more precisely trace the relative contributions of key contributors to workplace violence as it is manifested cross-culturally.

Despite the cultural complexities that such a cross-national study stirs up, our results highlight several important practical considerations for policy development and training efforts aimed at preventing worker victimization on the job. For example, in the United States, efforts to prevent victimization may best be targeted at inexperienced workers. Although further study can assist in untangling the relative importance of intrapersonal versus organizational dimensions of inexperience that heighten risk, professional education and training programs can begin to attend more directly to content on managing potentially risky client challenges. Research on human services professionals already provides helpful prescriptive guidelines on the prevention of victimization (e.g., Gilliland & James, 1993; Kaplan & Wheeler, 1983; Murdach, 1993; Newhill, 1995; Star, 1984), offering strategies on conflict resolution techniques, steps to take in potentially explosive situations with clients, and skill in asking questions nonprovocatively. Additionally, targeting training efforts at field instructors of students placed in agencies may serve as one particularly appropriate venue to "inoculate" novice professionals in the workplace.

Clearly, agencies themselves hold great leverage in preventing victimization behaviors from clients toward workers. Safety policies in agencies should, at a minimum, provide guidelines on events such as the need to restrain a client, procedures to alert other staff and evacuate a work environment when a client becomes violent, and procedures for making client visits in dangerous locations. However, as our findings suggest, agencies must assess their own client base, professional force, and cultural contexts in order to learn where the differential risks of worker victimization lie and to develop policies that fit the contexts in which the services are delivered.

Despite observed variations cross-nationally, the extent of the problem as reported in this study and those in other nations (Brown, Bute, & Ford, 1986; Rowett, 1986) point to the need for national and international organizations, such as the National Association of Social Workers or the International Association of Schools of Social Work, to spearhead efforts in policy formulation and spur the development of policies internationally that protect human services professionals from the commonplace risk of client victimization wherever they provide their services.

References

Bargal, D., & Guterman, N. B. (1994). *Working conditions of Israeli social workers: Report to the Warburg Fund*. Unpublished manuscript, the Hebrew University, Jerusalem, Israel.

Bernstein, H. A. (1981). Survey of threats and assaults directed toward psychotherapists. *American Journal of Psychotherapy, 35*, 542–549.

Brown, R., Bute, S., & Ford, P. (1986). *Social workers at risk*. London: Macmillan.

Carmel, H., & Hunter, M. (1989). Staff injuries from inpatient violence. *Hospital and Community Psychiatry, 40*, 41–46.

Carvajal, D. (1995, January 4). Farewell to a trusting heart. *New York Times*, p. B1.

Davis, S. (1991). Violence by psychiatric inpatients: A review. *Hospital and Community Psychiatry, 42*, 585–590.

Foster, C. (1990, September 27). The U.S.: Elder abuse on the rise. Protection limited. *Christian Science Monitor, 82*, p. 6.

Gilliland, B. E., & James, R. K. (1993). Violent behavior in institutions. In B. E. Gilliland & R. K. James (Eds.), *Crisis intervention strategies* (pp. 455–502). Pacific Grove, CA: Brooks/Cole.

Guterman, N. B., Jayaratne, S., & Bargal, D. (1995, January). *Health care social workers' stress, control and support on the job: A cross-cultural comparison of Israelis and Americans*. Paper presented at the First International Conference on Social Work in Health and Mental Health Care, Jerusalem, Israel.

Hatti, S., Dubin, W. R., & Weiss, K. J. (1982). A study of circumstances surrounding patient assaults on psychiatrists. *Hospital and Community Psychiatry, 33*, 660–661.

Hill, R., & Jennings, V. T. (1991, June 19). Baltimore caseworker is slain. *Washington Post*, p. C1.

Hillen, S. (1991, November). U.K. study: Half of therapists attacked. *APA Monitor*, p. 22.

Jayaratne, S., Vinokur-Kaplan, D., Nagda, B., & Chess, W. A. (in press). A national study of violence and harassment of social workers by clients. *Journal of Applied Behavioral Science*.

Kaplan, S. G., & Wheeler, E. G. (1983). Survival skills for working with potentially violent clients. *Social Casework, 64*(6), 339–346.

Leadbetter, D. (1993). Trends in assaults on social work staff: The experience of one Scottish department. *British Journal of Social Work, 23*, 613–628.

Levnon, S. (1992, September 9). V'meshehi tzaakah—t'vrachu, t'vrachu, hu horeg otanu [And someone cried—run, run, he's killing us]. *Yediot Acharonot*, pp. 4–5.

Loomis, J. F., & Halseth, H. H. (1993, April 1). Chapter shocked by member's murder. *NASW Newsletter*, Michigan Chapter, p. 1.

Madden, D. J., Lion, J. R., & Penna, M. W. (1976). Assaults on psychiatrists by patients. *American Journal of Psychiatry, 133*, 422–425.

Man kills child, shoots woman in Sacramento hostage drama. (1994, December 31). *San Francisco Chronicle*, p. A16.

McCarthy, K. (1991, November). Threat of violence leaves its mark: Analysts concerned about safety. *APA Monitor*, p. 22.

Murdach, A. D. (1993). Working with potentially assaultive clients. *Health and Social Work, 18*, 307–312.

Newhill, C. E. (1995). Client violence toward social workers: A practice and policy concern for the 1990's. *Social Work, 40*, 631–636.

Rosenfeld, J. M., Schon, D. A., & Sykes, I. J. (1995). *Out from under: Lessons from projects for inaptly served children and families*. Jerusalem, Israel: Joint Distribution Committee, Brookdale Institute.

Rowett, C. R. (1986). *Violence in social work*. Cambridge, England: Institute of Criminology.

Schultz, L. (1987). The social worker as a victim of violence. *Social Casework, 68,* 240–244.

Siegel, J. (1992, September 10). Shocked social workers confront own trauma. *Jerusalem Post*, p. 1.

Star, B. (1984). Patient violence/therapist safety. *Social Work, 29,* 191–199.

Sweeney, A. (1993, April 27). Slain social worker liked helping troubled kids. *Detroit News,* p. A6.

Tully, C. T., Kropf, N. P., & Price, J. L. (1993). Is field a hard hat area? A study of violence in field placements. *Journal of Social Work Education, 29,* 191–199.

U.S. Department of Health and Human Services, National Center on Child Abuse and Neglect. (1995). *Child maltreatment 1993: Reports from the states to the National Center on Child Abuse and Neglect.* Washington, DC: U.S. Government Printing Office.

Whitman, R. M., Armao, B. B., & Dent, O. B. (1976). Assault on the therapist. *American Journal of Psychiatry, 13,* 426–429.

9

Violence Against Nurses in Hospitals

Marilyn Lewis Lanza

The assault rate increase in hospitals, reflecting the rising violence in society, has become a major public health problem. Assault occurs in psychiatric and nonpsychiatric areas such as admitting areas and long-term care or nursing home care units (Veterans Administration, 1995). There is strong evidence of assault as a high risk in emergency rooms (Mahoney, 1991). Assault also affects nurses in home care (Fisher, 1994). Injury rates to staff from assaults by patients may surpass rates of injury in construction work, the country's most dangerous occupation (Lusk, 1992). The Bureau of Labor statistics documented 22,400 workplace attacks in which people were seriously injured and 1,063 workplace deaths; female nurses and nurses' aides were the prime targets ("Labor Letter," 1994). A recent review of five studies of injury from inpatient aggression showed that nursing staff in public psychiatric hospitals were at greater risk of occupational injury from violence alone than were workers in high-risk occupations such as mining, lumber, manufacturing, and heavy construction (Love & Hunter, 1996). If injuries to nursing staff from causes other than violence were included, the rates would greatly have exceeded these other occupational injury rates. The studies used a standard formula to calculate injuries per 100 employees, enabling comparisons across hospitals and employment categories.

National attention is beginning to be focused on the problem of hospital violence (American Academy for Nursing, 1993; American Psychiatric Association [APA], 1992; Joint Commission on Hospital Accreditation, 1994; Lipscomb & Love, 1992; Mikulencak, 1992; Veterans Administration, 1995; Worthington, 1993). On March 16, 1993, representatives from the American Nurses Association, the American Medical Association, the American Medical Women's Association, the American College of Emergency Physicians, and the American College of Obstetricians and Gynecologists held a press conference in Washington, DC, to call attention to the growing problem of violence in the workplace. The APA has documented assaults and fatalities on mental health workers across disciplines, including psychiatrists, psychologists, social workers, and nurses (APA, 1992). The APA advocates policy changes and research focus to address the problem of assault on health care providers.

The American Nurses Association cited an increase in injuries among hospital workers as a special characteristic of violence that has emerged in the 1990s (Worthington, 1993). Many of the patients nurses encounter use violence as a means to manage conflict in their everyday lives. More and more patients are arriving at the hospital with lethal weapons, up to 25% in some city trauma units. Contaminated syringes have been used to threaten or assault nurses. Visitors, intruders, and fellow employees also may introduce violence to the nurse's work environment. In a national, multiregion study, Poster and Ryan (1994) found that 76% of the nurses (N = 557) surveyed had been assaulted at least once in their careers.

To compound the problem is the acknowledgment that the reported statistics represent a tip of the iceberg. The assault rate is underreported by as much as 80% (Lion, Snyder, & Merrill, 1981) and reflects a critical-incidence measure at best (Lanza & Campbell, 1991; Silver & Yudofsky, 1987). A variety of reasons have been given for the underreporting of assault: the variable definition of assault (Lanza, 1988; Monahan, 1989; Pearson, Wilmot, & Padi, 1986), the degree of the patient's intent to commit harm (Lanza, 1988), staff inurement to assault (Lanza, 1988; Lion et al., 1981), peer pressure to not report and differential reporting based on the gender of the person assaulted (Lanza, 1988), fear of blame (Lion et al., 1981), excessive paperwork (Lanza, 1988; Lion et al., 1981), and incomplete or invalid information on reports completed by people who did witness the event (Drinkwater, 1982).

Staff Victim Reactions

Patients who are violent are perceived by staff members as being among the most difficult to treat (Colson et al., 1985, 1986). Lanza (1983) conducted a descriptive exploratory study in which nurses reported various short-term (1 week or less) and long-term (more than 1 week) reactions to patient assault, including family pressures to change jobs, leave nursing, or both. Reactions of nurse victims included emotional, social, biophysiological, and cognitive responses, which are summarized in Table 1 (Lanza, 1992). There are indications that some staff members felt they would be overwhelmed if they allowed themselves to admit their feelings. Some stated that if they allowed themselves to experience feelings about the likelihood of assault, they would not be able to function. Others felt they had no right to react or indicated that they expected to be hit because they believed being assaulted was part of the job. Staff members who received the most severe injuries indicated less fear of the patient who had assaulted them than did staff members who were less severely injured. Numerous studies have reported similar findings on the intensity and variety of victims' reactions (Bernstein, 1981; Browner, 1987; Carmel & Hunter, 1989; Cust, 1986; Janoff-Bulman, 1992; Lanza, 1985a; Lanza, Kayne, Hicks, & Milner, 1991; Lion et al., 1981; Poster & Ryan, 1989; Rix, 1987). Poster and Ryan (1989) and Whittington and Wykes (1992) documented that these reactions continued for up to 1 year, suggesting that nurse victims can suffer posttraumatic stress disorder.

Table 1. Victim Reactions to Patient Assault

Emotional reactions	Social reactions	Biophysiological reactions	Cognitive reactions
Short term			
Helplessness	Change in relation-	Startle response	Denial of thoughts
Irritability	ship with cowork-	Sleep pattern	about the assault
Fear of returning	ers	disturbance	Preoccupation with
to the scene of	Difficulty returning	Soreness	thinking about
the assault	to work	Headaches	the assault
Feeling of resigna-	Fear of other pa-		Considering change
tion	tients		in lifestyle job
Anger	Feel sorry for the		change
Anxiety	patient who hit		
Shock	them		
Apathy	Should have done		
Disbelief	something to pre-		
Self-blame	vent the assault		
Dependency			
Long term			
Fear of patient who	Feel sorry for the	Body tension	Anger toward au-
hit them	patient who hit	Soreness	thority
	them		Wanting protection
			by authority and
			from authority's
			criticisms

Note: Reprinted from "Nurses as Patient Assault Victims," by M. L. Lanza, 1992, *Archives in Psychiatric Nursing*, 7, p. 164. Copyright by W. B. Saunders. Reprinted by permission.

Role Conflict

Nurses who are assaulted report conflict between their role as a professional and a victim (Lanza, 1985a). Nurses are not socialized to expect to be assault victims, and most do not receive any academic education to prepare them for such a fate. Any formal training usually comes through employment in a psychiatric facility. There is intense conflict between conflicting realities when a nurse is assaulted (Lanza, 1985a). He or she generally believes that nurses are not assaulted and yet it has occurred. There also is divided loyalty between allegiance to one's professional functioning (i.e., putting the patient's needs first) and attention to one's own needs as a victim (Lanza, 1985a). For example, the nurse is hit by a patient and is required to continue working because staffing is inadequate to permit him or her to go home. Family members question why their mother or father works in "such a place." The victim often defends the institution to family members and denies his or her own feelings of victimization.

Stress for Coworkers

There is beginning to be an awareness of the impact of witnessing an assault. Many of the assaults that occur on nurses are witnessed by their coworkers. Although there has been no formal study, to my knowledge, I have gleaned the following from my extensive interviews of victim coworkers. Witnesses often identify strongly with the victim and imagine that the same thing could easily happen to them. Witnesses report heightened fear, anxiety, increased vulnerability, and irritability. Witnesses often feel guilty about the victim's plight. For example, witnesses will ruminate about what they should have done to prevent the assault of their coworker or that they should have intervened sooner. In an attempt to gain control over the situation, coworkers often give advice to the victim after the assault about "what to do" the next time, such as "Don't go into that patient's room alone" or "Maybe next time you shouldn't be so pushy with that patient about attending his activity." Obviously, this leads to enormous staff problems. While witnesses are trying to deal with their own anxiety and achieve some control, their efforts at identifying causative factors of the assault produce anger and a sense of being blamed in the victim. Witnesses do blame the victim as a way of distancing themselves from the assault situation and in an attempt to protect themselves from the strong identification with the victim.

These observations are consistent with a number of reports in the literature of the transmission of trauma to individuals close to the traumatized person. Some forms of stress responses are common in people who are closely involved with survivors of traumatic events. Danieli (1988) described the impact of parental traumatization on the children of Holocaust survivors and Vietnam veterans as a "secondary trauma." Maltas and Shay (1995) reported trauma contagion among the partners of survivors of childhood sexual abuse. McCann and Pearlman (1990a, 1990b) and Curtois (1993) described the vicarious traumatization in therapists working with trauma survivors. Herman (1992) reported traumatic countertransferences in therapists, and Davies and Frawley (1994) noted transference–countertransference enactments. Anxiety and depression in therapists and the intrusion into their waking and dreaming states of images associated with their patients' memories of past trauma and current reexperiencing of it were common occurrences.

Coping Strategies

The work of Janoff-Bulman (1992) is particularly useful in counseling assault victims. She detailed how three assumptions that are shared by most people are affected as a result of any victimization regardless of the cause. After victimization, the belief in personal invulnerability is severely damaged and the person is preoccupied with fear of reoccurrence. The perception of the world as meaningful and comprehensible is no longer applicable. One way for people to make sense of the world is that it is controllable (e.g., one can prevent misfortune by engaging in sufficiently cautious behaviors). The world does not appear meaningful to victims who feel that they were cautious and are good people. For the victim, the problem of loss of meaning focuses not on why the event happened but on why it happened to him or her. It is the selective incidence of victimization that appears to warrant explanation. Finally, seeing oneself in a positive light is affected. The trauma activates negative self-images. Victims see themselves as weak, helpless, needy, frightened, and out of control. They also experience a sense of deviance. They were "singled out for misfortune," and this sets them off from other people.

Coping involves coming to terms with shattered assumptions: coming to terms with a world in which bad things can and do happen to oneself. Although victims will probably never again view themselves as completely safe, they still need to feel that the world is not entirely bad or threatening. The assumptions of vulnerability, meaning, and self-esteem will be examined, altered, and reexamined until one's victimization and conceptual system are consistent.

Victims May Redefine the Victimization

Victims may selectively evaluate their victimization by comparing themselves with others who are less fortunate, comparing on a basis of who has the best attitude, creating hypothetical worse worlds, construing benefits from the experience, and manufacturing normative standards of adjustment. How one evaluates the victimization affects the extent to which the victimization functions as a stressor and threat.

Making Sense of the Event

One way of making sense of an event is to find some purpose in it. If the victimization can be viewed as serving a purpose, the victim is able to reestablish a belief in an orderly, comprehensible world.

Blaming oneself is one way of explaining why the event happened to that victim in particular. Self-blame can be functional, particularly if it involves attributions to one's behavior rather than enduring personality characteristics. Behavioral self-blame allows attributions to a controllable and modifiable source. Victims can alter their behavior. Thus, the victim believes that he or she can avoid being victimized in the future. Characterological attributions are associated with depression. Behavioral responses are not helpful for victims who believe that they engaged in safe or cautious practices before their victimization. Rules that had provided them with a personal sense of invulnerability did not work, and their perception of safety and security was destroyed. Those who feel most invulnerable before victimization may have the most difficulty coping after being victimized.

When Coping Fails

The awareness that medical personnel experience stress severe enough to benefit from intervention is a comparatively recent development (Lederberg, 1993). In the 19th and early 20th centuries, medical institutions often were staffed by religious people for whom the demands of caregiving were buttressed by their faith and vows of service. Intense and repeated exposure to stress leave staff feeling pain, sadness, fear, and revulsion. These feelings may in turn engender shame and guilt (Lederberg, 1993). Constructive sublimation is obviously commendable and need not be made conscious (Kernberg, 1978). However, staff members routinely have varying intimations of their suppressed and unconscious reactions and beliefs, which they experience as shameful and incompatible with their professional self-image. They keep them secret, reinforcing their belief that they are alone in having them. This can lead to increasing isolation and decreasing self-esteem. Lederberg (1993) and Abrams and Sweeney (1982) advocated the use of staff support groups to relieve suffering and conflict.

There must be interventions that recognize that staff members are victimized and that assault is a serious job stressor (Browner, 1987). A particularly useful intervention for staff members who have been assaulted is to offer supportive counseling. I use the word *supportive* to highlight the importance of counseling that focuses on the victim's perceived needs and not those of hospital administrators. If the latter scenario exists, there is danger that the victim will receive counseling to "improve his or her performance" and not to help the victim deal with his or her own unique reactions.

There are a variety of ways to offer counseling services to assault victims. A number of supportive counseling services for assaulted staff have been documented in the literature (Browner, 1987; Dawson, Johnston, Kehiayan, & Kyanko, 1988; Engel & Marsh, 1986; Flannery, Fulton, Tausch, & DeLoffi, 1991; Lanza, 1984, 1985b; Murray & Snyder, 1991; Whittington & Wykes, 1992). Most focus on individual counseling or group meetings having an educational focus. I describe several counseling services.

Counseling Services

The formation of a victim assault support team at the Edith Nourse Rogers Memorial Veterans Hospital (Lanza, 1984, 1985b) grew out of multidisciplinary concern for the plight of staff members who had been assaulted. Until the inception of the support team, staff victims often sought support from coworkers. However, it was felt that a recognized service needed to be available for staff victims.

Although the qualifications for counselors vary, the counselors are expected to have training as mental health professionals. Beyond that, specific qualifications require that counselors have great knowledge about the problem of patient assault. Counselors do not have to have been assaulted, but they do need to be able to empathize with the victim. Although understanding the assault situation from the victim's perspective is essential, it is necessary not to "take the victim's side." Counselors must be objective in order to be able to provide support and guidance to the victim. For example, victims often are angry at the administration for the assault. Counselors must be able to help the victim deal with the reality of those issues as well as any symbolic significance related to other areas in the victim's life.

It was decided that the services of the victim assault support team would be available to victims at their request. Other staff members can suggest the use of the support services, but there is no requirement to do so. This is to protect the victim's wish for privacy and provide freedom from unwanted pressure to seek counseling.

Because victim assault support services are available to the victim only at his or her request, it was necessary to widely publicize their existence. The services were announced at various staff meetings, explained during educational programs, and advertised in the hospital newspaper. The personnel health physician also was contacted because he or she generally examines the victim after an assault.

Most staff members who seek counseling do so 1 week after being assaulted. After the assault, victims report feeling upset but then feeling better. They seek counseling after unexpected episodes of fearfulness and crying are experienced. Victims are distressed by these symptoms because they thought that they had coped with their feelings. Other reactions reported by victims are anger at the patient, feeling criticized and not supported by coworkers, humiliation, fear of returning to work, stress in having to cope with their families' concerns and pressures to leave work, and anger at the amount of paperwork required to report the assault.

Victims are generally interviewed twice. During the first interview, victims review the symptoms they have experienced. The victims are helped to vent and understand the significance of their symptoms as part of what most victims experience after an assault. The counselor provides anticipatory guidance about any additional reactions that might be experienced. In addition, specific coping strategies are explored (e.g., how to deal with the fear of returning to work).

Two peer support programs, the assault support team (AST) (Dawson et al., 1988) and the Assaulted Staff Action Program (ASAP; Flannery et al., 1991), have been described in the literature. The AST provides emotional support and facilitates the resolution of role conflict. A training program for counselors includes the dynamics of assault, common victim responses, and supportive interventions. The AST uses a "buddy system" in which treatment teams are paired. When an assault occurs, phone calls are placed by the buddy team until an AST member is found who can respond to the staff victim. It then becomes the AST member's responsibility to contact the assaulted staff member. Depending on the needs of the staff victim, the AST member will make an immediate contact or schedule a meeting in the near future. Follow-up calls are made as needed. Written feedback is solicited from staff victims.

The ASAP team members debrief assault victims, assess the victim's sense of control, social supports, and ability to make sense of the incident. A short-term support group is offered. When an assault occurs, the ward charge nurse calls the hospital switchboard operator, who pages the on-call ASAP team member.

A nursing consultation support service (Murray & Snyder, 1991) is made up of psychiatric nurses who receive training from psychiatric clinical nurse specialists. A team member responds to an assault on his or her shift anywhere in the hospital. In the consultation, the staff victim is given the opportunity to describe and discuss the assault incident in its entirety. Questions are asked to aid the staff member in recalling and verbalizing additional aspects of the incident, including sensory experiences. The first problem that may require attention is staff feelings of shock, hurt, and anger. Another problem is critical, hurtful, blaming remarks by other staff to the person who was assaulted. The victim is seen one to four times for consultation and gives a written report to the chairperson of the consultation service. Consultation also is made available to the unit containing a violent patient regarding interventions and resources.

Some hospital programs include preparation for the new or inexperienced employee to anticipate and handle assaults. These usually are part of an orientation to a new place of employment or of an annual mandatory education program. For example, at the Edith Nourse Rogers Memorial Veterans Hospital, all new and current employees attend annual training programs on assessment, prevention, and intervention related to patient assault. A part of that program is focused on victims' reactions to the assault and the interventions available. Program participants also are introduced to a written policy outlining the rights of the assaulted employee.

Conclusion

In a time of austere measures and budget cuts, an adequate number of staff and support services to staff are among the first items to be eliminated. "Do more with less" is the common refrain. Top administrators often are unaware that assaults are vastly underreported, that adequate staffing levels are strongly related to safety and maintaining a quality therapeutic milieu, that staff suffer more than is apparent when victimized by assault, and that services to support the staff victim can improve staff morale and ultimately diminish rather than increase costs. Those in positions of leadership and influence can improve the quality of patient care by insisting that both patients and staff need to be safe in the hospital environment. The issue of patients' and staff's safety and well-being is not a contradiction in terms, as is sometimes alleged. Only when staff feel safe can they fully engage in their work of attending to patients' needs.

References

Abrams, R. C., & Sweeney, J. A. (1982). A critique of the process oriented approach to ward staff meetings. *American Journal of Psychiatry, 139*, 769–773.

American Academy for Nursing. (1993, November). *Violence: Nursing debates the issues* [conference]. Washington, DC.

American Psychiatric Association. (1992). *Clinician safety*. Washington, DC: Author.

Bernstein, H. A. (1981). Survey of threats and assaults directed toward psychotherapists. *American Journal of Psychotherapy, 35*, 542–549.

Browner, C. H. (1987). Job stress and health: The role of social support at work. *Research in Nursing and Health, 10*, 93–100.

Carmel, H., & Hunter, M. (1989). Staff injuries from inpatient violence. *Hospital and Community Psychiatry, 40*, 41–46.

Colson, D. B., Allen, J. G., Coyne, L., Deering, D., Jehl, N., Kearns, W., & Spohn, H. (1985). Patterns of staff perception of difficult patients in a long-term psychiatric hospital. *Hospital and Community Psychiatry, 36*, 168–172.

Colson, D. B., Allen, J. G., Coyne, L., Deering, D., Jehl, N., Kearns, W., & Spohn, H. (1986). Profiles of difficult psychiatric hospital patients. *Hospital and Community Psychiatry, 37*, 720–724.

Curtois, C. A. (1993, Spring). Vicarious traumatization of the therapist. *NCP: A Clinical Newsletter*, pp. 8–9.

Cust, K. (1986). Assault: Just part of the job? *Canadian Nurse, 82*, 19–20.

Danieli, Y. (1988). Treating survivors and children of survivors of the Nazi Holocaust. In F. Ochberg (Ed.), *Post-traumatic therapy and victims of violence* (pp. 278–297). New York: Brunner/Mazel.

Davies, J. M., & Frawley, M. G. (1994). *Treating the adult survivor of childhood sexual abuse*. New York: Basic Books.

Dawson, J., Johnston, M., Kehiayan, N., & Kyanko, S. (1988). Response to patient assault: A support program for nurses. *Journal of Psychosocial Nursing, 26*, 8–15.

Drinkwater, J. M. (1982). *Development in the study of criminal behavior* (Vol. 2). San Diego, CA: Academic Press.

Engel, F., & Marsh, S. (1986). Helping the employee victim of violence in hospitals. *Hospital and Community Psychiatry, 37*, 159–162.

Fisher, D. (1994). Violence puts home care nurses in harms way. *American Nurse, 26*, 16.

Flannery, R. B., Jr., Fulton, P., Tausch, J., & DeLoffi, A. Y. (1991). A program to help staff cope with psychological sequelae of assaults by patients. *Hospital and Community Psychiatry, 42*, 935–938.

Herman, J. (1992). *Trauma and recovery*. New York: Basic Books.

Janoff-Bulman, R. (1992). *Shattered assumptions*. New York: Free Press.

Joint Commission on Hospital Accreditation accreditation manual for hospitals (Vol. 1). (1994). Oakbrook Terrace, IL.

Kernberg, O. T. (1978). Leadership and organizational functioning: Organizational regression. *International Journal of Group Psychotherapy, 28*, 3–25.

Labor letter: A special news report on people and their jobs in offices, fields, and factories. (1994, September 27). *Wall Street Journal*.

Lanza, M. L. (1983). The reactions of nursing staff to physical assault by a patient. *Hospital and Community Psychiatry, 34*, 44–47.

Lanza, M. L. (1984). Victim assault support team for staff. *Hospital and Community Psychiatry, 35*, 414.

Lanza, M. L. (1985a). How nurses react to patient assault? *Journal of Psychosocial Nursing and Mental Health Services, 23*, 6–11.

Lanza, M. L. (1985b). Counseling services for staff victims of patient assault. *Administration in Mental Health Services, 12*, 205–207.

Lanza, M. L. (1988). Factors relevant to patient assault. *Issues in Mental Health Nursing, 9*, 239–258.

Lanza, M. L. (1992). Nurses as patient assault victims: An update, synthesis and recommendations. *Archives of Psychiatric Nursing, 6*, 163–171.

Lanza, M. L., & Campbell, D. (1991). Patient assault: A comparison study of reporting methods. *Journal of Nursing Quality Assurance, 5*, 60–68.

Lanza, M. L., Kayne, H. L., Hicks, C., & Milner, J. (1991). Nursing staff characteristics related to patient assault. *Issues in Mental Health Nursing, 12*, 253–266.

Lederberg, M. S. (1993). Staff support groups for high-stress facilities. In A. Alonso & H. Swiller (Eds.), *Group therapy in clinical practice* (pp. 171–184). Washington, DC: American Psychiatric Press.

Lion, J. R., Snyder, W., & Merrill, G. L. (1981). Underreporting of assaults on staff in a state hospital. *Hospital and Community Psychiatry, 32*, 497–498.

Lipscomb, J., & Love, C. (1992). Violence towards health care workers: An emerging occupational hazard. *Journal of the American Association of Occupational Health Nursing, 40*, 219–228.

Love, C., & Hunter, M. (1996). Violence in public sector psychiatric hospitals: Benchmarking nursing staff injury rates. *Journal of Psychosocial Nursing, 34*(5), 30–34.

Lusk, S. L. (1992). Violence in the workplace. *Journal of the American Association of Hospital Nurses, 40*, 212–213.

Mahoney, B. S. (1991). The extent, nature, and response to victimization of nurses in Pennsylvania. *Journal of Emergency Nursing, 17*, 292–293.

Maltas, C., & Shay, J. (1995). Trauma contagion in partners of survivors of childhood sexual abuse. *American Journal of Orthopsychiatry, 65*, 529–539.

McCann, L., & Pearlman, L. A. (1990a). *Psychological trauma and the survivor*. New York: Brunner/Mazel.

McCann, L., & Pearlman, L. A. (1990b). Vicarious traumatization: A framework for understanding the psychological effects of working with victims. *Journal of Traumatic Stress*, pp. 131–149.

Mikulencak, M. (1992, November–December). Personal safety emerging as a chief workplace concern. *American Nurse*, p. 7.

Monahan, J. (Speaker). (1989). Predicting violence among the mentally ill. *Audio Digest–Psychiatry, 18*(Cassette Recording).

Murray, M. G., & Snyder, J. C. (1991). When staff are assaulted: A nursing consultation support service. *Journal of Psychosocial Nursing, 29*(7), 24–29.

Pearson, M., Wilmot, E., & Padi, M. (1986). A study of violent behavior among inpatients in a psychiatric hospital. *British Journal of Psychiatry, 142*, 232–235.

Poster, E. C., & Ryan, J. A. (1989). Nurses' attitudes toward physical assault by patients. *Archives in Psychiatric Nursing, 3*, 315–322.

Poster, E. C., & Ryan, J. (1994). A multiregional study of nurses' beliefs and attitudes about work safety and patient assault. *Hospital and Community Psychiatry, 45*, 1104–1108.

Rix, G. (1987). Staff sickness and its relationship to violent incidents on a regional secure psychiatric unit. *Journal of Advanced Nursing, 12*, 223–228.

Silver, J. M., & Yudofsky, S. C. (1987). Documentation of aggression in the assessment of the violent patient. *Psychiatric Annals, 17*, 375–384.

Veterans Administration. (1995). *Report of assaultive behavior in Veterans Health Administration facilities during fiscal year 1991*. Washington, DC: Author.

Whittington, R., & Wykes, T. (1992). Staff strain and social support in a psychiatric hospital following assault by a patient. *Journal of Advanced Nursing, 17*, 480–486.

Worthington, K. (1993, June). Taking action against violence in the workplace. *American Nurse*, p. 13.

10

Workplace Violence in Federal Agencies

Caroline Freeman, Susan Fox, Barbara Burr, and John Santasine

Violent encounters that result in time loss from work or workers' compensation claims may be particularly good benchmarks for tracking workplace violence. Tracking is possible because such events are workplace related, records are available and convenient to study, cases of serious health outcomes are defined already, useful information is available on the occurrence of the event, and individual records are relatively complete. Such records can offer useful impressions about the peculiarities in the frequency of workplace violence in a population.

In fiscal year (FY) 1993, 2,185 cases involving fatal and nonfatal human violence were opened and recorded by the Office of Workers' Compensation Programs (OWCP) within the Department of Labor. These cases involved employees in approximately 30 different departments and agencies of the federal government. The highest case rates occurred in the Department of Veterans Affairs, the Department of Justice, and the Department of Transportation. Eleven fatalities were recorded; the highest case fatality rate occurred in the Department of Treasury. Fatalities also occurred in the Department of Labor and the Department of Justice and in the United States Postal Service. Of the total number of cases involving workplace violence, 1,222 cases involved "time lost from work." The highest rates of cases of time lost from work occurred in the Department of Justice and the Department of Veterans Affairs (U.S. Department of Labor, 1993). Preliminary information for FY 1994 shows similar findings. In FY 1994, a total of 7 fatalities occurred in the Departments of the Army, Justice, Treasury, and Labor (U.S. Department of Labor, 1994). In both years, cases were filed almost equally by sex, although for some occupations one or the other sex predominated.

Objectives of This Review

In this chapter we review data on claims of death and injury that resulted from human violence in the workplace among federal employees. We identify the uses of the database administered by the OWCP as a basis for enumerating and describing work-related injuries, examine the accuracy of the use of the terms *work related* and *human violence* in the OWCP database, and examine the reliability of these data as a method of case finding.

Background

Violence in the workplace is a concern to many Americans because of recent media reports depicting employees killed or harmed at work. Much of what is known about workplace violence comes from a small number of documents that focus on fatal work-related injuries, primarily homicides, that occurred within specific subsets of workplaces (Kraus, Blander, & McArthur, 1995).

In the general population for the decade 1980–1989, homicide was the leading cause of occupational death among women and the third leading cause of occupational death among all workers after motor vehicle accidents and machinery deaths (Jenkins, Layne, & Kisner, 1992; U.S. Department of Health and Human Services, 1993a, 1993b). In 1992, 1,004 deaths attributable to workplace violence occurred in the United States (U.S. Department of Labor, 1992). In 1993, the number of such deaths was 1,063 (Jensen, 1994). This is equivalent to more than 4 workplace homicides per day.[1] Homicide was the second leading cause of job-related deaths, accounting for 17% of the fatally injured workers in 1993 (Kraus et al., 1995; Toscano & Windau, 1993; U.S. Department of Labor, 1994). The majority of these homicides were the result of robbery attempts (U.S. Department of Labor, 1992). About 4% were caused by disgruntled employees (Jenkins, 1994). For women, most of the deaths were caused by unknown assailants (Jenkins, 1994).

Reviews of homicide data have provided information about work conditions associated with these higher risks (U.S. Department of Health and Human Services, 1993b). The following groups of workers are generally considered to be at high risk of workplace homicide: taxicab drivers (26.9 homicides per 100,000 workers); police and detectives (9.0 homicides per 100,000 workers); liquor store clerks and owners (8 homicides per 100,000 workers); gas station clerks (5.6 per 100,000 workers); security guards in protective agencies (5.0 homicides per 100,000 workers); and waitresses and bartenders (1.5 homicides per 100,000 workers; U.S. Department of Health and Human Services, 1993a). Workplace conditions that result in high risks of homicide in the workplace include working alone during the night and early morning hours, handling money, guarding valuables, having job tasks that require confronting violence (e.g., police work), being recently hired, and working with the public (Kraus et al., 1995; Service Employees International Union, 1993; U.S. Department of Health and Human Services, 1993b).

---

[1]4.4 cases of homicide times 240 workdays per year equals 1,056 cases.

Homicide accounts for only one type of workplace violence. Workplace violence includes verbal threats, assault, battery, and other deaths (e.g., manslaughter and suicide). For every worker-on-worker homicide, many more cases of nonfatal injuries, beatings, stabbings, shootings, rapes, suicides, near-suicides, and psychological traumas go unreported (Kraus et al., 1995). Workplace violence with or without injury and death has been classified into several basic types regardless of outcome. For reporting purposes, for example, the Bureau of Labor Statistics has categorized workplace violence incidents on the basis of type of circumstance, that is, whether the workplace violence resulted from a personal dispute or from client dispute (Kraus et al., 1995). The categories used by the California Division of Occupational Safety and Health include Types 1–3 and are based on the assailant's relationship to the workplace. There is, however, extensive overlap of important characteristics of such incidents regardless of whether the event resulted in injury, time lost from work, or death. For example, the motivation of the perpetrators, the action of the victims, and the relationship between the perpetrator and victim are not mutually exclusive factors (Kraus et al., 1995). Even though much of the current knowledge about workplace conditions associated with workplace violence comes from studies of groups of workers with high rates of homicide, those same workplace conditions may be associated with other types of workplace violence.

Data Set

The Occupational Safety and Health Act, passed by the U.S. Congress in 1970, mandates that the Occupational Safety and Health Administration (OSHA) ensure that all workers be provided with a safe and healthful place to work (OSHA, 1970). The Occupational Safety and Health Act covers more than 90 million workers in 50 states, including employees in more than 90 federal agencies. The Occupational Safety and Health Act also requires that employers keep records of illnesses and injuries. The Bureau of Labor Statistics collects most of the data, analyzes it, and makes it available to the public. Section 19 of the Occupational Safety and Health Act requires federal agencies to establish their own safety and health program and to comply with any OSHA standard developed under Section 6(b).

In FY 1993, more than 3 million workers were employed in the agencies of the federal government covered by the Federal Employee's Compensation Act (FECA). FECA is administered by the OWCP, which is part of the Department of Labor. This chapter focuses on the injury and illness data collected pursuant to the FECA. The OWCP database used covers all 90 federal agencies; only about 30 agencies, involving about 2.3 million workers, reported incidents of workplace violence (U.S. Department of Labor, 1993, 1994b). OSHA requires specific codes to identify workplace violence events; other information that is entered into the OWCP database is similar to that collected by Bureau of Labor Statistics.

The total number of cases per agency were enumerated for both FYs

1993 and 1994. For FY 1993 only, we also reviewed the number of workplace violence cases by job titles. (The calculation of the total number of cases and rates is discussed further in the method section.) Although there were some limitations and inaccuracies in the OWCP database, as discussed later, there are many overriding positive aspects to the use of these data for identifying cases of workplace violence.

We think that findings from this review are consistent with information from other reporting agencies. For example, the highest rates of workplace violence occur among workers with known risk factors (e.g., corrections officers and trainees; Service Employees International Union, 1993; U.S. Department of Health and Human Services, 1993b). This provides an internal validity check on the OWCP database. Further evaluation of these data and information about the existence of the OWCP database may therefore be useful.

Method

We reviewed fatal and nonfatal cases of human violence and violence among federal employees that were submitted as workers' compensation claims in approximately 30 federal agencies over 2 years.

In the OWCP database, information collected includes (a) *employee characteristics*, such as the age and sex of victim, the occupational code of the victim, and personal identification information; (b) *injury and illness type*, such as the date of the injury or death, the extent of the injury, the anatomical location of the injury, the nature of the injury, and the classification of the injury/illness (*International Classification of Diseases*, 9th revision); the OSHA type code; the OSHA source code; and the cause of the injury; and (c) *case reporting*, such as the zip code for the incident, the federal department code, and the date that the OWCP file was created or opened.

Two main ways of identifying workplace violence for this review were the (a) use of the source of injury/illness (SOI) code (SOI-940), an OSHA code that is entered into the database by federal management staff; and (b) use of the cause of injury (COI) code (COI-90), an OWCP code that is coded by OWCP clerical staff. Most cases were identified by the source category, or SOI, alone. As part of this process, incorrectly coded cases were examined and deleted. Cases were deleted if the coding for both source and COI did not clearly appear to be related to human violence. Some of these cases need further evaluation to identify whether they should have been deleted. The rates of injury, death, and illness were based on all cases, after deletions, coded by SOI (SOI-940; human violence), regardless of COI, plus all cases coded as COI (COI-90; violence), regardless of the source code. Cases that were coded as both SOI-940 and COI-90 were counted only once.

Results

Employment information for the federal government in FYs 1993 and 1994 indicates that about 3 million people were employed in federal government agencies for which workers' compensation data were supplied to the OWCP database. In FY 1993, a total of 2,185 cases of injury and illness caused by human violence were opened by workers in 26 federal agencies covered by the OWCP; these 26 federal agencies cover about 2.3 million workers. In FY 1993, there were a total of 1,706 cases, coded only by SOI-940, and an additional 479 cases for a total of 2,185 cases, when all COI-90s were included. Of these, 11 cases resulted in death; another 1,222 resulted in time lost from work. In FY 1994, there were 2,153 claims of injury and illness caused by human violence filed by workers. In FY 1994, there were a total of 1,680 cases, coded only by SOI-940, and an additional 473 cases for a total of 2,153 cases, when all COI-90s were included. Of these, 7 cases resulted in death; another 1,221 resulted in time lost from work. The remainder of the cases resulted in no time lost from work. This review covers only the cases of workers' compensation that were opened between October 1, 1992, and September 30, 1993 (FY 1993), and between October 1, 1993, and September 30, 1994 (FY 1994) regardless of the date of the incident.

There were 11 fatalities attributable to workplace violence in the federal workforce in FY 1993; these fatalities occurred in the United States Postal Service (4 deaths), Department of Justice (1 death), Department of Treasury (5 deaths), and Department of Labor (1 death). In FY 1993, fed-

Table 1. Departments (in Rank Order From Highest to Lowest) by Rate of Workplace Violence for Fiscal Year 1993

Department	Rate per 10,000[a]	COI-90
Veterans Affairs	26.19	30.17
Justice	20.92	31.63
Transportation	17.58	18.01
Securities and Exchange Commission	7.39	7.39
Treasury	4.56	7.61
Interior	4.30	7.85
Library of Congress	4.07	4.07
U.S. Postal Service	4.02	5.00
Labor	3.96	4.53
National Archives	3.17	3.17
Energy	2.41	2.41
Health and Human Services	1.67	1.97
Navy	1.66	2.18
Commerce	1.56	1.56
Army	1.25	1.57
Other	<1.00	—

Note. COI-90 = cause of injury code, which is equal to the source category plus the new COI.
[a]The rate is the source of injury/illness code.

eral agencies with the highest rates of violence were the Department of Veterans Affairs, Department of Justice, Department of Transportation, and Securities and Exchange Commission (see Table 1). Rates were based on total employed population per federal agency. In FY 1994, a total of 7 fatalities occurred as a result of workplace violence; fatalities from workplace violence occurred in the Departments of the Army (3 deaths), Justice (1 death), Treasury (1 death), and Labor (2 deaths).

For FY 1993, we conducted a review of violence cases (SOI-940 only) by job titles. The following are occupations that had 5 or more violence cases in FY 1993: nurses, 733 (43%); corrections officers, 219 (13%); customs or other inspectors, 105 (6%); workers in the United States Postal Service, 268 (16%); trainees, 180 (10%); and other, 64 (4%).

Occupations having fewer than 5 cases of workplace violence had another 137 cases (8%). When these numbers are standardized by the actual number of federal employees in that job classification, the relative rates of federal job titles that are likely to have violent experiences can be determined. Information on total employment in the federal sector by job title, based on federal civilian workforce statistics as of January 1994, was used to calculate rates for three job titles (U.S. Office of Personnel Management, 1994). These are presented as follows by relative ranking, from highest to lowest: corrections officers (19.4 per 1,000 workers); nurses (10.2 per 1,000 workers); and customs or other inspectors (7.9 per 1,000 workers). A preliminary review of FY 94 data indicate a high number of cases (SOI-940 only) in similar job titles. The following are the occupations that were most commonly reported as having workplace violence in FY 1994: United States Postal Service—postal collectors for delivery and other miscellaneous job titles (267 cases); Department of Veterans Affairs—nurses (133 cases) and practical nurses (93 cases), nursing assistants in several federal agencies (127 cases), police in several federal agencies (104 cases); Department of Justice—correctional officers (89 cases); and Department of Labor—apprenticeship and training (37 cases).

Discussion

The first purpose of our review was to identify any uses of this database as a basis for enumerating and describing work-related injuries. The OWCP database appears to have validity, in that cases occur where expected. The second purpose was to examine the accuracy of the use of the terms *work-related* and *human violence* in OWCP databases. Regarding accuracy, some misclassifications of cases appear to have occurred, and additional review is needed to determine whether some of these cases were inappropriately deleted from this analysis. There were some discrepancies and differences in coding; cases are reported differently by COI and SOI. The last purpose was to examine the reliability of these data as a method of case finding. We noted that the system of counting was not developed to capture information about workplace violence. Despite these limitations, these data appear to offer additional insight into the problems of workplace violence.

Our major findings are as follows: The highest rates of workplace violence occurred among workers with the job titles with known risk factors (e.g., corrections officers in the Department of Justice), providing an internal validity check on the OWCP data. Agencies with the highest rates of injury were the Departments of Veterans Affairs, Justice, and Transportation. Job titles with the highest rates of reported injuries were nurses and correctional officers.

One major difficulty in assessing the scope, dimensions, and characteristics of work-related injury is the definition of work-related activity (Kraus et al., 1995). The OWCP database enumerates violent encounters that result in time loss from work or workers' compensation claims. This database may be particularly good for tracking workplace violence because such events are workplace related, in that death or injury is caused where employees are engaged in work activities required as a condition of employment. The scope of the database covers employees with occupational injuries. Because records are available and convenient to study and cases of serious health outcomes are defined already, useful information is available from the OWCP database on the occurrence of workplace violence in federal agencies.

In the future, we would like to explore further the possible linkage of federal data; the outcomes, costs, or both per case; factors that affect the onset of workplace violence; the policies and procedures of each agency that affect reporting (e.g., the existence of agency entitlement for medical insurance coverage, outreach, domestic violence, and employee assistance programs); and differences in coverage (e.g., the length of shifts [events within an 8-hour shift versus events within a 24-hour shift]). In addition, federal agencies with no reported cases of workplace violence should be examined more closely.

Finally, we would like to determine the outcome of major incidents on the number of cases of workplace violence reported to the OWCP. For example, federal employees as a whole have never been considered to be at grave risk of workplace death or homicide. In the past, federal employees appear to have been at risk of nonfatal workplace violence; several thousand cases of nonfatal workplace violence are reported annually in the OWCP database; risks appear to be related to known workplace conditions. However, with the bombing of the Alfred P. Murrah Federal Building in Oklahoma City on April 19, 1995, federal employees as a whole became one of the groups of workers with higher risks of workplace death (5.6 per 100,000 workers).[2] With this one incident, we expect the number of cases of workplace violence reported to the OWCP database to increase in all federal agencies in the building.

Efforts should be made to evaluate all databases, such as the OWCP database, to determine whether causes of such workplace violence can be

---

[2]Assuming that about 3 million employees were employed by the federal government at the time of the bombing, and assuming that most of the 168 people killed in Oklahoma City in April were federal employees, the rate of workplace homicide among federal workers is about 5.6 per 100,000.

defined. Statistics on occupational injuries and illnesses for federal employees can be collected using the OWCP database.

References

Jenkins, E. L. (1994, January). *Workplace violence*. Paper presented at the biennial meeting of the National Advisory Committee on Occupational Safety and Health. U.S. Department of Labor, Occupational Safety and Health Administration, Washington, DC.

Jenkins, E. L., Layne, L. A., & Kisner, S. M. (1992). Homicide in the workplace: The U.S. experience, 1980-1988. *American Association of Occupational Health Nursing Journal, 40*, 215–218.

Jensen, M. (1994, December 5). *America On-Line*. New York: NBC.

Kraus, J. F., Blander, B., & McArthur, D. L. (1995). Incidence, risk factors and prevention strategies for work-related assault injuries: A review of what is known, what needs to be known, and countermeasures for intervention. *Annual Review of Public Health, 16*, 355–379.

The Occupational Safety and Health Act of 1970, United States Code Section 651(b).

Service Employees International Union. (1993). *Assault on the job*. Washington, DC: AFL-CIO.

Toscano, G., & Windau, J. (1993, October). Fatal work injuries: Results from the 1992 National Census. *Monthly Labor Review*, pp. 39–48.

U.S. Department of Health and Human Services. (1993a, August). *Fatal injuries to workers in the United States, 1980-1989: A decade of surveillance*. (DHHS [NIOSH] Publication No. 93-108). Washington, DC: National Institute for Occupational Safety and Health.

U.S. Department of Health and Human Services. (1993b). *NIOSH Alert: Request for assistance in preventing homicide in the workplace* (DHHS [NIOSH] Publication No. 93-109). Washington, DC: National Institute for Occupational Safety and Health.

U.S. Department of Labor. (1992). *Safer and healthier American workplaces through improving knowledge: Census of fatal occupational injuries*. Washington, DC: Bureau of Labor Statistics.

U.S. Department of Labor. (1993). *The Occupational Safety and Health Administration federal agency injury and illness database*. Washington, DC: Occupational Safety and Health Administration.

U.S. Department of Labor. (1994a, May). *Fatal workplace injuries in 1992: A collection of data and analysis* (USDOL Rep. No. 870). Washington, DC: Bureau of Labor Statistics.

U.S. Department of Labor. (1994b). *The Occupational Safety and Health Administration federal agency injury and illness database*. Washington, DC: Occupational Safety and Health Administration.

U.S. Office of Personnel Management. (1994). *Federal civilian workforce statistics: Employment and trends as of January 1994*. Washington, DC: Human Resources Systems Service, Office of Workforce Information, Statistical Analysis and Services Division.

11

Workplace Violence in an Urban Jail Setting

David A. Safran and Aldo J. Tartaglini

Correctional facilities are becoming increasingly violent workplaces (Holmes, 1995; Logan & Dilulio, 1993). As correctional theory has moved away from concepts emphasizing rehabilitation toward those emphasizing longer sentences and fewer amenities for inmates, there has been a dramatic increase in the size of the prison population (Cheek, 1984) and a corresponding increase in the proportion of inmates who are likely to engage in violent acts (Beck & Gilliard, 1994). Because exposure to violence is a significant aspect of correctional work, correctional facilities offer a unique perspective on violence in the workplace and may yield valuable insights into its correlates and concomitants.

Although exposure to violence is an inescapable part of correctional work, most research in this area has focused on violence *among* inmates. Thus, despite some evidence of a growing awareness of the adverse effects of law enforcement involvement with violence (Alkus & Padesky, 1983; Anderson & Bauer, 1987), there is a dearth of empirical literature on how exposure to violence affects corrections officers (Kratcoski, 1988). Even less is known about aspects of the correctional work environment (e.g., shift work, forced overtime, understaffing, prison design) and factors associated with the workforce itself that may potentiate workplace violence.

In this study we investigated exposure to workplace violence in a clinical sample of 807 correction officers. Demographic, employment, psychodiagnostic, and incident-related variables were examined to identify potential predictors of violence within the correctional milieu.

Given the inherent dangerousness of urban jail settings, we expected that most officers would report some exposure to workplace violence. As in previous studies (e.g., Shawver & Dickover, 1986), we hypothesized that male officers would report a higher frequency of exposure to violence than would female officers.

Consistent with Toch's (1969, 1992) observation of the importance of characterological attributes in individuals who are prone to violence, we expected that officers diagnosed with either a substance abuse problem or a personality disorder would report more episodes of exposure to violence. Substance abuse in particular was expected to be found among subjects most prone to violence exposure (Monahan, 1981). By contrast, officers diagnosed with a mood disorder were expected to report fewer exposures (Guze, 1976).

Method

The participants in this study were drawn from a clinical sample of 1,024 corrections officers who had been studied previously to determine the nature, scope, and work-related impact of psychological disorders among correction officers (Tartaglini & Safran, 1995). The subjects were employed in a large urban jail setting and were assessed at a departmental clinic after complaining of debilitating psychological distress. Psychologists who were employed by the department but who were not affiliated with the current investigation assessed the officers and diagnosed them according to criteria from the revised third edition of the *Diagnostic and Statistical Manual of Mental Disorders* (*DSM–III–R*).

Subjects' clinical charts were reviewed to obtain demographic and employment data (e.g., age, sex, age at time of entry into the department, current employment status); psychodiagnostic classification; and frequency and type of exposure to violence.

Because of the unreliability of self-report measures of violence, we used a more objective index: workers' compensation claims. The measure was understood to represent only a rough index of exposure to violence. For example, incidents that did not result in reported injuries were not counted. We also assumed that officers would tend to overreport incidents of violence exposure on workers' compensation forms to ensure future benefits should their injuries result in a disabling condition. Thus, although somewhat vulnerable to Type I error in cases in which injury was alleged, the measure was considered to be less prone to Type II error.

The following variables were coded from each subject's chart: (a) demographic data—age and sex; (b) employment data—length of tenure with the department, age at entry into the department, current status (i.e., active duty, retired, terminated); (c) clinical data—*DSM–III–R* diagnoses, which were grouped into clusters to facilitate statistical analysis (mood disorders; adjustment disorders; anxiety disorders; substance abuse; personality disorders; phase of life, life circumstance, and marital and family problems; occupational problem; uncomplicated bereavement; and malingering/none; and (d) data related to violent incidents—frequency, latency of first exposure to violence (i.e., length of time between when officer was hired and date of first episode of violence exposure), and mean interval between violent episodes (for subjects with more than two episodes).

A violence exposure episode was coded for each workers' compensation claim filed for an injury resulting from assaultive behavior by inmates, injuries received during the course of responding to inmate altercations, and injuries sustained in altercations with other officers. The severity of injuries and the overall veracity of claims were not assessed.

After initial study of the entire sample, the subjects were divided into subgroups for additional analysis. To categorize subjects according to degree of violence exposure, the following subgroups were examined: (a) subjects with no reported violent incidents, (b) subjects with only one reported exposure, (c) subjects who had two or more exposures to violence, and (d) subjects whose exposure to violence included an assault or altercation involving other staff. Subjects who left the department for various reasons (e.g., resignation, disability retirement, termination) during the study period also were examined.

Results

Whole Sample

Table 1 shows characteristics of the entire sample. The results suggest that direct, injury-producing exposure to violence was not necessarily experienced by the majority of officers. More than half (53.8%) of the sample reported no exposure to violence, 25.9% of the sample reported only one incident of direct exposure, and 20.3% reported two or more exposures.

Significant differences across sex and diagnosis were found for total frequency of exposure to violent episodes. Male officers reported involvement in more episodes of workplace violence than did female officers ($Z = 8.357$, $p = .000$, Mann-Whitney U test). Complementing this was that, of the officers who reported no exposure to violence, 72.6% were women ($M = 92.872$, $SD = 1$, $p = .000$).

Officers with a diagnosis of mood disorder reported significantly fewer exposures to violence than did officers in any other diagnostic category ($H = 23.43$, $p = .00$, Kruskal-Wallis test). Officers with a substance abuse diagnosis reported a greater frequency of exposure to violence than did those in the other diagnostic categories ($H = 23.43$, $p = .00$, Kruskal-Wallis test). There was a trend toward more exposures to violence in officers with a diagnosis of personality disorder, but this was not significant.

Officers Who Reported No Exposure to Violence

This group was composed largely of female officers (see Table 1). Life circumstance problems (including phase of life, marital and family problems) and mood disorders were the most prevalent diagnoses in this subgroup (see Table 2). The length of tenure for this group was shorter than that of the other groups studied ($H = 98.59$, $p < .005$), leaving open the possibility that these subjects' lack of exposure to violence was mainly a function of their not having been employed long enough to experience such episodes.

Officers With One Exposure to Violence

As in those officers who reported no exposure to violence, the most prevalent diagnoses in this group were life circumstance problems and mood

Table 1. Characteristics of the Sample and Exposure to Violence ($N = 807$)

Variable	Entire sample		No exposure		One exposure		>Two exposures	
	M	*SD*	*M*	*SD*	*M*	*SD*	*M*	*SD*
Men								
N	296		109		76		111	
Length of tenure (years)	9.4	4.0	8.1	3.6	9.0	4.0	11.0	3.8
Age at entry into department	26.4	3.8	26.9	3.9	26.2	3.8	26.0	3.8
Total number of claims filed[a]	3.6	3.4	1.5	1.7	2.4	1.5	6.3	3.6
Number of claims: Inmate violence	1.6	2.2	—	—	1.0	0.1	3.7	2.3
Number of claims: Staff-on-staff violence	0.0	0.2	—	—	0.0	0.1	0.1	0.2
Total number of claims related to violence	1.7	2.2	—	—	1.0	0.0	3.7	2.3
First exposure to violence posthiring (years)	—	—	—	—	4.0	3.0	2.3	1.6
Interval between violence exposures (years)	—	—	—	—	—	—	2.2	1.2
Women								
N	511		325		133		53	
Length of tenure (years)	7.5	2.8	7.1	2.5	7.8	2.6	9.4	3.7
Age at entry into department (years)	26.8	3.9	27.1	3.9	26.6	4.0	26.0	3.5
Total number of claims filed[a]	1.9	2.0	1.3	1.5	2.5	1.9	4.7	2.2
Number of claims: Inmate violence	0.5	0.8	—	—	0.9	0.2	2.3	0.8
Number of claims: Staff-on-staff violence	0.0	0.2	—	—	0.0	0.2	0.2	0.4
Total number of claims related to violence	0.5	0.8	—	—	1.0	0.0	2.5	0.8
First exposure to violence posthiring (years)	—	—	—	—	3.2	2.1	2.8	2.5
Interval between violence exposures (years)	—	—	—	—	—	—	2.3	1.4

Dashes indicate *not applicable*.

[a]Includes accidents and violent incidents.

Table 2. Distribution of Diagnostic Clusters Among Groups (%)

Diagnostic clusters	Entire sample	No-violence group	Low-violence group (1 exposure)	High-violence group (2 + exposures)	Staff violence	Staff attrition
Mood disorders	16.98	18.43	18.18	11.59	4.0	26.85
Adjustment disorders	10.53	11.52	8.61	10.37	0.0	12.04
Anxiety disorders	7.43	6.91	7.18	9.15	8.0	8.33
Substance abuse	4.83	3.00	3.83	10.98	0.0	13.89
Personality disorders	2.60	1.61	3.35	3.66	0.0	1.85
Life circumstances	39.41	41.94	39.23	33.54	56.0	25.93
Occupational problem	4.09	3.23	5.26	4.88	12.0	2.78
Bereavement	4.09	3.92	6.22	1.83	8.0	1.85
Malingering/none	10.04	9.45	8.13	14.02	12.0	6.48

disorders. Again, most of the sample was composed of female officers. The majority of officers in this group were exposed to violence during their first 3 years of employment. However, 47.37% of the officers reported that their exposure to violence occurred after 3 or more years on the job.

Officers With Two or More Exposures to Violence

Male officers reported more exposures to violence than did female officers in this subgroup ($Z = 4.355$, $p = .000$; see Table 1). The most prevalent diagnoses were the V Codes (clusters 6 to 9 in Table 2), followed by mood and substance abuse disorders. The rate of substance abuse for these officers (10.98%) was second only to officers who had left the department (see Table 2).

Staff-on-Staff Violence

This group was composed mainly of women (17 of 25 subjects). There were no significant differences across diagnoses for frequency of exposure to violence in these subjects. However, 88% of the sample were diagnosed with V Code conditions, and no subjects had diagnoses of either substance abuse or personality disorder. Of the 25 officers in the subgroup, 7 had their only reported exposure to violence in incidents involving other staff members.

The mean length of tenure for officers in this subgroup ($Ms = 10$ and 9.2 years for men and women, respectively) was longer than that observed in all other subgroups except for those who had two or more exposures to violence. Male officers entered the department later in life than subjects in any other subgroup ($M = 28.6$ years). Conversely, female officers entered the department at an earlier age ($M = 25.8$ years) than all other subjects.

Interestingly, staff attrition for these subjects (4%) was lower than in any other subgroup: 13.38% for the entire sample, 14.29% for the no-violence-exposure group, 11.48% for the single-episode group, and 13.41% for the high-violence-exposure group.

Staff Attrition

This group contained an equal number of male and female officers ($n = 54$). Again, male officers reported significantly more exposures to violence than did female officers ($Z = 2.197$, $p = .03$). The proportion of officers diagnosed with a substance abuse disorder was higher in these subjects than in all other groups (see Table 2). The longer officers had been on the job, the higher their total exposures to violence ($H = 10.62$, $p < .005$). No other significant findings were observed in this subgroup.

Exposure to Violence: Temporal Aspects

First exposure to violence. To examine the distribution of first exposures to violence over time, we measured the frequency of such episodes for the following intervals (reflecting length of employment): less than 1 year, 1–3 years, and more than 3 years. First exposures to violence (60.3%) occurred most frequently during the first and second intervals of employment (0–3 years; $M = 19.56$, $SD = 2$, $p = .000$). Officers whose first exposure to violence occurred earlier in their careers (0–3 years) subsequently experienced more exposures than officers whose first exposure occurred later (after 3 years; $H = 25.81$, $p < .005$).

Staff tenure and exposure to violence. An analysis of the entire sample was conducted to further explore time on the job as a predictor of exposure to workplace violence. As in the attrited personnel, length of tenure was directly related to the extent of violence exposure ($H = 98.59$, $p < .005$). The entire sample was then divided into a group of low-tenure (<8 years on the job) and high-tenure ($\geq$8 years on the job) participants. Female officers predominated in the low-tenure group (72.4%), whereas there was essentially an equal distribution of male and female officers in the high-tenure group. Subjects with more time on the job were more frequently given a substance abuse diagnosis, whereas subjects with less tenure were more frequently diagnosed as having a personality disorder or a V Code condition ($M = 16.12$, $SD = 1$, $p = .04$).

The proportion of male and female officers reporting high exposure to violence (>2 incidents) was lower in the low-tenure group than in the high-tenure group. The overall proportion of female officers in the low-tenure group was much higher than in the high-tenure group (approaching 3:1), raising the possibility that the presence of more female officers exerted a moderating effect on exposure to violence in the male officers. Moreover, the low-tenure group contained more officers who subsequently resigned their positions than did the high-tenure group, possibly indicating a relative lack of investment in the job. Finally, officers hired 8 or more years ago reported earlier exposure to workplace violence than did those hired less than 8 years ago, suggesting a possible cohort effect ($Z = 4.093$, $p = .000$, Mann-Whitney U test). That is, officers hired more than 8 years ago may represent a distinct cohort, one with demographic and psychological attributes that predispose them to a relatively high rate of exposure to workplace violence. Evidence that supports this hypothesis includes the fact that the high-tenure group had a more equal distribution of men and women, may have contained more officers with a military background, and may have included more individuals who had a specific interest in correctional work as a career.

When the officers in the low-tenure group were examined separately, we found that male officers again had a higher frequency of exposures to violence than did the female officers ($Z = 3.6$, $p = .000$). Male officers were diagnosed more frequently with a substance abuse disorder, whereas female officers carried more diagnoses in all other categories ($M = 25.05$, $SD = 1$, $p = .002$).

In a separate analysis of the high-tenure group, we found that male officers once again had a higher frequency of exposures to violence than did female officers ($Z = 6.78$, $p = .000$). Male officers were more frequently diagnosed with a substance abuse disorder, whereas mood and personality disorder diagnoses predominated among female officers ($M = 32.29$, $SD = 1$, $p = .000$).

The analyses of staff tenure basically reinforced the finding that violence exposure occurs more frequently in substance-abusing male officers. They also support the finding that early exposure to workplace violence is associated with an increased frequency of such exposures in the future.

Discussion

Overall, our findings suggest that long-term, substance-abusing male employees in urban correctional environments are at increased risk for exposure to workplace violence. Such individuals tend to experience their first exposure to workplace violence relatively early in their careers, and they subsequently experience more frequent episodes than female counterparts who do not engage in substance abuse.

Given the volatility of urban jail settings, where inmates are either serving short sentences for petty crimes, being held pending trial because they could not afford bail, are awaiting trial for serious offenses, or already have been sentenced and are awaiting transport to state prisons, the prevalence of exposure to workplace violence was not as high as expected. However, this could reflect a selection artifact, inaccurate or inconsistent reporting of violent episodes, or other factors. Nevertheless, a substantial proportion of the officers in our sample (46.2%) did report exposure to injury-producing violence on the job, confirming that the correctional workplace is indeed at times a violent one.

Among the more consistent findings of the study is the fact that male officers endured much more direct exposure to injury-producing workplace violence than did their female counterparts. It also appears that when there is a greater proportion of female officers, male officers experience fewer exposures to violence. This may be attributable to several factors. Female officers may bring skills and attributes to the job that have the effect of diffusing violence before it occurs (Zimmer, 1987). They may exert an overall moderating effect on the correctional milieu, raising the threshold for conflict or expressions of violence among inmates. Finally, female officers may tend to evoke less intense forms of resistance and destructive behavior from inmates and/or ameliorate provocative behavior on the part of male officers. Although female officers appear to have a violence-reducing effect on the inmate population, it also is the case that they are overrepresented in reported incidents of staff-on-staff violence. Nonetheless, these occurrences appear to be rare (17 of 25 incidents in a sample of 807 involved female officers).

Another finding is the close association between a diagnosis of substance abuse and a high rate of involvement with workplace violence. The relationship between these variables was most apparent for the male officers. In fact, all of the substance-abusing subjects in the high-violence group were men, as were most of the personality-disordered officers in the high-violence group. These findings suggest a possible profile of officers who are likely to experience workplace violence as being primarily male, characterologically impaired, and prone to addictive or impulsive behavior.

By contrast, officers diagnosed with a mood disorder or life circumstance problem were least likely to report exposure to workplace violence. Such officers may have been preoccupied with personal issues and relatively less "available" for exposure to workplace violence.

The analysis of staff tenure raises the issue of whether involvement in workplace violence is in fact an ineluctable aspect of the correctional work environment. The clear relationship between time on the job and incidents of reported exposure to violence would seem to indicate that such exposure is inevitable. However, the fact that more than half the sample had no reported incidents of violence exposure suggests that this may not be the case. In fact, violence exposure may reflect personal, interpersonal, and interorganizational dynamics as much as factors beyond anyone's control.

This is reinforced by the observation that, regardless of length of tenure, male officers with a diagnosis of substance abuse were more likely to experience exposure to workplace violence than were their male and female counterparts who did not meet criteria for this diagnosis. Was substance abuse a response to a harsh work environment, or was it a reflection of characterological impairment that somehow predisposes an individual to violent encounters? Is it possible to construct a profile of employees who are most likely to experience workplace violence? Is it possible to screen such individuals before they are hired to effectively reduce workplace violence? These questions, although beyond the scope of the current investigation, are nonetheless worth addressing in future studies if researchers are to expand the workplace violence database and broaden its practical utility.

Conclusion

In this investigation we explored incident-related, demographic, and clinical correlates of workplace violence in an urban correctional setting. The results point to empirical relationships among sex, diagnosis, length of employment, and reported exposures to workplace violence in corrections officers. These findings, although preliminary, may offer insights into the phenomenology of workplace violence.

That most subjects in this study reported no exposure to workplace violence raises the issue of whether passive exposure to violence (i.e., witnessing violence among inmates, violence between staff and inmates, etc.) has any unique significance for officers who experience it. For example, aside from untoward mental health effects, passive exposure to violence may lower the threshold for subsequent active participation in workplace violence in some officers.

To further elucidate the etiology and nature of workplace violence among correction officers and related populations, future researchers should use both clinical and nonclinical samples in diverse work settings to examine variables such as the extent and nature of preemployment screening, prior crisis management training, incidence or severity of violence exposure episodes (both direct and passive), nature of reported injuries, time of occurrence, location of incident, staff morale, and overall level of organizational functioning. Future investigators also should conduct a more thorough assessment of subjects' psychological characteristics using relatively objective psychometric indices such as standardized inventories, rating scales, symptom checklists, and so on. Finally, researchers should use prospective longitudinal designs to maximize data yield and reduce threats to validity.

References

Alkus, S., & Padesky, C. (1983). Special problems of police officers: Stress-related issues and interventions. *Counseling Psychologist, 11*, 55–64.

Anderson, W., & Bauer, B. (1987). Law enforcement officers: The consequences of exposure to violence. *Journal of Counseling and Development, 65*, 381–384.

Beck, A. J., & Gilliard, D. K. (1994). Prisoners in 1994. *Bureau of Justice Statistics Bulletin, NCJ-151654.*

Cheek, F. (1984). *Stress management for correctional officers and their families.* Lanham, MD: American Correctional Association.

Guze, S. (1976). *Criminality and psychiatric disorders.* New York: Oxford University Press.

Holmes, S. A. (1995, February 6). Inmate violence is on the rise as federal prisons change. *New York Times,* pp. A1, A14.

Kratcoski, P. (1988). The implications of research explaining prison violence and disruption. *Federal Probation, 52*, 27–32.

Logan, C. H., & Dilulio, J. J., Jr. (1993). Ten deadly myths about crime and punishment. *The Correctional Psychologist, 25*, 1–6.

Monahan, J. (1981). *Predicting violent behavior.* Beverly Hills, CA: Sage.

Shawver, L., & Dickover, R. (1986). Exploding a myth. *Corrections Today, 48*, 30–34.

Tartaglini, A. J., & Safran, D. A. (1995, September). *A topography of psychological disorders among correction officers.* Poster session presented at the American Psychological Association Work and Stress Conference, Washington, DC.

Toch, H. (1969). *Violent men.* Chicago: Aldine.

Toch, H. (1992). *Violent men* (rev. ed.). Washington, DC: American Psychological Association.

Zimmer, L. (1987). How women reshape the prison guard role. *Gender and Society, 1,* 415–431.

12

Correlates of Risk for Conflict Among New York City Traffic Agents

Elizabeth Brondolo, Thomas Jelliffe,
Christopher J. Quinn, Wendy Tunick,
and Elizabeth Melhado

New York City traffic enforcement agents (TEAs) issue summons for vehicular and parking violations. They travel by foot or in cars through all five boroughs and are frequently confronted by motorists and pedestrians who are angry about receiving these tickets. Since 1990, there has been an average of more than 500 serious confrontations or assaults per year. Although these physical confrontations are serious, agents also face a more chronic problem: frequent verbal harassment from the public. In this chapter we describe rates of assaults on agents and present the results of analyses conducted to evaluate demographic, psychosocial, and organizational predictors of verbal conflict with the public.

Background

The primary mission of the enforcement staff within the New York City Department of Transportation (DOT) is to facilitate safe and efficient traffic flow. However, the DOT also generates significant revenue for New York City, with the 5,340,600 tickets issued in 1994 providing approximately $159 million in revenue. More concretely, an average summons-issuance agent, writing 35 tickets per day at an average collectible cost per ticket of $29.75, is a source of almost $200,000 in revenue each year.

Preparation of this chapter was supported by Grant R03MH5930-01 from the National Institutes of Health and Grant 9500691 from the American Heart Association to Elizabeth Brondolo. We gratefully acknowledge the support of the agents and supervisors at the New York City Department of Transportation; the assistance of the St. John's research team, including Kwame Alexander, Caren Baruch, Cristina Benedetto, Jennifer Franklin, Robin Masheb, Elizabeth Melhado, Tanya Stockhammer, and Jackie Stores; and the statistical advice of Joseph Schwartz of the State University of New York at Stony Brook.

Table 1. Assaults and Confrontations for Enforcement Staff: 1990–1994

Year	FTE head count[a]	Assaults	Confron-tations	Total[b]	Summon count (in 1,000s)	Assault rate[c] adjusted for SPPD
1,990	—	158	372	530	7,628.9	2.07
1,991	1,947	176	432	608	8,909.5	1.98
1,992	1,895	190	392	582	8,909.5	2.13
1,993	1,818	184	346	530	6,394.1	2.88
1,994	1,459	134	296	430	5,340.6	2.53

[a]FTE = Full-time equivalent. The head counts are annualized averages reflecting the number of individuals with enforcement job titles whose duties involved risk of encounter with the public. Of these employess, 56% were involved in issuing summons.
[b]Combines assaults and confrontations.
[c]Rate of assault per 10 agents, per 100,000 summonses.

The DOT has several functions that involve contact with the public in an enforcement capacity. About half (56%) of the individuals in these enforcement positions are TEAs with ticket-writing responsibilities. Other functions include traffic control, towing, and emergency response. Average annualized head counts for employees in enforcement positions involving public contact are presented in Table 1.

There are three types of ticket-writing TEAs. Foot-patrol agents travel on foot in defined patrol areas and issue an average of 35 tickets per day. Motorized agents travel in cars throughout a larger patrol area and issue an average of 50 tickets per day. Business-district enforcement agents, whose mission is partially mandated by environmental regulations, patrol small, high-traffic areas. These agents have a dual mission: to issue tickets and to keep traffic moving, thereby reducing air pollution. These agents issue an average of 8–9 tickets per day. The DOT also has another independent unit, parking control, which includes 56 parking control specialists. These employees are more experienced, somewhat more highly paid, and travel throughout the five boroughs issuing tickets at a somewhat higher rate than the other groups of agents.

In general, agents travel alone throughout their patrol areas. Most are outfitted with portable radios and also are periodically visited by their field supervisors (lieutenants) who travel throughout the patrol areas. If they are confronted by a serious situation, they can radio for help. If the agents are injured seriously or if they will be able to press charges against the perpetrator, the agents can contact the Assault Investigations Unit (AIU). Personnel from the AIU then will work with the agent to get help for any injury and to press legal claims. The incidents reported to AIU are categorized as *assaults*, which involve a physical attack on the agent, or *confrontations*, which involve a motorist or pedestrian severely harassing the agent or attempting to destroy agency property (e.g., vehicles, meters, summons books, etc.).

Assault and Confrontation Rates: Data From the AIU

The rates of assault and confrontation for 1990–1994 are presented in Table 1. Of the assaults reported in 1994, 16 cases resulted in major injury to the agent, whereas 138 resulted in minor injuries.

The average annual rate of both assault and confrontation dropped since 1991, from a total of 608 in 1991 to 433 in 1994. However, this decrease appeared to be related to a drop in the head count for these enforcement functions. There were declines both in the number of agents overall and in the number of agents in some of the productive ticket-writing titles, including foot patrol. Because assaults and confrontations often, but not always, occur while an agent is issuing a ticket, the decrease in ticket issuance may represent a decrease in the opportunity for conflict.

Figure 1 contrasts the absolute number of assaults with the number of assaults adjusted for the number of tickets issued. Although the absolute number of incidents decreased, there was a small increase in the relative number of assaults adjusted for the rate of tickets issued.

An examination of the historical data suggests that a high percentage of the TEAs currently employed have been assaulted. Specifically, of the ticket-writing agents who are currently active, 26.8% have been assaulted at least once since 1992. Of those assaulted, 19.2% have been assaulted more than once. Among parking control specialists, 51.2% have been assaulted since 1992.

In February 1995, a new class of 117 agents began 2 months of training. By October, with just 6 months in the field, 30 agents (25.6% of the class) had been assaulted or confronted, with 11 of these agents assaulted or confronted more than once.

The fiscal costs of these assaults is significant, approaching $9.5 million per year. At any given time, there are about 100 agents on leave under workers' compensation grants authorized as a result of an assault. The DOT budget allows the agency to backfill roughly 70 of these positions each year, leaving 30 positions unfilled. Total costs are made up of costs related to workers' compensation payments to agents ($1,804,894), administrative costs for the workers' compensation unit ($137,000), costs associated with the replacement of 70 workers ($1,540,000), and lost revenue from unreplaced workers ($5,921,288). Lost revenue is calculated by considering the average number of tickets written for 30 agents, about 35 tickets per workday, for a collectible cost per ticket of $29.75.

Analyses are under way to evaluate demographic, psychosocial, and organizational predictors of assault. Currently, however, we have evaluated predictors of the more commonly occurring problem of verbal conflict with the public.

The St. John's University–New York City DOT Collaborative Project

Since 1992, St. John's University and the New York City DOT have been engaged in collaborative research. The goals of the research have been to

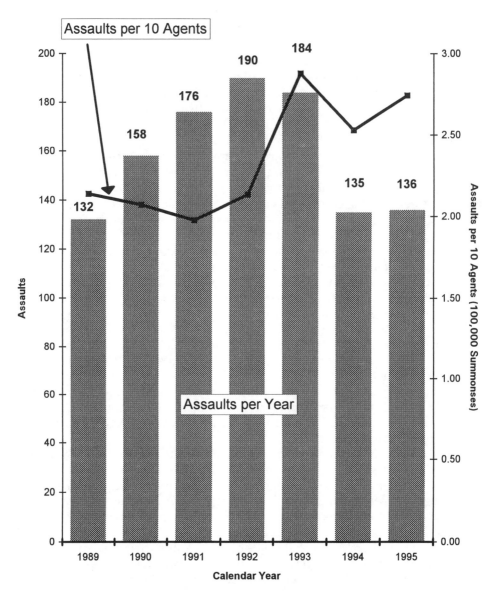

Figure 1. Assaults on traffic agents: 1989 through 1995. Absolute number of assaults versus assault rates adjusted for total tickets written.

study the cardiovascular correlates of interpersonal conflict and conflict coping style. As part of this research, and to help develop and evaluate a conflict management training program, we administered surveys inquiring about demographics, personality and coping, support, and conflict to TEAs and parking control specialists. Before administration, all protocols were reviewed with agency management and representatives of the four different unions representing these employees. Details of this study can be found in Brondolo et al. (1996) and are briefly reported here.

One purpose of the surveys was to identify predictors or correlates of interpersonal conflict between agents and the public. These conflicts often occur when agents are patrolling the streets and writing tickets. Motorists (or even pedestrians who once received a ticket) may attack an agent. Some of these conflicts involve verbal abuse consisting of insults, cursing, threats, or racial epithets. Physical abuse of the agents can include spitting, hitting, grabbing ticket books, among others. These conflicts, although predictable, are demoralizing for the TEAs.

Conflicts between TEAs and the public are somewhat different from the workplace conflicts typically investigated in communications and violence research. Unlike conflicts between supervisors and workers or among coworkers or family members, agent–motorist conflicts occur in public and between people who are strangers. These are short-term conflicts in which the TEA's goal is to end the conflict as quickly and safely as possible. A quick resolution is necessary to permit him or her to return to ticket writing. There is no need to resolve the conflict in a manner that encourages or facilitates further communication because the TEAs' patrol areas change regularly, so they are not likely to have ongoing relationships with the motorists.

The conflicts experienced by the TEAs are likely to evoke anger because they involve an attack that is perceived as serious, intentional, and unjustified (Harburg, Blakelock, & Roeper, 1979). From the agent's viewpoint, the motorist has violated the law. By issuing the ticket, the agent is simply doing his or her job. The harsh retaliatory responses shown by the motorists are perceived as being unfair by the TEAs.

Although all TEAs are at risk for conflict, there are wide variations in the frequency with which agents experience conflicts with the public. We examined whether we could identify demographic, organizational, and personality and coping correlates of verbal conflict with the public.

Study Description

Participants for this project were recruited from groups of TEAs and parking control specialists who were available in six large New York City DOT worksites. To date, surveys have been administered seven times (June 1993, October 1993, February 1994, June 1994, October 1994, January 1995, June 1995). The data presented in this chapter were obtained from the Time 1 sample in June–July 1993 and involved 227 experienced agents. These 227 agents represented 84% of the agents available at the worksites included in the study during the June 1993 test period.

Fifty-one percent of the Time 1 participants was women. The mean age of participants was 36 years (range = 21–64 years). Of these respondents, 52% were African American, 27% Hispanic, 14% White, 3% Asian, and 4% "other." The starting salary for TEAs was about $20,000 per year. Although there were no formal educational requirements for these positions, 88% of the agents had a high school diploma or a general equivalency diploma, and 35% had attended some college.

Method

The variables considered as potential correlates of conflict rate included demographic, organizational, and personality and coping variables. Demographic variables included age, sex, ethnicity, height, weight, and education. Organizational factors included years of experience, productivity (number of tickets issued the previous day), job title (foot agent, motorized agent, or midtown enforcement agent), shift (morning or evening), and worksite location (Manhattan vs. the other boroughs). At the time the study was initially conducted, the DOT was divided into two administrative structures, one for Manhattan and one for the other boroughs. Organizational variables also included perceived support from coworkers and supervisors and burnout. Perceived support was assessed with a modified version of the Job Content Instrument Support subscales (Karasek et al., 1985), and burnout was assessed with the Emotional Exhaustion subscale of the Maslach Burnout Inventory (Maslach & Jackson, 1981).

The personality and coping variables included in these surveys reflected our interest in examining the ways agents managed their anger during interpersonal conflicts. This was consistent with the primary focus of the larger study, which was investigating the relationships among conflict, anger, and workday blood pressure. Other research has demonstrated that hostile attitudes toward others and different styles of anger management have been linked with hypertension and other cardiovascular diseases (Harburg, Gleiberman, Russell, & Cooper, 1991; Helmers, Posluszny, & Krantz, 1994).

The scales chosen allowed examination of the effects of hostile attitudes toward others, characteristic methods for managing distress and anger, as well as more situation-specific methods of managing anger. Trait hostility was assessed with the Buss Aggression Survey Hostility subscale (Buss & Perry, 1992). Measures of trait anger and characteristic style of anger expression were drawn from the State-Trait Anger Expression Scale (STAXI; Spielberger et al., 1985). The characteristic anger expression scale has three subscales measuring an outward aggressive expression of anger (Anger-Out); an inward, resentful suppression of anger (Anger-In); and a calmer, reflective method of anger expression (Anger-Control).

Measures of job-specific coping also were included. These scales were designed to assess how agents managed their anger during conflicts with the public. The job-specific anger-expression scale included five items (i.e., During a conflict, I . . . "feel upset and show it," "speak sharply," "argue," "show my feelings," "express my feelings"). The job-specific anger-suppression scale included four items (i.e., During a conflict, I . . . "try to hide my feelings," "feel mad but hold it in," "feel upset but I don't show it," "boil inside but I don't show it"). The job-specific calm-communication scale included eight items (i.e., During a conflict, I . . . "calm down before I speak," "try to understand how the motorist felt," "think it through before speaking," "speak politely and calmly," "can stop myself from losing my temper," "calm down faster than most people," "am patient," "try to be tolerant and understanding").

Table 2. Percentage of Agents Experiencing Conflict With the Public

Incidents	Verbal conflict		Physical conflict (previous 2 months)
	Previous day	Average day	
0	37	9	81
1 or 2	28	35	13
3 or more	35	56	6

The dependent measures for the study included self-reported rates of verbal and physical conflict with the public. To assess the frequency of conflict, agents were asked to indicate (a) the number of times they were harassed (i.e., cursed at, insulted, threatened, etc.) by a member of the public on the day before testing; (b) the number of times they were harassed on a typical day; and (c) the number of times in the past 2 months in which they were physically confronted (i.e., punched, kicked, spit on, etc.). In the analyses reported here, the log of the previous day's conflict rate was the dependent variable. The previous day's conflict rate was hypothesized to be less affected by reporting biases than was report of the average number of conflicts.

Verbal and Physical Conflict

Verbal conflict was relatively frequent, occurring an average of 3.4 times per day. There were variations among agents in the frequency with which they experienced conflict (see Table 2). Thirty-seven percent of agents reported having no conflicts on the day before testing, whereas 35% had three or more. Physical conflict was reported less frequently, with only 19% of the sample reporting a physical confrontation within the previous 2 months. Not all physical confrontations reported in the survey data were reported to the AIU.

The frequency of verbal conflict was associated with the rate of physical encounters. Of the 40 agents who reported having had one or more physical confrontations within the past 2 months, all reported having one or more incidents of verbal conflict on an average day. Of those 78% (31 of 40) reported having three or more verbal conflicts on a routine day. None of the individuals who reported having no verbal conflicts on an average day reported having had physical conflicts within the past 2 months.

Correlates of Verbal Conflict

To examine the relationships among demographic, organizational, and personality and coping clusters and the rate of conflict on the previous workday, we conducted two types of analyses. To evaluate the combined effectiveness of these variables in predicting rate of conflict, we used a hierarchical multiple regression analysis with variables entered in clusters as described earlier. The overall R^2 for the full equation was .29; how-

Table 3. Cross-Sectional Regression of Risk for Conflict on Work-Related and Personality Variables ($n = 139$)

Variable	Standardized estimate	t	p
Work related			
Ticket rate	0.24	3.12	.002
Burnout	0.21	2.55	.012
Personality and coping			
Calm communication	−0.17	−2.13	.035
STAXI: Anger-In	0.26	2.81	.006
Trait hostility	−0.34	−3.68	.001

Note: For work-related variables, group $F(2, 138) = 8.48$, $p < .003$, partial $R^2 = .09$. For personality and coping variables, group $F(3, 138) = 6.00$, $p < .001$, partial $R^2 = .11$.

ever, the adjusted R^2 was only .11 because there were many nonsignificant variables included in the analysis. The significant variables in the full analysis were trait hostility (standardized estimate = -0.24, $p = .05$, STAXI Anger-In (standardized estimate = 0.33, $p = .03$), and job-specific calm-communication (standardized estimate = -0.28, $p < .02$).

To delete variables from the equation, we examined univariate effects. If variables were not significant in either the multivariate or univariate analyses, or if they were redundant with other variables, we deleted them from the equation.

Table 3 shows the best regression equation. Initially, we did not collect data on ticket-writing rates and had to use the average rate from the other time periods to generate an average rate of tickets issued. This average was available only for 139 of the agents who participated in later test dates, and this was the sample size available for the regression. Relations of the other demographic and personality variables to conflict rate remained the same when the full sample was used. With this combination of demographic, work, and personality and coping variables, we were able to predict almost 20% of the variance in the previous day's conflict rate. The most important of the work-related factors was the rate of ticket writing. The level of productivity or the number of tickets issued can be considered a proxy for the opportunities for conflict. The more tickets agents issue, the more opportunities for conflict they have. The correlation between the Time 1 conflict rate and the average ticket-writing rate was .25 ($p < .005$). The ticket-writing rate contributed about 6% of the variance. The other work-related variables (except for emotional exhaustion) were related to degree of opportunity for writing summons. Specifically, effects related to job title were primarily associated with differences among job titles in ticket-writing rates. For example, business district agents reported an average of 1.39 conflicts on the previous workday, foot-patrol agents reported an average of 2.31 conflicts, and motorized agents reported an average of 2.62 conflicts.

Similarly, the division between Manhattan and the boroughs proved to be nonsignificant when differences in the ticket-writing rate were controlled. This might have been a function of location differences in the distribution of different job titles. Many more of the Manhattan agents were business district enforcement agents, who customarily issue many fewer tickets than other agent groups. More fine-grained analyses of the differences among specific worksites might reveal additional information. Finally, the morning shifts issued more tickets than did the evening shifts, but the effects associated with time of shift were not significant when the level of ticket writing was controlled.

Emotional exhaustion or burnout contributed to the conflict rate. To evaluate this further, we divided agents at the median burnout score into high- and low-burnout groups. High-burnout agents reported more conflicts ($M = 2.72$) than did low-burnout agents ($M = 1.42$).

The variables that contributed the most to the equation were those assessing personality and coping, contributing about 11% of the variance. Again, agents were divided at the median into high- and low-calm-communication groups. Agents with high scores had fewer conflicts ($M = 1.66$) than did those with low scores ($M = 2.51$).

Both characteristic ($r = .15, p < .001$) and job-specific ($r = .12, p = .08$) suppressed anger was positively associated with conflict rate. The effects for characteristic suppressed anger become stronger when controlling for trait hostility ($r = .23, p < .0002$). Surprisingly, hostility was negatively associated with conflict rate. These effects were observed only when the level of suppressed anger was controlled ($r = -.20, p < .003$).

No demographic variable was significantly associated with conflict rate. There were no sex, race, age, education, or physical size effects. No social support variable was concurrently associated with conflict rate.

In summary, opportunity for conflict was a major predictor of frequency of conflict. The more tickets agents issued, the more likely they were to face an angry motorist. Not surprisingly, this finding has major implications for the agency. To increase traffic efficiency and generate revenue, managers must urge agents to patrol in high-traffic and high-congestion areas, which also increases the risk of conflict. The push for ticket-writing productivity engenders risk. Together, these findings suggest that the agency must work to find ways to balance the need for productivity against the deleterious impact of repeated conflict.

The issues related to the effects associated with personality and coping were more complex. It was clear that in cross-sectional analyses, a calm coping style was associated with relatively fewer conflicts. One possibility is that it is easier to avoid conflict if one is able to remain calm. The other possibility is that it is easier to remain calm if one has fewer conflicts. In focus and treatment groups, agents reported that they were able to start the day relatively calmly but became more agitated in the face of repeated assaults.

The findings also reveal a positive relationship between suppressed anger and conflict risk, combined with a negative relationship between trait hostility and conflict risk. One way to interpret these findings is that both measures tapped affect and cognition. However, the measure of suppressed anger (STAXI Anger-In) was a better measure of resentful angry affect, whereas the trait hostility measure was primarily a measure of suspicious attitudes, although it contains items assessing resentful angry affect. In fact, trait hostility was highly correlated with characteristically suppressed anger ($r = .52$, $p < .001$). Therefore, individuals who are habitually suspicious also are likely to suppress their anger in many circumstances.

The habitual suppression of angry affect appears to be relatively detrimental. Our research suggests that it is associated not only with increased risk for conflict but also with increased burnout and anger about the conflicts (Brondolo et al., 1996). The failure to adequately express angry feelings may leave agents sensitized to further hostile attacks. Attacks from the public may be problematic for this group because the majority of agents are members of minority groups and may experience racist comments in their personal lives as well. The agents recognize that aggressive retaliation directed at the motorist would violate standards of professional conduct. However, they need appropriate and effective strategies for handling the feelings evoked by these disturbing incidents because no one simply gets used to hostile attacks.

The cognitive dimension of hostility (i.e., the component left when the variance attributable to suppressed anger is controlled) potentially may be beneficial to agents. It may be appropriate to view motorists as being capable of acting in manipulative and selfish ways when trying to park in New York City. Our clinical experience suggests that agents who persisted in the belief that people "should" act nicely were more distressed than those who were able to accept that people often behave badly when they are being punished. Suspicious agents understood that it was unwise to trust sweet-talking motorists because they often get angry when their smooth words are not effective in persuading the agent to withdraw the ticket.

An example may help illustrate this idea. One agent was invested in trying to educate the public. A mother of several young children, she wanted people to think of her as a caring and intelligent person. For her, one of the benefits of the job was the opportunity to educate people about the traffic rules. When motorists asked her "Why did I get this ticket?" she often would try to explain in a reasonable way the reasons. However, many times when motorists say "Why did I get this ticket?" they really mean "How could you do this to me? How will I pay for this? Why did I have to get caught this time?"

If motorists are thinking these other thoughts, attempts to explain the technical violation will make them more angry. These reasonable explanations serve only to remind them that they are guilty and deserve their misfortune. Consequently, they may escalate the attack on the agent if the agent persists in trying to get them to understand that the agent was just trying to do his or her job (and is not really an unkind or uncaring individual). By contrast, agents who are less trusting and less invested in communicating with the public may offer a simple explanation when confronted with the question "Why did I get that ticket?" and then walk away. They do not require the motorists to display comprehension or understanding, and they do not become visibly disturbed if the motorist appears to think they are uncaring or unintelligent.

These suspicious attitudes, although potentially beneficial in dealing with motorists, are not necessarily beneficial in the workplace. Specifically, the findings from the surveys indicate that trait hostility is related negatively to perceived supervisor support. In clinical sessions, supervisors often reported feeling somewhat intimidated when approaching the agents to provide guidance or support. Consequently, supervisors may miss opportunities to bolster the morale and confidence of agents or to teach them new conflict management skills. This suggests that one challenge for the agency is to help agents develop a more distant approach toward the public without compromising their relationships with their coworkers and supervisors.

These data suggest that interventions aimed at reducing conflict between TEAs and motorists have several components. One component of the program might be targeted at the agents' behavior during ticket writing. For agents to be able to safely and efficiently issue many tickets, they need to be aware of their emotional impact on the street. Trainers could examine the agents' ticket-writing style, assessing the impact of nonverbal and verbal behavior displayed while agents are on patrol. By minimizing provocativeness and maximizing the communication of confidence and authority, agents may reduce the incidence of conflict. The second component of the program might target anger expression style. A variety of techniques, including communication skills training and exposure therapy, might be helpful to decrease the agent's use of a resentful, suppressed style and increase the use of a calm communication style (Brondolo, DiGuiseppe, & Tafrate, 1996). Finally, a cognitive intervention might be used to address agents' attitudes toward the public and supervisors. This might help agents develop one perspective for handling conflict in the field and another for handling conflict at the worksite or in other personal relationships.

In summary, our data suggest that conflict is a critical fact of life for New York City traffic agents. There are significant individual differences in the frequency of conflict, and organizational and personality and coping factors influence the rate of conflict. These findings suggest that the effects of personality style must be seen in the context of the workplace. Different components of a personality dimension, such as hostility, can have different effects depending on the demands facing the employee and his or her supervisors. Basic research on the nature of interpersonal conflict in different workforces can help tailor the design of interventions specific to the needs of the employees in high-risk occupations.

References

Brondolo, E., Contrada, R., Masheb, R., Stores, J., Harburg, E., & Schwartz, J. (1996). *Hostility and response to interpersonal conflict among NYC traffic agents.* Unpublished manuscript.

Brondolo, E., DiGuiseppe, R., & Tafrate, R. (1996). Exposure therapy for anger problems. Unpublished manuscript.

Buss, A., & Perry, M. (1992). The aggression questionnaire. *Journal of Personality and Social Psychology, 63*, 452–459.

Harburg, E., Blakelock, E., & Roeper, P. (1979). Resentful and reflective coping with arbitrary authority and blood pressure: Detroit. *Psychosomatic Medicine, 41*, 189–200.

Harburg, E., Gleiberman, L., Russell, M., & Cooper, M. L. (1991). Anger-coping styles and blood pressure in black and white males: Buffalo, New York. *Psychosomatic Medicine, 53*, 153–164.

Helmers, K., Posluszny, D., & Krantz, D. (1994). Association of hostility and coronary artery disease: A review of studies. In A. W. Siegman & T. W. Smith (Eds.), *Anger, hostility and the heart* (pp. 67–96). Hillsdale, NJ: Erlbaum.

Karasek, R. A., Gordon, G., Pietrkowsky, C., Frese, M., Pieper, C., Schwartz, J. E., Fry, L., & Schirer, D. (1985). *Job Content Instrument: Questionnaire and user's guide*. Lowell, MA: University of Massachusetts.

Maslach, C., & Jackson, S. (1981). *Maslach Burnout Inventory manual*. Palo Alto, CA: Consulting Psychologists Press.

Spielberger, C., Johnson, E., Russell, S., Crane, R., Jacobs, G., & Worden, T. (1985). The experience and expression of anger: Construction and validation of an anger expression scale. In M. A. Chesney & R. H. Rosenman (Eds.), *Anger and hostility in cardiovascular and behavioral disorders* (pp. 5–30). Washington, DC: Hemisphere.

13

Violence Turned Inward: Police Suicide in the Workplace

John M. Violanti

Violence in the workplace recently has gained the attention of occupational health and other professionals involved with the work process. The term *workplace violence* has been interpreted broadly. Braverman (1995) noted that workplace violence includes not only fatal interemployee violence such as homicide and assault but also daily instances of internal harassment, intimidation, abuse, and exposure to crime. Mantell (1994) defined workplace violence as "significant" events at work involving homicide, serious injury, assaults, and suicide.

Suicide is presently the eighth leading cause of death in the United States (Centers for Disease Control, 1992). Workplace violence research, however, has focused primarily on homicide and provides limited information on suicide. It is difficult to assess why suicide is committed in the workplace and equally as difficult to establish an association between work and suicide. Previous studies have suggested that work, increasing age, race, gender, and psychiatric status are potential risk factors in suicide (Boxer, Burnett, & Swanson, 1995; Burnett, Boxer, & Swanson, 1992).

The magnitude of suicide in the workplace is low compared with the overall suicide rate. This is likely because of the restricted amount of time that people spend in the workplace and the fact that everyone is not employed (Conroy, 1989). In addition, working populations are generally physically and psychologically healthier than the general population (McMichael, 1976). Conroy (1989) suggested that suicide at work is rare. Risk factors for workplace suicide are similar to the general population: (a) The risk for men is seven times that for women, (b) the risk for White people is 1.6 times that of African American people, and (c) risk increases with age.

Suicides at work may be related to access of readily available means. Rose and Rosow (1973), for example, found that a drug overdose was the means of suicide used in 55% of the cases for physicians, 40% for pharmacists, and 35% for dentists. Violanti, Vena, and Marshall (1995) found that 95% of the police officers in a municipal cohort study used their own gun to commit suicide. Studies of navy and marine personnel committing suicide have shown that guns are the most common means of suicide and that access to guns will more likely result in a successful suicide (Rothberg, Ursano, & Holloway, 1987). This may be one reason that men are at higher risk than women for suicide in the workplace, because almost 60% of male workplace suicide victims used available firearms (Conroy, 1989).

Occupational status also may be related to workplace suicide. Tuckman, Youngman, and Kreizman (1964) ranked eight professions in terms of socioeconomic status and found that suicide rates were higher among low-status workers. Labovitz and Hagedorn (1971) found no relation between suicide and occupational prestige. They suggested that other factors such as bureaucratic structure and dependency may be predictive of suicide. Stack (1982) found that the suicide rate of laborers was six times that of professional, technical, or managerial workers. Overall, the suicide rate for blue-collar workers was twice that of white-collar workers.

Police Suicide

In this chapter I focus on an occupational group that appears to be at particularly high risk for suicide: law enforcement officers. Police suicide has been associated with the availability of and expertise with firearms, continuous-duty exposure to death and injury, shift work, social strain, criminal justice inconsistencies, and a negative police image held by the public (Labovitz & Hagedorn, 1971; Nelson & Smith, 1970). Most epidemiological studies point to a police suicide rate higher than other occupations. Guralnick (1963) compared the death ratios of police 20–64 years of age with individuals in 130 other occupations in the United States and found the suicide ratio of police to be 1.8 times that of those in all occupations combined. Suicide accounted for 13.8% of police deaths and 3% of deaths in all other occupations. In addition, more officers killed themselves than were killed by others. Milham (1983) found that Washington State police officers and detectives between 1950 and 1971 had a suicide ratio higher than that in all other occupations. Police had a higher-than-expected proportionate mortality ratio than in any other occupation. Vena, Violanti, Marshall, and Feidler (1986) and Violanti, Vena, and Marshall (1986) found that police officers had a mortality ratio for suicide of approximately three times that of all other municipal workers. An analysis of the New York State Department of Health (1986) for the years 1980–1981 indicated that police officers in New York State had a mortality ratio for suicide of 1.79 times that of the general population. The majority of police suicides occurred among officers aged 35–54 years. A recent mortality study of police officers in Rome, Italy (Forastiere et al., 1994), indicated that the suicide ratio among police was 1.97 times as high as the general population in Italy.

Likely the first major study conducted was that of Friedman (1968), who studied 93 suicides among police officers in New York City from 1930 to 1940. Friedman found that the rate for officers was 6.5 times that of the general population. He attributed such high rates to two factors: aggression turned inward and the circumstances of the political climate.

Friedman's (1968) aggression hypothesis was based on a psychoanalytic concept of pent-up hostility:

> No one kills himself who has never wanted to kill another ... or at least wished the death of another .... The unconscious court condemns the self ... [an] eye for an eye, [a] tooth for a tooth .... It declares itself guilty of the death wish and condemns itself to death. (p. 87)

Schneidman (1970) provided a similar concept of suicide as being "murder in the 180th degree." Schneidman based his idea on Freud's (1955) formulation of suicide as hostility directed at the introjected "love object" and Menninger's (1938) components of suicide as "the wish to kill, the wish to be killed, and the wish to die" (p. 25). More recently, Romanov et al. (1994) found a 3.4-fold increased risk of suicide in individuals with high hostility scores.

Heiman (1977), in a secondary analysis of Friedman's (1968) data, concluded that police officers have problems that are more severe than aggression or politics. He concluded that the exposure of officers to tragedy and human misery is an important motivating factor in police suicide. Heiman conducted another study comparing suicide among New York City and London police officers between 1960 and 1973. He found that police suicide rates in New York were twice that of the city population, whereas London police suicide rates were at par with the population. Heiman attributed the high New York City rates to the availability of firearms in the United States (British police officers do not carry guns). Lester (1993) conducted a secondary analysis of Friedman's data and found that officers who committed suicide experienced depression (25%), had paranoid ideation prior to the suicide (13%), had problems at work (24%), were married (84%), were at a lower rank (84%), and had personal motives for suicide (65%). Alcohol abuse among these officers was significantly associated with depression, problems at work, and being at the lowest rank.

Danto (1978) studied the suicides of 12 Detroit police officers between 1968 and 1976. Two of the officers were older than age 40, 3 were in their early 30s, and 7 were in their late 20s. Most had served fewer than 10 years as a police officer. Six of the officers committed suicide at home, and 66% used a gun. Marital problems appeared to be the most important precipitating factor in the suicides. Danto noted the impersonal nature of the police military structure and the lack of services for troubled officers. He advised police departments to establish psychological counseling programs to provide ongoing assistance to officers.

Aussant (1984), in a study of Quebec police suicides, found that 80% of the suicide victims used guns, 50% had a history of psychiatric or medical problems, and many had a severe alcohol problem. Schwartz and Schwartz (1975) found that suicide rates were higher among older police officers and were related to alcoholism, physical illness, or impending retirement. Nix (1986) noted that the police bureaucracy, with its military structure, overbearing regulations, and negativism, was a primary catalyst in police suicides. Slater and Depue (1981) attributed police suicide to the isolation of victim officers from the police culture. Violanti (1984) viewed police suicide as an officer's response to a lack of control over work and his or her personal life.

Despite the abundance of research on police stress, little of this work can relate stress empirically to police suicide. Kappeler, Blumberg, and Potter (1993) argued that the connection between police stress and suicide is a myth that perpetuates public perception of "battered and blue crime fighters." Other researchers have attributed police suicide more to the following: (a) Police work is male dominated, and statistically men commit suicide more often than do women; and (b) officers have a readily available, lethal method with which to commit suicide (Alpert & Dunham, 1988). Still others attribute police suicide to the consequences of uncovering corruption in police departments. Friedman (1968), for example, noted that many of the suicides in the New York City police department in the 1930s might have been related to the Tammany Hall corruption scandal there. Recent police suicides in New York City possibly could be related to the drug ring scandal investigation. Several of the 12 officers who committed suicide in 1994 were part of that investigation.

It is possible that stress, or the inability to cope adequately with stress, may play an integral part in police suicide (McCafferty, McCafferty, & McCafferty, 1992). Stress may lead to attitudinal changes in police officers that may affect their perceptions of helplessness. Niederhoffer (1967), for example, found that cynicism among police officers varied positively according to the degree of "frustration" with the police role. Reiser (1974) wrote of officers who became "emotionally hardened" and isolated themselves from others. Police officers are not the only ones affected by job stress. At home, officers tend to shut down emotions toward the family, leading to detachment and the seeking of outside relationships (Hageman, 1978; Stratton, 1978, 1984). Officers experienced a high divorce rate, although this finding has been disputed by other researchers (Niederhoffer & Niederhoffer, 1978). Y. Daneili (personal communication, 1994) suggested that such a process may lead to the transgenerational transmission of stress to others in the police family. Future researchers might consider an analysis of suicides within the families of police officers.

Of the factors associated with stress in police work, incidents outside the range of normal activity appear to affect officers adversely. Such events are termed *critical incidents* and may include shootings, witnessing death and mutilation, attending to disasters, and dealing with abused or mistreated children. Critical incidents often are rated by police officers as being highly stressful. I found that "killing someone in the line of duty," "death of a fellow officer," and "physical attack" were ranked as the top three stressors by police officers (Violanti, 1994). Often associated with critical incidents is a prolonged reaction classified as posttraumatic stress disorder (PTSD). PTSD is defined as a severe reaction brought about by experiencing a serious threatening event (American Psychiatric Association, 1994). Symptoms of PTSD may occur when the officer has been exposed to a traumatic event and persistently reexperiences and avoids stimuli associated with that event. The officer also may experience symptoms of increased physiological arousal because of the trauma. These criteria can persist for several months and even years in some cases.

Suicide may be an attempt by police officers to restore feelings of mastery over the environment after exposure to a traumatic incident. Such deaths may be prompted by a perceived loss of coping abilities and a feeling of vulnerability that was never experienced before the incident (Allen, 1986; Bonafacio, 1991; Heiman, 1977; McCafferty et al., 1992; Violanti, 1984). It is known that people experience differential vulnerability because some cope satisfactorily with trauma and others do not (Fowlie & Aveline, 1985; Foy, Sipprelle, Rueger, & Carroll, 1984; Frye & Stockton, 1982; Kessler, 1979). Greening and Dollinger (1992), in their study of disaster victims, found that the effects of shattered notions of invulnerability lasted for as long as 7 years. Even time-limited shattered notions can have a permanent effect on the officer's sense of vulnerability for similar future events. Rangell (1967) suggested that trauma deals a strong blow to the ego, causing a feeling of lack of control, vulnerability, and not being able to cope with future occurrences. Although being emotionally impenetrable is considered necessary by police officers, it also may increase the likelihood of suicide when this cognitive armor is shattered by traumatic events. Police officers do not expect to feel vulnerable, and, when they do, it brings feelings of shame, fear, and a heightened sense of danger.

Aggressiveness serves as one method of adaptation to shattered perceptions of invulnerability. By dehumanizing the "enemy," aggressiveness may be expressed directly. The confrontation then becomes a war, with the police on one side and citizens (considered the enemy) on the other (McCafferty et al., 1992). The denial of mortality becomes progressively more difficult for officers, and the erosive effect of constant confrontation with hostile people takes its toll. To overcome the emotional numbing that pervades the police officer's life, an increased need for emotional stimulation develops. Outrageous behavior, involvement in casual sexual affairs, impulsiveness, and possibly suicidal ideation may develop as the police officer attempts to compensate (McCafferty et al., 1992).

Early studies have suggested an association between traumatic incidents and police suicide. Danto (1978), for example, found that many officers in the Detroit police department who committed suicide were exposed to some type of job-related trauma. Eleven of the 12 officers had been injured on the job because of confrontations with citizens, and all had been involved in a traffic accident during their careers. Two of the officers had received medals for being wounded during on-duty shootings. Danto's investigation also revealed that many of the officers expressed guilt about the shooting incidents. Loo (1986), in a study of the Royal Canadian Mounted Police, found that 15% of the officers who committed suicide had been recently exposed to a traumatic work incident involving either the suicide of a close friend or were in a serious motor vehicle accident.

Suicide frequently is thought of as an ultimate coping response to an intolerable condition. Suicidal police officers may, in effect, exhaust all available coping strategies to deal with their jobs. The result may be what Shneidman (1985) termed *constriction of thought*, a condition of limited response to a situation. Officers in a state of constriction may perceive only two alternatives: Remove the intolerable condition or die. Because it is unlikely that the conditions of exposure in police work will change, the suicidal officer may choose death.

Most people can find alternative ways other than suicide to cope with situations. Police officers as a group, however, tend not to cope well with psychological distress and often turn to maladaptive coping strategies (Violanti, 1993a). Coping skills may be defined as behavioral reactions to distress, and two primary categories of coping strategies have been identified: emotion focused and problem focused (Lazarus & Folkman, 1984). Hovanitz (1990) reported that emotion-focused strategies are generally less successful than are problem-focused strategies. Lennings (1994) found that police officers tend to use problem-solving coping strategies less than do nonpolice individuals (Toch & Grant, 1991). This was seen as unusual because police officers generally perceive themselves as problem solvers. Although police officers may use some problem-solving techniques, it appears that such techniques are primarily defensive in nature and may lead to an inaccurate appraisal of a stressful situation (Fridell & Binder, 1992).

Violanti (1993a) found that police officers turned primarily to two types of coping when confronted with stress: escape–avoidance and distancing. Escape–avoidance involves avoiding people and using alcohol or drugs; distancing involves emotional escape from the situation. Distancing is distinctly different from escape coping; one can distance oneself psychologically from a situation, but the individual may not be able to escape or avoid the consequences of that same situation. Highly distressed officers likely use escape–avoidance and distancing to deal with the lack of personal control in their work. Distancing may lead to depersonalization, which has been found to be a prominent feature of individual police behavior and culture (Pogrebin & Poole, 1991; Violanti, 1993c). For police officers, these strategies may be maladaptive, as evidenced by increasing alienation, stress, and reliance on alcohol to manage the stress (Violanti, 1983).

The police training environment may contribute to the type of coping police officers choose. Violanti (1993b) suggested that the use of distancing, self-control, accepting personal responsibility, and escape–avoidance were used significantly more by recruits under high distress. Escape–avoidance and distancing have an especially strong maladaptive potential. It also is possible that the training academy experience may increase the use of such strategies. If counterbalancing socialization does not occur after the recruit leaves the police academy, such strategies may carry over into the work environment. A lower stress training environment may allow for a wider choice of behavior conducive to proper coping and adjustment to police work.

Research suggests that police get into trouble at least some of the time because of perceived appraisal strategies. Either they are unaware of other people's feelings and situations, unaware of their own anxiety in a situation, or have made a judgment based on an inflexible plan that is followed rigidly (Fridell & Binder, 1992; Pogrebin & Poole, 1991; Stotland, 1991).

Even maladaptive coping techniques, however, may break down over time in officers (Selye, 1978; Somodevilla, 1986). Given evidence of the lack of viable coping alternatives in police work, and the primary socialization of officers into potentially maladaptive coping strategies, it is possible that suicide may become a final coping alternative. Perhaps training officers in problem solving, emotion focusing, and decision-making strategies may provide them with coping alternatives to suicide (Bayley, 1986).

Police Suicide and the Workplace

I first comment on the meaning of the term *workplace* as it applies to police work. Johnson (1995) noted that workplace violence does not have a uniform definition and that different kinds of violence require different insights and solutions. In addition, situational and contextual cues must be considered to define circumstances that lead to different kinds of violence. To clarify this important issue, the Association for Vital Records and Health Statistics, the National Institute for Occupational Safety and Health, the National Center for Health Statistics, and the National Center for Environmental Health and Injury Control have jointly developed classification guidelines for what is considered "injury at work." In the category "law enforcement officer," these guidelines state specifically that any injury or fatality experienced by a police officer either on or off employer premises must be considered as a "workplace injury or death" (National Institute for Occupational Safety and Health, 1993, Appendix I). The reasoning behind this classification guideline was not discussed by the joint committee. It appears, however, that researchers view police work as an occupation that encompasses the life of any individual within its ranks regardless of whether they are on or off duty (Niederhoffer, 1967).

On the basis of this definition, a suicide committed by a police officer away from or at the actual worksite may be considered a workplace death. It may be useful, however, to examine correlates of police suicides that occur at the actual physical worksite (e.g., at the police station) and those that occur somewhere else. Table 1 shows data on suicide in five major studies on police suicide.

Data in Table 1 indicate that the majority of police suicides in these studies occurred in the home (M = 64.8%) and that a small number occurred at the actual worksite (M = approximately 10%). An average 10% of the cases had no information about where the suicide took place. Chicago police officers committed suicide at home at a higher rate than did the officers in the other four departments. A further analysis was conducted on Buffalo police officers because they committed suicide at the worksite at a higher rate than did officers from the other departments and additional information was available. Table 2 shows data on Buffalo police officers who committed suicide at and away from the worksite.

The data in Table 2 should be interpreted with caution because of the small number (n = 6, 16%) of officers who committed suicide at the worksite. In general, officers who committed suicide at the worksite were older,

Table 1. Location of Police Suicides: Data From Five Police Departments

Location (%)	New York City[a] 1985–1994 (N = 66)	Chicago[b] 1970–1979 (N = 39)	Buffalo[c] 1950–1990 (N = 26)	Detroit[d] 1968–1976 (N = 12)	RCMP[e] 1960–1983 (N = 35)	Mean %
Home	68.0	76.9	64.0	66.0	48.5	64.8
Work	14.0	2.6	16.0	—	8.5	10.2
Other	18.0	10.3	12.0	25.0	31.4	19.3
Unknown	—	10.3	8.0	9.0	11.6	9.7

Note. RCMP = Royal Canadian Mounted Police.
[a]From Ivanoff (1994).
[b]From Cronin (1982).
[c]From Violanti (1995).
[d]From Danto (1978).
[e]From Loo (1986).

Table 2. Comparison of Buffalo Police Officers Who Committed Suicide at and Away From the Worksite: 1950–1990

Variable	Suicide at worksite ($N = 6$)	Suicide away from worksite ($N = 20$)
Mean age	54	50
Type of duty (%)		
Patrol	100	85
Administrative	0	5
Detective work	0	10
Police rank (%)		
Patrol officer	17	20
Detective	0	15
Lieutenant	0	0
Captain	0	0
Unknown	83	65
Employment status (%)		
Died in service	83	70
Retired	17	30
Disciplinary actions (%)		
None	100	80
Two or more	0	20
Precinct transfers (%)		
None	67	65
One	0	20
Two	33	5
Three or more	0	10
Documented sick leave (%)		
High (>100 days)	0	20
Low (<100 days)	100	80
Education (%)		
College	0	0
High school	100	90
< High school	0	10
Service veteran (%)		
World War I	0	5
World War II	0	25
Korea	0	15
Vietnam	17	5
No military service	83	50
Autopsy performed (%)		
Yes	17	44
No	83	56

Note. Data were taken from Violanti, Vena, and Marshall (1995).

were more likely to be at a lower rank, had fewer disciplinary actions and precinct transfers, and had less sick-leave usage. Except for one Vietnam veteran, officers who had been in the armed services tended to commit suicide away from the worksite. In short, unpromoted veteran officers who appeared to conform closely to organizational rules and attendance stan-

Table 3. Comparison of Locations of Suicide Among Police and Municipal Workers in Buffalo: 1950–1990

Location	Police officer		Municipal workers		Total	
	N	%	N	%	N	%
Away from worksite	20	77	13	100	33	85
At worksite	6	23	0	0	6	15
Total	26	100	13	100	39	100

Note. Data were taken from Violanti, Vena, and Marshall (1995). $\chi^2(1, N = 39) = 3.70$, $p < .05$.

dards were more likely to commit suicide at the actual worksite. These officers might have been unnoticed or unappreciated by the organization because they were good employees. Seemingly more attention might have been directed at officers who created problems at work and those who might have chosen an offsite location for suicide to escape that attention. It was interesting that an autopsy was not performed on 83.3% of the suicides committed at the workplace because any unattended or suspicious death requires an autopsy. There are indications that many police suicides may be misclassified as a result of workplace cohesiveness and that medical examiners may be influenced at the scene not to perform an autopsy (Violanti, Vena, Marshall, & Petralia, 1996).

An additional analysis was performed to examine differences between police work and other municipal occupations in terms of the location of suicide. Data were collected on suicides from a 40-year (1950–1990) epidemiological database of 11,000 municipal workers in Buffalo, New York (Violanti et al., 1995). The database included police officers and 25 other municipal job categories. Thirty-nine suicides were found involving 26 police officers and 13 municipal workers. Table 3 shows the results of analysis.

The data in Table 3 indicate that among those committing suicide, 77% of the police officers and 100% of the municipal workers committed suicide away from the workplace. Twenty-three percent of the police officers and none of the municipal workers committed suicide at the worksite. Analysis revealed a statistically significant association, $\chi^2(df = 1, N = 39) = 3.70$, $p < .05$, between committing suicide at work and being a police officer. Thus, being a police officer may increase the possibility of committing suicide at work compared with other occupations.

Our analyses provided some useful data concerning differences between worksite and off-worksite police suicides. Findings also indicate that police officers generally kill themselves more often at the worksite than do other municipal workers. We do not know, however, precisely why an officer would choose to commit suicide at or away from the worksite. I speculate that the police worksite (e.g., station house, precinct) is distinguished from other places by the presence of administrative organization. It appears that the worksite for many officers is an intrusive place wherein resides an administrative "enemy." Violanti (1994), for example, found that 10 of the 15 highest rated stressors mentioned by police officers involved the organization itself. Officers perceived the organization to be generally unsupportive and dehumanizing. The following hypothesis is based on my own work experience as a police officer and an analysis of more than 65 police suicide cases (Violanti, 1996).

For the police officer, committing suicide away from organizational influence may represent a quest for autonomy over one's own life. Common in police structures are military-style rank positions, specific work roles, and impersonal work relationships. The police organization is unique for others because of the intensity with which it restricts officers, intensity resulting from powerful combinations of militaristic and bureaucratic control methods. The typical police organization may be said to be punishment centered and to "compound the felony" against officers in terms of control (Gross, 1973). Officers are coerced into consistent behavior in a continuously changing environment and are punished when they do not conform.

The rigidity of organizational roles tends to diminish the ability of officers to assume other roles. The police organization places officers on the defense by what Kirschman (1983) termed the "deflection of blame," which is a form of individual control that protects the police organization at the psychological expense of its members. According to Kirschman, blame deflection occurs when there is a threatening intrusion from the outside system that may be detrimental to the image of the organization. Not only does the police organization demand rigid roles but it also prescribes precisely how officers must fulfill these roles. One result is what Harris (1973) called "false personalization," which forces officers to act out roles that are contrary to their true feelings (e.g., being polite to everyone even though one is extremely angry at them). Personalization may require superhuman individuals who must act as though they are unaffected by anything police work can throw at them. Kirschman (1983) spoke of an "occupational persona":

> One way to obfuscate occupational strain is to create an occupational persona, a mask of competence that belies ones' actual state of mind [sic] . . . . It becomes harmful only when the inherent deception becomes a substitute for reality and is ultimately more acceptable than one's genuine, yet imperfect self. It is then that individual needs synchronize with organizational and cultural elements, and the officer's vulnerability to job stress is increased. (p. 340)

The police organization may thus decrease the officer's ability to be flexible in life roles and relationships and, in doing so, increase their suicide potential. Officers may forsake themselves and other role identities for those of the police organization. The constrictive social influence of police organization on role identity may affect the self-representational cognitive structure of officers. This psychological structure defines the self as having purpose and meaning in the social environment. When this meaning is somehow lost, or the individual becomes isolated from the social environment, the risk of suicide may be present (Turner & Roszell,

1994). Just how great a potential risk may depend to some degree on the "psychological centrality" of the constricted role. Rosenberg and Pearlin (1978) and Gecas and Seff (1990) posited that if some cognitive self-representations are made to be more important to people, those representations will be affected more by life challenges. This may be the case for the police because police structure tends to emphasize and enforce the importance of the police role to the individual officer. Stryker and Serpe (1982) also suggested that individuals tend to organize multiple cognitive identities in relation to the social environment and to place these identities in a "salience hierarchy." The term *salience* refers to the level of commitment an individual has to each identity and determines the likelihood that a given identity will be invoked across different life situations. The more salient the identity, the greater will be the impact of a serious negative event on the individual's psychological well-being.

Thoits (1986) argued that individuals conceptualize the cognitive self as a set of social identities. The term *identity*, as defined by Thoits, refers to an assigned position in the social structure accepted by the individual. Identities are important for self-definition; they give meaning and purpose to individual social worth. Thoits hypothesized that the more social identities a person has, the less potential that person will have for depression or psychological distress. Her findings indicated that symptoms of distress varied inversely with the number of social identities and that changes in identities over time are psychologically beneficial or harmful depending on the direction of change.

Thus, because of restricted identity brought about by the police organization, the police officer may have limited flexibility in dealing with life problems. Officers who commit suicide away from the worksite may be initiating the only way they know how to gain control of their own behavior: to remove themselves from the influence of the organization. Officers who commit suicide at the worksite may be acting out more than a quest for role autonomy. Driven by personal and situational factors, these officers may choose suicide as a symbolic gesture of overt defiance. Suicide may be their final way of taking control and doing it blatantly at the site of the organization. According to the data in Table 3, it appears that police officers are more likely to act out such defiance than are those in other occupations. This may be indicative of the disdain that officers express for the organization.

Suicide Prevention Measures in Police Work

Suicide prevention may be difficult in police work because of a strong sense of denial that suicide is a problem. This denial likely is based on officers being socialized into thinking they have superhuman emotional and survival strength. From the first day in the police academy, recruit officers are told that they are unique, far different from the average citizen and certainly beyond harm. This pervasive illusion of invulnerability seems to be prevalent among new officers and is similar to Burger and Burns's

(1988) concept of "unique invulnerability" found in adolescents. One component of this concept is the "personal fable," a feeling that one is unique and has feelings and experiences unlike any other person. This feeling is reinforced by a strong belief in one's indestructibility (Greening & Dollinger, 1992).

Because of this carefully built perception of invulnerability, entire departments learn to deny feelings about emotionally charged situations. Such is the case with the suicide of a peer officer. Violanti et al. (1996), for example, found that approximately 20% of police suicides were misclassified as either an accident or an undetermined cause of death. Police investigators at the scene of a peer officer's suicide can effectively control (and explicitly deny) information about the suicide and lead medical examiners to consider other causes of death. Another example concerns a recent survey conducted by Susan Sawyer, chairperson of C.O.P.S. (Concerns of Police Survivors). Sawyer sent information requests about suicide to 14,000 police departments throughout the United States. Only 3 departments responded (S. Sawyer, personal communication, February 6, 1995).

A Police Suicide Prevention Model

Because workplace violence is multifaceted, all major components of the work environment must necessarily be involved in its reduction. Braverman (1995) pointed out that reducing workplace violence goes far beyond the initial screening and profiling of individuals employed. Instead, one should focus on a systemic-level assessment of risk and development of policies and procedures to mitigate against potential violence. Loo (1986) and Silverman and Felner (1995) suggested that a suicide prevention approach should focus not just on suicide but also on the more comprehensive approach of building a person's work and life competencies, thereby enhancing his or her resilience to stressors. It also must be realized that suicide can result not only from a single major crisis but also from the accumulation of apparently minor life events (Loo, 1995). The following is a proposal for a suicide prevention model that is readily adaptable to most police organizations. Police psychologists and others who work with police officers are cautioned about the primary purpose of a suicide prevention program: to assist the individual officer. Such programs, once implemented, tend to become entangled in organizational bureaucracy and this important goal may be lost.

Although recruit screening in most major police departments involves psychological testing, other personal and social factors often are not considered. Loo (1995), for example, stated that predisposing personality factors or precipitating family history variables (e.g., family violence, substance abuse) should be tracked for high-risk officers.

For officers already on the force who are being selected for special duty (special weapons and tactical teams, undercover, etc.), additional psychological assessments should be made to determine their suitability for such assignments. Loo (1995) suggested that officers on special assignments should be evaluated periodically for symptoms of distress, depression, and suicidal ideation. He also suggested that officers involved in critical incidents such as shootings be assessed psychologically.

Loo (1995) suggested that police departments should develop criteria to identify and track high-risk officers (e.g., officers with marital difficulties, substance abuse, work problems, and other life problems) so that timely support can be provided to avert a suicide. A behavior profile based on these stress indicators should be established for each officer and should be reviewed every 6 months by the medical department to determine which officers are under stress. Consultation with mental health professionals is essential when a police officer exhibits inappropriate behavior or a behavioral change that suggests that the officer may commit suicide. Other factors to consider are the police officer's personality structure, coping style, depression, substance abuse, personality or anxiety disorders, financial problems, physical illness, and problems with work. A past history of suicide attempts also is an important factor to consider. There should be documentation of changes in officers' behavior and problems (McCafferty et al., 1992).

A working example of tracking is being used by the New York City Police Department peer support group. Counselors assess a number of "points" for different types of problems for which officers request help. Points are weighted according to the seriousness of the officer's problem. When officers get too many points, they are offered additional professional help.

Certainly, the risk of suicide is increased in police officers because they carry firearms. Previous research has revealed that 95% of police suicides were committed with guns (Violanti et al., 1995). The practice of some departments of requiring police officers to carry firearms when they are off duty, 24 hour a day, may be an important target for police organizational policy change because such immediate access can facilitate impulsive suicidal tendencies. Reducing access may be successful because suicidal impulses often are transitory. Individuals whose preferred method of suicide is not available often do not resort to other means, and suicides are usually committed by means already available to the person rather than by means to be obtained specifically to commit suicide. Browning (1974) found that only about 10% of firearm suicides were performed by firearms purchased specifically for that purpose; the other 90% were committed by firearms already available to the person. In addition, there is some question about the necessity for officers to carry a firearm off duty. Although a firearm certainly may be necessary in life-or-death, off-duty emergencies, police officers may seldom use their guns for such purposes. An informal survey of four large urban police departments indicated that none of them kept statistical records of off-duty use of firearms by police officers (Violanti, 1996).

Seminars should be given for police recruits and their families so they understand the effects of police work. Marital problems can be one of the greatest stress producers in the suicidal police officer. The police department may become the "mistress" of the officer and "competition" for the officer's spouse (McCafferty et al., 1992). Ivanoff (1994), for example, found that 58% of the police suicides in New York City were the result of "relationship" problems with family members or significant others. Counseling services should be made available to families and officers.

An important area of suicide prevention is training that can help officers recognize and avoid psychological factors leading to suicide. Training should begin at the police academy before new officers are exposed to the powerful effects of police occupational socialization. Training on entrance is, in effect, an "inoculation" against future psychological crises and suicidal ideation (DeAngelis, 1993; Ivanoff, 1994). Ivanoff (1994) suggested that police suicide training programs should include recognition of psychological depression, communication skills, conflict resolution, and intimate relationship maintenance. Supervisors as well as line personnel should be trained to recognize the warning signs of suicide and suggest confidential referrals at the scene. Supervisors can be an important source of support to line officers having difficulties (Beehr, King, & King, 1990; Coyne & Downey, 1991; Etzion, 1984; Pearlin & Schooler, 1978).

Stress awareness is a psychologically sound method to help individuals cope with stress. A well-rounded stress education program should include identification of stress, the value and techniques of physical exercise, the benefits of proper nutrition, interpersonal communication methods, and coping styles. Stress awareness can make new members aware of potential problems they will face in the future. Once in service, officers should be instructed in coping strategies because they most likely have been exposed to the effects of job stress. Stress education for families should include identification of the police function, problems commonly encountered in police marriages, methods for effective communication, and using the family as a source of support.

Supervisors are equally susceptible to the negative effects of police work. Middle-line supervisors should be able to identify potential suicidal officers under their command. Suicide sensitivity training should allow supervisors to detect workers who are affected adversely by stress, alcohol, and other correlates of suicide. The responsibility for such detection should be incorporated into the role of the supervisor.

Executive-level training in suicide awareness also is important. Executives can play an important role in supportive functions, including organizational change and assistance with line-officer problems. "Support from the top" can give officers the impression that the organization cares. Also, executives are not immune to the effects of police work; they, too, have the potential for suicide.

Not only can an effective intervention effort save officers' lives, but it also can safeguard agencies from the devastating effects of suicide. Agencies must move beyond the morbidity of the subject to develop effective suicide countermeasures. Traditionally, no matter what their problems, police officers often refrain from asking for help. There are various reasons for this. Officers do not wish to appear weak or vulnerable in front of their peers; they perceive themselves to be problem solvers, not individuals with problems. To help officers take the first difficult step to seek intervention, the police organization should develop and increase accessibility to confidential psychological services. Essentially, officers need a safe place to go for help, out of administrative view. If police officers can approach such services without going through formal organizational channels, they will be more likely to seek help and less likely to commit suicide (Ivanoff, 1994). Because all police officers face similar challenges and pressures—regardless of the size of the agency in which they work—every officer should have access to comparable counseling resources.

Prior experience has demonstrated that easy accessibility is an important factor in the troubled person's decision to seek help. A 24-hour private phone service would provide such accessibility. This suicide hotline could be made available to any member of the department using an 800 number. A civilian answering service would accept calls anonymously and notify members of an early intervention program via a beeper system. The call then would be returned and the problem discussed initially over the phone. If further intervention is needed, an in-person contact can be made. This system can reach the greatest number of people with the least amount of cost while still maintaining confidentiality.

It is easier for troubled officers to talk to other police officers. Providing trained peer support for members would be important. Such counselors would not be expected to be psychologists but support people with whom to talk.

It is necessary to establish a professional network of psychologists, psychiatrists, or both who are familiar with police problems. When troubled members are in need of such services, they can be referred easily.

Retirement is not an easy transition for most people, and it is even more difficult for police officers. Gaska (1980) calculated a 10-fold risk of suicide among Detroit police retirees over the general population. The cohesiveness of police officers and the "protection" that being part of the police culture provides is lost at separation from police service (Violanti, 1992). Many officers do not have skills for other types of employment and are unprepared for retirement that generally occurs at a young age. Informational seminars and counseling should be made available to officers as early as 5 years before retirement. Spouses and other family members also should be included in such seminars.

Each police department is, in a sense, unique and has its own set of problems. Therefore, it is necessary to conduct ongoing research on the potential precipitants of suicide. Conducting "psychological autopsies" and epidemiological studies on previous suicides is an effective way to determine circumstances leading up to suicide.

Conclusion

The research discussed here reveals that police suicide in the workplace does not occur that often. It does appear, however, that police officers tend to commit suicide at the physical worksite more often than do other municipal workers. Therefore, it may be beneficial to focus further research on groups such as the police officers who choose the workplace to commit suicide.

The multidimensional character of suicide causality makes it extremely difficult to focus on specific attributes of the police occupation that may exacerbate suicide at work. In this chapter, I have identified several suspected factors that may be involved. First is the violent nature of the work and accouterments associated with protection from that violence. Police work inherently involves violence and death. The psyche of police officers may be battered continuously by the stress and trauma of this violence. Although some say that stress and trauma in police work is not associated with suicide (Kappeler et al., 1993), I still believe that researchers must consider them as part of the equation. In all probability, the multifaceted stress and trauma experienced over the course of a police career takes its psychological toll. Such exposure cannot be changed, but officers can be made aware of how to cope with it. If one believes that suicide is the ultimate coping response to intolerable conditions, providing ideas for other ways to cope may help reduce suicide in the police workplace.

A lethal method for suicide is readily and immediately available to police officers: the firearm. As discussed in this chapter, approximately 95% of all police suicides involve the use of a firearm, and police officers tend to use a firearm for suicide with greater frequency than do people in other occupations where guns are not present. Obviously, if firearms are less accessible, the impulse to commit suicide may pass. Police departments should consider enacting policies to help limit access to firearms, including providing locked storage for weapons during off-duty hours. The opportunity for intervention is much better at the workplace; once the officer takes a firearm home, the odds of a successful suicide may increase significantly.

The rigid nature of the police structure is another point that must be addressed. Police officers must be allowed greater flexibility at work in terms of decision making and control over their work environment. As I discussed earlier, demands by the organization for rigid adherence to the police role may truncate the coping flexibility of officers and lead to constrictive thinking about suicide. Police departments who use shared decision making and aspects of total quality management may fare better in reducing suicide among their officers.

I thought it interesting that the National Institute for Occupational Safety and Health (1993) would consider that any fatality of a police officer either on or off workplace premises should be considered a "workplace fatality." In my view, this is a recognition of the encompassing nature of police work. It is an occupation that pervades every aspect of an individual's life and brings with it a whole set of potential psychologically harmful attributes. Police work tests the coping ability of those doing it, and some cannot respond adequately. It is a task of future researchers, administrators, and policymakers to consider such devastating occupational effects and to plan for suicide reduction and prevention.

References

Allen, S. (1986). Suicide and indirect self-destructive behavior among police. In J. Reese & H. Goldstein (Eds.), *Psychological services for law enforcement* (pp. 412–416). Washington, DC: U.S. Government Printing Office.

Alpert, G. P., & Dunham, R. G. (1988). *Policing urban America*. Prospect Heights, IL: Waveland.

American Psychiatric Association. (1994). *Diagnostic and statistical manual of mental disorders* (4th ed.). Washington, DC: Author.

Aussant, G. (1984). Police suicide. *RCMP Gazette, 46*, 14–21.

Bayley, D. H. (1986). The tactical choices of police patrol officers. *Journal of Criminal Justice, 14*, 329–348.

Beehr, T., King, L., & King, D. (1990). Social support and occupational stress: Talking to supervisors. *Journal of Vocational Behavior, 36*, 61–81.

Bonafacio, P. (1991). *The psychological effects of police work*. New York: Plenum.

Boxer, P. A., Burnett, C. A., & Swanson, N. G. (1995). Suicide and occupation: A review of the literature. *Journal of Occupational and Environmental Medicine, 37*, 442–452.

Braverman, M. (1995, September). *Beyond profiling: An integrated, multidisciplinary approach to preventing workplace violence*. Symposium conducted at the Work, Stress and Health '95 Conference, Washington, DC.

Browning, J. H. (1974). Epidemiology of suicide: Firearms. *Comprehensive Psychiatry, 15*, 549–553.

Burger, J. M., & Burns, L. (1988). The illusion of unique vulnerability and the use of effective contraception. *Personality and Social Psychology Bulletin, 14*, 264–270.

Burnett, C. A., Boxer, P. A., & Swanson, N. G. (1992, November). *Suicide and occupation: Is there a relationship?* Paper presented at the American Psychological Association–National Institute for Occupational Safety and Health Conference on Workplace Stress in the 90s, Washington, DC.

Centers for Disease Control. (1992). *Position papers from the Third National Injury Control Conference: Setting the agenda for injury control in the 1990s*. Atlanta, GA: Author.

Conroy, C. (1989). Suicide in the workplace: Incidence, victim characteristics, and external cause of death. *Journal of Occupational Medicine, 31*, 847–851.

Coyne, J., & Downey, G. (1991). Social factors and psychopathology: Stress, social support and coping processes. *Annual Review of Psychology, 42*, 401–425.

Cronin, T. J. (1982). *Police suicides: A comprehensive study of the Chicago Police Department 1970–1979*. Unpublished master's thesis, Lewis University, Romeoville, IL.

Danto, B. I. (1978). Police suicide. *Police Stress, 1*, 32–35.

DeAngelis, T. (1993, September). Workplace stress battles fought all over the world. *APA Monitor*, p. 22.

Etzion, D. (1984). Moderating effects of social support on the stress burnout relationship. *Journal of Applied Psychology, 69*, 615–622.

Forastiere, F., Perucci, C. A., DiPietro, A., Miceli, M., Rapiti, E., Bargagli, A., & Borgia, P. (1994). *Mortality among urban policemen in Rome*. Unpublished manuscript.

Fowlie, D. G., & Aveline, M. O. (1985). The emotional consequences of ejection, rescue, and rehabilitation in the Royal Air Force crew. *British Journal of Psychiatry, 146*, 609–613.

Foy, D. W., Sipprelle, R. C., Rueger, D. D., & Carroll, E. M. (1984). Etiology of post-traumatic stress disorder in Vietnam veterans: Analysis of pre-military, military, and combat exposure influences. *Journal of Consulting and Clinical Psychology, 52*, 88–96.

Freud, S. (1955). Beyond the pleasure principle. In J. Strachey (Ed. and translator), *The standard edition of the complete psychological works of Sigmund Freud* (pp. 7–71). London: Hogarth Press.

Fridell, L. A., & Binder, A. (1992). Police officer decision making in potentially violent confrontations. *Journal of Criminal Justice, 20*, 385–399.

Friedman, P. (1967). *On Suicide*. New York: International University Press.

Friedman, P. (1968). Suicide among police: A study of 93 suicides among New York City policemen 1934–40. In E. S. Shneidman (Ed.), *Essays of self destruction* (pp. 414–419). New York: Science House.

Frye, J., & Stockton, R. A. (1982). Discriminant analysis of post traumatic stress among a group of Vietnam veterans. *American Journal of Psychiatry, 139,* 52–56.

Gaska, C. W. (1980). *The rate of suicide, potential for suicide, and recommendations for prevention among retired police officers.* Unpublished doctoral dissertation, Wayne State University, Detroit, MI.

Gecas, V., & Seff, M. A. (1990). Social class and self-esteem: Psychological centrality, compensation, and the relative effects of work and home. *Social Psychological Quarterly, 53,* 165–173.

Greening, L., & Dollinger, S. J. (1992). Illusions of invulnerability: Adolescents in a natural disaster. *Journal of Traumatic Stress, 5,* 63–75

Gross, E. (1973). Work, organization, and stress. In R. Levine & C. Scotch (Eds.), *Social stress* (pp. 54–110). Chicago: Aldine.

Guralnick, L. (1963). Mortality by occupation and cause of death among men 20–64 years of age. *Vital statistics special reports* (No. 53). Bethesda, MD: Department of Health, Education and Welfare.

Hageman, M. (1978). Occupational stress and marital relationships. *Journal of Police Science and Administration, 6,* 407–412.

Harris, R. N. (1973). *The police academy: An inside view.* New York: Wiley.

Heiman, P. (1977). Suicide among police. *American Journal of Psychiatry, 134,* 1286–1290.

Hovanitz, C. A. (1990). Life event stress and coping style as contributions to psychopathology. *Journal of Clinical Psychology, 42,* 34–41.

Ivanoff, A. (1994). *The New York City police suicide training project.* New York: Police Foundation.

Johnson, D. L. (1995, September). *Workplace violence: Practical strategies involving EAPs and mental health professionals.* Symposium conducted at the Work, Stress and Health '95 Conference, Washington, DC.

Kappeler, V. E., Blumberg, M., & Potter, G. W. (1993). *The mythology of crime and criminal justice.* Prospect Heights, IL: Waveland.

Kessler, R. C. (1979). A strategy for studying differential vulnerability to the psychological consequences of stress. *Journal of Health and Social Behavior, 20,* 102–108.

Kirschman, E. (1983). *Wounded heroes: A case study and systems analysis of job-related stress and emotional dysfunction in three police officers.* Doctoral dissertation (University Microfilms No. 8319021, pp. 337–340). Berkeley, CA: The Wright Institute.

Labovitz, S., & Hagedorn, R. (1971). An analysis of suicide rates among occupational categories. *Sociological Inquiry, 41,* 67–72.

Lazarus, R. S., & Folkman, S. (1984). Stress, appraisal, and coping. New York: Springer.

Lennings, C. J. (1994, February). *Suicide ideation and risk factors in police officers and justice students.* Paper presented at the Public Health Association Conference, Canberra, Australia.

Lester, D. (1993). A study of police suicide in New York City, 1934–1939. *Psychological Reports, 73,* 1395–1398.

Loo, R. (1986). Suicide among police in a federal force. *Suicide and Life-Threatening Behavior, 16,* 379–388.

Loo, R. (1995, September). *Police suicide: Issues, prevention and postvention.* Poster session conducted at the Work, Stress and Health '95 Conference, Washington, DC.

Mantell, M. R. (1994). *Defusing violence in the workplace.* New York: Irwin.

McCafferty, F. L., McCafferty, E., & McCafferty, M. A. (1992). Stress and suicide in police officers: A paradigm of occupational stress. *Southern Medical Journal, 85,* 233–243.

McMichael, A. J. (1976). Standardized mortality ratios and the healthy worker effect: Scratching beneath the surface. *Journal of Occupational Medicine, 18,* 165–168.

Menninger, K. (1938). *Man against himself.* New York: Harcourt, Brace, Jovanovich.

Milham, S. (1983). *Occupational mortality in Washington State* (DHEW Publication No. 83-116). Washington, DC: U.S. Government Printing Office.

National Institute for Occupational Safety and Health. (1993). *Fatal injuries to workers in the United States, 1980–1989: A decade of surveillance* (DHHS NIOSH Rep. No. 93-108). Cincinnati, OH: Author.

Nelson, Z., & Smith, W. E. (1970). The law enforcement profession: An incidence of high suicide. *Omega, 1,* 293–299.

New York State Department of Health. (1986). *Statistics on occupational deaths: Police officers*. Albany, NY: Author.

Niederhoffer, A. (1967). *Behind the shield*. New York: Doubleday.

Niederhoffer, A., & Niederhoffer, E. (1978). *The police family: From station house to ranch house*. Lexington, MA: Heath.

Nix, C. (1986, September 15). Police suicide: Answers are sought. *New York Times*, pp. B2–B4.

Pearlin, L. I., & Schooler, C. (1978). The structure of coping. *Journal of Health and Social Behavior, 19*, 2–21.

Pogrebin, M. R., & Poole, E. D. (1991). Police and tragic events: The management of emotion. *Journal of Criminal Justice, 19*, 395–403.

Rangell, L. (1967). The metapsychology of psychic trauma. In S. S. Furst (Ed.), *Psychic trauma* (pp. 412–442). New York: Basic Books.

Reiser, M. (1974). Some organizational stressors on police officers. *Journal of Police Science and Administration, 2*, 156–159.

Romanoff, K., Hatakka, M., Keskinen, E., Laksonen, H., Kaprio, J., Rose, R., & Koskenvuo, M. (1994). Self-reported hostility and suicidal acts, accidents, and accidental deaths: A prospective study of 21,443 adults aged 25 to 29. *Psychosomatic Medicine, 56*, 328–336.

Rose, K., & Rosow, I. (1973). Physicians who kill themselves. *Archives of General Psychiatry 29*, 800–805.

Rosenberg, M., & Pearlin, L. I. (1978). Social class and self-esteem among children and adults. *American Journal of Sociology, 84*, 53–77.

Rothberg, J., Ursano, R., & Holloway, H. (1987). Suicide in the United States military. *Psychiatric Annals, 17*, 545–548.

Schwartz, J., & Schwartz, C. (1975). The personal problems of the police officer: A plea for action. In W. Kroes & J. Hurrell (Eds.), *Job stress and the police officer* (pp. 130–141). Washington, DC: U.S. Government Printing Office.

Selye, H. (1978). The stress of police work. *Police Stress, 1*, 1–3.

Shneidman, E. S. (1970). Orientations toward death. In E. S. Shneidman, N. L. Farberow, & R. E. Litman (Eds.), *The psychology of suicide* (p. 7). New York: Science House.

Shneidman, E. S. (1985). *Definition of suicide*. New York: Wiley.

Silverman, M. M., & Felner, R. D. (1995). The place of suicide prevention in the spectrum of intervention: Definitions of critical terms and constructs. *Suicide and Life-Threatening Behavior, 25*, 10–21.

Slater, J., & Depue, R. (1981). The contribution of environmental and social support to serious suicide attempts in primary depressive order. *Journal of Abnormal Psychology, 90*, 275–285.

Somodevilla, S. A. (1986). Post-shooting trauma: Reactive and proactive treatment. In J. Reese & H. Goldstein (Eds.), *Psychological services for law enforcement* (pp. 203–205). Washington, DC: U.S. Government Printing Office.

Stack, S. (1982). Suicide in Detroit 1975: Changes and continuities. *Suicide and Life-Threatening Behavior, 12*, 67–83.

Stotland, E. (1991). The effects of police work and professional relations on health. *Journal of Criminal Justice, 19*, 371–379.

Stratton, J. G. (1978, April). Police stress: An overview. *Police Chief*, pp. 58–62.

Stratton, J. G. (1984). *Police passages*. Manhattan Beach, CA: Glennon.

Stryker, S., & Serpe, R. T. (1982). Commitment, identity salience, and role behavior. In W. Ickes & E. S. Knowles (Eds.), *Personality, roles, and social behavior* (pp. 199–218). New York: Springer-Verlag.

Thoits, P. A. (1986). Multiple identities: Examining gender and marital differences in distress. *American Sociological Review, 51*, 259–272.

Toch, H., & Grant, J. D. (1991). *Police as problem solvers*. New York: Plenum.

Tuckman, J., Youngman, W., & Kreizman, G. (1964). Occupation and suicide. *Industrial Medicine Surgeon, 33*, 818–820.

Turner, R. J., & Roszell, P. (1994). Psychosocial resources and the stress process. In W. R. Avison & I. H. Gotlib (Eds.), *Stress and mental health* (pp. 179–210). New York: Plenum.

Vena, J. E., Violanti, J. M., Marshall, J. R., & Feidler, F. (1986). Mortality of a municipal worker cohort: III. Police officers. *Journal of Industrial Medicine, 10*, 383–397.

Violanti, J. M. (1983). Stress patterns in police work: A longitudinal analysis. *Journal of Police Science and Administration, 11*, 211–216.

Violanti, J. M. (1984). Police suicide: On the rise. *New York Trooper, 1*, 18–19.

Violanti, J. M. (1992). *Police retirement: The impact of change* (pp. 75–81). Springfield, IL: Charles C Thomas.

Violanti, J. M. (1993a). Coping in a high stress police environment. *Journal of Social Psychology, 132*, 717–730.

Violanti, J. M. (1993b). High stress police training: What does it teach police recruits? *Journal of Criminal Justice, 21*, 411–417.

Violanti, J. M. (1993c). Sources of police stress, job attitudes and psychological distress. *Psychological Reports, 72*, 899–904.

Violanti, J. M. (1994). Ranking police stressors. *Psychological Reports, 75*, 824–826.

Violanti, J. M. (1995). Trends in police suicide. *Psychological Reports, 77*, 688–690.

Violanti, J. M. (1996). *Police suicide.* Manuscript in preparation.

Violanti, J. M., Vena, J. E., & Marshall, J. R. (1986). Disease risk and mortality among police officers. *Journal of Police Science and Administration, 14*, 17–23.

Violanti, J. M., Vena, J. E., & Marshall, J. R. (1995). [*Epidemiology of police suicide*]. Unpublished raw data.

Violanti, J. M., Vena, J. E., Marshall, J. R., & Petralia, S. (1996). A comparative evaluation of police suicide rate validity. *Suicide and Life-Threatening Behavior, 26*, 79–85.

14

Attitudes About and Experiences of Workplace Violence: Results of a Survey of Construction and Other Workers

Bernard A. McCann

As the modern American economy continues to transform and employment patterns continue to evolve, new and changing workplace health and safety risks have emerged. One example of these changing workplace risk factors is the apparent rise in workplace violence and related homicides. As a proportion of fatal occupational accidents, for the period 1980–88, homicides were the third leading cause of death in American workplaces, or 12% of total occupational injury deaths (Jenkins, Layne, & Kisner, 1992). Percentage rates for workplace homicides (Bureau of Labor Statistics, 1994c, 1995) rose from 17% in 1993 to 20% in 1994. Additional data collected for the years 1992–1993 reveal assaults and violent acts are the leading events associated with workplace fatalities for women and the second leading event for men (Bureau of Labor Statistics, 1995).

In seeking to discern the true magnitude of this growing workplace threat, many public and occupational health researchers and policy specialists have expressed concerns over the reliance on fatality statistics as a sole data base to define the true extent and nature of workplace violence. In addition, merely using existing occupational fatality research methodology to establish the parameters of workplace violence clearly underrepresents a significant component of this contemporary occupational health issue—the incidence of nonfatal workplace physical assaults, verbal harassment, and other violent incidents.

There are wildly divergent estimates of the total number and types of workplace assaults, ranging from tens of thousands to hundreds of thousands annually. Two widely quoted recent national surveys reveal both an awareness and concern about escalating workplace violence among Americans. A survey conducted by CNN (Cable News Network) and *Time* (Mantell & Albrecht, 1994) reported that 37% of the respondents viewed workplace violence as a growing problem. In addition, 18% reported being victims of workplace assaults and another 18% feared becoming a victim of violence in the workplace, suggesting that more than one third of working Americans could be affected by actual or potential workplace violence. Results of another survey by the Northwestern National Life Insurance Company (see Appendix A, this volume) estimated during a 12-month period ending July 1993 that 2.2 million workers were victims of physical attacks, 6.3 million were threatened, and 16.1 million were harassed. The same survey indicated that 24% of the physical attacks, 43% of the threats, and 58% of the harassment incidents went unreported. Additionally, 15% of those surveyed reported being physically attacked at some time in their lives while at work. One in six reported being attacked with a weapon.

Other research published by federal health agencies provides further data on this newly recognized occupational health hazard. A special report, "Violence and Theft in the Workplace" (Bureau of Justice Statistics, 1994), estimated that 1 million Americans become victims of violent crimes in the nation's workplaces each year, resulting in almost 160,000 injuries and accounting for 15% of the more than 6.5 million acts of violence experienced by people aged 12 years or older. Using data gathered in the National Criminal Victimization Survey (NCVS) from 1987 to 1992, the report projected that 17% of all simple assaults, 14% of all aggravated assaults, and 8% of all rapes occur at work. Additionally, 56% of all workplace victimizations in the study were not reported to police, a figure almost 10% higher than unreported nonworkplace victimizations. This same study projected that 500,000 victims of workplace violent crimes lose an average of 3.5 workdays per crime, costing more than $55 million in lost wages per year. Some researchers consider the cumulative costs to be considerably higher when the added expenses of litigation and workers' compensation also are tabulated. Other data gathered by the Department of Labor (Bureau of Labor Statistics, 1994c) report that 22,396 nonfatal workplace attacks occurring in 1992 resulted in a median of 5 days lost from work.

The large differences and variations in reports, estimates, and projections of workplace violence limit a comprehensive understanding of this occupational health hazard. A recent report by the National Institute for Occupational Safety and Health (NIOSH; 1993) proposed four areas for workplace violence research and prevention efforts. These areas were to (a) identify occupations and workplaces that could be deemed "high risk"; (b) teach employers about the risks of workplace violence; (c) encourage employers to assess their threat level and implement security measures; and (d) stimulate additional research on workplace violence and related subjects.

To address the lack of a research consensus on workplace violence and to obtain specific data regarding members of the Laborers' International Union of North America (LIUNA), the Laborers' Health & Safety Fund of North America, a joint labor–management trust fund serving LIUNA and its affiliates, investigated the nature and extent of workplace violence in LIUNA-organized work sites. LIUNA represents approximately 750,000 working people in the United States and Canada. Many of the members of LIUNA and its affiliates are employed in construction settings, but they also work in a variety of other occupations, including building services and maintenance, health care, food processing, and public service. The approximate percentages of occupational settings where LIUNA members are employed include construction (60%), industrial and manufacturing (10%), public service (10%), health care and service contracts (5%), and other occupations (15%). These settings vary in terms of members' exposure to and risk factors for workplace violence.

A review of occupational research specific to health hazards in the construction industry shows that certain occupational codes, particularly that of laborers, are at disproportionate risk for accidental death, the category in which statistics for workplace homicide are entered. A study of injury hazards for that 1980–1989 (Kisner & Fosbroke, 1994) indicated although the construction industry is the United States' sixth largest employer, fatal injuries rank among the highest in the nation. Results of a study of occupational mortality reports from various states and the United Kingdom (Robinson et al., 1995) suggest that construction industry workers experience elevated mortality for cancer, respiratory conditions, mental conditions, homicide, and fatal injuries. Data gathered for 1993 (Bureau of Labor Statistics, 1994b) revealed that the construction industry accounted for the largest percentage (15%) of all fatal occupational injuries by industry segment and that of those fatalities, the category designated as operators, fabricators, and laborers had the largest percentage (31%). Another data source, a NIOSH-funded mortality study of 11,865 death benefit records of LIUNA members from 1985 to 1988 (Laborers' Health & Safety Fund of North America, 1993), revealed that deaths from suicide and homicide for young LIUNA members (both on and off the worksite) were higher than in the general population of the same age group.

The LIUNA Member Poll on Workplace Violence

The instrument used in this research effort was a one-page, 13-item questionnaire. The instrument investigated three issues: (a) members' general attitude concerning their personal safety in the workplace (Item 1); (b) incidence of violent or harassing behavior experienced by members in the past 5 years, including specific details and any follow-up actions (Items 2–10); and (c) demographic information on respondents' type of workplace, age, and gender.

The survey questionnaire was sent to LIUNA local business managers and training center directors in LIUNA's Midatlantic, Midwest, and South Central regions. The surveys were subsequently distributed to and collected from current union members during local meetings and training sessions. The completed questionnaires then were returned to the Laborers' Health & Safety Fund of North America staff for tabulation. A total of 389 members representing 17 local unions in seven states returned completed questionnaires. Eleven of those questionnaires received were rejected because of incompleteness or contradictory answers, resulting in a final sample size of 378.

Survey Results

The majority (73%) of survey respondents were LIUNA members employed in construction. These respondents included those employed as laborers in diverse worksites such as heavy and highway construction; building and maintenance of roads, bridges, tunnels, and public works projects; new construction or rehabilitation of existing commercial or public buildings; and others.

The remainder of the survey respondents (27%) were employed in building maintenance or service contracts (13%), health care settings (3%), and others (11%). The building maintenance or service contracts category included members performing jobs such as exhibit setup at convention centers, facilities maintenance and janitorial services in public buildings and government installations, and related tasks. The health care setting included members employed as nurse's aides, orderlies, technicians, and dietary workers in institutional settings, such as Veterans Administration hospitals and nursing homes. The "other" category included members employed in light manufacturing, food processing, public service, and professional positions.

Of the 378 respondents, 89% were male union members and 11% were female members. Gender distribution by type of worksite was as follows: In construction settings, 96% were male and 4% were female; in building maintenance and service contracts, 70% were male and 30% were female; in health care settings, 63% were male and 37% were female; and in the "other" category, 68% were male and 32% were female. Sixty-one percent of the respondents were aged 25–44 years, 15% were aged 18–24 years, 18% were aged 45–54 years, and 6% were aged 55–64 years. Cumulative percentages for these and responses to survey content questions are provided in Exhibit 1.

The responses to the questions about general attitudes about workplace safety yielded what was the poll's most significant finding: The vast majority of workers in this sample (84%) considered their workplaces a safe place to work. More than one third of the respondents (37%) reported having personally witnessed assaults, violence, or harassing behavior at their workplace.

More than half of the incidents witnessed by respondents (52%) were classified as verbal behavior, whereas 39% of the reported incidents included both verbal harassment and physical assault, and 9% were classified as physical assaults.

When asked about the results of the incidents witnessed, the respondents classified 73% as having resulted in stress or emotional problems, 36% resulted in a work stoppage, and 22% resulted in physical injury. In identifying who was injured or affected by the incident, respondents reported most often their coworkers (69%) and themselves (39%) as the victims. Other responses to this item included supervisors (16%); others (9%); and customers, clients, or patients (1%).

In identifying the individual who committed the assault, violence, or harassing behavior, respondents reported nearly equally that it was their

Exhibit 1. LIUNA Workplace Violence Survey Results: 1995 ($n = 378$)

1. Do you consider your workplace a safe place to work?	Yes (84%)		No (16%)	
2. Have you ever personally witnessed an assault, violence, or harassing behavior on a LIUNA jobsite?	Yes (37%)		No (63%)	
3. If yes, how many times in the past 5 years?	1–5 (77%)	5–10 (11%)	10–20 (4%)	More than 20 (8%)
4. Was the assault, violence, or harassing behavior verbal, physical, or both?	Verbal only (52%)	Physical only (9%)	Both (39%)	
5. What was the result of the assault, violence, or harassing behavior?	Physical injury (22%)	Stress, emotional problems (73%)	Work stoppage (36%)	
6. Who was the person injured or affected by the assault, violence, or harassing behavior?	Self (39%)	Coworker (69%)	C/C/P (1%)	Supervisor (16%) Other (9%)
7. Who was the person who committed the assault, violence, or harassing behavior?	Coworker (51%)	Customer (2%)	Supervisor (47%)	Other (18%)
8. Was the incident reported to management (or anyone else)?	Yes (44%)	No (29%)	Don't know (27%)	
9. After the report, was any action taken by management (or anyone else)?	Yes (58%)	No (27%)	Don't know (15%)	
10. What was the action?	Police (7%)	Disciplinary action (42%)	Warning (28%)	Other (7%)
What type of work setting do you work in?	Construction (73%)	M/S contract (13%)	Health care (3%)	Other (11%)
Age (years) of respondent	18–24 (15%) 25–34 (23%)	35–44 (38%)	45–54 (18%) 55–64 (6%)	
Gender of respondent	Male (89%)		Female (11%)	

Note. Multiple responses may add up to more than 100%. LIUNA = Laborers' International Union of North America; C/C/P = customer/client/patient; M/S = maintenance/service.

coworker (51%) or their supervisor (47%). Other possible responses to this item included others (18%) and customer, client, or patient (2%).

Less than half of the incidents (44%) were reported to management (or others); of those reported, follow-up action was taken in 58% of the incidents. The postreport actions taken were disciplinary actions (42%), warnings (28%), and police (7%) or other (7%).

Discussion

Preliminary analyses of responses from this member poll are congruent with previous national polls on attitudes and experiences of workplace violence and related behavior. These findings help confirm suspicions that the actual incidence of worksite assaults, harassment, and violence are considerably larger than published federal agency statistics of either reportable injuries or fatalities attributable to workplace violence. This lends credence to the views of many occupational health experts that the number of homicides in the workplace is just the tip of the iceberg relative to the numbers of assaults and related behaviors.

Perhaps the most significant finding is that despite reports of harassment and related violence they personally witnessed, most respondents view their workplaces as "safe." I readily admit a considerable semantic variance in the use of the word *safe* to describe an occupational setting. LIUNA members responding to the poll were given no definitions or explanations of the word before completing the survey. I contend that definitions of the word *safe* can range from a lack of generalized danger from hazardous chemicals, toxic substances, electrocution, and other factors to specific concerns about a worker's immediate personal safety from violence or physical assault.

Existing financial projections of workplace violence, combined with the poll responses on the effects of the reported incidents, have clear financial implications for employers, labor organizations, and others in the areas of risk reduction, health care expenditures, corporate liability, and workers' compensation experience ratings. Data from the Bureau of Labor Statistics in 1994 (1994a, 1994b, 1994c) and from the 1987–1992 NCVS (Bureau of Justice Statistics, 1994) reported an average of 3.5–5 workdays lost per injury. The LIUNA finding that one fifth of the incidents resulted in physical injuries merely reinforces the widely held assumption that preventive measures certainly can reduce the human and financial costs of this occupational health issue.

Many employers, labor unions, and other employee groups have made considerable progress in identifying and reducing risks associated with workplace homicides by improving workplace designs, developing security procedures, and related efforts. Unfortunately, these measures often are only instituted after a workplace homicide illustrates the potential for tragedy. Research on other preventive measures, such as adopting staffing levels and shift schedules that maximize employee safety, is indicated and will assist in efforts to develop an integrated and comprehensive approach to this issue.

That nearly three quarters of the incidents reported in the survey resulted in stress or emotional problems suggests the psychological effects of actual or even potential workplace violence may exceed the actual cost of the physical injuries sustained by the individual victims. Certainly, the finding that more than one third of the reported incidents resulted in work stoppage is significant for efforts in maximizing workplace productivity. Additional data from field studies that have investigated how workers are affected psychologically by such incidents, how long these effects last, how soon they will be able to return to full productivity, and whether these occurrences contribute to higher levels of employee turnover are needed to enable a truly precise accounting of the multiple costs of this occupational health hazard.

That less than one half of workplace harassment and other violent incidents in this sample were reported to police, management, or other is reminiscent of the findings of the NCVS (Bureau of Justice Statistics, 1994) results and illustrates the "soft" nature of existing figures on workplace violence. Given the small sample size, homogeneity of gender, and occupation and union affiliation, further studies of these variables are needed to discern the reasons for low reporting rates. Obtaining more accurate prevalence data through greater reporting will enable those affected occupational groups and segments to research, identify, and implement preventive approaches. This in turn raises workplace policy questions about the appropriate roles and responsibilities of workers, coworkers, union representatives, managers, and employers in preventing, documenting, and responding to workplace harassment, assaults, and other violence. Educating those in supervisory positions as well as workers and others involved in workplace violence to recognize and to document these behaviors and incidents is an essential first step.

The finding that more than half the worksite incidents reported by respondents included verbal harassment suggests a direction for worksite violence prevention education. If further research can establish more than a causal link between verbal harassment and subsequent physical assault, a preventive approach including specific targeted efforts focused on reducing threatening verbal exchanges in workplace interactions might be beneficial in reducing the incidence of assaults.

Using the example of corporate efforts to reduce sexual harassment in the workplace, the use of workplace policy orientation briefings and educational presentations on sexual harassment has indeed raised awareness of this issue among employees. More specifically, these educational sessions and promotional activities have clearly established the parameters of acceptable and unacceptable behavior vis-à-vis identifying the creation, recognition, and prevention of a hostile work environment. A hostile environment is a workplace where inappropriate sexual or even suggestive behavior occurs. By identifying a hostile work environment as being included in the definition of sexual harassment and educating employees in this distinction, it is reasoned that more egregious and obvious acts of sexual harassment will be prevented. In many workplaces, these efforts have resulted in attitudinal and behavioral changes among coworkers. Additional research on the relationship between verbal harassment and subsequent physical assault is indicated. The development of a behavior modification paradigm that teaches individuals acceptable and unacceptable parameters in the workplace for verbal harassment might be one practical application of such research. As in the sexual harassment example, attempts to effect attitudinal and behavioral changes among individuals with regard to limiting verbal harassment then may prevent or reduce the occurrence of physical assaults.

These early results are preliminary. The represent only the beginning of an ongoing effort to gauge the incidence and effects of workplace violence in a representative sample of the membership of the LIUNA. Additional field research among workers and in various work settings is essential to adequately formulate realistic policy initiatives and effective prevention strategies aimed at reducing the frequency and impact of workplace harassment, physical assaults, violence, and related occupational fatalities. Other areas that merit further investigation include comparative studies of the frequency and proportions of harassing and assaultive behavior across differing occupational groups, in union-organized versus non-union-organized work sites, and across gender and ethnic groups. Subsequent research then can continue with the goal of developing preliminary intervention strategies. These strategies could focus on high-risk work settings, occupational groups, and workplace cultures that create environments conducive to conflicts, verbal harassment, assaults, and other violent behavior responsible for occupational injuries and, ultimately, fatalities.

References

Bureau of Justice Statistics. (1994, July). *Violence and theft in the workplace* (Publication No. NCJ-148199). Washington, DC: U.S. Department of Justice.

Bureau of Labor Statistics. (1994a, February). *Compensation and working conditions: Workplace homicides in 1992.* Washington, DC: U.S. Department of Labor.

Bureau of Labor Statistics. (1994b, August). *1993 census of fatal occupational injuries.* Washington, DC: U.S. Department of Labor.

Bureau of Labor Statistics. (1994c, August). *Violence in the workplace comes under closer scrutiny* (Summary 94-10). Washington, DC: U.S. Department of Labor.

Bureau of Labor Statistics. (1995, August). *1994 census of fatal occupational injuries.* Washington, DC: U.S. Department of Labor.

Jenkins, E. L., Layne, L. A., & Kisner, S. M. (1992). Homicide in the workplace: The U.S. experience. *American Academy of Occupational Health News Journal, 40*(5), 215–218.

Kisner, S. M., & Fosbroke, D. E. (1994). Injury hazards in the construction industry. *Journal of Occupational Medicine, 36,* 137–142.

Laborers' Health & Safety Fund of North America. (1993). *NIOSH death certificates report.* Washington, DC: Author.

Mantell, M. R., & Albrecht, S. (1994). *Ticking bombs, defusing violence at work.* Los Angeles: Irwin.

National Institute for Occupational Safety and Health. (1993). *Alert: Request for assistance in preventing homicide in the workplace* (DHHS) Publication No. 92-109. Washington, DC: U.S. Department of Health and Human Services.

Robinson, C. F., Halperin, W. E., Alterman, T., Braddee, R. W., Burnett, C. A., Fosbroke, D. E., Kisner, S. M., Lalich, N. R., Roscoe, R. J., Seligman, P. J., Sestito, J. P., Stern, J. P., & Stout, N. A. (1995). Mortality patterns among construction workers in the United States. *Occupational Medicine: State of the Art Reviews, 10,* 269–283.

Part IV

Workplace Violence Prevention and Management

Introduction

Many incidents of workplace violence can be prevented, and when they do occur, the consequences can be mitigated with appropriate measures. The individual worker bears some responsibility, but businesses, managers, and unions can do a lot, through properly designed programs, to inoculate workplaces against violence. The following chapters suggest a variety of measures that companies can take. The general outlines of prevention and management programs are given, and what management and unions must do are discussed. Two chapters review specific programs, that could serve as models, used by the U.S. Postal Service and Hughes Electronics Corporation. The final two chapters deal with workplaces that harbor specific types of threat, namely correctional facilities and health-care settings.

Though the likelihood of armed violence in the workplace is relatively small, organizations are continually confronted with numerous nonlethal but equally damaging and costly incidents—physical altercations, threats, destruction of company property, intimidation, harassment—that cause problems for management and involve potential liability. Nicoletti and Spooner describe a proactive violence and threat management program to anticipate and thwart incidents of this type and to reduce the possibility of minor events escalating into major tragedies. They recommend forming a team to handle reports or threats of violent incidents. The team should actively search for potential problems and respond in a swift and organized manner. It should cover three areas: preparedness and prevention, involving policies and procedures to forestall the development of potentially violent situations, particularly at times of hiring and firing; incident management, so that situations with the immediate potential for violence can be dealt through standardized and tested procedures, covering such matters as coordinated receipt and dissemination of information and timely and appropriate intervention; and assessment, analysis, and management of the consequences of any incident.

Kinney adds more psychological depth to the discussion of prevention and management. Most incidents, he notes, occur after identifiable threats. Consequently, threats and various forms of erratic behavior should be reported and adequately investigated to ensure safety and security. The threatening behavior should be examined in the context of the problem individual's entire life, taking account of stresses and risk factors and the presence or absence of stabilizing forces or psychological anchors that may deter violent behavior. Such intrusive measures, however, would only breed resentment if workers feel they are imposed from above. Instead, workers at all levels of the organization should be made aware of the dangers and involved in policy development. Managers need not only proper training and adequate leadership but also broad support within the organization. The foundation of an adequate program must be a comprehensive and mandated reporting system that encourages threat information to flow from within and from outside the workplace.

The variety of measures that companies have actually taken so far are illustrated by Bush and O'Shea from a study of 59 businesses. Most of the businesses used preemployment screening to reduce risk, specified employee grievance and harassment procedures to deal with complaints, and employee assistance programs, as well as outplacement services for terminated employees. Few had specific prevention and crisis-management plans, stress management programs, or employee training in threat recognition. Such external security measures as security guards and video cameras were common, but metal detectors were rarely used.

The U.S. Postal Service (USPS), despite all the media hype on particular workplace homicides in its facilities, is far from being a high risk environment for occupational fatalities. Relative to other work settings, the USPS is in fact a "safe" workplace environment—the occupational fatality rate of USPS workers is only 37% of the rate for all workers in the various occupations combined. The USPS has the largest employee assistance program in the world, considered by many professionals a model for clinical responsiveness, cost-effectiveness, and clinical efficacy. Kurutz, Johnson, and Sugden provide background on this program, discussing its history, structure, and scope and its role in violence prevention. The authors describe the six-strategy workplace violence prevention model that underlies the program and the threat management process. The nationwide data management and telecommunications systems that support these efforts are also discussed.

Corporate downsizing can trigger serious incidents, and should be accompanied by specific prevention programs. As an increasingly common measure in competitive industries, it is a major source of uncertainty, confusion, and distress for individuals, corporations, and communities. Attention to the practical and emotional needs of all employees can facilitate transition and lessen the trauma for affected workers. Root and Ziska provide a case study of a multifaceted violence prevention program linked to major downsizing and employee displacement. The Hughes Electronics Corporation (formerly known as Hughes Aircraft Company) in Southern California had a workforce composed predominantly of well-educated engineers and highly skilled technicians and maintenance workers who experienced long-term stability in employment and good career growth. When it underwent significant downsizing in 1994, Hughes formed a "People Team" to assist employees and ensure they and their family members were treated with dignity and respect during the difficult phase-down process.

Unions can contribute to violence prevention, especially by training their members. King and Alexander discuss the design and implementation of a week-long course for union leaders on dealing with workplace violence. The course is designed to raise the awareness of union representatives of the causes of violence and their familiarity with effective prevention methods. Besides training, unions can work with management in dealing with workplace issues of communication, safety, and prevention. Union interest in violence stems from concerns about member safety and health, but has to go beyond such partial solutions as post-incident grief counseling to address psychosocial relations in the workplace as a whole. This will require building constructive relations with management.

Workers in correctional facilities face significant threats from the inmate population. Dignam and Fagan describe the risks, which range from routine assaults faced every day to the danger of more serious and traumatic violence. Hostage-taking incidents, for instance, have involved 157 employees of the Bureau of Prisons in nine separate incidents since 1987; none of them received serious physical injury, but significant emotional trauma resulted in many cases. Dignam and Fagan describe the Federal Bureau of Prison's intervention system to respond to and ameliorate the impact of such traumatic events on employees and their families. They describe one such incident, provide an account of how the intervention system responded, and discuss the outcome for the employees over time.

Like corrections staff, health-care staff face threats from their clientele. Flannery et al. describe a comprehensive program, already in place in some health-care settings, that deals with the sequelae of assault: the Assaulted Staff Action Program (ASAP). This voluntary program puts clinicians and mental health workers on call 24 hours a day to respond not only to physical and sexual but also to verbal and nonverbal assaults. The team, essentially a peer support group, provides individual crisis intervention, post-incident debriefing for the staff of entire wards, counseling of victims and families, and professional referral when needed. Flannery et al. describe how the program has worked in four mental health hospitals. Besides providing support for victims, it appears to be associated with sharp reductions in the actual number of incidents. In one facility, violence was reduced by 63% in 2 years, and the program more than paid for itself by reducing employee medical expenses, sick leave, accident claims, and staff turnover. Flannery et al. provide detailed guidelines to develop, train, and field a team adapted to a particular facility (and to encourage worker participation and minimize resistance).

15

Violence in the Workplace: Response and Intervention Strategies

John Nicoletti and Kelly Spooner

Over the past decade, workplace violence has continued to gain momentum, with incidents escalating in both frequency and intensity (Johnson & Indvik, 1994). Workplace violence has become an important issue for corporate America in the 1990s. Bosses, coworkers, spouses, and supervisors are being murdered on the job at an ever-increasing rate. Corporate layoffs, downsizing, availability of firearms, and media attention are just some of the factors that seem to be fueling this trend.

Criminologists now identify workplace homicide as the fastest growing category of murder in America (O'Boyle, 1992). Targets of this violence are company employees, from management to front-line staff members (Johnson & Indvik, 1994). Perpetrators come from within and outside the organization and include disgruntled former workers, frustrated employees, angry customers, and estranged or jealous spouses who bring their rage to the worksite.

During the 1980s, the National Institute for Occupational Safety and Health found that an average of 15 people were murdered on the job each week, totaling approximately 800 deaths a year (Barker, 1994). A far greater number of workers are being physically attacked, threatened, or harassed each year (see Appendix A, this volume).

This phenomenon comes with a hefty price tag. The National Safe Workplace Institute estimates the average cost to employers for a single episode of workplace violence is $250,000, which encompasses lost work time, posttrauma interventions, and legal expenses (Anfuso, 1994). Additionally, an increasing number of negligence suits have been filed against companies who failed to take appropriate and reasonable action to prevent violent acts from occurring. In the case of wrongful deaths, monetary awards assigned by juries to victims' families average $2.2 million (Weisberg, 1994). Currently, workplace liability is the most rapidly expanding area of civil litigation. The courts have made it virtually impossible for companies to ignore their responsibility to keep workers safe.

Violence Prevention and Threat Management Programs

The rapid rise and incredible expense of violence in the workplace has prompted a few companies to find ways to combat this potential loss. In general, however, companies have been slow to react. A survey of human resource professionals by the Society of Human Resource Management, released in December 1993, indicated that more than half of the employers surveyed reported that two to five acts of violence occurred in their workplace over the past 5 years (Anfuso, 1994). Yet, despite these disturbing statistics, less than one third of the employers had any preventive program or crisis management policy to prevent a violent episode or handle the aftermath (Anfuso, 1994).

Corporations that have implemented programs differ greatly in their approach. Part of the reason for this is the diverse nature of companies; one standard policy would not necessarily be appropriate and applicable to all enterprises. However, the programs often vary along one dimension: the amount of proactive responsibility the employer is willing to assume. Some companies have only "clean-up teams," which are designed to deal with business details and reactions after a violent episode. Taking a more active role, the majority of programs emphasize education and training as key elements for prevention, with good reason. Unlike robbery and commercial crimes, workplace violence almost always happens after a predictable sequence of events, making the establishment of a specific protocol possible and paramount to ensuring the protection of all employees. The purpose of a preventive strategy is to recognize, detect, and address potentially violent situations before they escalate into tragedy. Additionally, almost all programs include a plan of action to be implemented after a violent incident has occurred.

The United States Postal Service's Program

In general, public offices have clearer policies and procedures than do private corporations (Barker, 1994). The United States Postal Service (USPS), for example, recently has introduced new policies to address employee job stress and hopefully to defuse violent situations. The USPS now maintains a 24-hour hotline for employees to report threats or safety concerns. It conducts employee focus groups regularly, thus providing a forum for workers to openly discuss past episodes of violence and present safety concerns and to generate ideas about violence prevention tactics. This serves to promote communication between employees and management and hopefully improves the working environment for all employees.

The plan unveiled by the USPS is, in many ways, prototypical of most company programs. It suggests guidelines for hiring and firing practices; emphasizes the use of appropriate reporting, assessment, and security measures; and attempts to promote a positive work atmosphere. The USPS's employee assistance program (EAP) is considered the cornerstone of the violence prevention program. Emphasis is on the creation of a work environment that fosters and maintains the ideals of value and respect for the individual employee's worth and dignity. Efforts are made to ensure that all employees are aware of the resources available to them to assist them in handling difficulties with work and everyday living.

The main thrust of this and many similar programs is to prevent violent episodes among current and former workers. The USPS's program has no provisions to address specifically threats from nonemployees, such as customers and employees' spouses. Historically, because violent episodes at the post office most often have involved employees, the program was designed with this perpetrator in mind. Yet, statistically, employees account for only 30% of workplace violence (see Appendix A). Most incidents are perpetrated by customers and a large portion are committed by strangers, who often enter the workplace to assault or kill their spouse or partner. The program proposed by the USPS is therefore limited by neglecting a large body of potential perpetrators. In their defense, the USPS has made great strides in implementing policies designed to reduce their previously overly authoritarian style and to improve employee treatment. This will no doubt help deter some offenders. However, a comprehensive violence prevention program needs to address threats stemming from the entire spectrum of potential perpetrators.

The Strategic Safety Association's Program

The Strategic Safety Association, a consulting firm for preventing workplace violence, and its executive director, Robert Pater, have developed a program with a similar emphasis on employees that underscores employer attunement to the individual employee's stress level (Barker, 1994). Recognizing the different contributors to employee stress, the plan proposes examination of environmental, personal, and organizational factors. Environmental contributors often are out of the control of the employer and include outside influences such as the media's attention and glamorization of violence, the changing roles of women in the workplace, and decreased insurance funding for psychological treatment. Pater also acknowledged that violence may result from the *fear* of violence in the workplace. Environmental contributors to this include a work environment that does not provide adequate cover and concealment, escape possibilities, or warning systems.

Personal factors that play a role in employee stress result from factors in the individual's background, motivations, and abilities. To counteract some of these personal factors, Pater recommended offering supportive intervention to help employees recover from difficult situations.

Organizational factors contributing to employee stress include downsizing, an increased push for productivity, poor communication, poor supervision, and a refusal to acknowledge workplace violence as a problem. To minimize the impact of the factors, some of which are inevitable, Pater suggested training supervisors to communicate effectively, recognize overstressed employees, and sensitively terminate employees. Most importantly, a strong plan for addressing workplace violence is crucial to make employees feel secure.

The focus of Pater's program is on treating employees sensitively and delicately, especially when they are experiencing a personal crisis or need to be terminated from the company. Pater also recognized how fear of violence in the workplace negatively affects employees and recommended the use of standard, practical security procedures to help decrease employees' fears.

Johnson and Indvik's Approach

In addition to education and interpersonal skills training, the plan proposed by Johnson and Indvik (1994) focuses on reducing the impact of personal contributors to violence. The plan includes provisions for increasing workers' self-esteem and empowering them through "compassionate leadership." They likened the employee–employer relationship to that of parent and child, and their program is based on the rationale that employees bring childhood and family dynamics to the workplace. Employees who feel empowered and united with the company in a significant way, like a strong family, are less likely to act out violently within the confines of the workplace. They advocated maintaining the sanctity of the "psychological contract" between employer and employee through open communication, conflict resolution, and mutual respect. They believed that this type of atmosphere maximizes the effort, output, and contribution by the employee and simultaneously reduces the propensity for aggression within the organization.

Johnson and Indvik's (1994) "paths to prevention" of workplace violence involve both the physical and psychological realms. Proper training for managers and employees is proposed, along with implementation of basic physical security measures. Their final plan advocates the following key procedures: preemployment guidelines, threat analysis and immediate security response, notifying law enforcement, security for executives and threatened personnel, policies for communicating with the workforce and the media, establishing psychological assistance programs, and disseminating information about violence to all employees.

The uniqueness of Johnson and Indvik's (1994) approach is their strong emphasis on ways employers can build employees' self-esteem and increase their sense of empowerment. They offered specific techniques of supervision that can foster employees' sense of belonging and increase their pride in their work and special skills. By using these techniques and making employees feel unique, competent, secure, empowered, and connected, Johnson and Indvik believed that this will decrease aggressive tendencies and increase the likelihood employees will make significant contributions to the organization.

Lindsey's Approach

In his workplace violence prevention program, Lindsey (1994) began with the premise that violence in the workplace takes many forms. Violent behaviors include sexual harassment, threats, violence, vandalism, belligerence, as well as verbal conflicts that escalate into physical altercations. He supported the view that violence is the end product of a process and that it therefore provides an opportunity for intervention at several points. He suggested performing a "cognitive ergonomic analysis" of the workplace approximately every 6 months.

Ergonomics involves adapting tools, procedures, methods, or the environment to meet the needs of the worker. Cognitive ergonomics analyzes the psychological factors that may be contributing to feelings of stress, discrimination, harassment, or fear in employees. From this information an intervention can be formulated and implemented.

Lindsey's (1994) proposal entails administration of a standardized survey to all employees, in which they anonymously rate their job stress and satisfaction level. They also are asked to report levels of distress experienced with discrimination, harassment, job security, and health and safety issues. In this way, the mental and emotional "pulse" of the company is available for review, and when problem areas or sudden changes become evident they can be addressed immediately. The data also can be readily compared with other indexes of problems such as health services use, frequency of claims, and accident or injury reports.

Lindsey (1994) offered another method of assessing attitudes, motivations, and perceptions of employees through the use of focus groups. Focus groups may offer employees the opportunity to verbally express their concerns, but, as Lindsey warned, these are subject to group dynamics and the influence of power differentials if middle and upper management personnel are involved. Additionally, because of the highly subjective nature of this information, it is extremely difficult to reduce to a usable database.

Baron's Approach

The program designed by Baron (1993) emphasizes understanding human behavior as a basis for predicting violence. He promoted training and education as key components in any corporation's threat management plan. He contended training should include information to familiarize employees with a "profile" of a violent person, which is based on traits found in former perpetrators. Characteristics of this profile constitute "red flags" and include the following: a past history of violence, psychosis, romantic obsession, substance abuse, depression, externalization of blame by the person, impaired neurological functioning, frustration with the environment, interest in weapons, and the presence of a personality disorder. In conjunction with this, he advocated that employees be taught to recognize the signs of stress in coworkers. Although admitting that the science of psychological profiling is imperfect, Baron believed that it is still invaluable when coupled with a list of warning signs and other reliable indicators and that it will assist companies in identifying volatile, possibly dangerous, employees.

Baron's (1993) program relies on employees reporting these signs as well as any threatening remarks or hostile actions to designated authorities. Of course, there needs to be an organized system in place to receive concerns and reports of threats and to evaluate them quickly. According to Baron, policy and procedure will determine which individuals will be responsible for evaluating the situation and assessing threat credibility. He noted that the method of reporting should ensure confidentiality for the reporter.

As part of his preventive program, Baron (1993) urged that management be trained in hiring, downsizing, and termination procedures to foresee and alleviate potential problems in these areas. Baron's program also offers guidelines to be followed in the event of a crisis situation and debriefing measures afterward. Specifically, he suggested the formation of a crisis management team that can be called on in the event of a violent incident.

Hardee's Program

In 1990, Hardee's Food Systems, Inc., created and implemented a comprehensive violence prevention program. The program is unique in that it addresses both internal and external threats of violence. The program entails extensive training and education to all employees about workplace violence and has a specific intervention policy to address threats, harassment, and domestic violence directed at any employee. In their plan normal security procedures play a secondary role, and the human resources department serves as the front-line defense. The human resources department actively uses extensive preemployment screening measures, trains managers to recognize and treat violent behaviors, and implements organized processes for reporting and responding to threats. The company's philosophy is to establish a working environment in which employees feel empowered and supported by company-run services such as the EAP. In addition to the education and assessment components, the plan calls for operation of a prevention task force to investigate, analyze, and intervene in threatening or potentially volatile circumstances. They established a 24-hour hotline for reporting safety concerns, which then are handled by their violence prevention task force. Their program also includes informational workshops on personal safety and protection for all employees.

Kinney's Program

The violence prevention program designed by Joseph A. Kinney of the National Safe Workplace Institute asserts that threat assessment begins with evaluation of the source of the threat, in conjunction with information known about characteristics of violent people (Kinney, 1995). He dispelled the myth that people just "snap" and become violent; instead, he offered various warning signs that predict aggressive actions. He cautioned that although only a small percentage of individuals who exhibit these signs will eventually become violent, one must be prepared. Kinney warned against using a profile because the workplace offender is varied and ever-changing. Decisions based on characteristics of previous perpetrators may be incorrect because evaluators could be lulled into a false sense of security when a potential assailant does not meet the profile criteria. With this caveat, he suggested some of the traits that many perpetrators have in common, such as a strong identification with their job and a sense of entitlement about their rights and privileges within the workplace.

In assessing threats, Kinney (1995; Kinney & Johnson, 1993) suggested that it is important to examine the overall life context of the individual, especially other stress and risk factors present in his or her life. Examples of such stress factors include the recent breakup of a relationship, being passed over for an expected promotion, financial problems, estranged or strained relationships with coworkers, and a perception of being targeted by management. Evaluators also should look for signs of violence toward property because this can indicate increasing hostility.

Another tactic in threat assessment is to examine the number of psychological "anchors" the individual possesses (Kinney, 1995; Kinney & Johnson, 1993). Anchors are personal characteristics and life circumstances that help stabilize and ground people during stressful times. Examples of anchors include a secure family life, stable finances, lack of substance abuse, outside interests, religious life, friendships, emotional stability, and a positive work history. Kinney asserted that the more anchors a person has, the less likely he or she is to behave in an irrational or violent manner. The absence or presence of these types of stabilizing forces are important to consider in determining an individual's propensity for violence.

In considering the level of threat posed, Kinney (1995; Kinney & Johnson, 1993) classified aggressive behavior according to a frequency pattern specific to the perpetrator. He distinguished three frequency levels: aberrational, periodic, and endemic. Aberrational is aggressive or threatening behavior that is unusual for the person. He or she has no history of violent behavior, and this type of outburst poses minimal threat if it is a one-time occurrence. Periodic or intermittent aggression is characteristic of a person whose temper routinely flares up. This suggests that the individual is functioning in a chronic state of hostility and that intervention by mental health professionals may be indicated, especially if the anger is accompanied by other disruptive behaviors or a decrease in organizational productivity. The final classification is endemic, which is defined as frequent aggressive or abusive behavior. At this point, the behavior is entrenched and has become a routine part of the person's behavioral repertoire. This high frequency of aggressive behavior requires prompt action and possible removal from the workplace.

Similar to other workplace violence prevention programs, Kinney

(1995; Kinney & Johnson, 1993) emphasized early intervention and preventive measures as the best defense. He recommended a mandated reporting system, with negative consequences to employees who fail to report suspicious situations. In evaluating and addressing threats, Kinney proposed several steps that need to be undertaken. Information from employees is first channeled to the appropriate human resources or security personnel, who document the specifics of the threatening situation and information on whether the employee in question has a history of previous incidents or violence. On the basis of this, the designated personnel determine whether the person poses a serious threat to other people or property. He found it useful to classify threats on a continuum of veiled, conditional, and direct. If the situation warrants it, the alleged perpetrator may be removed from the company until an investigation is completed. The threat assessment team is notified and then becomes responsible for determining a course of action. According to this plan, human resources, in consultation with security, will determine if the matter is of a medical or disciplinary nature. Depending on the conclusion, one of four courses of action then will be followed: (a) Have the employee undergo a fitness-for-duty examination by a qualified professional; (b) institute disciplinary measures; (c) remove the employee from the job with suspension or termination options; and (d) mandate counseling. Kinney thought it important for human resources, security, or both to take an aggressive role in reviewing all information and establishing and executing a course of action. Documenting the rationale for every step taken is highly recommended.

Kinney (1995; Kinney & Johnson, 1993) also addressed threats that originate from outside the workplace, such as customers and estranged spouses, and detailed some predictable patterns associated with these offenders. However, the main objective of his program is for employers to pay strict attention to the behavior of their employees, mainly because they have more leverage to intervene and manage this population.

The Nicoletti-Flater Approach

The intervention format we propose involves education and training as a means of violence prevention. The programs are tailored for presentation to major businesses, corporations, and governmental agencies. Like many other programs, we recommend formation of a committee or team to receive and handle reports or threats or violent incidents. This threat/violence assessment team (TVAT) should be proactive, capable of a swift and organized response, clear about its objectives, and cohesive in deployment of its goals. Achieving these qualities requires foresight and careful planning before an incident occurs.

Our strategy incorporates three phases, all of which are designed to address threats stemming from internal or external sources. The first two phases emphasize preparedness and prevention and are designed for implementation before and after threats have been made. The focus of the first two phases is on coordinated receipt and dispersement of information and timely, proactive intervention to prevent violence from occurring. The third phase entails action to be undertaken after a major incident. All three phases have provisions for self-assessment of the agency's program and a postincident analysis.

Our program is unique in that the overall plan has been conceptualized and reduced to "flow charts" detailing organized actions to be taken by designated individuals. The charts are designed to provide a step-by-step format with clear guidelines for the appropriate level of intervention given the presenting circumstances. The action charts provide the agency with the opportunity to respond to the threat or violence rather than react. In conjunction with corporate structure and needs, we developed three action flow charts. The first flow chart details prescribed action to be taken when violence is occurring and involves pretraining of personnel in evasion and tactical responses. The second flow chart is designed for situations in which violence appears imminent. This chart relies heavily on separating the potential perpetrator from the potential targets as the initial response. The third flow chart is used when there are only allegations, concerns, or veiled threats. This flow chart emphasizes verification and documentation activities.

The main thrust of our program is to assist companies in developing guidelines to recognize and thwart all levels of threats or violence that may occur within their workplace. We have observed that, for the majority of companies, the likelihood of an individual entering with a loaded weapon is relatively small. However, organizations are confronted continually with numerous nonlethal but equally damaging and costly incidents. Physical altercations, threats, destruction of company property, intimidation, and harassment cause trouble and potential liability. Our program describes measures that can reduce the possibility of minor events escalating into major tragedies.

Phase 1: Organization, Evaluation, and Prevention

The objective for Phase 1 of the program is to invoke all possible actions to forestall development of potentially violent situations, starting at the two end points where violence potential can most easily be avoided: hiring and firing. Companies are advised to develop policies and procedures regarding these practices. Strict preemployment guidelines with sufficient background checks are a good way to screen out high-risk individuals. Areas for background investigation can include the following: the applicant's past employment chronology, criminal record, workers' compensation history (pursuant to ADA guidelines; i.e., only after a provisional offer of employment has been made), education, experience, training, military service, credit history, and inquiries regarding general character and reputation. Because the information received involves significant legal ramifications, examination of local employment-related laws for each state is necessary. Releases of information should be obtained before a background investigation is conducted to protect all parties. The cost of background checks must be weighed with the risk of negligent hiring, with deference being given to reasonable rights to privacy by the prospective employee. Some programs recommend checking driving records, which may indicate the person's impulsivity or proneness to risk-taking behavior. Public records such as these are inexpensive to obtain and pose minimal infringement on civil liberties. We also recommend obtaining information on the individual's history of perceived injustices. All the previously mentioned areas of investigation should be reviewed and approved by the corporate legal counsel before implementation.

Regarding termination procedures, management needs to be trained in optimal downsizing and firing practices. Careful planning can lessen the negative impact on employees. Employees always should be treated with dignity and respect, but this is especially important during downsizing or termination. The company should establish and follow congruent, objective criteria when selecting employees for dismissal. Employers should be cautioned about getting rid of a problem employee through a layoff instead of addressing the performance or behavioral concern. Employees who are to be terminated should be provided with options to minimize their feelings of being "cornered" or out of control.

First, we, as well as most authorities examining this problem, recommend the development of standard operating procedures before the occurrence of any threatening incidents. We also recommend a company policy mandate, through explicit and implicit means, that employees immediately report any threat or security concern to the designated authorities. Our suggestion is to allow the TVAT to handle these reports. Any threat made by an individual is significant and has been shown to be predictive of later violence (Kennish, 1994). Without knowledge of potentially violent situations, the company is severely hindered in its objective of protecting employees. Because the most successful and valid approaches to violence prediction use multiple data sources, evaluation of any personal information on a potentially violent individual helps formulate a more accurate prediction. Information from multiple sources is necessary in this process, and thus employee reporting is crucial to this process.

For violence to occur, the perpetrator must have sufficient time, opportunity, ability, desire, and stimulus (Nicoletti, 1994). The objective of the TVAT is to remove some or all of these enabling factors, thereby decreasing the likelihood of violence. Preventive-oriented human resources programs, well-trained managers who recognize problems, and an immediate response to warning signs provide the best defense.

The composition of the TVAT should include representatives from security, EAPs, human resources departments, public relations, and legal factions. If the company is unionized, someone from labor relations also should be present. We strongly recommend that a professional trained in violence assessment procedures also be included on a regular or consultative basis. The main objective of the team is to be responsible for developing a protocol to handle threats and acts of violence directed at company employees. They must establish strict guidelines for dealing with threats that occur in any form (e.g., verbal, written, or nonverbal actions) and to actively address potentially volatile situations.

The team must have an organized method to formally evaluate situations and the people involved. The most important element to the functioning of the TVAT is an effective communication system among all members and a detailed flow chart of who is to take what action. Optimally, one person, the team leader (or on-call team leader), receives all pertinent information. The team leader should have expertise or, at the least, training and experience in such matters. Planned and coordinated pathways of communication between employees and the team, and among all team members, is the crucial first step in ensuring an effective and timely response.

Once a threat is made and reported, a meeting should be held to gather and evaluate data, determine the level of threat the situation poses, and take appropriate action. Determining the level of threat is a complex process and should be undertaken with consultation by competent professionals trained in violence prediction. We outline some guidelines for assessing threat in the next few sections. Actions that may be taken when a threat is determined to be serious include mandated counseling, temporary suspension, disciplinary action, and fitness-for-duty evaluation. Follow-up and monitoring of the situation is warranted, as is thorough documentation in a postincident report.

To determine the level of threat posed by an individual's behavior, the team must be able to identify and classify verbal and behavioral patterns. Employees can be abusive verbally or nonverbally. All behavioral factors must be analyzed together to establish a valid profile and determine the risk potential. Language often reflects the emotional or mental state of an individual and can provide clues to future action. Verbal statements fall on a continuum ranging from compliant to assaultive, with compliant being the most benign and indicating cooperativeness and lack of conscious hostility. Negative verbal communication is the next level and consists basically of the use of pessimistic, negative responding. After this, verbalizations can escalate into abusive and derogatory language, which involves name calling, accusations, belittling, and use of vulgar and offensive statements. The final category, verbally assaultive, is the most serious. At this point, the individual is overtly threatening and attempting to intimidate others. A person who is verbally assaultive may make death threats, threaten to perform industrial sabotage, or actually physically assault someone. The perpetrator presents a greater risk if the content is extremely destructive, sadistic, or bizarre.

In addition to verbal communication, aggressive behavior can be physical. These behaviors also range on a continuum from least to most threatening. Like spoken language, actions reflect the perpetrator's internal emotional state. Levels of physical abuse range from compliant to deadly assaultive. A compliant individual is one who is fully cooperative and essentially nonthreatening. A passive resistive person is one who does not follow directives but is not overtly confrontational. This individual may demonstrate slow but eventual compliance with instructions. The next category is active resistant, in which the physical behavior is a mixture of passive–aggressiveness and intentional noncompliance. At this point, the degree of resistance has intensified in scope. The person may destroy property or otherwise cause problems, such as engaging in covert sabotage or seeking vengeance through arbitration or other channels. The final categories, assaultive and deadly assaultive, are self-explanatory. The danger factor is extremely high at these levels, and the individual should be considered dangerous. Both verbal and physical aggression are evident. The individual's intention is to harm or destroy property or people, and attempts to gain compliance are met with hostile resistance or attack.

It is imperative that the TVAT be prepared to handle threats that come from outside the organization as well as from employees or ex-employees. Marital or personal relationship problems are increasingly entering the workplace in the form of domestic violence and stalking. Research done by Northwestern National Life Insurance Company (see Appendix A, this volume) has shown that domestic violence and stalking violence recently have accounted for more injuries and deaths in the workplace than that committed by disgruntled or ex-employees. This has been our experience as well. Currently, there is a discrepancy among authorities about the employer's responsibility to protect employees from their own personal problems. It is our contention that other, noninvolved employees are at risk in these situations and that because of this, it becomes the employer's duty to enact protocols to protect all employees.

Stalking is defined legally as "willful, malicious and repeated following and harassment combined with credible threat intended to make the victim fear death or serious injury" (Nicoletti, 1994, p. 13). Most stalking occurs because of the assailant's obsession with his or her object. The target usually is an estranged wife or girlfriend. Employees should be aware of indications of stalking and take all situations seriously. The first occurrence usually involves repeated telephone calls to the victim. The employer may help the victim obtain a restraining order to prevent this. In California, the courts are considering allowing companies to obtain similar restraining orders, and lawsuits have been won when companies failed to do so and employee deaths resulted. If the stalker persists, it may become necessary to contact law enforcement officials and have the individual prosecuted. Applicable statutes regarding stalking vary from state to state, and specific interventions will depend on the current legislation and the organization's resources.

Stalkers, like other violent perpetrators, go through predictable phases of behavior that begin benignly and, if unattended, may escalate. These phases include mental obsession, surveillance, harassment, and extermination. Similar guidelines to those detailed earlier regarding assessment of the level of threat should be used for stalkers. However, as Kinney (1995) noted, this is the most difficult individual on which to obtain information. This is because of the victim's frequent resistance to disclose information and the fact that the individual is outside the agency's scope.

The team's objective during Phase 1 should include notification of potential victims and the use of reasonable steps to ensure their safety while they are on or off the worksite. At this stage, it is important to record and maintain written documentation of actions effected by the team, the rationale for actions taken or not taken, and the expected and actual outcome. As part of the prevention phase, the team needs to compile a list of in-house and community resources to assist potential perpetrators and victims. Examples include EAPs, available therapists or counselors in the community, and safehouses. With information and access to available resources, the team can actively assist a potential target in devising a safety strategy.

We theorize that in violent behavior, unconfronted disruptive behaviors will either continue or escalate (Nicoletti, 1994). This has been echoed by other experts in the field. Pater explained that "if employees throw up red flags and they're ignored, they feel they have permission to go to the next level" (cited in Barker, 1993, p. 33). Kennish (1994) warned against the dangers of minimizing behaviors and failing to respond; "as a result, the problem remains and violence eventually ensues" (p. 34). On the basis of this, it is imperative that employers intervene at the lower ends of the continuum.

Phase 2: Handling Threats and Aggressive Action

The second phase of our intervention strategy involves implementing a standardized procedure to manage different types of situations that could precipitate violence. In each situation, there needs to be an established action threshold, a point at which verbalizations or gestures will not be tolerated by the company and will warrant intervention by the team. We recommend that companies subscribe to a "zero-tolerance" policy for verbal threats. In response to threats, the employer will investigate, document, and enact prescribe disciplinary actions. This policy should be clear and obvious. Each new and current employee should be given a written statement detailing such admonishments, and verification of the receipt of the statement documented by employee's signature should be retained.

Three types of employee actions command management intervention: abusive language, threats, and violent or aggressive actions. Most companies do not allow profanity or abusive language in the workplace, making it easy to identify it when it occurs. Threats can appear on different levels, however, and may not be recognized as easily. In a vein similar to Kinney (1995), we classify threats as direct, conditional, or veiled and think that it is important to determine the type because the risk of violence increases with each level. Direct threats are obvious statements that the individual intends to do harm, and these always warrant immediate intervention. However, conditional or veiled threats can be subtle and much more difficult to assess.

Assessing the specifics of the threat and its severity are important. When assessing the nature and seriousness of threats, it is particularly important to consult with an outside agency that specializes in violence and risk assessment. A complete and competent evaluation of the evidence is crucial in determining the lethality of an individual.

In any formal appraisal of threats or threatening actions, it is necessary to discover and record in detail the nature and circumstances of the suspect and his or her actions during the alerting incident. Interviewing all witnesses is crucial in gathering this information. At this point, it also is good to determine when the threat was made and if an accompanying complaint was filed quickly. This information provides the team with feedback about the effectiveness of their intervention strategy. If their education and prevention program is working, the complaint should have been made shortly after the threat was perceived. If the threat was not reported, it is important to discover the reason for this and to revamp any flaw in the program.

The presence or absence of any contradicting information also is important. For example, if the person has threatened to shoot someone and it is known that he or she has access to and knowledge of firearms, this is important information in determining the viability of the threat. On the other hand, if the threat is to plant a bomb and "blow up this place" and it is known that this person has no background in explosives, this information decreases threat credibility.

An investigation into the suspected perpetrator's background is useful at this point. Although we know of no verifiable "profile" of the workplace violence perpetrator, there are several validated risk factors for general violence that should be considered and examined for a match. These include the following: history of violence, poor impulse control, unsuccessful personal history, injustice history, obsession, substance abuse, interest in or ownership of weapons, preoccupation with violence, current situational stressors, and mental illness.

Positive correlations with these risk factors proportionally increases the chances that the individual will act violently. However, the absence of these variables does not necessarily indicate minimal risk. The totality of the situation and the personal dynamics of the individual must be taken into account.

If the suspicious person is an employee, a meeting should be held by the TVAT to confront him or her with allegations of his or her activities and to explain the reasons for the intervention. Evaluation of the accused person's reaction is important, but it should never be accepted at face value. For example, an apparently contrite person should not be allowed leeway in established disciplinary or intervention policies. On the other hand, a person who feels justified and continues to make threats warrants serious cause for concern and most likely requires stringent security measures.

Phase 3: Posttrauma Debriefing

The third phase of the intervention plan designates action to be undertaken by the TVAT after a violent or near-violent incident or even if just a threat was made. Threats and violence significantly affect employees' comfort zones and shatter their perceptions about the world, thus creating a traumatic reaction. The team's responsibilities in this phase are to coordinate timely, organized action and intervention for all involved parties. The targeted group should be as comprehensive as possible, but should at the least include victims and other affected employees and witnesses. We also recommend that families of the victims and employees who are not directly involved should not be included. Contact with outside agencies is crucial at this stage because there may not be sufficient in-house resources to handle the demand for therapeutic services. At this point, the focus is on debriefing the individuals involved and assisting them with the traumatic aftermath. Research demonstrates that the earlier the intervention, the less likely there will be negative, long-lasting psychological effects. It also is cost-effective for the company because therapy, when implemented immediately after a trauma, has been shown to be relatively brief compared with therapy implemented later. Additionally, individuals are less likely to be litigious if given reasonable and appropriate care immediately after an incident.

Violent episodes almost always attract media attention. It is therefore important that the team predesignate someone to act as a company spokesperson and assume responsibility for releasing information to the community.

Conclusion

Because workplace violence is a relatively new field, there is little outcome data available on the effectiveness of violence prevention programs. Hardee's reported decreased criminal-related violence after implementation of their program but did not provide data on employee-related violence. We have found similar reports and results from the companies we have trained over the past 3 years. Almost all authorities agree, as we do, that time is of the essence in these situations and that the implementation of standard policies and procedures is the best way of ensuring a timely response to this disruptive, possibly lethal behavior.

In designing a program, companies need to first decide whether the program is intended to defuse and deflect violence from a specific perpetrator, much like the USPS has done, or whether it will attempt to educate and help protect employees from a host of potential perpetrators, either within or outside the workplace, such as the program developed by Hardee's. Regardless of the specific focus, core elements need to include the following: a centralized reporting system, an organized and standard way to evaluate and address threats, physical security or a plan to secure such, training for all employees on violence prevention, and a plan for postincident action. Supplements to this may include enhanced EAPs, focus groups or other assessment tools, education for employees on personal safety issues and domestic violence, increased security measures, employee training on conflict resolution and management, and implementation of a TVAT.

A new era of treating employees respectfully also is emerging from increased awareness of this problem. Increased sensitivity to employee issues and viewpoints can be an effective adjunct to a sound, comprehensive violence prevention program. Intuitively, this seems to promise a decrease in employee frustration and alienation and perhaps will forestall violent responses within the workplace.

References

Anfuso, D. (1994). Deflecting workplace violence. *Personnel Journal, 73*(10), 66–77.

Barker, T. (1994). How to prevent violence in the workplace. *Safety and Health, 150*(1), 32–38.

Baron, S. A. (1993). *Violence in the workplace.* Ventura, CA: Pathfinder Publishing.

Johnson, P. R., & Indvik, J. (1994). Workplace violence: An issue of the nineties. *Public Personnel Management, 23*(4), 515–523.

Kennish, J. W. (1994). Violence in the workplace: Stemming the tide. *Professional Safety, 40*(6), 34–36.

Kinney, J. A. (1995). *Essentials of managing workplace violence.* Charlotte, NC: Pinkerton Services Group.

Kinney, J. A., and Johnson, D. L. (1993). *Breaking point: The workplace violence epidemic and what to do about it.* Chicago: National Safe Workplace Institute.

Lindsey, D. (1994). Of sound mind? Evaluating the workforce. *Security Management, 38*(9), 69–71.

Nicoletti, J. (1994). *Violence goes to work.* Englewood, CO: Mountain States Employers Council.

O'Boyle, T. F. (1992, September 15). Disgruntled workers intent on revenge increasingly harm colleagues and bosses. *Wall Street Journal,* pp. B1, B10.

Weisberg, D. (1994). Preparing for the unthinkable. *Management Review, 83*(3), 58–61.

16

Workplace Violence: Comparative Use of Prevention Practices and Policies

David F. Bush and P. Gavan O'Shea

Violent behavior associated with the workplace has become increasingly common in the past 15 years (Kinney, 1995; Kinney & Johnson, 1993); between 1980 and 1989, 7,660 deaths were attributed to workplace violence, and homicide was the nation's second leading cause of death on the job (Travnick, 1994). Additionally, the consequences of violence in the workplace are costly for organizations where such events occur, regardless of whether they have effective contingency programs to respond to such events.

Practices implemented to prevent workplace violence include internal and external security measures. External prevention methods often include security guards, limited-access areas, fences, and closed-circuit TV monitoring, whereas internal measures often consist of preemployment screening, employee assistance programs (EAPs), efficient grievance and harassment processing, and training in the recognition of potentially violent situations. The goal of our research was to examine what types of programs were in place in a myriad of companies in a large, northeastern metropolitan region.

Different prevention practices and policies apply to external and internal threats. Practices and policies directed at external threats are generally concerned with preventing penetration of the organization's boundaries by the external threat. Those directed at internal threats must deal with a complex set of human resource management problems. In this chapter we describe a study of the policies and practices currently being used to deal with these threats by the companies that responded to our survey. We also discuss the strengths and weaknesses of the companies surveyed and implications of the results.

We acknowledge the assistance of the Philadelphia regional chapter of the Society for Human Resource Management in the data gathering for this research. We express our appreciation for critical comments from Richard Andrulis and Ralph Earl and help preparing the manuscript from Kerry Geran.

The Study

We surveyed organizations in the Delaware Valley Region (southeastern Pennsylvania, New Jersey, and Delaware) to determine the frequency with which organizations used various approaches to prevent acts of violence in the workplace. Questionnaires were mailed to senior human resources managers who were members of the Society for Human Resource Management (SHRM).

The Questionnaire

The questionnaire is presented in Exhibit 1. The items that dealt exclusively with external threats were those related to physical security measures (e.g., security guards, videocamera surveillance, fences). The other items dealt with practices and policies that focused on minimizing internal threats or on minimizing the threats presented by individuals who are in transition from an internal status (employees) to an external status (terminated employees). The items targeted as methods to reduce the threat of internal violence include screening, communication training, violence prevention plans, grievance processing procedures, harassment policies, EAPs, outplacement services, stress management programs, crisis management, meetings between supervisors and subordinates to discuss issues of mutual interest, and training to recognize potential violent threats in the workplace.

Survey Results

The survey results were based on the responses of 59 organizations from the southeastern Pennsylvania, New Jersey, and Delaware area. The responding companies ranged in size from small to large. Table 1 shows the categories to which the responding organizations belonged. The most frequently occurring categories were health care ($n = 10$), insurance ($n = 9$), and manufacturing ($n = 7$). The questionnaire was designed to elicit anonymous responses, requesting only information concerning the number of employees and the type of organization. We thought that managers would be more honest about their company's prevention policies if they were not required to identify themselves or their organizations. However, in many cases, the responding organization returned the questionnaire in a company envelope. In other cases, several organizations failed to complete the item regarding the type of organization. The responses to each survey item are discussed separately, beginning with the description of the data from the 59 responding organizations. Table 1 also shows comparisons of the most frequently occurring prevention policies for each category of responding organization. These data are expressed in terms of the percentages of companies responding yes to each item. Further statistical analyses were not warranted because of the small number of companies in most of the

Exhibit 1. Prevention of Workplace Violence Survey

Instructions: Please circle your responses and write your comments. Please return as soon as possible.

1. Does the organization hold regular meetings so that employ-   yes   no
   ees and supervisors can meet to openly discuss topics of mutual interest?
   Comment:
2. Are supervisors and employees trained to negotiate and com-   yes   no
   municate effectively?
   Comment:
3. Does your company implement physical security measures to
   protect employees and customers from any form of violence?
   If so, indicate by marking an X next to all that apply.
   Fences ___   Metal detectors ___   Videocameras ___
   Security guards ___
   Other (specify) _____
4. Does your company screen and evaluate potential employees?   yes   no
   Comment:
5. Is there a prevention plan in place for dealing with potentially   yes   no
   troublesome employees to help prevent any violent incidents
   from occurring?
   Comment:
6. Is there a crisis plan for dealing with violent incidents while   yes   no
   they are occurring?
   Comment:
7. What (if any) employee assistance programs does your com-   yes   no
   pany currently have? Do you have stress management plans?
   Comment:
8. Does your company provide training for employees to recog-   yes   no
   nize potential violent threats to employee safety?
   Comment:
9. Are outplacement services (counseling, retraining, or other   yes   no
   support) provided for laid-off or fired employees?
   Comment:
10. How are employee grievances dealt with in the organization?
11. Are there clear policies in your organization to deal with em-   yes   no
    ployee harassment?
    Comment:
12. Please describe your organization's size and industry. How
    many employees? ___
    What industry? (e.g., banking, insurance, computers, phar-
    maceuticals, etc.) _____

organizational categories. Attempts to make follow-up calls produced no additional responses.

Physical Security

The most commonly used response to external threat was the use of security guards, which was listed by 56% of the responding organizations.

Table 1. Percentages Using Security Practices by Type of Company

Security practice	All companies (n = 59)	Health care (n = 10)	Insurance (n = 9)	Manufacturing (n = 7)	Consulting (n = 6)	Financial (n = 4)	Utilities (n = 4)	Pharmaceutical (n = 4)	Other[a] (n = 10)	Unknown (n = 5)
Screening	95	100	89	72	100	100	100	100	90	100
Harassment processing plan	88	90	67	100	67	100	100	50	100	100
Grievance processing plan	73	70	67	57	67	50	100	50	80	100
Employee assistance program	69	30	78	43	100	75	100	75	90	60
Supervisor–subordinate meetings	68	50	67	86	50	75	75	50	80	60
Outplacement services	58	50	33	43	50	75	50	25	90	60
Security guards	56	50	56	29	67	75	50	25	70	60
Communication training	53	70	33	57	67	50	25	50	40	80
Videocamera surveillance	41	50	33	14	67	50	0	25	60	20
Crisis management	36	50	78	29	50	25	0	0	20	40
Fences	25	20	44	14	33	0	0	0	30	40
Stress management programs	24	10	33	43	33	25	50	0	70	0
Violence prevention plan	24	20	33	29	0	25	0	0	24	60
Training to recognize potential threats	10	0	11	0	0	50	25	0	10	20

[a]Other organizations include nonprofit, retail, legal, service, publishing, food, computers, government, and education.

Videocamera surveillance was reported by 41% of the respondents and fences by 25%. The percentages of organizations using a particular type of physical security measure are shown in Table 1. A number of deterrents to entry were included as open-ended responses, and, because they were listed infrequently, they are not included in Table 1. These deterrents included security cards, identification access badges, turnstiles, and locked exterior doors. Several companies also reported using buzzers and alarms as preventive measures. The questionnaire did not, however, include an exhaustive list of such items because we wanted to keep it to one page to increase the likelihood that it would be completed.

In many organizations, the prevention of violence from external agents will have more involvement from corporate security personnel than from human resources professionals. As a consequence, human resources managers may have greater awareness of practices aimed at internal threats. However, in many organizations, human resources policies can influence susceptibility to external threats. For example, security issues have received substantial attention in businesses with high levels of exposure to nonemployees, such as retail outlets (especially convenience stores, fast-food outlets, and gas stations) and banks, because of the relative frequency of workplace violence episodes on their premises. However, the companies responding to the survey tended, except for several hospitals and a bank, to have less exposure to nonemployees on the premises.

In increasing numbers, American businesses are growing accustomed to the reality of living with security guards and having limited-access areas, metal detectors, and bulletproof glass. When deciding what type of physical security measures to implement, companies should consider their size, the type of product or service they provide, and the frequency of contact with the public (Overman, 1993). Using the classifications presented in Table 1, we analyzed the use of specific security practices by type of company for those that occurred with frequencies of four or more.

Although approximately 41% of the responding organizations used videocameras, particular types of organizations used them more than others. Fifty percent of the financial and health care companies and 67% of the consulting firms had installed videocameras, whereas only 14% of the manufacturing organizations and none of the utilities companies used them. Additionally, although 44% of the insurance agencies had installed fences around their businesses, none of the pharmaceutical, utilities, or financial firms had done so. The use of security guards was more uniform, with at least 25% of the agencies in each category using their services.

In addition to the issues revealed in these data, there were several other security practices being used. The physical layout of an office also can aid or inhibit a quick response to an outbreak of violence. Security-conscious office designs have been used in a number of organizations. Before a violent episode, one company decided to install high walls between cubicles because workers wanted to increase their sense of privacy. However, after an armed assailant stalked the office and the employees could not see him because of the high partitions, the walls were taken down to allow each worker to have a full view of the larger room (Overman, 1993).

It also is important to design and practice a physical evacuation plan. If a violent incident occurs, each worker should know where to go and how to exit the building (Travnick, 1994). Too often a violent incident can reduce an office to a chaotic mess, with some employees running down the halls and others hiding behind their desks. Overman (1993) recommended integrating security guards, who were used frequently by our respondents, into the company. In many cases the employees of a given business do not even know the security guards' names, nor do they care to. However, Overman suggested inviting the guards to total quality management meetings, introducing them to the staff, and generally fostering a close relationship between employees and security guards. From this perspective, employees will be more likely to approach security personnel with concerns about safety and potential violence, and the security personnel will have a greater understanding of the safety needs of the organization.

A new physical-security approach to preventing workplace violence and a possible industry benchmark is Crime Prevention Through Environmental Design (CPTED; Thomas, 1992a). The main points of such an approach are natural surveillance, access, territoriality, and activity control. These principles can be demonstrated by describing a newly designed gas station. In the area of natural surveillance, the station has both bright interior and exterior lighting, windows are free of clutter, and the clerk has a clear view of entering and exiting customers. During late-night hours, two clerks are on duty, and the store is always monitored by a camera. To control access, the isles channel customers so that the clerk is always able to see them. Also, the clerk is behind a protective barrier. To emphasize territoriality, the business is located along a well-traveled road, and its boundaries are clearly marked and well lit. Activity control is enhanced by capitalizing on the presence of legitimate users by having them become part of the natural surveillance strategy. The gas station is combined with the facilities of a convenience store, and the increased amount of customers thereby provide "safety in numbers." In line with the recommendations inherent in the CPTED model, the State of Florida has been studying the possibility of requiring dual-shift workers during particular hours (Thomas, 1992b).

Preemployment Screening

Preemployment screening was the most commonly used practice of those listed in the questionnaire, with 95% of the responding organizations indicating that they used screening before hiring. The questionnaire did not, however, probe the extent to which an applicant's background was investigated. Given the legal catch-22 involved in the conflicts among negligent hiring, negligent referral, and interference with contract (future employment), the specifics of preemployment screening practices and policies may merit their own questionnaire.

Preemployment screening of prospective employees can be an effective means of preventing an external threat from becoming an internal threat, thus reducing the probability of workplace violence (Kuzmits, 1992). In many cases, screening potential employees is not a simple task; an examination of the privacy of information statutes and the heightened awareness of defamation suits have made it clear that it is often difficult to find out a good deal of information about a potential job applicant's violent tendencies. However, there are other ways to find out this information. When reviewing employment histories, one can examine gaps that might appear in the list of previous jobs (Feliu, 1994; Martucci & Clemow, 1995; Overman, 1993). These gaps could be the result of a simple period of unemployment, a prison term, or a hospitalization. In addition, it is imperative that the interviewer probe the reasons for various job terminations (Quirk, 1993). When contacting former employers about job references, it also has been suggested that the caller emphasize that if the former employer withholds information about an applicant's prior violent behavior, the previous employer could be named as a co-defendant in a lawsuit (Filipczak, 1993). When the characteristics of a job do warrant a criminal background check, it is becoming easier to conduct such searches inexpensively thanks to new computerized databases of criminal information (Di Lorenzo & Carroll, 1995).

Screening, however, raises some of the most complex legal issues of any of the prevention measures we consider. As noted previously, current employee law places constraints on the use of screening measures such as preemployment reference checks, criminal background checks, credit checks, and testing (Gerson, 1993; Quirk, 1993). The rationale for using any of these practices is based on the assumption that the data from previous behavior will provide a basis for predicting future behavior. In general, it is this assumption that serves as the legal stumbling block to using such information. The pervasive belief in an individual's right to privacy, coupled with the increasing demands to create safe and healthy working environments, has created a legal tension that has been experienced in corporate boardrooms across the country in recent years (Feliu, 1994). Essentially, an employer may be sued for taking aggressive actions to prevent violence in the workplace (and subsequently violating privacy rights); the employer also may be sued for not taking specific cautions to protect the company from a violent employee (Di Lorenzo & Carroll, 1995). Although a complete discussion of the legal issues pertaining to workplace violence is beyond the scope of this chapter, it should be obvious that the legal guidelines concerning employer liability are, in many cases, muddled, unclear, and seemingly contradictory. Or, as one human resources professional eloquently stated, "If a potentially violent employee is a serious problem, a potentially violent employee with a lawyer is even worse" (Filipczak, 1993, p. 40).

Several human resources professionals recently have recommended various new ways of obtaining information about violent tendencies using a particular style and type of interview question. Specifically, San Diego psychologist Michael Mantell noted that "you can get into questions such as anger management—when it is relevant to the job—temper control, how you handle customers who give you a hard time. You can offer scenarios and ask people to think through them" (cited in Barrier, 1995, p. 23). Other questions that could help to shed light on violent proclivities are "When have you felt that you have been treated unfairly in your life?" and "What has a supervisor done in the past to make you really angry?" (Stone, 1995, p. 9). By asking these questions carefully, the interviewer can assess violent tendencies while remaining well within legal boundaries.

Testing

The use of standardized tests as tools in the screening process to identify potentially violent employees in the workplace has led to few positive results, but a test that is both a valid and reliable indicator of predicting violent behavior has not been identified (Feliu, 1994; Quirk, 1993). However, the accepted model used when attempting to validate most tests as accurate predictors of violent behaviors is the clinical model, which relies heavily on case histories and often uses the criminal population as a subject pool. Slora, Joy, and Terris (1991) suggested that tests rooted in a statistical model using actuarial data are able to predict violent proclivities, although supporting evidence for such a claim is limited. In the clinical model of prediction, the human decision maker forms a decision on the basis of clinical judgment, a skill garnered through education, training, and experience. In the actuarial model, "the human judge is eliminated and conclusions rest solely on empirically established relations between data and the condition or event of interest" (Dawes, Faust, & Meehl, 1988, p. 1668). In a review of clinical and actuarial decision making in contexts as diverse as diagnostic categorization, clinical judgment, and patient life expectancy, the actuarial method was significantly better at prediction than was the clinical model (Dawes et al., 1988).

In a 1983 brief filed with the U.S. Congress, the American Psychological Association (APA) estimated that psychiatrists and psychologists are correct in only one out of every three testing or assessment estimates they make about a person's proclivity to commit violent acts in the future (Di Lorenzo & Carroll, 1995). The American Management Association estimated that only 2% of most recent acts of violence in organizations can be attributed to a past violent criminal history (Stone, 1995). Mental health professionals have indicated that it is virtually impossible to predict violent behavior, mainly because of the relative infrequency of violent events. Therefore, they recommend that the focus should not be violence prediction per se but on violence prevention.

Using this perspective, tests can be best used to assess the safety of the organizational culture or climate. Workplace violence instruments, such as those being developed commercially by organizations such as Hilson, can be used to determine how many individuals appear to present some risk. Organizational development or training interventions then can be designed to modify environmental influences within the organization and modify the culture to create a safer workplace. Other instruments, such as the Ethical Dilemmas in Computing Test (EDICT; Bickel, Larrondo-Petrie, & Bush, 1991, 1992) or the Defining Issues Test (Rest, 1979), can be used to assess the type of thinking used by employees to select a particular course of action in dealing with coworkers or managers. The EDICT can be particularly useful for employees who work with computer systems, serving as a basis for small-group interventions to reduce the likelihood of computer crime.

Threat Assessment Teams

In addition to screening and testing, threat assessment teams are an integral part of a comprehensive internal violence prevention program. Such teams often are multidisciplinary and can be either permanent or action oriented; they usually consist of a human resources manager, law enforcement personnel, an attorney, a medical staff member, a psychologist, and an EAP professional (Di Lorenzo & Carroll, 1995; Thornburg, 1993). The hybrid nature of the group allows each professional to contribute a unique perspective and offers a more complete picture of the needs of the organization. The threat assessment team is responsible for conducting an agencywide safety needs assessment, monitoring the workplace for violent activities, assessing each individual threat and planning a course of action, and possibly drafting an informal list of managers who would be effective members of a crisis management team (Overman, 1991). In addition, the effective team regularly conducts workshops pertaining to stress management, effective communication, conflict resolution, team building, dealing with difficult people, the management of change, and termination training (Bensimon, 1994). IBM developed threat assessment and management teams after the occurrence of several violent incidents in the workplace and has since reduced significantly the severity of such incidents (Johnson, 1993). Table 1 shows the percentage of each type of organization with a violence prevention plan for dealing with potentially troubling employees.

Training in the aforementioned issues is increasingly becoming a focal point in the search for effective violence prevention programs. In addition to these topics, threat assessment teams often teach supervisors how to lead effective discussion groups centering on diversity in the workplace and the management of anger (Overman, 1993). One study noted that although law enforcement officials are often thrust in the face of danger in the line of duty, on-the-job fatalities are actually less than might be expected (Hales, Seligman, Newman, & Timbrook, 1988). They hypothesized that this low ratio may reflect the training and experience of law enforcement officials in dealing with dangerous situations and highlights the need for violence prevention training in other professions.

Human resources supervisors often play a key role in creating effective training programs because they are usually the critical link between employees and the threat assessment team. In this regard, supervisors are able to gather critical employee input toward the creation of a quality violence prevention plan (Barrier, 1995). A relatively high percentage of responding organizations sponsored meetings between supervisors and employees to discuss issues of mutual interest. Fifty percent of the health care, consulting, and pharmaceutical companies reported implementing such practices, whereas 67–86% of the manufacturing, utilities, financial, and insurance businesses sponsored such meetings. Table 1 shows the percentages of companies that conducted meetings in which topics of mutual interest to employees and management can be discussed.

Training

Overall, 53% of the organizations responding to the survey indicated that they provided their employees with training in effective communication and negotiation skills. Twenty-five percent of the utilities and 33% of the insurance companies provided communication training, and 70% of the health care, 57% of the manufacturing, and 67% of the consulting organizations offered such services. Communication and negotiation skills are particularly important for supervisors, enabling them to be more effective in defusing potentially violent situations. However, although the skills that are indirectly applicable to the prevention of violence in the workplace are fairly common, those that are more directly applicable are not. The percentages of organizations that provided training in effective communication and negotiation are shown in Table 1.

Our respondents reported little training designed to prepare employees for the recognition of potentially violent individuals. Only 10% of the companies responding used this type of training, which would be particularly helpful for supervisors who need to be able to recognize potential violence before it occurs. Interestingly, none of the health care, manufacturing, consulting, or pharmaceutical businesses reported providing such training. This finding is consistent with other recent surveys by the SHRM and the American Management Association, which revealed that even after episodes of workplace violence, companies remained unlikely to offer such training. The percentages of organizations that provided training to recognize potential threats are listed in Table 1.

Training designed to aid in the recognition of potential threats is often linked to violence prevention plans and crisis management plans. Effective programs operate in both prevention and response phases, ensuring preparation for both violence avoidance and event aftermath management. We found that only 24% of the responding organizations had a violence prevention plan in place. In addition, 36% of the organizations had formed a detailed crisis management plan in the event of a violent situation in the workplace. Effective crisis management plans often will provide an opportunity for organizational learning through systematic debriefing concerning the antecedents of the violent event. Effective training also will prepare employees for mutual support, similar to other crises or disasters.

When the companies were examined according to the seven major categories of responding organizations, many differences emerged. For example, none of the pharmaceutical, consulting, or utilities companies had established violence prevention plans, and 20–33% of the insurance, financial, manufacturing, and health care firms reported having violence prevention plans in place. Similarly, none of the pharmaceutical or utilities businesses had crisis management programs in place to aid in the effective response to an outbreak of workplace violence. On the other hand, 50% of the health care and consulting firms and more than 75% of the insurance firms reported such programs. The percentages of responding organizations having violence prevention plans, crisis management programs, or both are listed in Table 1.

Grievance Processing and Harassment Prevention Programs

Most responding organizations (73%) reported having employee grievance processing policies; the prevalence of such policies was fairly evenly distributed across the seven types of organizations (see Table 1). These grievance policies generally specify procedures for processing employee complaints. As long as employees understand that such specific procedures exist and they perceive them as being fair, the likelihood of frustration reaching the breaking point should be reduced.

Surprisingly, employee harassment policies were reported more frequently than were grievance policies. Eighty-eight percent of the responding organizations had such policies in place; it is encouraging that this percentage increases when only the manufacturing (100%), health care (90%), financial (100%), and utilities (100%) companies are examined. Table 1 shows the percentages of organizations having an employee harassment policy. Such services should minimize the extent to which coworkers or superiors can engage in behavior that constitutes harassment. This is important for avoiding violent events in two ways. First, harassment, whether sexual or nonsexual, is a form of violence and as such needs to be monitored and minimized. Second, harassment often can become the stimulus for more deadly violence, especially when the victim of harassment feels trapped and desperate.

EAPs

A majority of the responding organizations (69%) had implemented an EAP, which provides a spectrum of counseling and support services to employees who have a variety of personal problems (e.g., drug and alcohol abuse, marital conflict). Although the overall percentage of organizations offering such services was high, the percentages among the different types of organizations differed greatly, as can be seen in Table 1. In the utilities businesses and consulting firms, the establishment of EAPs seemed to be "standard practice"; 100% of the companies in each category offered EAP services. Additionally, 75% of the pharmaceutical and financial and 78% of the insurance companies offered such programs. However, only 43% of the manufacturing businesses had an EAP program in place, and 30% of the health care organizations offered such services.

EAP programs became popular after World War II as an effective method for employees to receive alcohol and drug counseling, but they have since expanded their roles by focusing on general counseling needs, referral services, and employee wellness issues (Kuzmits, 1992). In many cases, the EAP staff also can provide managers and supervisors with training in interpersonal skills, conflict negotiation, and methods for identifying troubled or potentially violent employees. In Ameritech's "two-tiered" EAP program, middle managers who have been laid off receive $2,000 worth of services in the form of group workshops that include how to conduct a job search, how to interview, and a general guide to the marketplace. Upper management members who have been laid off receive all of the aforementioned workshops but also are allowed to use an office and have access to secretarial services. The employee transition program set up at the Tennessee Valley Authority provides laid-off employees with 6 months' worth of compensation and benefits while they are searching for a new job, along with monthly counseling on job skill development (Kinney & Johnson, 1993). Such services undoubtedly aid in preventing many violent incidents from occurring when employees have lost their jobs, suffered from substance abuse addictions, or simply needed counseling for family or general life problems.

If an EAP outplacement program is unavailable to employees who have been laid off, managers have been advised to conduct an exit interview. Aside from providing the laid-off employee with a venue to voice potential concerns, the exit interview can be an excellent opportunity to identify a person who "might come back in three weeks to show management what he really thinks of his severance package" (Filipczak, 1993, p. 43). As mentioned earlier, employees who are likely to become violent offenders often are highly job identified. For such people, a layoff is much more than a loss of income; it is a loss of identity. Providing proper placement services, humane layoff procedures, and detailed exit interviews can help alleviate some of the impact that a job loss is bound to have. When conducting exit interviews and laying off employees, Thornburg (1993) advised focusing on economic cutbacks and job performance rather than on personal factors that might have led to the dismissal.

Stress Management Programs

We were somewhat surprised by the lack of organization-sponsored stress management programs: Overall, only 24% of the organizations offered such programs. There also was a great deal of variation between the different types of organizations. Although 43% of the manufacturing and 50% of the utilities organizations had stress management programs in place, 33% of the consulting, 25% of the financial, and 0% of the pharmaceutical businesses had implemented such practices. Table 1 shows the percentages of organizations offering stress management programs.

Given the increasing levels of organizational stress, particularly in the face of extensive downsizing and the survivor syndrome (Noer, 1993), stress management programs may be more needed now than in the past. These programs, through a variety of techniques, reduce the level of perceived threat for employee participants, allowing them to live with a lower level of frustration and to experience a number of healthy benefits.

A major stressor in today's economy is the specter of job loss. Outplacement continues to be a popular means of ameliorating employee distress during a job loss by providing assistance in obtaining a new position in another organization. Outplacement services range from workshops on job-seeking skills to temporary offices with complete support services and the availability of an experienced career counselor for more senior executives leaving their jobs. Fifty-eight percent of the responding organizations provided outplacement services for their employees. When examining only the pharmaceutical and insurance businesses, this percentage fell to 25–33%. Table 1 shows the percentages of organizations that provided outplacement services for laid-off or fired employees. We expected that this service would be much more common, on a level comparable to the availability of EAPs. Note, however, that although outplacement services may serve to reduce the resentment and potential for violence by terminated employees, it may in fact increase the resentment of the surviving employees, who face the reality of more work and less support (Noer, 1993).

Conclusion

The prevention of violence in the workplace is of critical importance if employers want to continue the national trend toward increased productivity. Deming (1986), the late founder of the quality improvement movement, extolled managers to "drive out fear." One source of fear that Deming did not anticipate was the fear of violence in the workplace. Yet it is clear that the aftermath of such violent episodes is associated with substantial drops in productivity as workers are traumatized, distracted by fear, and spend time seeking reassurance and social support. Thus, the prevention of violence is in the best interest of productivity and profitability. It also is in the best interest of management because, as Losey (1993), chief executive officer of the SHRM, noted, the firing manager and the human resources manager are the most likely targets of retribution by an employee going through the process of termination. Executives also have been the targets of kidnappers and terrorists. The motivation for prevention should be clear.

Several prevention practices were represented well within the companies surveyed. For example, nearly all of the companies screened new employees before hiring, and a relatively large number of companies have implemented effective grievance and harassment processing programs. Many of the businesses also sponsored meetings between managers and subordinates to discuss topics of mutual interest. Finally, except for metal detectors, many of the companies used security guards and other physical prevention methods to prevent external threats of violence.

In other areas, selective strengths and weaknesses were found. For example, although 43% of the manufacturing and 50% of the utilities agencies had adopted stress management programs, 33% of the consulting and insurance firms and none of the pharmaceutical businesses had implemented such practices. The formation of EAP programs also was a standard practice at the utilities (100%) and consulting firms (100%), whereas a low percentage of the manufacturing (43%) and health care (30%) organizations offered their employees such services. Additionally, although 78% of the insurance and 50% of the health care organizations had a clearly defined crisis management plan, none of the pharmaceutical or utilities businesses had such a plan in place.

One key area related to the prevention of workplace violence involves training supervisors to recognize potential violent threats. Through this type of training, supervisors are able to respond to violent threats before they erupt into violence. Although such training is a critical part of a comprehensive violence prevention program, few of the responding companies offer such training. In fact, although 50% of the financial companies and 25% of the utility companies offered training to help supervisors recognize and respond to threats of violence, none of the pharmaceutical, health care, manufacturing, or consulting organizations offered equivalent training.

The results of our survey indicate that in several key areas related to the prevention of workplace violence, various organizations of all sizes have not yet taken seriously these threats. Given the similarity between our findings and the SHRM and American Management Association data, it would appear that American organizations are still not implementing a wide range of effective violence prevention policies. However, as in other areas of business excellence, such as quality, organizations such as Polaroid are clear leaders. The organizations that have had policies in place to help prevent workplace violence can serve as benchmarks for other organizations. As Camp (1989) noted, the fastest way to gain a competitive advantage is often by benchmarking the best practices. At this time, such an approach can save a company millions of dollars in legal fees, insurance charges, and lost productivity.

References

Barrier, M. (1995). The enemy within. *Nation's Business, 83,* 18–24.

Bensimon, H. F. (1994). Violence in the workplace. *Training and Development Journal, 48*(1), 26–32.

Bickel, R. W., Larrondo-Petrie, M. M., & Bush, D. F. (1991). EDICT [Ethical decisions in computing test]: A tool to assist computer ethics education. *International Business Schools Computer Users Group Quarterly, 2*(4), 13–23.

Bickel, R. W., Larrondo-Petrie, M. M., & Bush, D. F. (1992). EDICT for computer ethics education. *Journal of Systems Software, 17,* 81–89.

Camp, R. C. (1989). *Benchmarking.* Milwaukee, WI: ASQC Quality Press.

Dawes, R. M., Faust, D., & Meehl, P. E. (1988). Clinical versus actuarial judgment. *Science, 243,* 1668–1674.

Deming, W. E. (1986). *Out of the crisis.* Cambridge, MA: Massachusetts Institute of Technology, Center for Advanced Engineering Study.

Di Lorenzo, L. P., & Carroll, D. J. (1995). Screening applicants for a safer workplace. *HR Magazine, 40*(3), 55–58.

Feliu, A. G. (1994). Workplace violence and the duty of care: The scope of an employer's obligation to protect against the violent employee. *Employee Relations Law Journal, 20*, 381–406.

Filipczak, B. (1993). Armed and dangerous at work. *Training, 30*(7), 39–43.

Gerson, A. (1993). A violent state of mind? *Occupational Health and Safety, 62*(11), 64–67.

Hales, T. H., Seligman, P. J., Newman, S. J., & Timbrook, C. L. (1988). Occupational injuries due to violence. *Journal of Occupational Medicine, 30*, 483–487.

Johnson, D. L. (1993, July 19). The best defense against workplace violence. *Wall Street Journal*, p. B1.

Kinney, J. A. (1995). *Violence at work.* Englewood Cliffs, NJ: Prentice Hall.

Kinney, J. A., & Johnson, D. L. (1993). *Breaking point: The workplace violence epidemic and what to do about it.* Chicago: National Safe Workplace Institute.

Kuzmits, F. E. (1992). Workplace homicide: Prediction or prevention. *S.A.M. Advanced Management Journal, 57*, 4–7.

Losey, M. (1993, November). Managing in an era of workplace violence. Paper presented at the national leadership conference of the Society for Human Resource Management, Alexandria, VA.

Martucci, W. M., & Clemow, D. D. (1995). Workplace violence: Incidents—and liability—on the rise. *Employment Relations Today, 21*, 463–470.

Noer, D. M. (1993). *Healing the wounds.* San Francisco, CA: Jossey-Bass.

Overman, S. (1991). You may not be able to deal with this. *HR Magazine, 36*(11), 46–47.

Overman, S. (1993). Be prepared should be your motto. *HR Magazine, 38*(7), 46–49.

Quirk, J. H. (1993). HR managers face legal aspects of workplace violence. *HR Magazine, 38*(11), 115–122.

Rest, J. R. (1979). *Development in judging moral issues.* Minneapolis: University of Minnesota Press.

Slora, K. B., Joy, D. S., & Terris, W. (1991). Personnel selection to control employee violence. *Journal of Business and Psychology, 5*, 417–427.

Stone, R. A. (1995). Workplace homicide: A time for action. *Business Horizons, 38*(2), 3–10.

Thomas, J. L. (1992a, June). A response to occupational violent crime. *Risk Control*, pp. 27–31.

Thomas, J. L. (1992b). Occupational violent crime. *Journal of Safety Research, 23*(2), 55–62.

Thornburg, L. (1993). When violence hits business. *HR Magazine, 38*(7), 40–45.

Travnick, J. (1994). Averting workplace violence. *Risk Management, 41*, 13–20.

17

The Dynamics of
Threat Management

Joseph A. Kinney

Employers are increasingly aware of the risks and costs that violence imposes on organizations. As is commonly recognized, violence can originate from inside or outside of an organization. Inside threats or acts of violence can be associated with employees, contractors, or temporary employees. Outside threats or acts of violence can be associated with intruders such as former employees, stalkers, romantically disaffected individuals, or customers.

Employers wish to know about what should be done to respond to threats and behaviors that may predicate violence. Concerns about aggressive behaviors are influencing employers to develop multifaceted violence and aggression prevention programs. As part of such efforts, employers are mandating a zero-tolerance for violence and are establishing employee awareness initiatives, hotlines, and supervisor training programs. What is less clear is how organizations can prevent or control the problem through threat management strategies of various types. Although authors have written about threat management for lay audiences, there is little about this concept in the academic literature (Kinney, 1995a; "Techniques to Manage Violence in the Workplace," 1993). To understand the dynamics of threat management, the reader can examine the practical experience upon which this article draws, which is founded, in part, on psychological and epidemiological concepts. There are appropriate ways to train primary responders (security, human resources, and employment attorneys) on how to respond to threats of violence. Instruction that does not meet clear standards will limit an employer's effectiveness in reducing the risk of violence.

Definitional and measurement issues complicate our understanding of

Some of the material presented in this chapter appeared in *Violence at Work: How to Make Your Company Safer for Employees and Customers* by Joseph A. Kinney. Copyright 1995 by Prentice Hall, Inc. Reprinted by permission.

The author wishes to acknowledge James Cavannaugh, MD, Isaac Ray Center, Chicago; Dennis A. Davis, PhD, San Diego; Barbara Lambert, PhD, Confidante, San Francisco; and John Monahan, PhD, University of Virginia for their insightful comments and encouragement.

occupational violence and what should be done to address this problem. In an organizational context, violence is often associated with homicide. Because homicide is relatively rare in most organizations, that is hardly a useful yardstick to measure or understand occupational violence. However, coemployee homicide away from the workplace is a very serious and unrecognized problem. To the extent that the conditions of such homicides or assaultive acts have their source in the workplace, then a failure to adequately supervise or properly intervene with an employee would contribute to a subsequent violent act.

For the purpose of this chapter, I define violence in broad terms. I include both physical and psychological attacks and nonphysical acts of destruction, sabotage, and theft of property belonging to the employer or a coworker. This range encompasses different types of incidents and circumstances. However, it is appropriate to develop a definition that is realistic and that can lead employers to impose reasonable control measures that will prevent less serious problems (e.g., abusive language) from becoming significant to the organization. This is the essence of violence risk reduction.

Although it is difficult to predict the precise time when violence may strike,[1] there are steps that employers and workers can take to prepare for such a possibility—and to effectively manage a crisis once it occurs. Employers and employees alike can begin by understanding that most incidents of violence follow recognized threats, and that the reasonable and prudent course of action is to adequately prepare for violence as a life-threatening hazard that can be minimized or prevented. Employers must realize that violence is an identifiable risk much like a safety hazard in the workplace. Employers should also recognize and accept the growing reality, which law requires and good management dictates, that a recognized threat must be met by a response that will reduce the possibility that physical harm will come to the employer's workers or customers.

Use of Threat Management Teams

The use of teams reflects the complexity of some threats and the need to have a response that builds upon the talents of specialists within the organization. This chapter highlights the steps that should be taken to ensure that proper procedures are followed to manage threats of violence and actual incidents.

Dealing with threatening behaviors or communications is as much an art as it is a science. Nonetheless, it is crucial that employers have practical processes for handling threats because failure to respond poses enormous risks and problems. In this chapter, I provide useful pieces of information that experts have woven together in their understanding of threats

---

[1]There are few individuals who have been more thoughtful about the prediction of violence than John Monahan, PhD, of the University of Virginia School of Law (e.g., Monahan, 1992).

and how people act out violently in a work environment. But there are no ready-made plans for violence prevention: Circumstances and personalities vary from location to location and from situation to situation. Although there are cases involving "copy cats," the vast majority of cases have many unique qualities that require a sophisticated and individualized response.

All threats and bizarre behaviors should be investigated by trained professionals. Investigations can be supplemented by contributions from licensed psychologists or professional investigators, working in tandem with an individual who coordinates threat management on behalf of the employer. In most cases, threats can be brought to an effective conclusion without substantial damage to the organization or its workers. Normally, management's involvement with an existing employee can end with referral to the employee assistance program (EAP) or a mental health treatment facility, reassignment to another position, placing the individual on medical leave, or other courses of nonpunitive discipline. If an employee's behavior or communications reflect elevated anger or bizarre acts, then it is appropriate to mandate—if the employee does not accept a recommendation—a psychological assessment. In some cases termination may be necessary. The important consideration is that threats must be taken seriously, investigated appropriately, and brought to a logical conclusion that ensures the safety and security of the work environment.

Threats from an intruder (e.g., former employee, stalker, or other third party) typically pose greater risks and complexity in the threat management process. Whereas employers can exercise some control over employees, intruders have freedom of movement and rights that make them difficult to contain. Nevertheless, there are steps that can be taken when threats are made known to appropriate personnel. Some of those steps will be discussed in this chapter. But before I begin, I will examine exactly what is meant by *threats*.

Threats

There is no question that a person who makes threats to an employer or to a worker represents a recognized hazard that must be addressed in an effective and timely manner. Even though most threats will not result in violence, management must respond to threats as if violence were a real possibility. There are different types of threats—*direct, conditional*, and *veiled*—that must be distinguished during the threat management process. Threats, along with behavior, should be the focus of the first step of the threat management process.

Management of threats from outside the organization involves far more sophisticated skills and sources of information than management of threats from an existing employee population. If a threat involves a former employee or stalker, getting information may be difficult. However, there are almost always sources of information, including information directly from the perpetrator. In many cases, it is appropriate to employ a private investigator to obtain information. Indications of past violent acts and an individual's perception of themselves and what they have to lose in a violent act are very important in determining how seriously a threat should be regarded. Employers must analyze information with care to achieve the proper result. Typically, a coordinator should involve someone skilled in threat management (usually a clinical psychologist) and an employment attorney.

There are three types of threats:

1. *Direct threats* involve clear and explicit communications such as "I am going to kill you." Direct threats leave the unmistaken impression that the perpetrator intends to do bodily harm.
2. *Conditional threats* involve a condition. An example: "If you report me, I will get even with you and you will be sorry."
3. *Veiled threats* usually involve body language or behavior that leaves little doubt in the mind of the victim that the perpetrator intends harm.

Understanding the type of threat that has been made is critical to threat management. Conditional and veiled threats, if seldom made, can be subject to misinterpretation. Perpetrators often deny making conditional or veiled threats. Denial may be part of a person's behavior or reflect genuine differences in point of view. In the case of isolated conditional or veiled threats, it is probably best to document the reported behavior or communication and to counsel the employee on appropriate conduct. If the perpetrator repeats a veiled or conditional threat on multiple occasions, then appropriate action, referral to an employee assistance program or the application of discipline, must be taken.

Bizarre Behavior

My investigations and case studies demonstrate that the perpetrators of violence sometimes do not exhibit elevated anger. Instead, these perpetrators engage in bizarre forms of behavior. They are likely to do things that are uncharacteristic but clearly abnormal, even to the untrained observer. For example, one perpetrator left brown paper bags of kittens or puppies on the loading dock where he worked. Another perpetrator would come to work wearing underwear on his head. Still another talked about being an alien from outer space. This last perpetrator, Paul Calden, eventually murdered three employees and wounded two others in a cafeteria in the office building of his former employer, Fireman's Fund Insurance in Tampa, Florida.

Bizarre or aggressive behavior can be described in many ways. In most cases, it is appropriate to think in terms of the frequency and severity of such behavior. Examples of classifications might include

- *Aberrational*: A "bad day" that is unusual for individual.
- *Periodic anger*: Behavior is infrequent yet pattern exists.

- *Endemic* or *chronic*: Part of a person's behavioral pattern.

Often, individuals make comments of a bizarre nature or challenge the boundaries of their supervisors and managers. If an employee engages in such behavior, the possibility of violence must be considered in addressing that individual's behavior. Like threats, behaviors—especially those that involve aggression—should be documented and reviewed by specialists. In general, a skilled threat manager will be looking for patterns of behavior. If in doubt, a psychological assessment may be appropriate. Again, mandating such an assessment may be an appropriate course of action if an employee will not voluntarily participate in such a process (Kinney & Lambert, 1996).

Behavior in a Context

Behavior typically occurs in a context, not in a vacuum. As human beings, there tends to be a method to our madness, a reason for why we do things the way that we do them. Employers need to be aware of deviations from trends and patterns—a possible warning sign that trouble may lie ahead. Violent actions, in the context used here, often occur in response to the way a person perceives his or her environment. If a person believes that they have nothing to lose or believes that they have been unjustly harmed by an organization, they are much more likely to become violent.

Early warning mechanisms, including behavioral observation systems (BOS), are reasonably helpful methods to measure and evaluate behavior over time.[2] Early warning mechanisms can provide a foundation from which to evaluate more extreme behaviors or threats.

More often than not, a desirable level of information from which to evaluate perpetrator behavior does not exist. If adequate information does not exist, decisions are likely to reflect more of an art form than a science. If employers lack a desirable level of information about a person or their behavior, the level of uncertainty increases a corresponding level. This means that threat managers must use caution in determining an appropriate course of action. Under these circumstances, it is highly appropriate to seek professional assistance in plotting a course of action.

Coordinating Threat Management

There are proper ways to investigate and manage threats. Once the information is received, it must be carefully evaluated. Ideally, a coordinator (the primary threat manager) will receive information from a reporting center (e.g., hotline) within hours of the report. The coordinator will conduct a preliminary investigation, typically by conferring with witnesses, victims, experts, or others familiar with the circumstance. The coordinator

---

[2]See Appendix C, Model Behavioral Observation Program, pp. 267–276 in Kinney, 1995b.

will be able to handle most cases without involving additional individuals, such as threat team members or consultants.

The first issue for the coordinator to evaluate is the immediacy of the threat. If a high level of risk exists, then prompt defensive action must occur. If there is no sense of urgency, then there should be a systematic attempt to carefully and thoughtfully weigh the nature of the threat against the person's likely capacity to carry out acts of physical violence. The ultimate goal is to protect people and property. There are a number of questions that a coordinator should attempt to answer in assessing the potential for violence:

1. Has a direct or explicit threat of violence been made?
2. Does the person have weapons or capacity to inflict physical damage?
3. Does the person have a history of violence?
4. What does the person believe he or she may lose by an act of violence?

These questions are meant as a general guideline, not a precise formula.

It is interesting to note that much information about the potential for violence from outside the organization comes from family members, friends, or other third parties rather than employees. Often spouses or other family members see the acute stress that has been imposed on the victim or recipient of a threat. Because a victim is often embarrassed by the apparent inability to remedy his or her situation, he or she is reluctant to come forward. But family members, because they are concerned over a loved one's safety, are more inclined to take steps to ensure the protection of that individual. Although the coordinator should welcome information from any source, he or she also must acknowledge that this information is sometimes difficult to evaluate. There have been occasions when third parties have made false or misleading reports in order to punish or embarrass an employee. Similarly, it is also true that one may receive information from someone close to the perpetrator of a threat. This information, if received and acted upon in a timely fashion, can be very important.

Identifying Potentially Dangerous Individuals

There is no sure way to determine if a person will eventually engage in a violent act. Competent, licensed psychologists and psychiatrists have failed to diagnose individuals as dangerous when that same person committed a lethal act just a few days later. Also, there are probably hundreds of individuals with many of the characteristics of past lethal perpetrators, none of whom may actually kill in the workplace. No one can say with any degree of certainty who will kill and who will not. This lack of certainty results in the need to intervene to try to control the perpetrator's behavior and choices.

The method of identifying dangerous individuals poses enormous risks and uncertainties for those involved in the threat management process. For example, there is a tendency to compare the behavioral characteristics and features of those individuals to whom threats have been attributed with the personal characteristics of those who previously committed acts of violence. Undue emphasis on the use of profiles can be harmful for many reasons. For openers, there are many individuals who are likely to have some of the characteristics of past perpetrators. Because these individuals fit a profile does not mean that they will become violent.

Profiling runs the risk of severely damaging the reputations of otherwise innocent individuals, with the possible result of unjustly blamed individuals who may wish to pursue defamation lawsuits. Moreover, an undue focus on certain *types* rather than on *behaviors* can divert attention from individuals who are much more serious threats to the organization. The use of profiles should be limited to psychiatrists or licensed clinical psychologists. Even then, profile data should be used only in the later stages of a threat evaluation.

Perhaps a more systematic and objective way to make decisions has to do with the sequence in behavior of someone making threats. Research by the National Safe Workplace Institute confirms the notion that there is a sequence in the steps of behavior of perpetrators of violence (Kinney & Johnson, 1993). Generally, the individual will deteriorate over time, becoming isolated from others as they grapple with frustration and their sense of failure. Often, the process begins when the individual suffers from a significant traumatic event or the cumulation of many smaller traumas. As shown in Exhibit 1, the individual perceives that the situation is unsolvable and begins to project all blame onto the situation rather than on himself or herself. Gradually, the individual begins to think that violence is the only way out.

Employers with threat management responsibility should place more emphasis on behavior and behavioral patterns and the sequence of behavior than on other factors. The actual act of making a threat or bizarre patterns of behavior should be the "trigger" for further investigation and, possibly, action. Investigating an individual simply because that person has been angry and fits a statistical profile not only runs certain risks that are detrimental to corporate and individual welfare, but is likely to be a waste of time and resources.

One of the most important factors is the presence of weapons or the

Exhibit 1.   Routine Experiential Sequence of Violence Perpetrators

1. Individual suffers trauma which creates extreme tension or anxiety; may be a single major event (e.g., job loss or divorce) or cumulative minor events.
2. Individual thinks that problems are unsolvable.
3. Individual projects all responsibility onto the situation.
4. Individual's frame of reference becomes increasingly egocentric.
5. Self-preservation and self-protection gradually become sole objectives.
6. Violent act perceived as only way out.
7. Violent act is attempted or committed.

Source: Kinney, 1995a, p. 90.

capacity for violence. A perpetrator with weapons or a history of physical violence (e.g., spousal beatings) poses a much higher degree of risk than those without weapons or such histories. However, although there are examples of individuals who have utilized recently acquired weapons in lethal acts in the workplace, there are also individuals who have used other methods to kill coworkers. Perpetrators have used guns and other forms of lethal force, including strangulation or stabbing. As part of the assessment process, one must consider the presence of weapons and the capacity of an individual to use force. Information about prior incidents of violence and disregard for established authority are very important to the assessment process. If a person has exercised violence in the past, then one must assume that the potential perpetrator has the capacity to become violent in the future.

Potential Inhibitors or Anchors

Experience from psychology and other behavioral sciences convincingly shows that there are numerous *inhibitors* or *anchors* that are likely to diminish the possibility that an individual may become violent (Kinney & Johnson, 1993). For example, a person who is financially secure with a stable family and community life is less likely to commit violence than an individual with "nothing to lose." On the other hand, a person who does not have a family life and who is badly in debt may be more inclined to become violent.

A capable threat manager may wish to develop an inhibitor or anchor profile for each individual who is a source of threats. The threat manager will collect data on a person's finances, their health, family and community life, supervisory relationships, and other pertinent factors. In general, this information can be obtained from coworkers or public sources without violating an individual's right to privacy. If necessary, the threat manager may need to consult with an attorney about appropriate investigative standards.

Although such information may not be conclusive, it will likely help determine what steps may be prudent in a particular situation. Some of the anchors that may inhibit violence are

- Secure family life (spouse and children)
- Reasonably rational, somewhat future-oriented
- Stable finances (good credit rating; savings, reasonable debt load)
- Drug and alcohol free, with no history of abuse
- Emotionally stable, steady personality
- Community ties, may own home
- Outside interests (hobbies, sports)
- Friendships (externally driven)
- Good work history (continuous employment)
- Character (no real pattern of criminal conduct)
- Religious life (involved in church)

The reader should not think about this information in a rigid fashion. It is possible that there may be some factors not on this list that may be as important. Likewise, it is highly possible that one or two anchors (e.g., religious) may be disproportionately significant.

Measuring the Response on the Basis of the Level of Violence

In developing a response to a violent act, it is important to consider the level of violence. There are options that a manager has available at his or her disposal if a worker has made threats or engaged in low-level acts of violence. Managers must be aware of these options in order to make decisions that hopefully will result in "win–win" choices that will eventually protect the interest of both the employer and worker.

As one can determine by examining the incident or behavior types associated with Level One Violence (see Exhibit 2), the appropriate response should be taken at the supervisory level, with likely input from human resources (personnel). It is important to distinguish levels of violence because consistent definitions or classifications help provide appropriate and just responses. It is crucial that management not overreact to a Level One act of violence. Although an intervention is appropriate, management must make the remedy fit the injury or problem.

Levels Two and Three Violence, as described in Exhibit 3, represent much more serious situations, with the need for correspondingly serious responses in order to control damage or reduce risks. In many cases, it may be appropriate to involve law enforcement, for both legal and moral reasons, in cases where laws may have been broken. In fact, California and other states are now considering legislation that permit an employer to seek restraining orders and other interventions. These acts of violence, by almost any measure, will result in injury to employees and possibly others.

Exhibit 2.   Incidents or Behaviors Associated With Level One Violence and Responses

---

Level One Violence
  • Refuses to cooperate with immediate supervisor
  • Spreads rumors and gossip to harm others
  • Consistently argues with coworkers
  • Belligerent toward customers or clients
  • Constantly swears at others
  • Makes inappropriate sexual comments
Available Responses
  • Discipline or referral to EAP

Source: National Safe Workplace Institute, 1989.

Exhibit 3. Incidents or Behaviors Associated With Levels Two and Three Violence and Responses

---

Level Two Violence
- Argues increasingly with customers, vendors, coworkers and management
- Refuses to obey company policies and procedures
- Sabotages or destroys equipment or property of employer or coworker
- Verbalizes wishes to hurt coworkers or management
- Sends sexual or violent notes to coworkers or management
- Sees self as victimized by management ("me vs. them")

Level Three Violence
Frequent displays of intense anger resulting in
- Recurrent physical fights
- Destruction of property
- Recurrent suicidal threats
- Utilization of weapons to harm others
- Murder, rape, or arson

Available Responses
- Psychological assessment, discipline, or law enforcement intervention

---

Source: National Safe Workplace Institute, 1989.

Understanding and Maximizing Options

By being informed of the available options, managers can make rational decisions that will achieve a favorable result and withstand scrutiny over time. Proper planning will result in appropriate action that will help limit and control damage. Especially when the potential for violence is very high, there must be a concerted effort to consider available options.

If an employee is the source of a threat, it may be necessary that a professional evaluation by a licensed mental health professional be undertaken. This should involve a "fitness for duty" or "dangerousness assessment" by a licensed psychologist who is trained to conduct such assessments. Employers have a number of options after such an evaluation is conducted: They may discipline or transfer an employee, change a supervisor, or restructure the job. Unfortunately, experience demonstrates that many of these options are simply not considered.

The options that exist for managers if the perpetrator is not an employee are more limited. However, there are a number of options, especially if the perpetrator is a former employee or known to management. In such situations, as much information should be obtained as possible in an effort to determine what steps are necessary to ensure that the employer has taken prudent action. Substantial data on employment histories, financial and credit information, criminal records, and so forth, can be obtained through various sources.

If violence does occur, a number of steps must be taken for the employer to assert control of the work environment.

1. Control and secure the workplace (i.e., contact law enforcement; account for all personnel; ensure employee, customer, and public safety; and evacuate all individuals).

2. Provide law enforcement information (i.e., perpetrator data, and information on physical plant).
3. Take caution in making statements to the press.
4. Plan for posttrauma care.
5. Conduct investigations and postincident analysis.
6. Conduct debriefings of relevant personnel (Kinney, 1995a, p. 94).

Hopefully, an employer will have properly planned for such a crisis so that key individuals, such as threat management team members, know their individual and collective roles. Acts of violence nearly always result in laws being broken, either in terms of injury to individuals or in terms of damage to the employer's property. Ultimately, violence becomes a legal issue, with necessary law enforcement consequences.

Effective managers, however, should be able to control and manage most incidents, bringing them to a logical conclusion that does not involve action by law enforcement. If law enforcement becomes involved, employers run the risk of losing control of the work environment. By definition, their decisions and performance in preventing violence have failed.

Employers must be prepared to address crucial issues that inevitably arise during serious incidents. Typically a violent act that is underway will ultimately require involvement by law enforcement. Nonetheless, there are many steps that prepared employers should consider in developing crisis management plans. For example, employers should have a licensed clinical psychologist who can debrief "survivors" of violent events or those who have experienced serious threats. Experience demonstrates that such measures are crucial in terms of identifying workers and others who will require long-term care while "returning" others to full productivity. Many law enforcement agencies routinely contract with such professionals to debrief officers after fatal accidents, shootings, violent acts, and other events that may disrupt an officer's psychological well-being.

Defenses Against Violent Intruders

In some cases, threats of violence are made against individuals as opposed to indiscriminate threats against an organization. (I estimate that there are far more homicides, maybe five times as many or more, of coworkers being murdered by coworkers away from the workplace than in the workplace.) A commonplace example of a revenge-oriented act of workplace violence would involve a person who is stalking his or her spouse. If individual employees are threatened there are prudent ways to defend them against the possibility of violence. Sometimes, organizations will hire investigators to track the movement of perpetrators. They also may employ bodyguards to protect those who have been threatened. These decisions are expensive and may have questionable effectiveness. For example, there is very little that can be done to stop a truly determined perpetrator. The Secret Service employs literally hundreds of individuals to protect the president on a daily basis, when there are no unusual threats. Deployment

Exhibit 4. Steps to Take to Protect Employees From Intruders

- Provide protective services to potential victims (e.g., having a security officer walk by victim)
- Relocate work station of threatened employee
- Alter employee's work schedule
- Provide photographs of perpetrator to security, receptionists, and so forth
- Encourage law enforcement to enforce restraining order
- If threat is acute, provide employee with time off
- Place silent alarms or buzzers at employee's work station
- Deploy security camera near entrances to victim's work area
- Provide preprogrammed cellular telephone

of a bodyguard may give the target a greater sense of security but will probably have minimal effect against a truly determined perpetrator.

Exhibit 4 illustrates a number of steps that can help protect individuals who have been threatened. If a perpetrator knows a person's whereabouts and schedule, then the element of confusion may, in effect, serve as an effective means of protection. This Exhibit is important because it illustrates the need for creativity in such cases. These steps may be particularly effective in situations involving threats by stalkers.

Training for Threat Management

Employers are using role-playing, scenarios, and other techniques to train those who have the primary threat management responsibility (e.g., security, employment counsel, human resources). There is a considerable advantage in being trained using such methods. Such preparation can prevent incidents from becoming serious, minimize the damage from the crisis when it does take place, or facilitate a smoother transition to normalcy following the incident. Such training should be conducted by individuals outside the organization who have significant experience in threat management. Using an employee assistance program provider, as some employers are doing, raises the potential of damaging the EAP's credibility and even subjecting the employer to litigation involving negligent training.

Some employers are not aware of the risk of training negligence. There is a belief that training can be internalized if not done by the EAP. Certainly, those involved in training do not want to lose control over training resources and budgets. Although training negligence is not a serious problem with most training in organizations, the risks are very substantial if training involves decisions that can affect life and limb. If injury to customers or employees occurs, there will be a determined effort in litigation to discover how appropriate individuals were trained and supervised. Those employers who have weak responses to such a challenge will face the risk of a law settlement or judgment.

The use of scenarios is an especially valuable training method. Appropriate scenarios would include threats from (a) a stalker or romantically disaffected individual, (b) a potentially dangerous employee who is being terminated, (c) a former employee who has made threats, and (d) a menacing or threatening employee. A trainer should be able to direct his or her class to consider various contingencies during the development of such a scenario. If properly done, such training will leave participants empowered to manage many threatening situations.

The Rise of Psychological Terrorism

During the past few years, there have been a number of cases where individuals—usually fired employees or angry customers—will exercise acts in what can best be described as *psychological terrorism*. Psychological terrorists are individuals who prey upon the fears of managers trying to cope with the unknown. Psychological terrorists often are very intelligent and creative individuals who understand the line between behavior that is legally permissible and that which is not. Their goal is to terrorize the organization, diverting management attention in the process, without bringing undo legal attention upon themselves.

One documented case of a person who can be called a psychological terrorist involves John Kliebert, a fired Kidder Peabody bond salesman. *The Wall Street Journal* published an exposé on Mr. Kliebert's psychological terrorist campaign against his former employer in a page-one story published on April 29, 1994 (Siconolfi, 1994). Key features of this story are highlighted in Exhibit 5.

Two facts are beyond dispute. Mr. Kliebert certainly captured the attention of senior Kidder Peabody executives. According to the newspaper account, Kidder Peabody spent $1 million investigating Mr. Kliebert. According to the author's sources, Kidder's funds were expended for psychiatric assessments and for investigative reports on Mr. Kliebert, as well as for protective services for Kidder executives. After 10 frustrating months, beleaguered Kidder Peabody called off the full-court press. Almost as quickly, Mr. Kliebert ceased his obnoxious threats.

Exhibit 5.   The Saga of John Kliebert, a Fired Kidder Peabody Bond Salesman

---

Acts by 41-Year-Old Mr. Kliebert
- Threatened former boss at Kidder's headquarters, saying "his shirt would look good with a red splotch in the chest area."
- Phoned threats, promising to "get even" with four coworkers.
- Sent long-stem black roses and abusive faxes to secretaries in the bond trading area.
- Employed an attorney to advise him on legalities.
- Threatened to expose a "scandal" at the firm's Board meeting.

Response by Kidder and Law Enforcement
- Spent more than $1 million on private investigators, who even followed him on a vacation to the Caribbean.
- Had Kliebert arrested on third-degree menacing charges, a misdemeanor. Charges were dropped when he agreed to see a therapist and honor a court order.

Source: Kinney, 1995a, p. 97.

The Kliebert saga is increasingly common in U.S. business. Employers are facing terminated employees or disgruntled customers who are extremely threatening. Although these individuals appear well-anchored and otherwise stable, employers are often fearful that threats will be transformed into reality.

In all likelihood, Kidder's reaction to Kliebert was overkill. Few workplace murderers had the intelligence, financial resources, and disposition of Kliebert. Moreover, there is no evidence that suggests that murderers go on vacation to the Caribbean to plot acts of violence. However, there is no reason to believe that Kidder was following anything but a prudent course. Although there is little evidence that Kliebert had the emotional state of mind (e.g., present-time oriented, isolated, and irrational) that suggested he was about to kill anyone, Kidder, however, felt that it could not take a chance.

There may be ways to manage psychological terrorists like Kliebert. Possible steps would include

- Brief affected Kidder personnel on the individual's state-of-mind and the likelihood that he will not be violent.
- Investigate the perpetrator on a periodic basis to evaluate whether the person's emotional state of mind is changing.
- Protect targets of the individual's wrath (see Exhibit 4).

It is possible that Kidder's overreaction, especially the diversion of management personnel from primary duties, is precisely what Mr. Kliebert wanted. Few individuals are able to divert management attention and resources like Kliebert was able to do. In fact, it is possible that Kliebert, aided by disloyal Kidder employees, played a role in providing details of this incident to the *Journal*.

Conclusion

Threat management is a complex but reasonably logical process. Ideally, management will involve workers from all levels of the organization in policy development in order to ensure that such a policy is well received and credibly implemented. The foundation for any policy must be a reporting system that is comprehensive, encouraging threat information from both internal and external sources. If threat managers are properly trained and supported by senior management, most challenges can be successfully overcome. Senior management must be committed to effective threat management; policies, to be credible, must be effectively communicated to employees and other stakeholders.

The threat coordinator—the individual who manages this information—plays a key role in an effective violence prevention program. It is the coordinator who must make a crucial determination on how far a matter should be investigated and managed prior to convening a team. It is obvious that few employers can afford the luxury of assigning a team to every situation. In many cases, the coordinator will be able to manage an issue to an appropriate conclusion. In cases where the problem is more complex or intractable, the coordinator will have to employ further resources, which may include a team.

In most organizations, a coordinator will have other responsibilities than responding to reports. In most cases, a coordinator will likely be a security or human resources professional who spends whatever time is necessary addressing problems related to violence. However, irrespective of that person's position in the organization, it is crucial that information management be the coordinator's first responsibility. In general, the coordinator should receive substantial training in interviewing, incident documentation, and other skills that will be of assistance in this important role.

Like other processes, threat management can be done poorly. Failure can be costly in terms of financial and human resources. Employers must make every effort to undertake the threat management mission with adequate resources and skills. If done properly, a threat manager or coordinator can go a long way to making workplaces the safe and healthy environments that they should be.

References

Kinney, J. A. (1995a). *Violence at work. How to make your company safer for employees and customers*. New York: Simon & Schuster; and Englewood Cliffs, NJ: Prentice Hall.

Kinney, J. A. (1995b). *Preventing violence at work. A step-by-step program to protect your employees, company and assets*. New York: Simon & Schuster; Englewood Cliffs, NJ: Prentice Hall.

Kinney, J. A., & Johnson, D. L. (1993). *Breaking point: The workplace violence epidemic and what to do about it*. Chicago: National Safe Workplace Institute.

Kinney, J. A., & Lambert, B. (1996). *Mandating psychological assessment of employees*. Charlotte, NC: National Safe Workplace Institute.

Monahan, J. (1992). Mental disorder and violent behavior: Perceptions and evidence. *American Psychologist, 47*(4), 511–521.

National Safe Workplace Institute. (1989). Levels of violence and anger in the workplace. *The Healthy Office Report, 2*(7), 2–3.

Siconolfi, M. (1994, April 29). An employee fired by Kidder Peabody casts a pall of fear. *The Wall Street Journal*, pp. A1, A6.

Techniques to manage the threat of violence in the workplace. (1993, November 25). *Security Management Bulletin* (Bureau of Business Practice), No. 2222, 1–8.

18

Unions Respond to Violence on the Job

Judith L. King and David G. Alexander

The recent media attention to workplace homicides has produced a spate of articles in the human resource and security management literature. Most put their focus on the potentially dangerous disgruntled employee— the "ticking time bomb" (Graham, 1992) or the employee "on the edge" (Filipczak, 1993). Many provide a profile to help managers recognize this employee before he or she explodes (Baron, 1993).

Union representatives, too, are concerned about violence in the workplace, in no small part because their members are the likely targets of violence. To union leaders, however, the focus on the crazed employee is misplaced: To reduce violent encounters, the lens must move beyond a particular employee to scan conditions both inside and outside the work site. As tragic, dramatic, and frightening as many recent and well-publicized incidents have been, zeroing in on the employee who fits the profile misses the bigger picture of workplace violence.

Over the past year, our work with local and national leaders in the labor movement has centered around one issue: How can we remove the hysteria from the issue of violence so that we can look for ways to make workplaces safer, and still protect the rights of individual members? Some of the most important and innovative work in the safety and health arena is being done by unions trying to protect their members from violence on the job. In this chapter, we will report on some of those efforts. We will also relate the results of a survey of local union leaders, and will describe some education programs currently underway. We hope to place the subject of violence into a much broader context than it usually appears in the literature. In doing so, we hope to increase the reader's understanding of union leaders and their legal responsibilities—responsibilities that often place leaders in a most awkward position when confronted with threats of violence in the workplace.

A Look at the Numbers

By now, many readers are familiar with the statistics: Violent acts account for 20% of occupational deaths; homicide is the leading cause of on-job deaths for women; in five states, murder is the leading cause of death on the job. Less widely reported, however, are these figures from the Bureau of Labor Statistics (BLS) (Toscano & Weber, 1995):

- In 1993, robbery was the motive in 75% of workplace homicides.
- Family disputes were involved in 4% of workplace homicides.
- About 6% of workplace homicides were committed by current or former employees; another 4% were committed by customers or clients.

What increases workers' risk of murder on the job? The National Institute of Occupational Safety and Health (NIOSH) has identified several factors (NIOSH, 1993):

- Working alone
- Working with money
- Working late at night or in the early morning
- Working in high-crime areas
- Working in community settings.

Less is known about the number and types of nonfatal workplace assaults, but BLS reports the following (Toscano & Weber, 1995):

- In 1992, over 22,000 workers were injured in nonfatal assaults resulting in loss of work time. These assaults averaged 5 lost work days.
- Nonfatal violent acts usually involved hitting or kicking, and often occurred in health care facilities.
- In contrast to workplace homicides, where men were the likely victims, women accounted for 56% of workplace assault victims.

Workplace assault and homicide, then, are likely to result from contact with a stranger, a patient, or a client—not from a coworker. This fact has led international unions to call upon employers to look at all factors that expose their employees to risk. Health-care workers, teachers, librarians, corrections personnel, social service employees, and those in retail sales are particularly concerned with the potential for violence in public contact jobs. They feel that, in many cases, violent acts may be both predictable and preventable.

Action at the International Union Level

For years, those unions whose members deal with the public have been concerned with violent acts toward their members. The American Federation of Teachers (AFT), for example, has response teams to investigate incidents of assaults on teachers (Alexander, 1995). After an assault, the union provides support for the member, including dealing with the police, hospital, or family. Follow-up counseling is also available.

The United Federation of Teachers (UFT), New York City, an AFT affiliate, has been collecting data on violent incidents for over 20 years. The union has its own school safety department, which works with the New York City Office of School Safety to improve school security. UFT has published a handbook, *Security in the Schools* (Muir, 1989), and has been involved with community efforts to keep guns out of the hands of young people.

The Service Employees International Union (SEIU), representing large numbers of health-care workers and workers in community settings, has one of the most extensive training programs in the labor movement. SEIU has produced a video, *Private Horror/Public Issue: On the Job Assault*, that puts a human face on the potential violence facing those who work with the public. Their booklet, *Assault on the Job: We Can Do Something About Workplace Violence* (1995), provides information on safety and security programs, sample contract language, an employee survey, and an incident reporting form.

The New York State Public Employees Federation (PEF) has a comprehensive surveillance program and provides members who are victims of workplace assault with special insurance benefits (PEF, 1991). PEF has also joined with other public sector unions in the state to lobby for legislative action, to set safety standards, and to educate authorities about funding, understaffing, and workplace design issues.

The Civil Service Employees Association (CSEA), Local 100 of the American Federation of State, County, and Municipal Employees (AFSCME) has produced its own booklet on workplace security (CSEA, 1994). CSEA has been particularly concerned with modifying worksites to make them safer and with procedural changes that eliminate the risks of assault to employees.

Some unions have devoted special attention to different aspects of the violence question. AFSCME (1995) and the United Food and Commercial Workers (UFCW, n.d.) have each produced materials relating domestic violence to the workplace. The Association of Flight Attendants (Mirsky, 1995) uses its peer counselors to deal with posttraumatic stress syndrome after violent incidents. The National Association of Letter Carriers (1994) has joined with the Postal Service to educate the citizens of Los Angeles about attacks against letter carriers.

One pioneering joint labor-management effort is now underway with the United Auto Workers (UAW)–Ford's Behavioral Emergency/Critical Incident Stress Debriefing Program. The program is designed to respond to traumas and to prevent incidents on the shop floor. Stemming from language proposed in the 1993 collective bargaining agreement, the model seeks to recognize workers who may be exhibiting, through unusual behavior, signs of stress, and then to intervene with those workers through counseling. Special teams, using resources both within and outside the workplace, confront workers who may need help, defuse potentially dangerous situations, and debrief workers after an incident. Training sessions for team members, union committeemen, and supervisors are being conducted in Ford facilities throughout the country (UAW–Ford, 1994).

Finally, international union safety and health representatives have joined in coalition to press the Occupational Safety and Health Administration (OSHA) for a standard dealing with violence on the job. The members of the coalition are pooling educational materials and working together politically to strengthen state and federal laws to protect workers from attack on the job.

Because most of the unions leading the way on the issue have large numbers of members working in public contact jobs, and because the numbers suggest that these are the workers most at risk, training efforts have focused by and large on protecting workers from clients, patients, students, or strangers. The UAW–Ford program, however, suggests that at least some attention is being given to potential worker-on-worker violence. The interest in coworker problems surfaces again in a survey of local union leaders.

The View From the Local Union Level: The Alabama Survey

In the past few years, both union and university-based labor education programs have sponsored training to deal with the issues of violence. The Center for Labor Education and Research (CLEAR) at the University of Alabama at Birmingham, for example, has conducted seven sessions, reaching over 300 unionists (King, 1994). In addition, the subject is now routinely covered in their safety and health classes.

The interest among Alabama unionists has been curious. On the one hand, Alabama is one of the states where homicide is the leading cause of on-the-job death. On the other hand, few Alabama unionists work in the public contact jobs that typically expose workers to violence.

To get a better sense of why Alabamians seemed to be so interested in the topic, CLEAR conducted a survey of local union leaders in late 1994. Questionnaires were mailed to local union presidents and safety committee chairs; about 50 responded. The respondents represented 14 different unions, reflecting a cross-section of Alabama industry: paper, steel, rubber, telecommunications, printing, transportation, construction, retail food, and food processing. Some of the respondents were in public contact jobs; only a few were in the public sector.

Local union leaders view the issue of violence in the workplace from a very intimate perspective. Classroom discussion and the survey yielded six observations:

1. The concern with violence stemmed from direct experience with it. Of the 50 leaders, 38 reported incidents of violence in their workplaces. Although most involved threats of assault or fights, 17 incidents involved guns, and 15 involved other weapons. Vir-

tually any item could become a weapon, according to the respondents: Irate customers would pick up a tin can and strike a cashier, or a tool could be raised in anger. At least a dozen injuries were reported, including gunshot and stabbing wounds. Police were involved in some cases. Local leaders perceived a great potential for harm.

2. The most serious incidents occurred in those workplaces with public contact. Grocery store clerks reported armed robberies, countless scuffles with shoplifters, and assaults over price disputes. In CLEAR classes, as well, teachers and health-care workers reported assaults by students and patients. Librarians reported incidents involving gang members, displaced mental patients, and homeless patrons. Many of these episodes involved weapons or excessive force.

3. Statistics notwithstanding, survey respondents saw that the potential for violence was simmering among workers in many workplaces. The most likely expression of this violence, however, was not mass murder but fights, or threats to "get" someone. Some 40 fights and 80 threats were documented in the survey.

    In the few cases where union leaders feared a worker could seriously harm him or herself and others, they were caught in a terrible quandary: Should they try to handle the situation themselves, or should they take their concern to management? Union leaders are bound by a legal duty to fairly represent all members, and a leader reporting a member to management could conceivably face a lawsuit if his or her suspicions were in error. Beyond that, many leaders believe deeply that it violates their oath of office to report a brother or sister to management. Balancing the well-being of the membership while protecting the rights of the individual member is a thorny legal and moral issue for local leaders.

4. In most cases, workers knew what needed to be done to alleviate the problems they saw on the job. The grocery clerks knew that they needed security guards after dark, procedures that made money less visible, increased staffing, and access to telephones in different areas of the stores. Other leaders were able to identify stress, long hours, forced overtime, racial tensions, production pressures, rotating shifts, fear of plant shutdown or job loss, harassment, and heat as contributing factors to the outbreaks of fights and threats on their job sites.

    Rarely, however, did these leaders find that management was ready to respond. In the survey, none of the employers had a plan for handling violent situations, nor had any conducted training for supervisors or employees. Of the 50 respondents, 7 had approached management to work together on the issue, and each of the 7 had been rebuffed. Employee assistance programs (EAPs) were not involved in any way.

5. Local leaders were also clear that they needed not only more co-

operation from management, but also more training for themselves. The training they wanted was specific to their problems:
how to respond to a robbery attempt; how to recognize and deal
with patients and patrons who may not be stable; how to defuse
tensions among those working together under stress.

6. Finally, the survey and discussions with local leaders uncovered
one other disturbing facet of workplace violence: Union representatives, in their capacities as leaders and problem solvers, may
themselves become the victims of violence by irate members. Of
the 50 respondents, 11 reported being the target of threats. One
international representative received long and frightening letters
from a member; one steward finally went to the police after being
stalked by the husband of an employee who had been terminated.
Employees inclined to exact revenge may well include the union
representative who could not resolve the problem to the employee's satisfaction—whether that was possible or not.

The Meany Center Program

The Alabama survey was one impetus for the development of a weeklong
class, Dealing With Workplace Violence, held at the George Meany Center
for Labor Studies. In addition to its college degree program, the Meany
Center offers at its Silver Spring, Maryland, campus weeklong, noncredit
courses designed to provide practical and portable information to union
representatives. A class of this nature, however, involved more than what
a planner might face in coordinating the more traditional contract nego-
tiations or organizing programs.

How could we design a course that would provide useful information
for local union officers and staff who are struggling to assess and prevent
violence in the workplace every day? We faced one major obstacle: We had
to create a program to meet the needs of two separate and distinct audiences. As mentioned earlier, unions in the public and service sectors are
particularly sensitive to ways to protect their members from attacks from
a member of the public, be it a patient, customer, or robber. In designing
the program, however, we could not ignore the needs of private sector
unionists who face the more difficult problem of worker-on-worker violence. The private sector leaders needed to develop a quite different set of
skills.

Finding adequate resources for the program was less of a problem. As
with a number of other issues in the labor movement, there were many
people working on the problem of workplace violence. The Interunion
Workplace Violence Coalition, composed of representatives from approximately 35 international and national unions, was able to provide a number
of instructors and resource materials.

The program was held November 5–10, 1995, at the Meany Center's
Silver Spring campus. Fifteen participants from nine different interna-

tional unions attended. About a month prior to the class we mailed a survey to the participants, asking for information about themselves, their unions, their industries, and the kinds of workers they represented. We planned to use this information to assess the problems they were dealing with in their workplaces.

The participants' responses fit some predictable patterns. The private sector representatives were looking for ways to defuse tensions between workers, or between workers and management, before conflict erupted. The public sector representatives, in contrast, were looking for ways to create a more secure workplace to eliminate assaults from people they were unlikely to know. Several participants wanted specific skills to help them prepare and present arbitration cases in which workers were disciplined for fights, threats, or possession of weapons. Others were unable to identify specific instances, but were increasingly uneasy about the potential for violence in their workplaces.

We began the first day with two sessions to give the participants a frame of reference. A representative of the National Institute for Occupational Safety and Health provided statistical information in a session on the "Epidemiology of Violence." The second session helped students view violence as an occupational safety issue. This was useful to the participants for a number of reasons. First, it helped them recognize that the problem could be approached in ways that were already familiar to them: through their local union safety and health committees. Second, it provided a view of the issue that was distinctly different from that of most employers, who tend to see the issue of violence strictly as a human resources matter and pay little attention to other important environmental factors. Part of what this program was about was educating union leaders on how to encourage their employers to approach the issue from a wider perspective and share in joint action.

The first afternoon's session was devoted to helping the union establish a workplace violence program. As mentioned above, the New York State Public Employees Federation has been very successful in program development, worksite analysis, hazard prevention and control, and training. We wanted the participants to examine how they could incorporate these components into their own workplace plans. Throughout the week, then, the students applied what they heard to develop their own programs, containing these elements:

- *Program development.* What steps should the union take to insure employee involvement and management commitment? What kinds of resources would be needed to develop an effective program?
- *Worksite analysis.* How would the union do a worksite assessment? What documents would be needed? How would the union gather information about incidents in the workplace? What kinds of information about the work environment would be needed? How would organizational hazards be identified?
- *Hazard prevention and control.* What changes in workplace design,

security measures, incident reporting, administrative policies and procedures, and staffing would need to be implemented to prevent assaults?

- *Training programs.* What kinds of training should employees receive? What job-specific training would be needed? What role should the union play in any training program? What kind of training would be needed for supervisors and managers?
- *Medical management.* What kinds of post-incident services, including counseling, medical assistance, and workers' compensation, should be offered? What role should an employee assistance program (EAP) play?
- *Post-incident.* How should a follow-up program be designed?

Much of the second day was devoted to work being done at the international union level. Representatives from SEIU, AFSCME, and the AFT discussed how their unions were responding to situations that led to violence. Representatives from the UAW–Ford Behavioral Emergency/Critical Incident Stress Debriefing Program described their model of joint labor-management cooperation.

A 3-hour session was devoted to post-incident response. Participants were asked to think about new ways of using existing resources, such as EAPs, local union community service committees, and crisis-related organizations in their own areas. Unions as diverse as the Association of Flight Attendants, the American Federation of Government Employees (AFGE), and the Laborers' International Union of North America (LIUNA) have been training union representatives to participate in post-incident programs. Representatives from these unions, as well as from the AFL-CIO Community Services Department, spoke to the group.

The message of this particular session was to encourage local union leaders to participate in post-incident debriefings, recognizing that the union has a responsibility as an equal partner in any joint program. These responsibilities include participation in the selection of any outside facilitators who may work with the parties in the design and implementation of the debriefing; setting rules to protect confidentiality and to ensure that nothing said is used against an employee at a later time; and ensuring follow-up referrals, evaluations, and counseling.

Another important part of the program covered domestic violence. Workplace violence is the number one killer of women in the workplace, and women involved in abusive personal relationships often find that the abuse carries over to their jobs. Abuse is not always physical, and the signs of such abuse may not be readily apparent. Participants examined differing levels of abuse and discussed strategies to provide constructive responses to this problem.

In Canada, as in the United States, there is growing concern about protecting members from violence, and a representative of the Canadian Union of Public Employees described efforts of that union. Highlighted were examples of legislation being enacted in four provinces to set standards that would apply to all employers, no matter what size, industry, or sector. This session reinforced the need to use political strength to deal with workplace violence.

A final session related violence to dispute resolution, featuring an arbitrator who detailed the evidentiary standards in cases in which violence, or the potential for it, has to be decided by a neutral third-party. This session raised some troubling issues for union representatives, who are forced to deal with the unique problem of violence in the context of traditional disciplinary and grievance structures.

The typical grievance and arbitration process is designed to assess and correct conduct only *after* an offense has occurred. With the increasing use of threat assessment programs by employers, there will undoubtedly be more cases in arbitration where a grievant is removed because he fits a "high-risk profile." The fact that some employees who engage in violent behavior fit this profile does not mean that employees who fit the profile engage in, or are even significantly more likely to engage in, violent behavior. The use of these profiles to identify employees as threats and to take action against them may create significant opportunities for harm because of bias, personal conflicts, or even union activity. As with the issue of substance abuse, arbitration is probably the wrong place to effectively deal with an employee's larger problems.

As mentioned earlier, the centerpiece of the week was the development of the workplace action plan. On the final day of the institute, the participants reported back to the class on their particular plans. It was clear from the reports that each participant realized the importance of approaching this problem with all available resources. It was also clear that each union has to spend more time educating members about the union's role in keeping their workplaces free from assault. It is up to the union to help formulate policies and procedures, not merely to react to the employer's policies.

On their evaluations, the participants made many suggestions for improving the training sessions. Several mentioned the need to spend more time on targeting and defusing racial tension. With the prospect of an increasingly diverse workforce struggling with fewer opportunities to progress, unions must provide a model for tolerance and understanding. Others felt a need for a law enforcement perspective, and information on how unions should work with local police. Some participants raised the issue of threats to union representatives, as the Alabama survey also revealed. As frustrations in the workplace continue to fester and union leaders attempt to perform their responsibilities with fewer and fewer resources, more union leaders may find themselves targeted. Being a union leader is a perilous job under the best of circumstances: Fearing for one's safety is a burden no one should have to bear.

All in all, however, the participants felt they gained a great deal, particularly from interacting with others in small group exercises, simulations, and in the development of the action plan. Working with leaders from different unions, different economic sectors, and different parts of the country provided valuable insights for each participant to apply back home.

Conclusion

This chapter highlights just some of labor's responses to the problem of workplace homicide and assault. Other materials and labor education programs abound.

Whatever the union, whatever the industry, whatever the region of the country, one theme is sounded over and over: Place the issue of workplace violence into the total context of workplace safety and health. Management is hardly credible if it focuses on coworker incidents and ignores the much larger threat from those who enter the workplace from outside. Management is hardly credible if it rushes to install screening programs and zero tolerance policies while refusing to attend to electrical, chemical, fire, and ergonomic hazards. Violence is, at heart, a safety issue.

That said, it is also true that unions are moving, albeit cautiously, toward addressing the problem of worker-on-worker violence. Drug abuse, the ready availability of guns, a social climate that tolerates violence to solve problems—all these can be lethal when combined with the stresses of modern workplaces. The respondents in the Alabama survey recognized the flash points: threat of job loss, pressures in the "do more with less" workplace, racial tensions, and intransigent management. What they need to know is how to defuse those tensions while remaining within the bounds of their legal and ethical obligations to their members.

This issue will demand some new approaches from both labor and management. The UAW–Ford program is a giant step away from the traditional disciplinary system toward a joint program that seeks help for the troubled worker before he has irretrievably damaged himself, his career, or other people. It requires a great deal of faith on both sides: Others in the labor community await the results of this experiment. Will management really turn to counseling instead of discipline or removal for someone who appears to be a threat to others? Will union members really report to management a brother or sister who exhibits signs that might foreshadow danger?

The labor movement must also attend to the threats that face their own representatives. In a world where every institution from government to education is increasingly suspect, the grievance handler or local officer is the most visible symbol of one more institution that cannot seem to satisfy the disaffected. Local leaders often complain that their members have little understanding of the limits of the union; nowhere is that more apparent than with the worker who holds both the company and the union to blame for his misfortune.

One thing is certain: The labor movement has already begun to marshal the resources to uncover and address the many facets of workplace violence. As unions move forward to negotiate, administer their contracts, and lobby for political action, the interactions—within the union and with management—will be difficult. They will also save lives.

References

Alexander, D. (1995, November 7). Presentation given at Dealing With Workplace Violence Conference, George Meany Center of Labor Studies, Silver Spring, MD.

American Federation of State, County, and Municipal Employees. (1995). *Domestic violence: An AFSCME guide for union action* [brochure]. Washington, DC: Author.

Baron, S. A. (1993). *Violence in the workplace: A prevention and management guide for businesses*. Ventura, CA: Pathfinder Publishing.

Civil Service Employees Association. (1994). *Security in the workplace* [brochure]. New York: Author.

Filipczak, B. (1993, July). Armed and dangerous at work. *Training*, pp. 39–43.

Graham, J. P. (1992). Disgruntled employees—Ticking time bombs? *Security Management, 36*, 83–85.

King (Catlett), J. L. (1994, Fall). Violence in the workplace: A new quandary for unions. *Labor Studies Forum, 7*, 1.

Mirsky, S. (1995, November 9). The AFA [Association of Flight Attendants] Emergency response program. Paper presented at the Dealing With Workplace Violence Conference, George Meany Center, Silver Spring, MD.

Muir, E. (1989). *Security in the schools*. New York: United Federation of Teachers.

National Association of Letter Carriers. (1994, January 13). Davis praises Branch 24 program to curb assaults against carriers. *NALC Bulletin, 94*(1).

National Institute for Occupational Safety and Health. (1993). *NIOSH alert: Request for assistance in preventing homicide in the workplace*. Washington, DC: U.S. Department of Health and Human Services.

New York State Public Employees Federation. (1991). *ATAC: Assault trauma and captivity insurance program* [brochure]. New York: PEF Membership Benefits Program.

Service Employees International Union. (1995). *Assault on the job: We can do something about workplace violence* [brochure]. Washington, DC: Author

Toscano, G., & Weber, W. (1995, June). Violence in the workplace. *Fatal workplace injuries in 1993: A collection of data and analyses* (BLS Report 891). Washington, DC: Government Printing Office.

UAW–Ford Employee Support Services Program. (1994). National behavioral emergency/critical incident "stress debriefing" procedures [manual]. Detroit, MI: UAW–Ford.

United Food and Commercial Workers Union. (n.d.). *Domestic and workplace violence: Breaking the cycle* [brochure]. Washington, DC: Author.

19

The Assaulted Staff Action Program: Guidelines for Fielding a Team

Raymond B. Flannery, Jr., Walter E. Penk,
M. Annette Hanson, and Georgina J. Flannery

As violence has been increasing in the country at large, there has been a similar increase in violence in the workplace. In the past quarter century, violence at the worksite has increased in frequency, extent, severity, and lethality (Flannery, 1995). Such aggression affects not only direct parties to violent acts but also other employees who witness the event.

A recent review of the published findings (Flannery, 1995) suggests at least five major types of assailants: the angry customer, the medically ill individual, domestic batterers, criminals, and disgruntled employees. The violent acts of these assailants result in human suffering, medical expense, and lost productivity (Hunter & Carmel, 1992), and research has been undertaken both to identify possible worksite assailants and to address the aftermath that the worksite violence creates.

This worksite literature is most developed for psychiatric health care settings (Blair, 1991; Davis, 1991; Dietz & Rada, 1982; Flannery, Hanson, & Penk, 1994), where thirty years of published findings have identified some consistent characteristics of medically or psychiatrically ill assailants. Often these assailants are young, male, psychotic patients with a past history of violence and a diagnosis of substance abuse. They are likely to attack younger, male, lower level mental health employees who have less formal education.

Health care organizations have begun efforts to address the aftermath of these violent episodes. With increasing evidence of the deleterious consequences of assaults, including posttraumatic stress disorder (PTSD; Caldwell, 1992; Flannery, 1994b), clinicians have begun to address the psychological sequelae of these assaults (Dawson, Johnson, Kehiayan, Kyanko, & Martinez, 1988; Flannery, Fulton, Tausch, & De Loffi, 1991; Flannery,

---

The authors wish to thank the ASAP team leaders, Kenneth Allen, RN, Mary Barry, RN, Barbara Glick, RN, Russell Mulhearn, MHW, Lenore Pollen, LICSW, Virginia Stevens, RN, Phyllis Stone, LICSW, Bruce Schwartz, PhD, and all of the ASAP team members for their excellent service to their colleagues.

Hanson, Penk, Flannery, & Gallagher, 1995; Flannery, Hanson, Penk, Pastva, & Navon, 1996; Storch, 1991). Dawson and her associates utilized a peer-help intervention to provide understanding and support for assaulted staff, whereas Storch developed an ongoing staff support group for employee victims in a large state mental hospital.

The Assaulted Staff Action Program (ASAP; Flannery et al., 1991; Flannery, Hanson, Penk, Flannery, & Gallagher, 1995; Flannery et al., 1996) appears to be one of the more comprehensive data-based programs to date. This voluntary, peer-help approach provides needed support for employee victims; it is one of the first programs to report sharp reductions in violence in the facilities where it has been fielded. Although ASAP was developed and fielded in health care settings, the flexibility of this approach makes it suitable for other worksite settings, including corporate–industrial settings, police and correctional facilities, and schools or colleges. The steps to fielding a successful ASAP program in a variety of worksite settings are outlined in these pages.

A Description of the Assaulted Staff Action Program

The Assaulted Staff Action Program (Flannery et al., 1991; Flannery, Hanson, Penk, Flannery, & Gallagher, 1995) is a voluntary, peer-help, crisis intervention, systems approach for addressing the psychological sequelae of patient assaults on staff in mental health care settings. It is based on the principle from military medicine of proximity, immediacy, and expectancy (Grinker & Spiegel, 1945). The employee victim is treated near the site where the assault took place, as quickly as possible, and with the expectation that the employee will return to work quickly.

Philosophy

Four assumptions guide the ASAP program:

1. Staff members may experience a traumatic crisis as a result of patient assaults.
2. Employee victims are worthy of compassionate care.
3. Employee victims who are able to speak to peers with the same risk for assault will be more likely to talk about the event, and will cope more effectively in the short-term and avoid long-lasting disruptions, including PTSD.
4. ASAP is committed to the belief that the episode of violence is not the employee victim's fault. This approach assumes employee victims did not deliberately cause the assault. Although they may have made technical errors which need to be corrected, they did not seek to harm with deliberate intent. (True criminal assaults by staff are dealt with according to state legal procedures.)

Assaults

ASAP responds to four known classes of assaults (Flannery, Hanson, & Penk, 1995):

1. *Physical assaults* are unwanted physical contact with intent to harm (e.g., punching, kicking, slapping, or spitting).
2. *Sexual assaults* are any unwanted sexual contact (e.g., fondling, attempted rape, or exposing).
3. *Nonverbal intimidation* refers to behavior or acts meant to frighten or intimidate staff (e.g., throwing an ashtray across the nurses' station).
4. *Verbal threats* refer to verbal statements meant to frighten staff.

ASAP Structure

ASAP teams vary in size and composition based on the needs of the facility both in terms of frequency of assaults and the number of patient care sites. In a typical state mental hospital setting of 200 to 400 beds and 200 to 400 direct-care staff, an ASAP team would require about 15 volunteer members. The team would include clinicians in all disciplines as well as mental health workers. In addition, it would include the hospital's switchboard operators. ASAP members are not paid for their services. However, if they respond to assaults that occur off shift, they do receive compensatory time.

Eleven of these volunteers constitute the first-line responders. They are on-call by page beeper for 24-hour periods on weekday rotations, and are on-call one weekend every 3 months. Members respond to each individual episode of patient assault on staff, and attend a weekly team meeting to review cases as well as a monthly inservice training program.

Three additional volunteers comprise the ASAP supervisors. They are also on-call by page beeper on a weekly rotation for second opinions, multiple assaults, and for critical incident stress debriefings (CISD; Mitchell & Everly, 1993) of entire ward units. They also attend the weekly team meeting to review cases as well as the monthly inservice training. The ASAP supervisors are usually senior nurse supervisors or senior staff development personnel. This allows for informal outreach on the units, where indicated, and assessment of needs for further staff training in patient-care issues.

The final volunteer is the ASAP team leader, who is charged with administering the program and monitoring the quality of the services delivered. The team leader chairs the weekly team meeting, co-leads the support group for employee victims, provides for inservice training, monitors team members for vicarious traumatization (McCann & Pearlman, 1990), and provides ASAP debriefing for ASAP team members who may be directly assaulted in the course of their hospital duties. Finally, the team leader meets with the hospital switchboard operators. Although not formal team members, the operators are an integral part of the service delivery system, and are debriefed weekly by the team leader. They are also included in all ASAP inservice trainings and ASAP social gatherings.

ASAP Services

There are five services offered by ASAP:

- individual employee victim debriefing
- staff victims' support group
- ward unit debriefing
- employee victim family debriefing
- professional referral

A detailed description of each one follows.

Individual employee victim debriefing. If an assault occurs, the ward charge nurse is required to notify the hospital switchboard. The ASAP first-line responder is summoned to the site by beeper, checks to be sure safety and medical issues have been addressed, and then proceeds to gather specific information about the assault to determine what has actually happened. Then, because mastery, attachment, and meaning have been demonstrated to be hallmarks of adaptive functioning (Flannery, 1994a, b), the first responder assesses the employee victim for disruptions in these areas as well as for any symptoms usually associated with psychological trauma and PTSD. The first responder then assists the employee victim to return to some level of preincident functioning. The same first-line responder calls the employee victim 3 and 10 days later to evaluate the need for any further support and assistance.

In those cases where an assault occurs during off-shift times, the first responder calls the unit, assesses the nature of the critical incident, and decides, with the aid of the charge nurse (or supervisor, if it is not a medical setting) and the employee victim, if the debriefing needs to be done immediately or can wait until the next day. If it needs to be addressed immediately, the first-line responder returns to the facility, does an ASAP interview, and receives compensation time for travel and services rendered.

Staff victims' support group. The staff victims' support group, which is led by the team leader and one ASAP supervisor, meets weekly to provide short-term, ongoing support to employee victims who may need additional support. Staff victims are given release time and paid their hourly wage for group attendance.

Ward unit debriefing. Occasionally, a particular episode of assault may involve multiple victims or be especially violent and disruptive to the entire ward community. In these cases, the team leader and ASAP supervisors provide CISD (Mitchell & Everly, 1993) for the entire ward unit. They may provide a group debriefing for the ward unit managers, the clinical and nursing staff, and then the entire patient and staff community together.

Employee victim family debriefing. Sometimes, especially in the case of single parent employee victims, other family members may fear further harm to the employee victim if the employee victim returns to the facility. If requested, ASAP team members will meet with family members to process the impact of the assault on the family.

Professional referral. From time to time, employee victims of patient assaults may have memories of previous episodes of violence in their personal lives. If the recurring memories of personal violence are distressing to the employee victim, the ASAP team leader has a list of therapists who specialize in trauma counseling, and the option of a referral is offered to the employee.

With the exception of private counseling, all of the ASAP services are a free employee benefit. All ASAP information is kept completely confidential and does not become part of the employee's personnel record or medical file. ASAP information is available from the ASAP team leader only upon receipt of an ASAP release of information form signed by the employee victim.

Findings of the Assaulted Staff Action Program

Because the ASAP findings have been reported previously (Flannery et al., 1991; Flannery et al., 1994; Flannery, Hanson, Penk, & Flannery, 1995; Flannery et al., 1996; Flannery et al., in press), only the main findings are reviewed here.

ASAP teams have been fielded in four state mental hospital settings in which one team was fielded for 2 years, and three others where ASAP teams have completed 1 year of implementation as of this date. These teams have responded to 452 episodes of patient violence during 3 years of service. ASAP was accepted in 387 incidents and declined in 65 other episodes (17% refusal rate).

Assaults were more likely to involve junior-level mental health workers (over 60%) or nurses (over 15%), and bruises with swelling were the most likely injuries. Female staff victims were more likely to be victims of random assaults, and male staff victims were more likely to be assaulted in restraint and seclusion procedures. These findings are consistent with 30 years of previously reported findings (Blair, 1991; Davis, 1991; Dietz & Rada, 1982; Flannery et al., 1994).

Several employee victims reported symptoms associated with psychological trauma and PTSD, especially hypervigilance, sleeplessness, and intrusive memories of the assaults. For most, these symptoms cleared within 10 days, but 10% were still experiencing disruptions after 10 days, a finding consistent with Caldwell (1992).

In each facility there was a 40–50% decline in the number of assaults within 1 year after the ASAP program was fielded. In the original ASAP facility, which was on-line for 2 years, the reduction in overall facility violence declined even further to 63% below base rate. These declines in violence have resulted in less suffering, less medical expense, less use of sick leave, fewer industrial accident claims, and less staff turnover. Over a 2-year period, the original ASAP program saved its facility $268,000 over and above team costs in staff turnover costs alone, and thus paid for itself.

Taken together, these findings suggest the efficacy of the ASAP program in addressing the psychological needs of individual employee staff victims and of reducing the level of violence in the facility. The fielding of an ASAP team may be of importance in those facilities of any type where workplace assaults have reached an unacceptable level of occurrence.

Fielding an ASAP Team at Work

The development, training, and fielding of an ASAP team, which is adapted to the needs of a particular worksite, is best addressed in a series of five stages. These stages include (a) considering the organization's administrative issues, (b) designing the team for a particular setting, (c) selecting the team members, (d) training, and (e) fielding the service. ASAP teams are fielded with less resistance and greater workforce participation, if these stages are addressed in the sequence just noted.

Administrative Issues

The ultimate success of any ASAP program depends on the support it receives from senior managers. Their public support of the team, and in some cases becoming ASAP team members, enhances workforce acceptance and the continuous functioning of ASAP services. In health care settings, the senior managers would include, at the least, the chief executive officer, the medical director, the director of nursing, and the department heads. Each of these interested parties needs to be included from the beginning. Although there may be particular individual administrative issues in any particular organization, senior managers in most worksites must address common and reasonable concerns as they consider fielding a team.

Legal matters. The most common set of issues are legal concerns that arise within the context of the confidentiality of ASAP debriefings. Because staff often have an initial concern that the ASAP team may be a management policing mechanism to determine fault or misuse of sick leave in cases of assault, ASAP team records must remain fully confidential if the team is to succeed. ASAP records are not to be part of the employee's personnel file or medical record, and are kept locked in the team leader's office.

If this system of confidentiality is to be put in place, administrators may have understandable concerns about employees committing crimes against patients and other violations of human rights. The ASAP program addresses these concerns in two ways. First, every ASAP team member arriving on-site for any debriefing always tells the employee victim(s) that all ASAP information is confidential unless the employee reports a crime. At that point, legal reporting requirements of abuse become paramount. Second, ASAP teams can be designed so that the ASAP first-line responder will not be someone who was also a witness to or participant in the incident, and so that the first-line responder is not the employee victim's supervisor or otherwise indirectly responsible for the incident that occurred. In this way the ASAP team member has no direct observational information or responsibility for the assault, and, therefore, will not generally be subject to related investigations.

A second possible legal interface may arise with the collection of ASAP data, and its possible use in anonymous, nonaggregate form for publishing findings and for conducting routine quality management reviews. This is a legitimate issue. However, gathering informed consent at the moment of the assault is impractical, often clinically contraindicated, and would probably not be valid in many instances where employees are in distress due to disabling critical incidents. ASAP policies have addressed this matter by drafting a letter for all employees in conjunction with guidance from the legal department and the research of the institution's Human Subjects Review board. The final approved draft indicated that all data would be coded and reported in the aggregate so that no individual employee victim could be identified. All employees were informed of this by a letter that stated the policy. The letter also stated that they could refuse the service, or accept the service but request that the data on a particular incident not be coded and submitted.

Two other legal matters may also arise. The first is the need for a legal contract if the ASAP team will involve the cooperative efforts of two or more agencies that will share the same team. Here standard contract law applies as joint responsibilities are outlined. The final common legal issue is the matter of employee victims pressing charges against patient assailants. The ASAP program is guided by specific facility policy, which states that every employee has a legal right as a citizen to press charges. The ASAP team will inform employee victims of facility policy but, because ASAP is primarily a post-incident debriefing service, it remains neutral in any specific incident. Such a decision is usually left to the employee victim and counsel. Because legal conventions may vary from one facility to another, whether to press charges is best resolved with the legal authorities in a specific setting.

Financial matters. A second general area of administrative concern involves the financing of an ASAP program. In an era of severe fiscal budgets and corporate downsizing, mergers, and layoffs, fiscal concerns become critical. Although it is true that an ASAP team may save money over time (Flannery et al., 1994), start-up costs are immediate and include staffing issues, needed support services (e.g., beepers), and compensation, if any. (See designing a team below.) These require budget allocations or reallocations and must be weighed against competing fiscal requests. Depending on the composition of the team, the facility must be sure that its malpractice insurance covers the various ASAP services and all classes of members on the team (e.g., nonclinical mental health personnel). In addition, any possible overlap with any current company employee assistance programs (EAPs) must be resolved to avoid duplication of services.

Finally, management needs to meet with all unions that will be involved. The ASAP program needs to be explained in detail, its possible benefits to employees outlined, and all union issues must be addressed. Unions need to agree with the compensation for their members for being on-call, and, if there is no compensation, unions need to be in agreement with compensatory time as a resolution to the matter. In our experience, unions understand that patient assaults may place their members at risk, so they are supportive of ASAP, and regard such peer support as helpful in developing safer work environments.

Systems issues. Administrators must also consider the general functioning of the facility. Ongoing issues for power and influence within the facility may present themselves around the development of the ASAP program. What is the role of ASAP in the Nursing Department? What is the role of ASAP with regard to unit chiefs and department heads? To whom is the volunteer ASAP team member primarily responsible as an employee? Issues such as these need to be addressed directly and early on, or there may be subsequent attempts to sabotage ASAP service delivery.

If the social system is in upheaval due to mergers, downsizing, and so forth, it is probably better to delay implementing an ASAP team until some stability is present. Although an ASAP team that is in place prior to the changes can assist in reducing violence as the system is modified, it is likely to remain problematic if the start-up occurs with the changes themselves (Flannery, Hanson, Penk, Pastva, & Navon, in press; Snyder, 1994).

Lastly, in addition to ASAP, administrators at all levels will want to be aware of general information about risk management strategies for reducing violence in specific facilities. For example, research in health care settings (Blair, 1991; Davis, 1991; Flannery et al., 1994; Flannery, Hanson, Penk, & Flannery, 1995) has shown that strong unit leadership, adequate staffing levels, and structured wards and activities will contribute to reductions in violence in their own right.

Designing the Team

Basic considerations. In designing a team, each organization needs to consider its own physical structure as well as its own organizational chart to understand both the potential number of sites to which ASAP team members could be deployed, and how much time would be needed to travel the distances between sites. Each organization needs to assess what types of violence may occur at the worksite, how frequent these events are likely to be, and the total number of employees in the labor force that the team will need to serve.

With this information in hand, the design of a specific team for specific needs can proceed. Initial decisions need to include what staffing is available for the team and how many sites will be involved. If staffing is limited, a team might begin with only individual debriefings and only those for a specific type of violence, such as physical assaults only. As a general rule of thumb, it is better to provide limited services to all sites and on all shifts than to select partial groups for services. This latter strategy contains the risk of some members of the workforce perceiving themselves as second-class employees. If an ASAP team begins by serving only selected members of the facility, it will not be readily accepted if it seeks to expand its mission at a later date. The general design of the team further needs to consider the issues of compensation for on-call services and how the ASAP team member's responsibilities at his or her worksite will be covered when the team member responds to a critical incident. The team's membership should also reflect the cultural diversity of the workforce to be served. If it is at all possible, the ASAP team should include representatives of all of the cultural groups represented by the employees. Bilingual skills may also prove to be helpful in assuring that ASAP can address the needs of all employee victims. Finally, all paperwork should be standardized and brief in nature.

Specific matters. Each organization will need to develop specific solutions to problems that may emerge in some facilities. Mandated reporting of violence is a case in point. Some facilities have clear policies for reporting all episodes of threats or of actual violence. However, in some cases, there may be selective reporting of violent events (Lion, Snyder, & Merrill, 1981). For health care settings, ASAP has a three-step reporting system. When an assault occurs, the charge nurse must complete both an incident report and a call to the ASAP team. In addition, a report of the assault must be presented at nursing rounds the next morning. It is necessary that each facility have clear, operationally defined types of violence, and that reporting of violent acts be mandated facility-wide. Each of these steps helps to ensure that critical incidents are, in fact, reported. An organization may want to consider having this reporting system in place for 1 or 2 months prior to fielding ASAP so that there is baseline data with which to compare the possible impact of the ASAP project.

A second unique issue may arise if organizational policy requires a review of policy and procedures with every act of violence. This is true for the health care facilities where ASAP is fielded, and it has proven to be helpful to have the ASAP debriefing first and to separate it in time from the administrative review. This approach avoids the potential of retraumatizing the employee victim during the administrative review (McCann & Pearlman, 1990).

A third potential special problem arises if the post-incident response teams are operational. As word of an ASAP program spreads, interested parties both within and without the facility will ask to use this resource.

From within may come requests to counsel laid-off employees or employees who are dealing with the deaths of family members. From without may come requests to provide debriefing for municipal emergency services personnel and the like. Although there may be occasional exceptions, in general it is better for ASAP to direct its energies toward its original mission.

When the basic general considerations and any specific problems have been thought through, it is imperative that the final proposed design be reevaluated and approved by all of the senior managers.

Selecting the Team

The team leader. Arguably, the most important decision in an ASAP program is the choice of the team leader. In many ways the success of the program will rest in the hands of this one person. There are several qualities that have proven to be important in the successful management of an ASAP team. The ASAP team leader needs to be knowledgeable about psychological trauma and human behavior in general. The debriefings are a clinical service, and trained clinicians of any discipline have a clear advantage in understanding the needs of victims. Team leaders also need to be good managers. They need to be able to elicit input and act decisively. They need to be able to think clearly in times of crisis, to set limits on the team and the facility when necessary, and to do this without interruption of services. Finally, team leaders need to be attentive to detail, such as is needed for record keeping and on-call coverage scheduling. ASAP services have been disrupted with changes in leadership, and it is helpful to seek at least a 2-year commitment from the designated team leader. If staffing shortages exist, it may be helpful to have ASAP co-leaders. In any case, a good team leader has a sense of ownership of the team, its mission, and its members, and both energy and enthusiasm for the task.

Team members. Team members should be chosen from all disciplines or departments and should reflect the workforce that they will serve, as was noted earlier. Team members should have at least 2 years of mental health services experience, be concerned with and motivated to help others, and should feel comfortable with being on-call. Potential members with a past history of being victimized are welcomed, if the issue has been addressed. Job trainees have not been included because of the possible privacy issues that might arise in the debriefing of supervisors and employees. ASAP team supervisors should be senior employees, especially if they are in positions that permit informal ASAP follow-up or outreach. Employees in human resources or staff development are good choices as supervisors.

All team members need to know the length of time of their commitment to the team (at least 1 year); the amount of time for team needs per month; who will cover their unit responsibilities when they are on ASAP calls; what extra compensation there will be, if any; and how they will be trained.

Team supplies. ASAP teams operate with a minimum of support needs. Teams do require beepers for paging, sanctioned time for service calls and meeting times, paper supplies for records, and access to the in-house mail service to send notices to all employees. Sometimes there are additional space needs, but, by and large, ASAP teams are lean, efficient, and pay for themselves in times of reduced medical and sick leave costs.

Buddy–buddy system. As ASAP teams have continued to evolve, the original teams have paired themselves with the new facilities that are starting to field ASAP teams. The established team leaders and the novice team leaders have monthly meetings to design and field teams, answer questions of any nature, and build a sense of support and rapport among all ASAP teams. An annual training day, including recognition through the presentation of awards, is currently being planned for all members of all teams.

Training the Team

ASAP training begins with a day-long program for all potential team members. It focuses on violence in the workplace and the nature and role of ASAP in that context; the nature of psychological trauma; principles of crisis intervention; and basic ASAP administrative procedures. The course content is drawn from three books: *Violence in the Workplace* (Flannery, 1995), *Post-Traumatic Stress Disorder: The Victim's Guide to Healing and Recovery* (Flannery, 1994b), and *Critical Incident Stress Debriefing (CISD): An Operator's Manual for the Prevention of Traumatic Stress Among Emergency Services and Disaster Workers* (Mitchell & Everly, 1993). Each team has tended to have one copy of each and to circulate it among its members. In addition, each team member receives an ASAP training manual that includes administrative procedures, blank report forms, and over 50 reprints of articles with relevant information about trauma and various trauma interventions.

Interspersed role-plays build on the content material throughout the day, and are arranged in levels of increasing severity. In the first role-play, team members pair off in twos and take turns being the ASAP member debriefing an employee victim. The next role-plays are done in groups, and include examples of real assault cases. In these small groups, members are divided into teams. Some role-play the employee victims, and one is chosen to be the ASAP team member. The remainder act as "advisors" to the ASAP member, and offer suggestions on how to conduct the debriefing as the role-play proceeds. The day's trainers then instruct all team members except for those involved in the role-playing to leave the room. The role-played victims range from distraught employees in severe agitation to employee victims unable to speak because of psychological shock, to deceased employee victims or patients. Scenes are made as real as possible to facilitate learning and to desensitize team members to what they may actually encounter on the unit. When the scene is ready, the remaining team members return to the room and through the ASAP designee conduct a debriefing of the employee victims. The third role-play is an example of a CISD (Mitchell & Everly, 1993) debriefing for an entire unit. The trainees role-play the ASAP debriefers, the staff, and the patients.

The day itself begins with an informal continental breakfast so that the staff volunteers can begin to interact as ASAP team members. This is followed by a formal welcome by the chief operating officer and other select senior managers so that the new team members understand the importance of the ASAP mission and the senior management's full support of it.

Formal training begins with an overview of violence in the workplace (Flannery, 1995) and the role of ASAP as a workplace intervention for addressing the psychological sequelae that may occur in the aftermath of patient assaults. The overview is followed by a discussion of the nature of psychological trauma and its symptoms (Flannery, 1994b). The team members then role-play in dyads interviewing employee victims. After a coffee break, basic principles of crisis intervention are reviewed and the more complex case examples of assaults are conducted in groups.

After the luncheon provided by the facility, formal training continues with a presentation of CISD (Mitchell & Everly, 1993) and a role-play of a ward debriefing. After a small break, the team members return to review all ASAP policies, procedures, and record keeping, and to practice relaxation exercises (Flannery, 1994a). The day closes with each participant receiving a certificate that states they are qualified ASAP team members.

The ASAP team supervisors have a second half-day training in which they review the principles of CISD (Mitchell & Everly, 1993) for debriefing ward units. They also practice various role-plays in which the CISD service might be fielded by an ASAP team.

Additional training continues for all team members at monthly inservice meetings. These meetings include presentations by guest experts on various aspects of psychological trauma and its treatments, and role-playing difficult situations that were actually encountered by ASAP where additional thought and practice may prove helpful. The role-playing at these monthly inservice meetings is of particular importance in keeping ASAP members' skills fine-tuned during periods when service calls may be minimal. The ASAP team leader is responsible for these ongoing trainings as well as training new staff at later dates.

Fielding the Team

As the team members are being trained, it is helpful to begin to educate the workforce to this new employee benefit. This is best done by meeting with departments, ward units, unions, and so forth, where interested parties can learn of the new employee benefit as well as have their questions answered. These initial meetings can be followed up by letters or memos with employee payroll checks as an added method of reaching all members of the workforce. The meetings and letters should explain the ASAP program fully, detail the methods that will be used to ensure confidentiality, and explain how any published findings will be done anonymously and in the aggregate so that each employee victim's privacy is assured.

If management wants to establish baseline data, as was noted earlier, this should be implemented before the ASAP start date. When this is completed, the workforce is notified of the start date, and the ASAP team begins its service.

Resistance should be expected initially. The more common forms include the mind-set that assaults "come with the turf," the fear that an assault on a unit will somehow reflect poorly on the unit management and staff, and systems paranoia about the management using ASAP as a policing tool of some form. These resistances are best addressed directly through monthly memos discussing aspects of trauma, the team's services, and how confidentiality is always maintained. As employees realize that ASAP can be trusted to keep matters confidential, employee victim participation will increase. The development of the ASAP program is an ongoing process. For each facility there has often been a defining moment for ASAP where the ASAP program has earned full respect. This may occur in a particularly gruesome assault, the death of a staff member or patient, or the like. The ability of ASAP to be present in times of true organizational distress demonstrates both the need for ASAP and its helpfulness in difficult times.

When an ASAP team is on-line, the next step is consideration of any employee victims of assaults already on sick leave or industrial accident claims. With union permission, letters are sent to all of these employees to tell them of the team, offer its service, and provide phone numbers to contact team members at home or at the facility if they can be of assistance. ASAP teams have provided extra steps for such employees, including meeting those who are anxious about returning to the worksite at the unit, and spending the first day back with them until their apprehension has subsided.

Finally, if an employee victim wants his or her ASAP team records, the employee meets with the ASAP team leader and the specific ASAP debriefer for the incident to review the ASAP notes, answer any questions, and sign the ASAP release of information form.

An ASAP Team at Work: The Experience of Its Members

Although it is true that each organization has its own unique issues, and although it is also true that there are infrequent but more complicated ASAP issues that have not been addressed, the preliminary guidelines noted here should permit any agency to field an ASAP team that successfully reduces human suffering and medical expense and maintains productivity and morale. But what of the team members themselves? What is their experience of an ASAP program?

In those ASAP programs that are successfully fielded and managed by the team leader, there is usually a strong sense of mission present in the membership. Patient assaults on staff are an extensive problem in health care settings (Blair, 1991; Davis, 1991), and employee victims are usually left with informal supervision or their own resources in the aftermath. ASAP members bond strongly and form a cohesive group that has a sense of responsibility for this issue in terms of the psychological welfare of the workforce. ASAP team members have presented their work and its importance at professional meetings in six states. Being an ASAP member usually has prestige within the organization. Often there are waiting lists to join the team, and it is rare for a team member to resign unless the member has been transferred or is retiring. Certificates of ASAP training and acceptance often grace the walls of the members' offices.

Professional development is a second common theme among ASAP members. They become specialists in psychological trauma and emergency services, and may continue to develop skills for individual practice as clinicians. The process of developing a feedback system, where ASAP members and management together can evaluate the outcome of ASAP efforts and identify areas for improvement, enhances one's sense of professional growth. Not surprisingly, some have gone on to join emergency services programs beyond their own worksites. The ASAP program provides its members with opportunities to develop for themselves the domains of optimal health and well-being that they seek to develop or restore in employee victims. ASAP teams provide many opportunities for enhancing a sense of mastery, a network of caring attachments, and personal meaning in one's work.

There are problems. Some team members experience feelings of rejection when ASAP services are declined; this usually resolves itself, however, with the passage of time. Members have issues with multiple responsibilities and finding time to attend ASAP meetings. This is especially problematic if the health care delivery system is downsizing (Snyder, 1994). ASAP paperwork is an additional burden, and team members must be reminded to turn in needed ASAP records. A more fundamental problem is repeated exposure to episodes of violence. This may result in vicarious traumatization in some (McCann & Pearlman, 1990), but it is also an ongoing lesson in how vulnerable any of us are in the face of violence.

In spite of the problems, ASAP team members are proud of their service. Perhaps one meaningful indicator of ASAP participation is that ASAP team members, similar to employee victims, seek to extend their service by establishing ASAP services at their next postings.

References

Blair, D. T. (1991). Assaultive behavior: Does provocation begin in the front office? *Journal of Psychosocial Nursing, 29*, 21–26.

Caldwell, M. E. (1992). The incidence of PTSD among staff victims of patient violence. *Hospital and Community Psychiatry, 43*, 838–839.

Davis, S. (1991). Violence in psychiatric inpatients: A review. *Hospital and Community Psychiatry, 42*, 585–590.

Dawson, J., Johnson, M., Kehiayan, N., Kyanko, S., & Martinez, R. (1988). Response to patient assault: A peer support program for nurses. *Journal of Psychosocial Nursing and Mental Health Services, 26*, 8–15.

Dietz, P. E., & Rada, R. T. (1982). Battery incidents and batteries in a maximum security hospital. *Archives of General Psychiatry, 39,* 31–34.

Flannery, R. B., Jr. (1994a). *Becoming stress-resistant through the project SMART program.* New York: Crossroad Press.

Flannery, R. B., Jr. (1994b). *Post-traumatic stress disorder: The victim's guide to healing and recovery.* New York: Crossroad Press.

Flannery, R. B., Jr. (1995). *Violence in the workplace.* New York: Crossroad Press.

Flannery, R. B., Jr., Fulton, P., Tausch, J., & DeLoffi, A.Y. (1991). A program to help staff cope with psychological sequelae of assaults by patients. *Hospital and Community Psychiatry, 42,* 935–938.

Flannery, R. B., Jr., Hanson, M. A., & Penk, W. E. (1994). Risk factors for psychiatric inpatient assaults on staff. *Journal of Mental Health Administration, 21,* 24–31.

Flannery, R. B., Jr., Hanson, M. A., & Penk, W. E. (1995). Patients' threats: Expanded definition of assault. *General Hospital Psychiatry, 17,* pp. 451–453.

Flannery, R. B., Jr., Hanson, M. A., Penk, W. E., & Flannery, G. J. (1995). Violence in the lax milieu? Preliminary data. *Psychiatric Quarterly, 67,* 47–50.

Flannery, R. B., Jr., Hanson, M. A., Penk, W. E., Flannery, G. J., & Gallagher, C. (1995). The Assaulted Staff Action Program (ASAP): An approach to coping with the aftermath of violence in the workplace. In G. P. Keita (Ed.), *Job stress intervention: Current practices and future directions* (Vol. III, pp. 199–212). Washington, DC: American Psychological Association.

Flannery, R. B., Jr., Hanson, M. A., Penk, W. E., Pastva, G. J., & Navon, M. A. (1996). The Assaulted Staff Action Program (ASAP): Replicated findings. Cambridge, MA: Department of Psychiatry, The Cambridge Hospital. Manuscript submitted for publication.

Flannery, R. B., Jr., Hanson, M. A., Penk, W. E., Pastva, G. J., Navon, M. A., & Flannery, G. J. (in press). Hospital downsizing and patients' assaults on staff revisited. *Journal of Mental Health Administration.*

Grinker, R. R., & Spiegel, J. P. (1945). *Men under stress.* New York: McGraw-Hill.

Hunter, M., & Carmel, H. (1992). The cost of staff injuries from inpatient violence. *Hospital and Community Psychiatry, 43,* 586–588.

Lion, J. R., Snyder, W., & Merrill, G. L. (1981). Underreporting of assaults on staff in a state hospital. *Hospital and Community Psychiatry, 32,* 497–498.

McCann, L., & Pearlman, L. A. (1990). *Psychological trauma and the adult survivor: Theory, therapy, and transformation.* New York: Brunner/Mazel.

Mitchell, J. T., & Everly, G. S., Jr. (1993). *Critical incident stress debriefing (CISD): An operations manual for the prevention of traumatic stress among emergency services and disaster workers.* Ellicott City, MD: Chevron Publishing Corporation.

Snyder, W., III. (1994). Hospital downsizing and increased frequency of assaults on staff. *Hospital and Community Psychiatry, 45,* 378–379.

Storch, D. D. (1991). Starting an in-hospital support group for employee victims of violence in the psychiatric hospital. *Psychiatric Hospital, 22,* 5–9.

20

The United States Postal Service Employee Assistance Program: A Multifaceted Approach to Workplace Violence Prevention

John G. Kurutz, Dennis L. Johnson, and Brian W. Sugden

Workplace violence is an issue that has become increasingly prominent in recent years. Harassment, threats, stalking, and overtly violent behaviors that lead to potential loss of life or property, as well as litigation, are a growing concern for businesses nationwide. Employers, who have a legal obligation to provide a safe and healthful work environment, have become acutely aware of the need to respond to these problems. Although still relatively rare, homicide is now the second leading cause of occupational injury death (U.S. Department of Labor, 1995). The potentially devastating and long-lasting effects of these episodes demand a coordinated and comprehensive response on the part of employers.

The United States Postal Service (USPS) has developed a workplace violence prevention program that stands at the forefront of contemporary efforts to combat this growing concern. The USPS program involves a multidisciplinary effort including participation at the executive level as well as local coordination at the district level. The program is designed to promote comprehensive assessment of potential threats, provide extensive educational and prevention efforts, and to intervene promptly and effectively in both threats and actual occurrences of violence.

The USPS Employee Assistance Program (EAP) plays an active role in the workplace violence prevention and threat management efforts of the Postal Service. EAP professionals serve on workplace violence prevention committees, monitor and assess employee attitudes and workplace climate issues, and serve as part of the critical incident response team along with management, union, security, and medical personnel (U.S. Postal Service, 1995).

History of the Postal Service EAP

The United States Postal Service's EAP was established in 1968 as the Program for Alcoholic Recovery in response to management surveys which had identified alcohol abuse as a major impediment to customer service and employee productivity. During 1986, the program was expanded to include treatment for other forms of chemical dependency in the face of the growing incidence of drug abuse in the United States. A committee composed of Postal Service management, EAP representatives, and the national unions was convened in 1990 to develop the employee assistance program for the future, an effort that culminated in 1993 (Kurutz, 1994). Since that time, the program has undertaken a new and greatly expanded mission that now encompasses a wide range of individual and organizational issues affecting the culture of the Postal Service. The USPS Employee Assistance Program has been particularly active in the development and implementation of programs aimed at the prevention of violence in the workplace and increasingly involved in issues of organizational culture and climate.

Scope and Philosophy of the USPS EAP

In 1994, the Postal Service ranked 33rd among the largest corporations in the world, generating nearly $50 billion in revenue and delivering 40% of the world's mail. The United States Postal Service Employee Assistance Program is the largest in the world (Kurutz, 1994). It is a unique partnership of Postal Service staff, union officials, consultants, and contract service providers that serves employees, their families, and the organization nationwide. The EAP operates proactively to promote employee well-being and job satisfaction, as well as attempting to reduce absenteeism, tardiness, workplace conflict, and disability claims. The range of services offered by the EAP includes professional assessment, short-term counseling (or referral, if appropriate) and follow-up. Employees and their families may self-refer or may be referred by supervisors, union stewards, medical unit personnel, or other family members for job-related or personal problems.

To service this enormous need, the Postal Service has contracted with the Public Health Service, which in turn has contracted with individual vendors within two major regions of the United States. The result is a team of more than 240 full-time professionals who staff the 170 USPS counseling sites. All Postal Service EAP counselors have a master's degree or doctorate in a counseling field, 3 or more years of relevant experience, and licensure or certification as required. In addition, counselors are provided with specific training to help them better understand the unique culture and climate of the Postal Service organization. They provide direct counseling services to employees and their families and consult with Postal Service management and union officials.

In addition to the full-time counseling staff, the EAP contracts with a nationwide network of more than 10,000 affiliate counselors to ensure that services are readily available to all Postal Service employees. Counseling services are provided at sites both on and off Postal Service premises. Off-site locations are chosen to facilitate ready access and are typically within a one-hour drive for any employee. Full-time EAP counselors may choose to refer clients to outside affiliates for reasons of accessibility or for expertise in a given area. In regions where the number of workers does not warrant a full-time staff person, vendors may subcontract for services with affiliate counselors.

In addition to face-to-face counseling and referral services, the USPS's EAP maintains a nationwide toll-free telecommunications system with a counselor available 24 hours a day to assist with personal emergencies and critical incidents. During 1995, the system responded to an average of 7,000 calls per month. A second toll-free number is also available to address organizational or job-related issues (U.S. Postal Service, 1995).

Employee Assistance Program Information System

An important tool for the management of the Postal Service EAP is the Employee Assistance Program Information System (EAPIS). EAPIS is a state-of-the-art, custom-designed, software program that allows counselors to enter their work directly into a national database. EAPIS allows for the collection and aggregation of information on the utilization of the program and training activities, client demographics, clinical activity, and outcome data, while maintaining strict confidentiality of identifying information. In addition, consumer satisfaction data are collected from each client and maintained by EAPIS. The automated system was instituted in 1994 and became available nationwide in July of 1995 (U.S. Postal Service, 1995). The EAPIS system helps to assure that current and future decisions about the direction of EAP programs and services are based on reliable data.

Nature of Client Population and Services Provided

During 1995, the USPS EAP responded to 53,312 initial contacts and opened nearly 30,000 new cases, a greater than threefold increase over 1991 figures (the latest available data from the previous EAP; see Figure 1; U.S. Postal Service, 1995). Frequently seen problems include troubled interpersonal relations, depression, anxiety, drug and alcohol abuse, other addictions (e.g., gambling, overeating), stress, bereavement, and personal or job-related conflicts. Risk of violence was indicated in 8% of the precase contacts in 1995. Five percent of callers were prompted by an emergency situation to contact the EAP. Services to the family members of employees represented an increasing percentage of the client contacts during 1995, accounting for about 10% of the new cases seen (see Figure 2). Other trends observed included increases in the percentage of new cases that involved supervisory personnel (U.S. Public Health Service, 1995).

NEW CASES OPENED

Figure 1. During 1995, the EAP responded to 53,312 initial contacts. From these, a total of 29,689 new cases were opened (U.S. Postal Service, 1995).

PROBLEMS ASSESSED

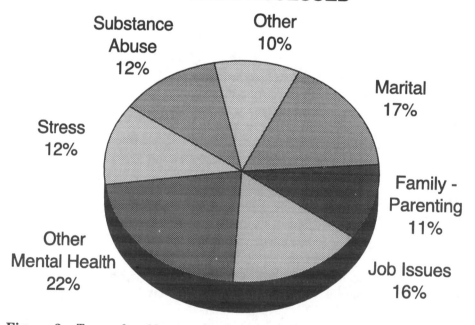

Figure 2. Types of problems assessed by the USPS EAP. Relative percentages have remained generally consistent over time (U.S. Postal Service, 1995).

SOURCE OF TREATMENT

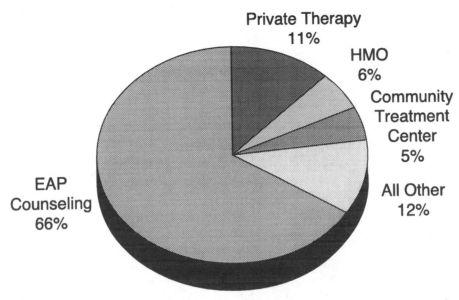

Figure 3. Two thirds of clients were treated by EAP professionals (rather than outside agencies), resulting in cost savings to the clients and benefit cost containment to the USPS (U.S. Postal Service, 1995).

The 12-session model. The Postal Service operates under the philosophy that many problems can be successfully treated with brief counseling. The Employee Assistance Program offers 12 free, voluntary, and confidential sessions to employees and family members. For those problems that are determined to be more extensive, or otherwise inappropriate for the 12-session program, the EAP counselor may refer the employee to a community resource. The EAP also provides regular follow-up, during which counselors ensure that treatment recommendations are being carried out. During 1995, 66% of the EAP clients were provided short-term services by EAP counselors. The remaining 34% were referred out, for a variety of specialized clinical services, to HMOs, managed care providers, private therapists, inpatient or outpatient substance abuse treatment centers, or other health services, or for financial or legal assistance (U.S. Postal Service, 1995; see Figure 3).

Other services provided. In addition to counseling and counseling-related services, the EAP also provides information and training on a broad range of organizational issues: wellness seminars; workplace violence prevention efforts; critical incident debriefing; child and eldercare resources; supervisor training and employee orientation; AIDS education; cultural diversity training; and supervisor and union shop steward consultation. The USPS also disseminates information and provides assistance with numerous mental health issues through the publication of newsletters, brochures, and pamphlets. More than 3.5 million pieces were produced and distributed in 1995. Topics included AIDS, posttraumatic stress, family relations, coping with grief and loss, and alcohol and other chemical abuse.

The special role of the USPS EAP Coordinator. Under the USPS model, EAP Coordinators in each of the 85 USPS districts nationwide play a unique and essential role. Coordinators, all employed directly by the Postal Service, have at least a master's degree; and many have doctorates. EAP Coordinators provide no direct clinical services or counseling. Instead, they operate at a systems level, serving as "change agents" responsible for (a) helping to assess, change, and monitor the organizational climate and culture in their district; (b) coordinating the EAP operations in their district; (c) facilitating and marketing the programs, encouraging supervisors and employees to use the EAP as a problem-solving resource; (d) identifying organizational issues at the district level; and (e) advising management on potential ways to resolve issues. Thus, the coordinators serve to manage the activities of the EAP at a district level, and to implement and coordinate Postal Service headquarters' initiatives.

Each district has a committee that addresses the prevention of violence in the workplace whose membership includes the EAP Coordinator. If there is a potential critical incident, it is typically the EAP Coordinator who is in the most strategic position to initiate the appropriate proactive procedures to prevent the incident. If a critical incident does occur, the EAP Coordinator functions as the organizer and manager of support and intervention efforts.

The Six-Strategy USPS Violence Prevention Program

The United States Postal Service has developed a six-strategy model that is designed to access and engage all of the major resources within the Postal Service related to violence prevention. The model focuses on prevention and early intervention. The strategies include:

1. *Selection.* The goal of this strategy is to ensure that the USPS employs the right persons. The EAP consults with management regarding the employee selection process.
2. *Security.* Both security teams at Postal facilities and law enforcement professionals from the Inspection Service and Postal Police play critical roles in prevention and intervention.
3. *Policy.* The Postal Service, its unions, and management associations authored a joint statement on violence in the workplace that includes an unequivocal commitment to "do everything within our power to prevent further incidents of work-related violence" (U.S. Postal Service, 1992). The joint statement also affirms the right of all employees to a "safe and humane working environment." Also included in the statement is a strong stance on violence in a number of forms:

There is no excuse for and will be no tolerance of violence or any threats of violence by anyone at any level of the Postal Service; and there is no excuse for and will be no tolerance of harassment, intimidation, threats, or bullying by anyone. We also affirm that every employee at every level of the Postal Service should be treated at all times with dignity, respect, and fairness (U.S. Postal Service, 1992).

The statement also expresses a commitment to enforcement of policies related to basic human rights, and to remove from their positions those who do not respect those rights. All reports of threats or weapons in postal facilities are investigated promptly and appropriate actions taken. The Postal Service is committed to the prohibition of weapons of any kind on USPS property.

4. *Climate.* The EAP is involved particularly with organizational development interventions that are designed to ensure a safe and healthful workplace and positive corporate culture.
5. *Employee support.* The EAP is committed to early identification and prompt intervention, allowing problems to be dealt with before they escalate to the point of loss of behavioral control.
6. *Separation.* The USPS is actively involved in the refinement of procedures designed to make the termination process safer and more effective. The EAP becomes actively involved if an individual being terminated requires support and assistance, or if he or she may represent a potential threat to self, other individuals, or the organization.

Workplace Violence Prevention Committees and the Threat Management Process

The EAP Coordinators also maintain a central role in the Postal Service's workplace violence and critical incident response and threat assessment activities. Each postal district has its own workplace violence critical incident response team and threat assessment team. These teams are usually composed of representatives from EAP, medical, human resources, labor relations, operations management, and the Inspection Service. The overall threat management process consists of (a) policy development, (b) threat reporting procedures, (c) threat assessment, (d) case management, (e) critical incident response, (f) critical incident stress debriefing, and (g) post-incident analysis. The EAP Coordinator's role includes threat assessment, needs evaluation, and awareness training.

Threat assessment teams are charged with evaluating situations involving threats or overt acts of violence and developing appropriate plans of action. The teams conduct a systematic assessment of any dangerous or threatening circumstance and develop a risk reduction strategy that is reviewed by management. The recommendations of the threat assessment team are reviewed by management at the local facility and the District Manager. Implementation of a threat assessment plan, as well as follow-up, are often directed by the Human Resources Manager in consultation with the EAP Coordinator.

The EAP Coordinator plays a principal role, not only in the design and organization of the threat assessment team, but also as the pivotal point-of-contact for intervention and support resources during and following a critical incident. In addition, it is the EAP Coordinator who directs the stream of communications regarding the incident both upward to postal headquarters as well as through chain-of-supervision to employees. The Coordinator is also responsible for contacting the families of victims and may assist, as appropriate, with media relations and rumor control.

During and following a critical incident, the EAP Coordinator facilitates the provision of services to employees and their families by (a) assessing the severity of impact on the employees in the workplace, (b) identifying employee victims, obvious and nonobvious, (c) organizing critical incident stress debriefing groups, (d) coordinating on-site and off-site counseling, (e) coordinating the services of contracted providers, and (f) developing a follow-up plan for services for affected employees.

In addition to the personal costs, the stress-related symptoms that are known to occur following a threat or act of violence may translate into higher rates of absenteeism, loss of productivity, increased turnover, and reduced organizational cohesiveness. USPS EAP coordinators function to reduce and then positively redirect critical incidents by initiating debriefings within 72 hours after a potentially traumatic incident. EAP Coordinators and counselors facilitate these debriefing meetings for employees, victims, and family members as needed. The purpose of these meetings is to provide affected individuals with an opportunity to process thoughts and feelings about their experience of the incident. The debriefing meetings also afford EAP Coordinators and counselors an occasion to educate employees about the symptoms related to trauma and to identify persons who may be in need of further professional services. The USPS EAP responded to a total of 377 critical incidents during 1995 including, among others, homicide, bomb threats, suicide, robbery and assault, threats of violence, and accidents. Critical incident stress debriefings were conducted for 5,728 individuals and grief groups for 2,440 (U.S. Postal Service, 1995).

Workplace violence awareness training. In keeping with an emphasis on prevention as the most effective form of intervention, the EAP has developed an 8-hour violence awareness training program. The program is composed of modules on recognition, prevention, and appropriate response to violence. More that 14,000 participants took part in 276 training classes during 1995 (U.S. Postal Service, 1995). Plans call for the training to be presented to more than 40,000 postal supervisors, union leaders, and postal managers throughout the United States. Information on the early identification of signs and symptoms of troubled employees is an important part of supervisory training within the USPS.

Threatening Correspondence Program. The Threatening Correspondence Program evaluates and rates potential risk for violent behavior.

Threats are assessed on the basis of (a) direct threats to individuals, (b) organizational threats to employees, (c) volatility of the current worksite or nexus to a site currently or previously experiencing threats of violence, (d) risk indicators suggesting psychiatric disorder or serious alcohol or drug abuse, and (e) expression of a specific plan of violence. The program is focused upon identifying individual or organizational risk before a crisis stage is reached. When potential problems are identified, a threat management model, which emphasizes respect and dignity for individuals and maintenance of a positive organizational culture, is put into operation. A total of 253 such assessments were conducted during the past year with 148 deemed to require a priority response.

Critical incident response. Despite intensive and ongoing preventive efforts, violent and critical incidents inevitably occur. Such incidents have an immediate and profound impact on employees and operations, and may cause severe and debilitating personal distress. Following a critical incident, the Postal Service EAP provides critical incident stress debriefings. Early and comprehensive intervention is intended to promote a restored sense of order and normality for employees as soon as possible. EAP Coordinators serve to direct response efforts, communications, and, as appropriate, media relations.

Current Directions

As the largest, and probably most visible, program in the world, the Postal Service EAP continues to play a prominent leadership role in national efforts to reduce workplace violence. In April 1995, the USPS sponsored *Workplace Violence Forum '95: Prevention Strategies.* An audience of 250 government, military, and industry leaders gathered to examine and discuss the latest research and thinking in the area of workplace violence prevention. Keynote speeches by Tipper Gore, wife of Vice President Gore; James Brady, former press secretary to President Reagan; and Dr. Mary Jane England, Chief Executive Officer of the Washington Business Group on Health and President-elect of the American Psychiatric Association, highlighted the day.

Conclusion

The Employee Assistance Program is profoundly active within the United States Postal Service at every stage of employment, from selection to termination. The EAP is advertised and promoted extensively within each of the 85 districts and is well-known to USPS employees. Individual counseling continues to be central to the mission of the USPS EAP and thousands of employees and their family members receive services each year. Additionally, the Employee Assistance Program has become increasingly involved with organizational development and climate issues, and is a vital component of the nationally prominent USPS workplace violence prevention program.

References

Kurutz, J. G. (1994, March/April). Service EAP: Then and now. *EAP Digest*, pp. 30–34.

U.S. Department of Labor, Bureau of Statistics. (1995, April). Compensation and working conditions. *Violence in the Workplace, 47*(4), 1–8.

U.S. Postal Service. (1992, February 14). *Joint statement on violence and behavior in the workplace.* Washington, DC: Author.

U.S. Postal Service. (1995). *Employee Assistance Program: Activity summary FY 1995.*

U.S. Public Health Service, Division of Federal Occupational Health, Region V. (1995, November 8). U.S. Postal Service Employee Assistance Program information system, national summary report, 1 Oct 94–30 Sept 95. Chicago, IL: Author.

21

Violence Prevention During Corporate Downsizing: The Use of a People Team as Context for the Critical Incident Team

David A. Root and Mark D. Ziska

Corporate downsizing causes uncertainty, confusion, and distress for individuals, corporations, and communities. Attention to the practical and emotional needs of all employees can facilitate the transition and lessen the negative impact on affected individuals. The development of a *critical incident team* (as part of a *people team*) to assess and handle threats and aggression can provide a humane service to employees, prevent work disruption, and save corporate funds. A Hughes Fullerton site served as one of the major Southern California locations for what is now called Hughes Aircraft Company, a business unit of Hughes Electronics Corporation. During a recent downsizing, Hughes Fullerton utilized a multifaceted strategy to minimize psychological harm and workplace violence. The authors of this chapter were cofounders of the people team and of the critical incident team at Hughes Fullerton.

The Fullerton Ground Systems Group Operations, which is part of the Aerospace and Defense sector of Hughes Aircraft Company, experienced years of successful development of new products and continued application of technical systems worldwide. This history began in the late 1950s and continued through the end of the Cold War. The workforce was predominantly well-educated engineers, with other employees, such as highly skilled technicians and maintenance employees, involved in the manufacturing operations. The production and maintenance employees were represented by a union. Hughes Fullerton employees experienced long-term stability in employment and good career growth. Many of the employees were active in the local community, including serving in volunteer leadership positions. The employee population was also highly involved at the facility through clubs, sports, continuing education, and social activities. Hughes Fullerton was recognized as a good place to work. At its peak, the Fullerton site had some 16,000 employees (Hughes Employee Database).

As in many aerospace firms, Hughes has been involved in downsizing in recent years. In September 1994, it was announced that, due to an excess of space throughout the company, the Fullerton site would be significantly downsized and most of the property would be sold. There were approximately 6,000 employees on site at that time. Many of these employees had been with the company for 15 to 30 years. The employee population included salaried exempt professionals (engineering), salaried nonexempt workers (clerical and administrative), and hourly workers (union). By the time the downsizing was completed in December of 1995, 2,000 employees remained at the site, employed in two different Hughes business units. The majority of the Fullerton employees retained employment within Hughes. The hourly employees were the hardest to place due to the limits created by union contracts, lower demand in manufacturing occupations, and unwillingness on the part of many hourly employees to relocate. Compounding the plight of these employees has been the general economy, the economy in Southern California in particular, and the significantly shrunken Defense Department budget. These factors conspired to make a job search outside of Hughes difficult.

The Hughes Fullerton Approach

Hughes implemented a multifaceted approach to mitigate the negative impact and psychological distress of the downsizing and displacement. This would involve the use of a career resource center, a flexible transition benefit package, and an internal placement program. All of this was done in the context of the creation of a *people team*. Some of the specific resources included were as follows:

1. A *Career Resource Center* was established on site, funded by a federal grant to an outplacement firm for the retraining of aerospace workers. Once an employee received a 60-day plant closure notice, he or she was eligible for the services offered in the career resource center. These services included what one would expect: classes in such subjects as resume writing, vocational selection, job search techniques (networking), and job interview skills. Each employee had a personal job counselor. Additionally, a representative from the California State Employee Development Department was on site daily (to assist with application for unemployment benefits and in a job search using the California State Employee Development Department's database). Furthermore, employees were provided the opportunity of attending a once-a-week job club, with special speakers, discussion, and peer support for their job search process. The career resource center continued to be available to the displaced employees after layoff. In January 1996 its primary operation was moved off site, with a satellite office remaining on site.
2. *Laid-off employees were eligible for up to 12 weeks severance pay, 3 months of continued health benefits, and educational reimburse-*

ments upon layoff. Many employees took advantage of the retraining opportunities. These employees were more often nonexempt and hourly. The employees were given a minimum of 60 days advance notice of layoff. Upon notice of layoff, the employees were given release time during work hours to attend the career transition training, to conduct job searches, and to interview with prospective employers.

3. *Internal Selection Process*. Hughes put in place mechanisms to assure that displaced employees from any Hughes site had first preference on job opportunities within the company. Managers at Hughes Fullerton worked very hard to place their people within Hughes. This program was largely successful as witnessed by the level of placement noted above. The company believed that the resources outlined above were deserved by the laid-off employees. Further, it was understood that what was good for the employees was, at the same time, an essential part of prevention of workplace violence.

People Team

Prior to the announcement of the plantsite reductions, a *people team* was formed. The people team at Hughes Fullerton was a cross-functional team with the sole purpose of keeping focus on important people issues. The people team had a twofold charter: (a) serve as a communication liaison between executive leadership (with overall phase-down responsibilities) and the plantsite population, as part of the commitment to help identify and coordinate actions affecting employee morale, health, safety, and productivity; and (b) initiate actions that help maintain a focus on people, ensuring that all employees (and family members) were treated with dignity and respect during the difficult process of phase-down.

What is a people team? It is a cross-functional team with representatives from human resources, employee assistance program, medical, security, communications, and line organizations. The formation of the people team was considered important in and of itself and an important component in preventing workplace violence. Our premise, supported by the literature on workplace violence, was that the good treatment of employees (along with effective communication, forums for conflict resolution, and outplacement services) was the best way to prevent workplace violence.

The people team provided us a ready means of two-way communication between the employees and executive leadership. The leadership was concerned about how the placement of Hughes Fullerton employees in other Hughes organizations was going, and the members of the people team, working in those various organizations, were able to garner that information. The team served as an important symbol that emphasized the value and importance of each employee. We have come to believe that any company of size would serve itself well by creating the equivalent of a people team. It is an effective way to raise consciousness of the need for everyone to treat one another with dignity and respect.

Employees were able to raise issues of concern to the people team via the representatives. The executive leadership, given the task of phase-down management, was kept aware regularly of the prime people issues. Both the people team leader and its executive champion regularly participated in the executive transition meetings. This, of course, facilitated effective communication with the executives and enabled the team to put employee concerns before them.

As noted above, the key message articulated by the existence of a people team was: People issues are important. The team provided a readily available forum for addressing these issues. The people team had several subteams: a human resource team, a communications team, a health services team, an employee assistance team, a spirit team, and a critical incident team.

The *human resource team* kept in focus the issue of a fair selection process within Hughes for Fullerton Ground Systems employees, and devised organizational practices and processes to assure fairness. Managers were strongly urged to champion the placement of their people within other Hughes organizations (the two remaining on site, several organizations in the El Segundo area, and elsewhere).

The *communications team* produced a weekly newsletter distributed to all employees. This newsletter kept employees apprised of what was happening at the plantsite, on resources for job search within and outside the company, on personal resources for coping with the enormous changes, and so forth. Focus groups, all-hands meetings, staff meetings, and public address announcements were also used to keep communication flowing. Most of us are aware that during times of great change, many companies tend to shut down communication rather than increase it.

The *health services team* sponsored monthly forums on health-related topics, from eating right to handling stress. It conducted an onsite blood drive through the Red Cross. It also sponsored a health fair, with many of the primary providers of health-care to site employees present, providing such things as cholesterol screenings, blood pressure checks, lung examination, and even massages.

The *employee assistance team* provided intensive and proactive EAP services. This was made possible by the site contracting for additional EAP staff. This enabled us to provide the regular EAP services of assessment and referral to community-based counseling and services. Additionally, we were able to offer special workshops, staff training, and personal sessions to deal with problems related to the downsizing and reorganization. The workshops and training covered such topics as managing change, handling stress, and understanding the new economy and the information age. The training was provided to departments (upon request) and in open-enrollment workshops. The overall theme was constant: providing personal resources to employees for handling the changes occurring.

The *spirit team*, staffed with employee volunteers, provided social events for the plantsite. Even in the circumstances of a severely downsizing plantsite, employees responded well to the events, ranging from a Western barbecue to a "Keep Smiling" campaign. This campaign utilized buttons with a happy face on them and cards attached on which 10 employees' names could be registered. An employee who had a button handed it to another employee upon "catching" them smiling. Each employee signed his or her name on the attached card, and every week these cards were drawn randomly and prizes were awarded. This 5-month campaign was fun, and emphasized that we could all be pleasant with one another even during tough times. As part of the spirit events, many gifts were raffled, helping to foster positive expectations and goodwill.

The *critical incident team* was also a subteam of the people team. This itself created a message we wanted to provide to management and employees: We can all participate in maintaining a safe and healthy plantsite by keeping focus on the kind and courteous treatment of employees.

Critical Incident Team

The first thing to notice about the critical incident team (CIT) at Hughes Fullerton is what we have already articulated. The emphasis was on treating employees with dignity and respect by communicating with them regularly, fostering goodwill via social events, providing personal resources to help them manage change, lobbying for their placement within Hughes, having in place a method for conflict management, and providing outplacement services.

The critical incident team had a twofold charter: (a) foster prevention of workplace violence and (b) act in the case of actual workplace violence. In addition, all of the functions represented on the CIT had roles to play in case of *any* workplace trauma, including actual workplace violence.

One of the first items of business for the CIT was to hammer out a policy statement. The security manager took the lead in this, with inputs from all members of the CIT and the executive leadership. The statement was signed by the site executive and distributed to all supervisors. The membership of the CIT was typical, including representatives from security, human resources, legal, medical, and employee assistance. Due to the phase-down of the plantsite, the members of the CIT changed over the 17 months of its existence, but the functioning and procedures of the team remained constant.

Training in workplace violence was provided for all supervisors and selected others (security, human resources, department administrators, etc.). The training was designed to be completed within 1 hour. It was organized to answer two key questions:

1. What does one look for when assessing the potential for violence in employees?
2. What are the procedures if one perceives an employee to be at risk for violence?

Groups of 50 to 100 employees at a time were trained over a 2-week period, with nearly all supervisors (and others) participating in that training. This training was sponsored by the CIT, endorsed by executive management, and conducted by the EAP professionals.

Attendees at the training were given handouts including (a) *Key Findings* regarding workplace violence as reported in the Northwestern National Life publication (1993), reprinted as Appendix A in this volume; (b) "The personal and interpersonal characteristics of employees at-risk for violence" (Baron, 1993; Kinney & Johnson, 1993); (c) "Warning signs of the employee at-risk" (Baron, 1993, pp. 49–52); (d) "Levels of Violence" (Baron, 1993, p. 31); (e) "Ways to Prevent Violence in the Workplace" (Northwestern National Life, pp. 14–15); (f) "The Membership and Charter of the Critical Incident Team" at our plantsite; and (g) "The Hughes Fullerton Process for Reporting and Dealing With Potentially At-Risk Employees."

There is an interesting, not-unexpected sidelight: The reports of employees perceived to be potentially at risk increased just subsequent to the training. This underlines the importance of the training for all supervisors. Had time allowed, we may well have included department secretaries, executive secretaries, union representatives, and others who have much contact with a fairly wide selection of employees.

The CIT was announced to all employees via the Hughes site newsletter. The article was entitled: "Hughes Introduces Safe Workplace Policy." Employees were told to report perceived threats or at-risk employees to their supervisors. In case of actual violence, employees could call an onsite emergency number (our own 911, which rang security). Supervisors were urged to discuss workplace violence and the responsibility of all workers to maintain a plantsite that was as safe and healthy as possible. In the Hughes culture, it has remained true that employees want to learn about significant issues from their own supervisors. We honored and emphasized that tradition in making employees aware of the CIT via staff meetings.

In cases of actual violence in the workplace, or any natural disaster or trauma, the CIT was set up to respond as a central command and communications team. In this role, the CIT plan was tied in to the emergency response plan of the plantsite.

We should say a word about the training of the critical incident team members. Soon after the formation of the team, every team member was provided a copy of Anthony Baron's *Violence in the Workplace* (1993). The members, of course, experienced the training designed for supervision, outlined above. And the entire CIT participated in a training, sponsored by Corporate Human Resources (HR) and provided by the University of Southern California Center for Crisis Management. By the time this training was offered, we discovered we were doing virtually all that the USC trainers recommended.

Our CIT utilized Baron's "Levels of Violence" (1993, p. 31) to assess what was happening on the plantsite. Each CIT member shared what she or he saw happening from the vantage point of his or her function. Of course, security knew of most any incident that happened, because our company culture has long emphasized referring such matters to security. However, other members of the CIT were able to pulse the plantsite from various vantage points. Our assumption was that it is important not only to know of specific incidents but also to have an awareness of the *level of violence* at which our plantsite was functioning at any given time. For those not familiar with Baron's three levels of violence (seen on a continuum), they are, in sum

- *Level 1*: Behaviors companies see often—arguing with coworkers, much swearing at others, belligerence toward customers, and so forth.
- *Level 2*: Refusal to obey company policies and procedures, sabotage, threats of violence, sexual harassment, and so forth.
- *Level 3*: Recurrent suicidal threats or physical fights, destruction of property, rape, arson, and the ultimate violence of killing self or others.

By the same manner, we were also able to discover various *hot spots*—departments or employee groups who particularly expressed feelings of disenfranchisement.

Let us walk through a typical case involving the CIT assessment of an employee potentially at risk. Generally, we would be called by a member of supervision. Sometimes, the original reporter of the incident would be a fellow employee, other times a supervisor. The CIT was convened as soon as possible—normally the same day, depending on the apparent severity of the situation. The CIT would convene whomever was appropriate, including supervisor and manager. The CIT would agree on an action plan. The components of the fact-finding included an investigation by security or human resources, sometimes both; the facts as presented by the supervisor or manager; an EAP assessment, involving a supervisory directed referral to the EAP of the at-risk employee; if required, immediate exclusion of the employee from the plantsite, generally with pay.

The EAP, upon assessing the employee, generally referred him or her for a psychological evaluation. Our preference came to be an assessment by a psychologist, conversant with workplace violence and capable of psychological testing (MMPI, TAT, etc.). More helpful information was gained in the psychological assessment when it included both an inperson interview *and* testing.

Once the assessment from the mental health expert was received, the CIT was reconvened. At that time, the results of the psychological evaluation and the security or HR investigations were shared. Often, the employee was judged as not at risk and could be readmitted to the plantsite, with no loss of pay. The EAP continued to monitor the employee for as long as was deemed necessary. It was not unusual for a counseling referral to be made, separate from the assessment by a psychologist, with a release of information so that the EAP counselor could speak with the treating mental health provider.

The EAP files are, of course, separate from personnel files. The appropriate entries were made in the personnel file. The EAP assessment and the written summary of the psychological assessment were held in the confidential EAP file. Most reported incidents involved threat, implied threat, or at least perceived threat. We experienced no evidence of "witch hunts" or other malicious reports by employees or supervisors.

The Critical Incident Team in Action

The following incidents show the range of situations in which the CIT was involved. Of course, details that might identify any employee have been changed to protect their right to privacy.

Incident 1

An employee was upset by criticism of his work by his manager. In venting about the criticism to his supervisor, the employee said regarding his manager: "Tell him he's dead!" The supervisor immediately went to the manager and, together they confronted the employee. They concluded he did not, in fact, intend to do violence to the manager, but was merely spouting off in anger.

Nevertheless, the supervisor and manager told the employee they were referring the matter to the CIT, which they did. From the evidence the supervision provided, it was decided that security would do a background check and the EAP would assess the employee face-to-face. This was the action plan.

The security check turned up no prior convictions of any type, including violence. The EAP assessment concluded the employee was, indeed, just venting. He was warned by the EAP and his supervisors that his use of language was not at all acceptable, that it was akin to yelling "fire" in a crowded theater, whatever the intent might be. The employee admitted his wrong and fully accepted the constructive confrontation.

As a result of his revelation to the EAP professional that he was under a great deal of stress at work and in his personal life, the employee was referred for mental health counseling. He very willingly attended. Conversation with the treating provider validated that the employee was not at risk for violence. He responded well to psychological treatment.

Incident 2

A long-term employee was confronted by his supervisor for excessive use of the telephone during work hours (the phone was near the supervisor's office). The employee, still on the phone, got very angry, hung up, and tossed some metal objects toward the supervisor, which fell harmlessly to the floor.

The CIT was called by the manager. The supervisor and manager attended the CIT session. The employee had already been excluded from the campus pending the investigation of the matter. An action plan was agreed upon, including an EAP assessment and investigations by both HR and security.

The employee attended the EAP inperson assessment and was referred for a psychological assessment. The assessor saw no risk for violence by the employee. The HR investigation revealed ongoing conflict between the supervisor and the employee, partially because the employee spent too much time away from his work station, on the phone or otherwise. There had been an ongoing supervision issue that had been addressed by supervision, with only short-term change on the employee's part. We clearly distinguished to the supervisor and manager the difference between assessment for at-risk behaviors and other performance issues. The employee had no conviction record per the security investigation. The EAP professional did not see the employee as at risk.

The employee was allowed to return to work after the completion of the investigation by HR and security. He was off for approximately a week, including some disciplinary time off without pay. Follow-up sessions were conducted by the EAP counselor for several months after. It turned out he was very anxious about all the changes occurring at the plantsite and about his potential layoff. So he was referred for biofeedback training, which uses electronic instruments that monitor various bodily responses (pulse, heartrate, galvanic skin response) and show how successful the participant is in achieving a relaxation response. He responded with good success to the biofeedback training. The treating psychologist confirmed that the employee was not at risk for violence and, indeed, needed training in the handling of stress. He had medical problems, among other things. His eventual layoff occurred without incident.

Incident 3

A couple of employees reported to their manager a comment that others heard a fellow employee make while at work. The comment was to the effect that if he were laid off he would blow away 20 people. In this comment, he was making obvious reference to a recent incident in the Los Angeles area in which a disgruntled employee shot four employees at their place of work after receiving a poor performance appraisal. This incident was widely publicized in the national media.

Upon the manager's call to the CIT, we were convened immediately. The manager indicated that the employee was frequently moody and his work performance of uneven quality and quantity. This employee was in his 50s, was relatively long-term, and rightly perceived he was a candidate for layoff, especially in light of the fact that he had refused for years to upgrade his skills. The employee's name was, in fact, on the layoff notice, but the manager did not notify him of his pending layoff after hearing of this implied threat.

The CIT agreed on an action plan. The employee would be excluded from the plantsite. He would be sent to see the EAP (which is outside the secured area of the plantsite) with an HR representative present, first thing the next morning.

The HR representative reviewed with the employee the allegations of his threat of violence. He informed him of his rights and of the necessity of an HR investigation into the matter. He was further told he would be excluded from the campus pending his investigation. In keeping with this, the employee gave up his badge to the HR representative.

The employee did not appear at risk for violence to the HR representative or the EAP professional. When confronted with what he had been heard to say, the employee said he owned no guns and was not a violent man, but was concerned about layoff. This made clear he understood how his comment was being perceived. He admitted making a comment to the general effect of what the HR representative quoted him as having said. He did downplay the incident even though admitting he was wrong.

The EAP sent him for a psychological evaluation that day. The psychologist administered the MMPI and other psychological tests. He reported verbally, then in writing, that he did not see the employee as at risk for violence.

The CIT reconvened. The EAP reported the employee did not appear at risk for violence. It was decided he would be disciplined a couple of days for his inappropriate comment. The manager insisted the employee would be disruptive back at the work area. So a management decision was made to give the employee his layoff notice in a meeting with HR and the EAP. He would remain excluded from campus, other than attending the career resource center (which was entered from outside the secured area). Furthermore, there was an EAP professional skilled in outplacement and job-search issues working in the career resource center. The employee was handed off, so to speak, to this EAP professional. Also, the CRC was to notify security when the employee was at the center. The employee was given full pay during this 8-week period, and so could devote all his time to a job search.

Incident 4

The last incident on which we wish to report is rather more complex than the other situations we have outlined. It involved an actual act of sabotage. The perpetrator was never positively identified.

A few weeks prior to the incident we are reporting, someone threw a brick through the glass front door of one of the buildings. After investigation, security decided it was an act of vandalism. However, after this second incident, it was hypothesized that the two incidents were most likely linked and committed by an employee. Both incidents occurred late on Sunday or very early Monday (11 p.m.–1 a.m.).

An employee (investigation clearly implied) started small paper fires in one upstairs office, each one under a fire sprinkler. An employee sounded the fire alarm upon seeing all the water from the sprinklers running down the hallway.

The next morning, an extended CIT meeting was convened. Due to the nature of the incident, most members of the executive transition team were included and also representatives from facilities and finance and a security investigator from the corporate office.

The basic facts were ascertained. The glass door to the lobby of the building was broken, apparently from the inside out. A fire had been set in one of the offices upstairs. The type of fire was bound to create maximum water damage and minimum fire damage. So the person knew what he or she wanted to accomplish. Indeed, several thousands of dollars of water damage was incurred. Several offices were damaged: Carpeting was ruined and equipment was also damaged.

The local fire and police departments took a frontline role in the investigation due to its criminal nature. The company investigation was coordinated by corporate security.

Employees arriving at the affected building Monday morning were met by their managers and given a brief written description of what had occurred. After the extended CIT meeting, a public address announcement offered critical incident debriefing to any employees wishing it.

It was ruled out that the hostile act was directed at the employee in whose office the fires were set. He was out of the country at the time. Nonetheless, he was called by his manager and apprised of the incident. Counseling was offered both to him and his wife. He was reassured that all the evidence pointed to sabotage aimed at the company and not violence directed toward him.

A public announcement was provided to the press. The local city manager was debriefed on the incident by representatives from Hughes. A communication plan for customers was formulated.

A safety investigation was conducted. Some employees were moved to other office space due to allergic reactions. Furthermore, added security measures were instituted to prevent further sabotage. Employees were given a flyer and a newsletter article was written explaining the primary details of the incident, without revealing information that would inhibit the investigation of police, fire, and Hughes's security. All of this was part of the action plan agree upon by the extended CIT.

As noted above, the saboteur was never conclusively identified. However, there were no succeeding incidents of this manner. We believe that the presence of an active CIT helped in the handling of this incident and in the flow of information to employees throughout the plantsite.

Conclusion

Hughes Electronics Corporation is fully committed to prevention of violence at all of its worksites. Corporate leadership has clearly articulated that employees are the company's most important resource and must, under all circumstances, be treated with dignity and respect. Furthermore, Hughes recognizes that the health and safety of employees and the success of the enterprise are inseparable. It realizes that downsizing in the modern corporation is a fact of life and that this reality calls for careful consideration of employees. This careful consideration includes a corporation-wide method for conflict resolution between employees and management, including the utilization of an executive advisor for employees who desire one. Further, Hughes has for many years utilized outplacement services and a generous transition package for laid-off employees. Now most Hughes sites have a critical incident team for the purpose of preventing of workplace violence and dealing with actual violence, should it occur. In August 1995, corporate human resources sponsored training for all of the existent CITs within Hughes, provided by the University of Southern California Center for Crisis Management. Finally, the leadership of Hughes has endorsed the role of a people team, whose sole focus is on fostering the treatment of all employees with dignity and respect.

What are the essential components of a critical incident team? The first requirement is that executive leadership at the top of the corporation and at the top of all business units fully understand and clearly endorse the role and activities of the CIT. A second requirement is that all management staff learn that the best prevention of violence is the kind and courteous treatment of employees. Third, there must be in place a clear policy statement that articulates zero tolerance for workplace violence and that summarizes the function of the CIT. Fourth, the appropriate members for a cross-functional CIT must be assembled; they must then be educated about workplace violence and about the functioning of the team. This is an ongoing process as members on the team change. Fifth, all members of management and supervision must be trained in how to detect and deal with potential or actual workplace violence. It is useful to extend this training to other persons who have a clear pulse of their organization and its employees (i.e., executive secretaries and administrative assistants). Sixth, the CIT must meet regularly and be ready to respond immediately to situations requiring their assessment of employees' potential risk for violence. Seventh, these activities must be carried on discretely, with careful consideration for confidentiality. Eighth, the team (in our model, through its employee assistance program) must have capable outside mental health professionals (usually psychologists and psychiatrists) to assess employees deemed potentially at risk for violence. Ninth, the activities of the CIT must be documented carefully, with the documentation only accessible to appropriate personnel.

In closing, companies must remain aware, as we stand on the vestibule of the 21st century, that the world is in the midst of a major socioeconomic revolution, called by some the Information Age. An essential characteristic of this new socioeconomic reality is constant change. This heightens the potential for workplace violence. Enlightened companies recognize that people are their most valuable resource and that the fair and dignified treatment of these employees is an essential component of successful business practice. The challenge is to hold in careful balance the competitiveness of the company and the well-being of employees. In the end, the two cannot be separated. This, after all is said and done, is the best any company can do to prevent workplace violence.

References

Baron, R. A. (1993). *Violence in the workplace: A prevention and management guide for business*. Ventura, CA: Pathfinder Publishing.

Kinney, J. A., & Johnson, D. L. (1993). *Breaking point: The workplace violence epidemic and what to do about it*. Chicago: National Safe Workplace Institute.

Northwestern National Life Insurance Company. (1993). *Fear and violence in the workplace: A survey documenting the experience of American workers*. Minneapolis, MN: Author.

22

Workplace Violence in Correctional Settings: A Comprehensive Approach to Critical Incident Stress Management

John Dignam and Thomas J. Fagan

Much of the available workplace violence literature is fraught with definitional and conceptual problems; this is understandable given the relatively recent emergence of the field as an area of study and practice. Both popular and professional writings on the subject focus almost exclusively on disgruntled employees and their potential for violent behavior, when in fact they are responsible for a small fraction of the violence that occurs in the workplace overall (cf. National Institute for Occupational Safety and Health, 1992).

A more accurate and inclusive typology of workplace violence was provided in the California Division of Occupational Safety and Health's (1994) guidelines for workplace security. Three distinct types of workplace violence were described in that typology. Type I events are those where the perpetrator of violence has no legitimate relationship to the workplace, such as a criminal who commits a violent act during a robbery of a retail work setting. In Type II events, the perpetrator is a customer or recipient of service at the workplace, such as a hospital patient or prisoner. Type III events involve an assault or other violent behavior committed by a current or former employee or a friend, relative, or lover of an employee who has some grievance or dispute.

For correctional workers, Type I and Type III incidents are probably no more prevalent than at other work sites. Indeed, one can argue that they are probably less prevalent. Type I incidents are unlikely to occur in correctional settings for obvious reasons, including the emphasis on physical plant security that renders such incidents virtually impossible. Such tight security also greatly reduces the threat of Type III incidents, where nonemployees are the perpetrators. Type III incidents involving employee

The views expressed in this chapter are those of the authors and do not necessarily represent official views of the Federal Bureau of Prisons.

perpetrators are also less likely insofar as correctional agencies typically conduct more thorough background investigations than the average employer when hiring staff. Preemployment background checks to screen out job applicants with histories of violence and other criminal behavior is a practice universally recommended by experts in this area (cf. Mantell, 1994).

Conversely, Type II workplace violence events are undoubtedly the kind most frequently experienced by correctional workers. Although this is probably also true for other human service professionals, such as police officers or psychiatric nurses, it can be argued that correctional workers represent a unique high risk occupational group for workplace violence. Those who work in prisons and jails are quite vulnerable to acts of violence by prisoners or inmates in their charge. Incarcerated offenders are obviously more likely as a group to have personal histories of violence and to act out aggressively compared with other "customer" populations served by human service workers. Moreover, the fact that they are held against their will and certainly do not view themselves as "customers" generally results in a work climate often less than cordial and occasionally quite antagonistic, an atmosphere obviously more conducive to violence than other human service-oriented work relationships.

Harer (1992) reported that the rate of assaults by inmates against Federal Bureau of Prisons staff, for example, was 55 per 1,000 employees during an 18-month period in 1988 and 1989. More recent data indicate that this rate has increased: Over an 18-month period between 1994 and 1995, during which time the ratio of inmates to staff remained essentially the same as in 1988 and 1989, the rate of inmate assaults against staff was 70 per 1,000 employees. The incidence of inmate assaults against prison staff members in state and local institutions is probably as high and presumably higher; offenses that are prima facie crimes of violence, such as murder or assault, are more likely to be adjudicated and the perpetrators incarcerated in state and local jurisdictions (cf. Light, 1994).

In addition to the possibility of routine individual assaults, those who work in correctional facilities also have a greater chance of being victims of more serious and traumatic violence. The Centers for Disease Control and Prevention (1993) cited correctional workers as one of the occupational groups with the highest rate of work-related homicide. Prison riots and other violent disturbances, which place correctional employees at great risk of physical harm, have increased dramatically in the last part of this century. Of the more than 300 prison riots reported in the past 200 years, approximately 90% have occurred since 1950 (Martin & Zimmerman, 1990). Hostage taking incidents also occur at a high rate. In the Federal Bureau of Prisons alone, there have been 157 employees held hostage in nine separate incidents since 1987. Remarkably, none of those employees were seriously injured physically, but significant emotional trauma resulted from such victimization in many cases.

Responding to Workplace Violence in Correctional Settings

Violence of any kind within prisons and jails is preventable to a great extent. It is undoubtedly true that inmates' violent behavior has been and continues to be successfully deterred by proven and effective prison management techniques (DiIulio, 1987; McCorkle, Miethe, & Drass, 1995). Strict adherence to established security procedures, staff training in interpersonal communication as well as self-defense, ensuring sufficient staff-inmate ratios, and providing meaningful self-improvement programs to prisoners are just a few of the many management strategies that can reduce the likelihood of violence and other problems within correctional facilities. Unfortunately, despite such prevention, assaults and other aggressive acts by prisoners against correctional staff do occur on occasion. When they do, there are a variety of other safety, security, and emergency response procedures that staff may follow in order to contain volatile situations, to maximize the safety of both staff and other inmates, and to ensure swift justice and appropriate punishment for perpetrators.

In the Federal Bureau of Prisons, among the many established emergency procedures activated in response to violent incidents is a component devoted entirely to ensuring that employees and their families receive appropriate psychological support services in the event of a workplace violence incident or other crisis. This is accomplished generally through the agency's employee assistance program (EAP) and, in the case of catastrophic or critical incidents, through a specific program within the agency's EAP called the family and employee assistance team program. This comprehensive approach to providing support services in response to critical incidents is best described as a multifaceted system that can be expanded or contracted depending on the nature and severity of an incident and the particular needs of staff, their families, and the organization during and following an incident.

What follows is a description of the different types and levels of services available, and the kinds of workplace violence incidents that have prompted mobilization of those services. The chapter concludes with a detailed account of how this system was originally implemented during a critical incident considered to be one of the most challenging and potentially disastrous prison disturbances in the history of the Federal Bureau of Prisons. This account includes a discussion of outcome data that suggests that this comprehensive approach to critical incident stress management is effective and beneficial to correctional staff and their families.

Individual and Family-Level Interventions

At its most basic level, the Bureau of Prisons' response to the psychological needs of staff who are victims of assaults or other violent acts is essentially the same as it is for any other job-related or personal problem staff may experience. The agency's employee assistance program is organized in such a way that staff and their families at all locations have immediate access to counseling services if necessary or requested. Although some of those services are available through private agencies under contract, the bulk of employee assistance services are provided by qualified Bureau of Prisons staff. Each correctional facility has a psychology services department staffed by doctoral-level psychologists whose primary duty is to provide mental health services to inmates. However, the provision of confidential employee assistance services to institution staff is an important collateral duty of all Bureau of Prisons psychologists.

The chief of psychology services at each facility serves as the local EAP coordinator. She or he is responsible for the following: educating all staff about available services (including how to access services, how to tell what types of problems services can and should be used, and what the nature and limits of confidentiality are); identifying local community mental health resources to be used for referral purposes; training supervisors on topics such as when to refer staff for EAP counseling; and personally providing, or ensuring that other psychologists on staff are available to provide, whatever crisis intervention, assessment, referral, and follow-up services may be necessary to assist staff, and any immediate family members, in resolving any emotional or other problems.

In the event of an inmate assault on staff, a local EAP counselor is available to provide the necessary and appropriate services for the victimized staff member. In most cases of this kind, serious emotional trauma does not result and extensive services are not needed, but they are always available if management wishes to refer staff or if victimized staff request them. On occasion, staff who have been assaulted have had difficulties such as increased fear of inmates, avoidance of work situations or areas associated with the assault, or other acute stress reactions that are common and understandable for trauma victims. In those cases EAP staff intervene through supportive counseling and education about traumatic stress symptoms for the victimized staff and his or her family, referrals to qualified mental health providers in the community to treat and prevent exacerbation of symptoms, and whatever advocacy or recommendations for accommodation (e.g., temporary job or shift changes) may be necessary in order to successfully reintegrate on the job.

In some cases, there may be significant emotional sequelae or unique needs of victims that require additional intervention. For example, a recent assault involved the serious biting of two employees by an HIV-infected inmate. The employees and their families experienced profound psychological distress and disruption as a result. In addition to the usual assessment and referral services, local EAP staff determined that the affected employees and their families should be provided with psychoeducational sessions on AIDS and its transmission to allay undue fear and anxiety. Also, the agency provided immediate funding for that part of the community mental health services recommended by EAP staff not covered by insurance, so that those staff and their families would not have to wait for lengthy processing of workmen's compensation claims in order to obtain appropriate services.

Group-Level Interventions

If a larger group of correctional employees are potentially affected, usually by a relatively more severe workplace violence incident such as a homicide or a riot, additional interventions may be necessary. One such intervention is critical incident stress debriefing (CISD), a procedure designed to buffer the effects of traumatic stress on victims and thereby prevent or reduce posttraumatic stress symptomatology (Mitchell, 1983, 1988). CISD is a highly structured, psychoeducational group technique that is often used as a crisis intervention tool to assist any group of emergency response workers (law enforcement, fire rescue, medical personnel), or any other group who may be victims or witnesses to a traumatic event, in coping with the stress of such direct involvement in a critical incident. Over the past two decades, this intervention has been used to help thousands of workers who respond to disasters and other critical incidents, and appears to have significant beneficial effects in terms of preventing employment separations and the need for subsequent mental health services (Mitchell & Everly, 1993).

A subcomponent of the Federal Bureau of Prisons' emergency response procedures within its EAP is the family and employee assistance team (FEAT). FEATs are composed of Bureau of Prisons psychologists and chaplains who undergo an extensive training program in CISD techniques and other matters such as death and dying issues, crisis intervention, and posttraumatic stress disorder with an emphasis on team building and other role-playing exercises. Donovan (1983) recommended the use of both psychologists and chaplains for staff debriefing sessions in prison settings. The Bureau of Prisons' experience is that those two disciplines complement each other quite well in providing staff and their families with the necessary psychological, supportive, and spiritual counseling in times of crisis.

Each correctional institution has a local FEAT and all regional office and national headquarters administrators of both psychology services and religious services are also trained so that such services are always available, and the deployment of additional teams can occur if necessary. CEOs of all facilities are directed through various national policies to utilize FEATs to assist staff during and after any institutional crisis as appropriate. FEAT composition and other relevant information necessary for rapid deployment of the FEAT(s) are typically part of all local institution-written emergency plans.

A recent example of how FEATs are used in response to workplace violence incidents took place following the tragic murder in December 1994 of a Bureau of Prisons correctional officer by an inmate at a penitentiary located in the Southeastern region of the United States. This kind of workplace violence event is emotionally devastating to most staff, especially those who worked closely with the victim and, most certainly, staff who are witnesses to the incident. In this case, the regional administrators for psychology and religious services were dispatched to the site to assist the local FEAT in providing group debriefing sessions for affected staff.

During the weeks following this tragic homicide, which had occurred only days before Christmas, over 500 penitentiary staff participated voluntarily in group debriefings. Facilitated by trained staff, those sessions provided a safe environment in which staff could express their anger, guilt, sorrow, and other emotions in constructive ways and with the support of fellow correctional workers. Themes that emerged from those sessions included a shared sense of helplessness and loss of control, the collective sense of loss and grief for a fallen comrade, and a reaffirmation of the need to work together and to function as a cohesive unit. A memorial service was also held at the institution to assist staff in their grieving. Supportive counseling and referral services were provided on an individual basis if required or requested and, of course, such services were available to family members of victims. Finally, group debriefing sessions and another memorial service were offered to staff on the recent anniversary of the officer's death. These activities helped promote a sense of community and healing among employees at a stressful time, when divisiveness, bitterness, and significantly more individual emotional trauma were just as possible.

A more recent example of workplace violence events during which FEATs were deployed highlights the importance of having multiple teams available to assist staff. In October 1995 the Bureau of Prisons experienced a number of simultaneous inmate disturbances of varying severity. In some of the most severe cases, inmates burned down structures and caused other significant damage within facilities, assaulted staff and other inmates, and trapped some employees for a time before they were rescued by other responding staff. Fortunately, there were no serious injuries sustained by staff or inmates during these simultaneous disturbances, and the agency regained control of all affected institutions very quickly. Nonetheless, the potential for significant emotional trauma existed given the experience of many victimized staff.

At most affected facilities, local FEAT members were not directly involved in responding to the disturbances and were available to provide services to those in need. However, at two facilities where local FEAT members had been immediate responders and where large numbers of staff were affected, the respective regional offices simultaneously sent their FEATs to conduct group debriefing sessions. At both facilities the visiting FEATs conducted group sessions over a few days to accommodate scheduling and other needs of staff and management, all of whom were still dealing with the aftermath of the disturbances. Debriefing sessions were provided separately for primary victims (those who were directly victimized by inmate physical attacks or being trapped by rioting inmates) and for responding staff who witnessed the events or had other issues that were helpful to process (e.g., critiquing the overall emergency response, concerns about inmate management immediately following the disturbance).

Multisystem-Level Interventions

Along the spectrum of potential workplace violence events faced by correctional workers, perhaps the most unsettling prospect is being involved in a hostage taking incident. Although recent experience has suggested that the risk of serious physical harm to those taken hostage in correctional hostage incidents is generally low, especially if effective hostage negotiation techniques are brought to bear, the psychological impact of being held hostage can be devastating. Individuals who have been held hostage typically exhibit significant psychological symptoms and follow a predictable pattern of symptom changes and recovery over time (Strentz, 1987; Symonds, 1983).

A preventive intervention provided to all Bureau of Prisons staff regarding this kind of workplace violence event is annual training in "hostage survival skills." In this class, correctional staff are reminded that, although the chance of actually becoming a hostage during their careers is generally low, they work in an occupation that carries a higher risk of hostage taking than the average profession. They are then taught a number of survival strategies that former hostages have reported helped them maintain a relative sense of calm and hope under such severely stressful circumstances. This training is designed as a form of stress inoculation against the significant emotional trauma that would result from being taken hostage. Staff are also encouraged to discuss the possibility of becoming a hostage with their loved ones and to inform them of the services that would be provided to families and employees in the unlikely event of a hostage situation. Those services are described below.

When an actual hostage taking event occurs, especially a protracted hostage situation that lasts over many days, there is obviously more than one identifiable victim. The primary victims, of course, are the hostages themselves. But there are many other secondary or tertiary "victims" as well: the hostages' spouses, children, relatives, and friends who are left to wonder when or if their loved ones will come out safely; on-scene emergency personnel who, in some cases, may risk their lives through rescue attempts or other emergency procedures; management officials responsible for making life and death decisions during the crisis; families of the hostage takers who are concerned about the safety and future of their loved ones; and other responding staff whose jobs and lives have been disrupted as a result of the incident. At different points in time throughout this kind of crisis and well after it has been resolved, those various groups require different levels and types of services to cope successfully with the unique stressors and strains of the event and, for some, the resulting psychological trauma and readjustment difficulties.

When a protracted hostage situation occurs in the Bureau of Prisons, a family services center is organized at the crisis site to provide the necessary psychological and other support services to the various victim groups. The family services center typically is established in a building fairly close to the crisis site but sufficiently distant to avoid interfering with efforts to manage and resolve the incident. The center is staffed by FEATs, the number of which is determined by the size of the crisis. FEATs from other correctional institutions in the same geographic region as the crisis site are deployed first. If the needs of the center demand additional FEAT personnel, or if the situation endures and existing center staff need relief, then FEATs from other regions may be deployed. The center may remain open for some time after a hostage situation is resolved, depending on the number of primary victims, the severity of resulting symptoms, and the complexity of job reintegration issues.

A wide range of services for different groups is typically provided at the family services center. For families of hostages, those services include, but are not limited to, supportive counseling or any other mental health services deemed necessary; special children's groups and day care activities; shelter and meals for those family members who wish to remain at the center during the crisis; routine information updates conducted by a management representative; and psychoeducational sessions to prepare family members to expect certain behaviors or symptoms upon the hostages' release. Selected FEAT personnel may also be available to assist families of hostage takers in similar ways, but not in the same location as the hostage families. Center staff also provide counseling and support services to all levels of staff responding to the crisis who may be experiencing fatigue, emotional exhaustion, or other symptoms.

As hostages are released, after medical screening and intelligence debriefing, there are a number of interventions by family services center staff that follow a structured sequence. First, FEAT members conduct individual sessions with each former hostage to reorient them psychologically. This is accomplished by providing information about what has transpired during the crisis (including information about services provided to their families), educating them about acute stress symptoms they may experience as they return home, conducting a general assessment of their psychological well-being to identify those who may require more intensive immediate services, and scheduling them for a group debriefing session within the next 1–2 days. These individual "defusing" sessions, also referred to as "demobilization" or "decompression" in other writings on critical incident stress intervention (Mitchell & Everly, 1993), are very brief so that former hostages can be reunited with their loved ones with minimum delay.

Next, group critical incident debriefing sessions are held approximately 24–36 hours later. Two FEAT members, typically a chaplain and a psychologist, facilitate each session, during which former hostages discuss and share their experiences, fill in information gaps for each other to better attain some sense of closure, process emotions felt during and since the crisis, learn more about possible symptoms still to come, and discuss coping strategies to be used during the recovery process. Depending on the needs of former hostages, multiple debriefing sessions may occur over the initial days following the crisis. An aftercare plan is also developed for each former hostage and his or her family. Individual counseling and referrals to community mental health or other social services are provided for those who appear to be struggling and unable to cope in their recovery or who have clearly developed significant psychiatric symptoms as a result of the psychological trauma of being a hostage. Finally, center staff assist management in job reintegration difficulties that may arise over time.

A Case Example: The Atlanta Hostage Crisis

Implementation of the critical incident stress management system described above can be complicated in a protracted hostage situation. The following is a case example describing how this system was first developed and implemented in Atlanta, Georgia, during the largest and longest hostage event in the history of the Federal Bureau of Prisons.

In November 1987, two Bureau of Prisons facilities, the U.S. Penitentiary in Atlanta and the Federal Detention Center in Oakdale, Louisiana, were simultaneously taken over by Cuban detainees for several days. Most of these detainees had come to America during the Mariel Boatlift in 1980 when Fidel Castro briefly relaxed Cuban emigration requirements. Included in this group of emigrants were Cubans with known criminal records and histories of mental illness. Many of these, as well as other detainees, failed to acclimate to their new surroundings and, because of the severity of their actions, found themselves confined in various prisons and jails awaiting deportation to a country from which they had either fled or been expelled.

An agreement between the U.S. State Department and Cuba was finally reached in November 1987 that allowed for the repatriation of approximately 2,400 Cuban detainees. The Cuban detainees incarcerated in Atlanta and Oakdale, assuming they would be among those deported back to Cuba, expressed their dissatisfaction with the agreement and with their uncertain status within the United States by rioting. During these riots they set fire to a number of buildings, ran freely through these institutions destroying government property and records, and took 138 Bureau of Prisons employees hostage.

It was in response to these scenes of chaos and destruction that the Director of the Bureau of Prisons dispatched a small group of Bureau psychologists and chaplains to both locations with the simple instruction that they meet the personal needs of victimized staff and their loved ones. Of the two disturbances, the incident at the Atlanta penitentiary was the larger and is therefore the focus of the remainder of this section. Over the course of 11 days, 110 staff members at Atlanta were held hostage for varying lengths of time and approximately 1,400 Cuban detainees participated in the disturbance.

Although the psychologists and chaplains who arrived on site were relatively untrained in established critical incident response procedures, victims and their needs were evident right from the beginning. In the early hours of the disturbance, all available Bureau staff were involved in attempts to quell the disturbance and to identify staff who had been captured. Media, quick to respond, were televising live pictures of the penitentiary burning. Family members of employees, seeing these images on TV and unable to reach their loved ones at the penitentiary, began to arrive on the scene in an effort to seek information about the safety of their loved ones.

Acquiring a meeting space to provide information to family members became the first goal. A space on federal property, but away from the actual incident, was established as the family services center. Arriving family members were directed to report to this area. The area was equipped with televisions, VCRs, telephones, and cots so that family members could monitor events as they were reported on television, could talk to family members not present, and could take brief naps without leaving the scene. Center staff asked on-scene commanders to come to the family center periodically to brief family members about the incident and, more specifically, about the status of their loved ones. Negotiators were also able to convince hostage takers to photograph captured staff and to allow them to write brief notes to family members. Tower officers were also able to videotape hostages as they were moved from one location to another by their captors. These materials were shared with family members and were very helpful in allaying their fears.

As hours turned into days, the number of immediate and extended family members at the family services center grew to over 300. Effectively managing and meeting their most basic informational and practical needs became the second goal for center staff. Interventions in this category included establishing a telephone notification system (i.e., telephone chains) that could be activated by family members in the event that hostages were released; organizing food delivery, preparation, service, and clean-up; screening new arrivals to determine their relationship to captured staff; establishing schedules for telephones, sleeping accommodations, and so forth; providing day care and baby-sitting services to allow adult loved ones time for counseling and other activities; and staffing an information hotline for family members who were unable to come to the family center. It quickly became obvious that additional psychologists, chaplains, and other staff would be needed to manage the center given the number of family members and the growing needs of the group as the crisis continued. Thus, additional staff from selected institutions throughout the Bureau of Prisons were dispatched to the scene. At its peak, the family center was operated by 14 psychologists, 14 chaplains, 3 support staff, and numerous family member volunteers.

After family members' initial relief that their loved ones were unharmed for the moment, they naturally began to react to the reality that this situation posed inherent dangers and uncertainties. Emotional displays were frequent and tensions ran high. Center staff members began offering family members crisis counseling on an individual basis. Later, group counseling sessions were organized on an array of topics, such as household finances, Bureau of Prisons' operating procedures, and dealing with school systems. Group sessions were also used to provide more traditional forms of brief therapy for PTSD-like symptoms. As days passed, these services continued and were augmented by the naturally occurring emotional support families began to provide to each other.

An uneasy emotional equilibrium was reached and maintained within the family center. There were long periods of relative calm with occasional flare-ups that typically paralleled stressful moments and events inside the penitentiary. Center staff used those periods of relative calm to educate family members about what to expect when their loved ones were released. Miniseminars on such topics as the Stockholm Syndrome (a phenomenon where hostages begin to identify with and develop positive feelings toward their captors), critical incident debriefing procedures, and posttraumatic stress disorder were presented to family members. These miniseminars were used as much to focus their attention away from the minute-to-minute stresses of the incident as they were to prepare them for things to come.

Center staff also used periods of calm to begin researching and establishing procedures on how to handle hostages as they were released. The defusing and debriefing procedures described above were developed during this period. Community mental health practitioners, agencies, and facilities were canvassed to determine which of them had experience dealing with PTSD issues and law enforcement personnel and which of them would be willing to serve as referral sources for hostages who might need long-term care. This period was also used to begin training center staff in debriefing techniques and procedures. Local community resources experienced in such operations were brought in to provide this instruction and were also used to actually conduct defusing and debriefing sessions with some of the 21 hostages who were released before the incident was resolved. Center staff participated in these sessions and refined their own defusing and debriefing styles under the tutelage of an experienced practitioner.

Development of telephone chains, discussion of the defusing and debriefing procedures at miniseminars for family members, and on-the-job debriefing training for center staff paid handsome dividends on the 11th day of the incident, when the remaining 89 hostages were released. Selected center staff members began notifying family members of the release. Others began conducting defusing sessions with released hostages. By the time defusing sessions were completed, most family members had arrived and were united with their loved ones. All released hostages were escorted home by either a family member or by a coworker so that no hostage would have to return to an empty house on their first night of freedom. Thirty-six hours after release, hostages returned for their group debriefing sessions. During the debriefing process, many released hostages admitted that they probably would not have come to the debriefing had it not been for the urging of family members who had been previously instructed about the importance of debriefings.

All hostages who were debriefed were asked to complete a brief questionnaire as part of the aftercare process. A copy of this questionnaire is

Table 1. Symptom Comparison Before and After Incident

Symptom	% of Hostages reporting symptoms prior to the incident	% of Hostages reporting symptoms after the incident
Sleep difficulties	0	77
Nightmares	1	49
Anxiety	2	68
Depression	3	48
Anger	1	62
Irritability	1	60
Fatigue	3	52
Concentration difficulties	0	51
Memory problems	2	38
Guilt	4	12
Intrusive thoughts	0	18
Physical problems	3	26
Marital stress	4	31
Parenting difficulties	2	18
Other (e.g., alienation, confidence problems, etc.)	1	7

$N = 95$.

Table 2. Hostage Stressors During the 12 Months Before the Incident

Stressor	% of Hostages reporting stressors in 12 months before the incident
Death in family	14
Change in residence	25
Job change	18
Serious illness	8
Marital difficulties or divorce	7
Financial difficulties	10
Legal problems	1
Disciplinary action on job	6

Note. Individual hostages may have endorsed more than one item.
$N = 95$.

presented in the chapter Appendix. The questionnaire focused on four key areas: presence of PTSD-like symptomatology, both pre- and post-incident; past life stressors that might exacerbate current symptomatology; and self-assessed current and long-term needs. Questionnaire results were reviewed with each hostage and used to assist them in the development of an aftercare strategy. Although not meant as a research tool, questionnaire results in aggregate did provide a good snapshot of hostage status shortly after their release.

Ninety-five hostages completed this questionnaire. As Table 1 demonstrates, hostages reported increased physical, emotional, and cognitive symptomatology following the disturbance. Most frequently cited

Table 3.   Short-Term Services Requested by Hostages After Incident

Service	% of Hostages requesting service after incident
Financial assistance	7
Medication	10
Relocation	19
Mental health counseling	45
Medical exam or treatment	21
Religious counseling	1
Information from personnel	38

$N = 95$.

symptoms included: sleeping difficulties, anxiety, anger, and irritability. Table 2 presents the percentage of hostages who reported significant life-stressors in the 12 months preceding the incident. The obvious conclusion to draw from this table is that a number of hostages entered the incident already stressed by other life events; this presumably increased their vulnerability to the negative effects of traumatic stress. Table 3 reflects the types of services in which hostages were most interested immediately following the incident. Almost half of the group clearly saw the need for mental health counseling. A little over one third of the group were interested in the types of information provided by personnel staff (e.g., workman's compensation questions, tort claim questions regarding personal property lost or damaged during the disturbance, etc.). Some hostages were interested in job relocation information and in scheduling a physical examination to reassure themselves that their 11 days in captivity living under relatively primitive conditions had not resulted in any serious physical complications. Thirty-nine percent of the hostages reported career counseling and 22% reported mental health services as long-term needs.

At the conclusion of group debriefings, hostages were offered the opportunity to meet individually with a center staff member to discuss any private concerns they might have or to develop an individual treatment plan to assist them with their recovery and job reentry. To assist hostages and their family members with post-incident problems, the family center, now referred to as the hostage and family services center, remained in operation for 3 additional months. At the end of this 3-month period, active cases were transferred to the institution's local EAP coordinator for continued follow-up, and remaining center staff returned to their parent institutions and normal job duties.

Approximately 18 months after the Atlanta disturbance, a team of staff who had worked at the family services center returned to Atlanta to follow up and assess the status of former hostages. Only former hostages who volunteered to participate in a follow-up interview were scheduled for an individual session. Thirty-nine former hostages chose to participate in the 18-month follow-up. This follow-up session was initiated to ensure that the agency was doing everything it could to meet the needs of its victim-

Table 4.   1987–1989 Symptom Comparison

Symptom	% of Hostages reporting symptoms in 1987	% of Hostages reporting symptoms in 18-month follow-up
Sleep difficulties	82	52
Nightmares	56	46
Anxiety	76	41
Depression	36	30
Anger	69	37
Irritability	64	46
Fatigue	64	22
Concentration difficulties	62	35
Memory problems	56	13
Guilt	25	2
Intrusive thoughts	28	33
Physical problems	31	15
Marital stress	31	33
Parenting difficulties	15	13
Other (e.g., alienation, confidence problems, etc.)	5	7

$N = 39$.

ized employees, not as a research vehicle. However, aggregate results do provide limited outcome data regarding the effectiveness of family center services offered both during and after the incident.

Each former hostage was asked a series of questions about the following: ongoing problems and symptoms related to the incident; services (e.g., EAP, medical, mental health, personnel, etc.) utilized after the incident to assist with recovery and job reentry; and an assessment of the value of those services actually used by former hostages and family members. Using a list of PTSD-like symptoms (same symptom list as was used in the initial post-release questionnaire), all former hostages were also screened for the presence and severity of each symptom expressed or observed during this interview.

Table 4 presents comparisons between symptoms reported by these 39 hostages immediately following the disturbance and symptoms reported by this group during the 18-month follow-up. These data suggest that former hostages were still experiencing symptoms 18 months after the event, although the percentage of staff troubled by most symptoms had decreased. An exception was that former hostages reported slightly more difficulty managing intrusive thoughts about the incident 18 months after the event. Marital and parenting problems continued to trouble former hostages at about the same level 18 months after the incident as they did just after the incident.

Of the 39 former hostages who participated in the follow-up, 35 indicated that they had participated in individual counseling activities offered through the institution's local EAP. All participating former hostages rated the support and counseling they and family members received through the family services center and local EAP both during and after the incident positively. They felt that these services helped moderate the negative impact of the disturbance on their overall mental health and well-being.

Conclusion

Correctional workers represent a unique high risk occupational group for certain types of workplace violence. The Federal Bureau of Prisons' comprehensive approach to helping its employees manage critical incident stress in the aftermath of a variety of workplace violence incidents has many advantages. The multifaceted nature of the system allows for maximum flexibility in matching type and amount of resources to employee assistance needs in the event of any workplace violence situation. Services can easily be expanded or contracted as appropriate. Flexibility is also evident in terms of the scope of other problems to which this approach can be applied. FEATs have responded to other crises of varying size in the Bureau of Prisons. Examples include natural disasters that affect the working conditions or personal lives of staff (e.g., Hurricane Andrew in the Southeast U.S. in 1993 and the 1994 Los Angeles earthquake); staff suicides; and accidental deaths, such as one that was witnessed by fellow employees in the Northeast region in 1993 when a correctional officer accidentally fell from a vehicle on the way back from an emergency response training exercise.

The use of agency staff as employee assistance providers also offers greater accessibility of services to employees. This is certainly the case given that in-house staff are already on site or are easily deployed to various locations. But it is also true in a less tangible sense. Helpers who are also fellow correctional workers have more credibility with victims insofar as they know what it is like to work with inmates every day, they share the same potential for violent encounters in the workplace, and they understand "the system." As a result, victims tend to trust them more and are not as resistant to help as they might be if outside mental health resources were used exclusively or as the front-line employee assistance force.

The nature of crisis intervention obviously limits the degree to which carefully controlled research can be conducted in this area. Although the outcome data from the Atlanta hostage crisis is not easily interpreted given the inability to rule out alternative explanations of results, the overall benefit of this approach in buffering the impact of and directly managing traumatic stress is clearly suggested by the self-report data about satisfaction with and use of services. In employing this strategy of providing assistance directly to staff in times of crisis, the agency itself also accrues benefits in terms of staff morale and the shaping of an organizational culture that is viewed by all as positive and proactive. This, in turn, presumably leads to more positive job outcomes in general (e.g., increased productivity, ability to recruit and retain experienced staff).

One aspect of workplace violence that is certainly not unique to any occupational group is the need for employers to be responsive to this increasingly more visible problem. Prevention is key, but when incidents inevitably occur it is equally important to provide effective assistance to employees who otherwise have to cope and recover from the effects of traumatic stress on their own in the aftermath of workplace violence. There are many benefits for both employees and employers in having a comprehensive critical incident intervention plan. The approach described above can be easily modified and replicated across a variety of public and private workplaces.

References

California Division of Occupational Safety and Health. (1994). *Guidelines for workplace security*. Sacramento, CA: Author.

Centers for Disease Control and Prevention. (1993). *Fatal injuries to workers in the U.S., 1980–1989: A decade of surveillance*. Cincinnati, OH: National Institute for Occupational Safety and Health.

DiIulio, J. J., Jr. (1987). *Governing prisons*. New York, NY: Free Press.

Donovan, E. J. (1983). Responding to the prison employee-hostage as a crime victim. In *Correctional officers: Power, pressure and responsibility* (pp. 17–24). College Park, MD: American Correctional Association.

Harer, M. (1992). Assaults on BOP staff and inmates—Where and when they occur. *Research Forum, 1*, 1–20.

Light, S. C. (1994). Assaults on prison officers: Interactional themes. In M. C. Braswell, R. H. Montgomery, Jr., & L. X. Lombardo (Eds.), *Prison violence in America* (pp. 207–226). Cincinnati, OH: Anderson Publishing.

Mantell, M. (1994). *Ticking bombs: Defusing violence in the workplace*. New York: Irwin Professional Publishing.

Martin, R., & Zimmerman, S. (1990). A typology of the causes of prison riots and an analytical extension to the 1986 Virginia riot. *Justice Quarterly, 7*, 711–737.

McCorkle, R. C., Miethe, T. D., & Drass, K. A. (1995). The roots of prison violence: A test of the deprivation, management, and "not-so-total" institution models. *Crime and Delinquency, 41*, 317–331.

Mitchell, J. T. (1983). When disaster strikes . . . the critical incident debriefing process. *Journal of Emergency Medical Services, 8*, 36–39.

Mitchell, J. T. (1988). Development and functions of a critical incident stress debriefing team. *Journal of Emergency Medical Services, 13*, 43–46.

Mitchell, J. T., & Everly, G. S., Jr. (1993). *Critical incident stress debriefing: An operations manual for the prevention of traumatic stress among emergency services and disaster workers*. Ellicott City, MD: Chevron Publishing.

National Institute for Occupational Safety and Health. (1992). *Homicide in U.S. workplaces: A strategy for prevention and research* (DHHS [NIOSH] Publication No. 92-103). Morgantown, WV: U.S. Department of Health and Human Services, Public Health Service, Centers for Disease Control, National Institute for Occupational Safety and Health.

Strentz, T. (1987, November). A hostage psychological survival guide. *FBI Law Enforcement Bulletin*, pp. 1–8.

Symonds, M. (1983). Victimization and rehabilitative treatment. In Eichelman (Ed.), *Terrorism: Interdisciplinary perspectives*. Washington, DC: American Psychiatric Press.

**Appendix.   Hostage Questionnaire
(Post Incident)**

Name: _____   Position: _____

Date of Birth: _____   Length of Service (BOP): _____

Age: _____ Race: _____   Length of Service (Atlanta): _____

Marital Status: _____   Date of Release: _____

Education Level: _____   Date: _____

I. PLEASE CHECK IF YOU WERE EXPERIENCING THE FOLLOWING
    SYMPTOMS BEFORE THE HOSTAGE EXPERIENCE, OR IF YOU HAVE
    EXPERIENCED THEM AFTERWARDS:

	BEFORE	AFTER
Sleeping Difficulties	( )	( )
Nightmares	( )	( )
Loss of Appetite	( )	( )
Anxiety (Nervousness)	( )	( )
Depression	( )	( )
Anger	( )	( )
Irritability	( )	( )
Fatigue	( )	( )
Difficulty Concentrating	( )	( )
Memory Problems	( )	( )
Guilt	( )	( )
Intrusive Thoughts	( )	( )
Physical Problems	( )	( )
Marital Stress	( )	( )
Parenting Difficulties	( )	( )
Other	( )	( )

II. PLEASE CHECK THE FOLLOWING THAT APPLIED TO YOU IN THE
     PAST YEAR:

Adverse Personnel Action	( )
Job Change/New Job	( )
Financial Difficulties	( )
Marital Difficulties/Divorce	( )
Legal Difficulties	( )
Serious Illness	( )
Change in Residence	( )
Family Death	( )
Other	( )

III. WHAT ARE YOUR CURRENT OR IMMEDIATE NEEDS?

Personnel Information	( )
Physical Exam/Treatment	( )
Chaplaincy Services	( )

Mental Health Services   ( )
  a. Counseling   ( )
  b. Medication   ( )
Financial Assistance   ( )
Other   ( )

IV. WHAT ARE YOUR LONG TERM NEEDS?

Relocation Assistance   ( )
  (Region/Institution) _____
Career Planning/Counseling   ( )
Mental Health Services   ( )

_____

Signature of Staff Member

Appendix A ————————————————

Fear and Violence in the Workplace: A Survey Documenting the Experience of American Workers

This study examines the incidence of workplace stress, harassment and violence and the conditions at work that create them. The report offers recommendations for preventing violence in the workplace.

Executive Summary

Violence in America is spilling into the workplace, putting at risk the safety, productivity and health of American workers. In fact, chances are one in four that a worker may be attacked, threatened or harassed on the job in the next year.

In July 1993, Northwestern National Life Insurance Company (NWNL) conducted a survey and study on workplace fear and violence among 600 representative civilian workers (excluding business owners and sole proprietors). *The study is the first comprehensive assessment of the incidence of fear and violence and their effect in the workplace.*

The study revealed several significant findings:

KEY FINDING 1: Violence and harassment in the workplace are pervasive. More than 2 million Americans were victims of physical attack at the workplace during the past year. Another 6 million American workers were threatened and 16 million were harassed. Between July 1992 and July 1993, one out of four full-time workers was harassed, threatened or attacked on the job.

KEY FINDING 2: Violence and harassment affect the health and productivity of victims and other workers. Victims said they felt angry, fearful, stressed and depressed. While victims reported varying degrees of physical injury or illness, three out of four reported psychological distress. Violence and harassment also reduced productivity and increased the desire to change jobs.

KEY FINDING 3: There is a strong relationship between job stress and workplace harassment and violence. Job stress can be both a

Reprinted with permission of Northwestern National Life. All findings noted are statistically significant.

cause and an effect of workplace violence and harassment. Highly stressed workers experienced twice the rate of violence and harassment as less stressed employees. In turn, threats of violence in the workplace were linked with higher burnout rates.

KEY FINDING 4: American workers believe social issues—especially substance abuse, layoffs and poverty—are major causes of workplace violence. Most workers blamed alcohol or drug abuse, layoffs or firings, and poverty in society as major causes of on-the-job violence. To a lesser but important degree, the availability of guns, violence on TV or in the movies, job stress and job-related conflicts were identified as major causes.

KEY FINDING 5: Harassers are usually co-workers or bosses, while attackers are more likely to be customers. Most attackers and harassers were people that victims dealt with on a daily basis. Coworkers and bosses accounted for most of the harassment at work. Customers, clients and patients accounted for the largest segment of attackers. Victims identified interpersonal conflicts as the most likely reason they were harassed or threatened, and believed irrational behavior precipitated most attacks.

KEY FINDING 6: Improved interpersonal relations and effective preventive programs can result in lower levels of violence and harassment. Employees who said their employers have effective grievance, harassment and security programs reported lower rates of workplace violence. In addition, these employees reported lower levels of dissatisfaction with their jobs, lower rates of burnout and lower levels of stress-related illnesses.

Northwestern National Life commissioned the study in response to concern for the overall health and safety of employees in the workplace. The study is an outgrowth of earlier research on the effects of workplace stress on American workers, which includes *Employee Burnout: Causes and Cures, 1992; and Employee Burnout: America's Newest Epidemic, 1991.*

Definitions

Full-time Worker: Civilian employee (excluding the self-employed) who worked 35 or more hours per week for eight or more months between July 1992 and July 1993.

Harassment: The act of someone creating a hostile work environment through unwelcome words, actions, or physical contact not resulting in physical harm.

Threat: An expression of an intent to cause physical harm.

Physical Attack: Aggression resulting in a physical assault with or without the use of a weapon.

Note: NWNL used common—not legal—definitions of harassment, threatening behavior and physical attack.

Key Finding 1

> The threat of violence in two of our major social institutions, the school and workplace, is clearly more prevalent than people realize and completely intolerable. Employers and employees must work together to establish a climate of safety and respect in the workplace.
>
> Richard H. Price, PhD,
> University of Michigan, Ann Arbor

Violence and harassment in the workplace are pervasive. Violence in America is spilling into the workplace, putting at risk the safety, productivity and health of American workers. According to NWNL's study, one out of four full-time workers in America was harassed, threatened or attacked on the job in the past year. More than 2 million Americans were victims of a physical attack at work during the past year. Another 6 million American workers were threatened and 16 million were harassed. (*see Table 1*)

Overall, 15 percent of workers surveyed said they had been physically attacked at some time during their working life. (*see Table 2*) Of those workers, one in six (18 percent) was attacked with a lethal weapon. Meanwhile, 21 percent of workers have been threatened with physical harm, and one in seven (15 percent) of those incidents involved a lethal weapon.

However, the majority of harassment victims and a large share of attack and threat victims did not report the offense:

- Fifty-eight percent of harassment victims.
- Forty-three percent of threat victims.
- Twenty-four percent of attack victims.

When victims did report the incident, most informed their employer and more than 70 percent were satisfied with the actions taken.

Table 1. Approximately 2 Million Full-time Workers[a] Were Physically Attacked on the Job Between July 1992 and July 1993

On-the-job incident experienced	Percentage of workers	Rate per 100,000 workers	Number of workers (millions)
Harassment	19%	18,667	16.1
Threat of physical harm	7%	7,333	6.3
Physical attack	3%	2,500	2.2

Sample size: 600 full-time American workers.
[a]Based on 1991 Census Bureau estimates of 96.575 million full-time workers less 10.341 million self-employed workers, or a total of 86.234 million workers.

Table 2.   Violence and Harassment in the Workplace Are Pervasive

Violence, threat, harassment, or fear	Percentage of workers
Worker was harassed, threatened, or attacked on the job in the past 12 months	25%
Someone was threatened with physical harm in employee's workplace in the past 12 months	22%
Worker was threatened with physical harm on the job during lifetime	21%
Worker was harassed on the job in the past 12 months	19%
Worker was physically attacked on the job during lifetime	15%
Someone was physically attacked in employee's workplace in the past 12 months	14%
Worker considered carrying teargas or mace for protection on the job	11%
Worker is often worried about being a victim of violence on the job	10%
Worker considered bringing a gun or other deadly weapon to work for protection	4%

Sample size: 600 full-time American workers.

Some workers are at greater risk. Employees who work evenings or nights were more likely to have been:

- Attacked on the job (25 percent vs. 14 percent of those working daytime hours).
- Threatened with physical harm (37 percent vs. 19 percent).
- Harassed (29 percent vs. 17 percent).

Women reported a higher incidence of harassment (23 percent vs. 16 percent), while men were more likely to experience threats of physical harm (25 percent vs. 16 percent).

Key Finding 2

> Managers need to confront workplace violence head on. They must develop preventive education programs, just as many have done in dealing with sexual harassment. Our experience with crisis management has shown conclusively that even the threat of workplace violence has a damaging effect on morale, productivity and health.
>
> > Mark Braverman, PhD,
> > Susan Braverman, MEd, MSW,
> > Crisis Management Group, Inc., Boston

Violence and harassment affect the health and productivity of victims and other workers. Victims said they felt angry, fearful, stressed and depressed. While victims reported varying degrees of physical injury or illness, three out of four experienced psychological distress (*see Table 3*).

Table 3. Workplace Violence and Harassment Affect the Health and
Productivity of Victims

| | Percentage of . . . | | |
Effect on worker	Workplace attack victims ($n = 89$)	Workplace threat victims ($n = 127$)	Workplace harassment victims ($n = 112$)
Affected psychologically[a]	79%	77%	88%
Disrupted work life[b]	40%	36%	62%
Physically injured or sick	28%	13%	23%
No negative effect	15%	19%	7%

Sample size: 600 full-time American workers.
[a]Victim was angry, fearful, stressed, intimidated, or depressed.
[b]Victim reported at least one of the following effects: interpersonal problems, quit or changed jobs, wanted to quit, lowered productivity, or adjusted work schedule or routine.

The psychological trauma can be more distressing than the physical. A victim of a workplace robbery said, "I was very fearful. For about a year I couldn't go out by myself at night. The knife didn't hurt me, but the attack made me very nervous."
Victims of violence or harassment:

- Experienced twice the rate of stress-related conditions, including depression, anger, insomnia, headaches and ulcers (35 percent vs. 18 percent of non-victims).
- Were 20 times more likely to say their productivity was reduced (21 percent vs. 1 percent).
- Were 10 times more likely to change jobs (39 percent vs. 4 percent).

Non-victims are also affected. Just the fear of violence and harassment disrupted employees' lives.

- Twenty-one percent of workers reported that fear of harassment or violence on the job resulted in one or more of the following consequences in the past year:
  —Mental or physical distress,
  —Desire to change jobs,
  —Reduced productivity on the job,
  —Changes in what hours of the day are worked,
  —One or more days of work being missed, or
  —Changing jobs.
- Fear of harassment and violence was more likely to disrupt workers' lives in companies with recent layoffs (28 percent vs. 15 percent of companies without layoffs).

Workplace violence and fear can translate into costs to the employer in the form of increased medical and stress-related disability claims, lower productivity, higher turnover and possibly greater legal liability.

Key Finding 3

Violence is recognized as an important cause of injury and death in the workplace. What the present data teach us is that we need to begin thinking more broadly about violence at work—as a source of chronic stress and threat to productivity—and about the possible role of job stress as a cause of workplace violence.

> Steve L. Sauter, PhD,
> Naomi G. Swanson, PhD,
> National Institute for Occupational
> Safety and Health (NIOSH), Cincinnati

There is a strong relationship between job stress and workplace harassment and violence. Job stress can be both a cause and an effect of workplace violence and harassment.

- Highly stressed workers experienced twice the rate of violence and harassment as less stressed employees (40 percent vs. 19 percent).
- In turn, threats of violence in the workplace were linked with higher burnout rates (49 percent vs. 34 percent of companies where no threats occurred).

    "My boss' negative attitude made me very stressed, to the point that I didn't want to go to work," a secretary said. "I was always fearful about what he would explode about next, and it was almost impossible for me to do my best work under those conditions."

Describing an attack, an emergency room worker said, "It was very stressful. The patient's relative was upset and he struck me. I was angry because of the lack of protection."

Employee burnout—and its costs—are likely to increase with escalating workplace violence. Thirty-seven percent of those polled expected to burn out on the job in the next year or two, showing no improvement from 34 percent documented in NWNL's 1991 research on workplace stress and employee burnout. Burnout victims experienced four times the rate of stress-related illnesses and conditions (42 percent vs. 10 percent), which are often linked to lower productivity and higher health care costs. The factors contributing to stress—particularly layoffs and economic hardship—are still on the rise. Four out of 10 workers (44 percent) said their employer had layoffs in the past year, compared with 37 percent in 1991.

These findings suggest that as employee stress increases, violence, harassment and fear in the workplace are likely to escalate as well.

Key Finding 4

With today's rampant violence, no place, including the workplace, can be complacent about safety. Although the workplace may for the moment be relatively safe compared to the streets, both employers and employees must prepare for a more risky future. NWNL's study provides a good foundation for understanding the nature and extent of workplace violence.

Keith Baker, PhD,
Milton S. Eisenhower Foundation,
Washington D.C.

American workers believe social issues—especially substance abuse, layoffs, and poverty—are major causes of workplace violence. Most workers blamed alcohol or drug abuse, layoffs or firings, and poverty in society as major causes of on-the-job violence. To a lesser but important degree, the availability of guns, violence on TV or in the movies, job stress and job-related conflicts were identified as major causes. (*see Table 4*).

Other findings among workers' beliefs about major causes of workplace violence included:

- Women were more likely to believe media violence is a major cause of workplace violence (47 percent vs. 28 percent of men).
- Minorities were more likely to believe poverty is a major cause of workplace violence (62 percent vs. 50 percent of Caucasians).
- The availability of guns was considered a major cause of violence more often by women (58 percent vs. 36 percent of men) and metropolitan and suburban workers (50 percent vs. 38 percent of rural/small town workers).

A shoe salesman who was attacked by a former employee said, "He felt I did something that made him lose his job. It started out as a shouting match, and then a shove here and a shove there."

Table 4. American Workers Believe Social Issues—Especially Substance Abuse, Drugs, Layoffs and Poverty—Are Major Causes of Workplace Violence.

Factor	(*n*)	Cause of workplace violence (percentage of workers)		
		Major	Minor	Not a cause
Alcohol abuse or illegal drug use	(594)	59%	31%	10%
Layoffs or firings	(596)	53%	38%	9%
Poverty in society	(592)	52%	36%	12%
Availability of guns	(596)	46%	31%	24%
Violence on TV or in movies	(595)	36%	45%	19%
Pressure of too much work on the job	(594)	34%	53%	13%
Overly controlling management	(589)	32%	55%	12%
Conflicts with co-workers	(592)	28%	62%	11%

Sample size: 600 full-time American workers.

"I was threatened by a former employee because I had to fire him," reported a warehouse supervisor. "He threatened to destroy my vehicle while I was at work. I was worried what would happen to me."

Key Finding 5

Harassers are usually co-workers or bosses, while attackers are more likely to be customers. Most attackers and harassers were people that victims dealt with on a daily basis (*see Table 5*):

- Customers, clients and patients accounted for the largest segment of attackers (44 percent).
- Co-workers and bosses accounted for 86 percent of all harassment at work, one third of threats, and one fourth of workplace attacks.

"My boss knocked me around in the hall. It didn't hurt me as much physically as mentally," said a machine operator. "I don't think my work has gone down, but I cry a lot. He humiliates and intimidates me. I try to stay away from him but it's been two years."

Interpersonal conflict is considered the main reason for harassment; irrational behavior is likely cause of attacks. Victims cited reasons for the violence and harassment they experienced.

- Forty-six percent of workplace harassment victims and 27 percent of workers who had been threatened identified job-related interpersonal conflict as the likely cause.
- Irrational behavior, such as mental disturbance or influence of al-

Table 5. Harassers Are Usually CoWorkers or Bosses, While Attackers Are More Likely to be Customers

	Percentage of		
Perpetrator	Workplace attack victims[a] (n = 89)	Workplace threat victims[a] (n = 127)	Workplace harassment victims[b] (n = 112)
Customer or client[c]	44%	36%	15%
Stranger	24	16	2
Co-worker other than boss	20	32	47
Boss	7	5	39
Former employee	3	6	2
Someone else	3	7	2
Total	101%	102%	107%

Sample size: 600 full-time American workers.
Note: Columns total more than 100 percent if more than one person attacked, threatened or harassed the worker.
[a]Most recent event in lifetime.
[b]Most recent event in past year.
[c]Includes students, patients and inmates.

cohol or drug use on the part of the perpetrator, was the reason given by 26 percent of workplace attack victims and 21 percent of workplace threat victims.

- Twenty-three percent of workplace threat victims and 19 percent of workers who had been attacked on the job cited the customers' dissatisfaction with service as the reason they were victimized.

A truck driver described work conflicts that escalated into harassment. "My boss felt threatened and began pitting employees against each other. You would have to check your work because sometimes co-workers would mess with it to make you look bad. When you're worried all the time you can't do your job."

Key Finding 6

Violence and its threat sabotages the fundamental human need for a sense of security and place in the world. While the temptation to take strong actions against violence after the fact is attractive to many, a wiser and ultimately more effective course is that which looks at prevention.

Michael Resnick, PhD,
University of Minnesota, Minneapolis

Improved interpersonal relations and effective prevention programs can result in lower levels of violence and harassment. Employees who said their employers have effective grievance, harassment and security programs reported lower rates of workplace violence. In addition, these employees reported lower levels of dissatisfaction with their jobs (5 percent vs. 21 percent of workers whose employers don't have programs), lower rates of burnout (28 percent vs. 44 percent) and lower levels of stress-related illnesses (13 percent vs. 29 percent) (see Table 6).

"A patient came after me with a lit cigarette," a psychiatric nurse said. "I was angry that the incident occurred because there wasn't adequate staffing at the time, and I felt it could have been avoided if more security precautions had been taken."

The rate of workplace violence was substantially reduced if employers:

- Promoted harmony in work groups.
- Allowed employees adequate control in how they did their work.
- Were supportive of employees.
- Encouraged teamwork and supportiveness among co-workers.
- Provided training in how to reduce interpersonal conflicts.
- Handled grievances effectively.
- Protected employees from harassment.
- Provided effective security.

Table 6. Improved Interpersonal Relations and Effective Preventive Programs
Can Result in Lower Levels of Violence and Harassment

	Percentage of workers	
Employees report they:	Employer has grievance, harassment, and security programs	Employer does not have all three programs
Will burn out in the next year or two	28%	44%
Experience a lot of job stress	22%	32%
Have been attacked, threatened or harassed in past 12 months	18%	31%
Worry about being laid off or fired in the next year	14%	21%
Experience high levels of stress-related illness	13%	29%
Have no harmony in their work group	13%	27%
Have been harassed on the job in the past 12 months	13%	23%
Cannot rely on supervisor for support	11%	30%
Were attacked or threatened on the job in the past 5 years	11%	21%
Are dissatisfied with their job	5%	21%

Sample size: 600 full-time American workers.

"I was kind of afraid to go to my employer," said a school bus driver who had been fondled by a co-worker. "But my boss took care of it immediately, and then I was fine."

Top 10 Ways to Prevent Violence in the Workplace

There is no single prescription for reducing violence in the workplace. Each organization is unique and operates in a different social and economic environment. When planning workplace safety issues, employers may want to consider the organization's culture, history, size, industry and work force.

These 10 solutions are based on responses from survey participants and recommendations from experts who guided the research. The suggestions should be modified to best accommodate the needs of an organization.

1. Foster a supportive, harmonious work environment. Creating a culture of mutual respect can help reduce harassment and hostility in the workplace. In such a culture, employers strive to communicate openly, give employees adequate control in their work and provide them with support and recognition. Conflict and stress are lower when employees feel empowered to work independently and are motivated to work cooperatively.

2. Train supervisors and employees how to resolve conflicts. Conflicts on the job can be reduced by developing employees' skills in negotiating, communicating effectively, team building, and resolving disputes. Furthermore, programs that encourage respect for diversity can help to lessen interpersonal conflicts.

3. Develop effective policies to protect employees from harassment. While all companies strive to build a culture free of harassment and discrimination, they can advance this goal by having systems in place to address infractions. The key is a company harassment policy that clearly denounces harassment and states unequivocally that it will not be tolerated. A thorough policy defines harassment, specifies how to report it, explains how complaints will be investigated and presents the consequences.

4. Establish procedures for handling grievances. Employees need to understand grievance procedures for reporting complaints of unfair treatment, discrimination or harassment; believe that those procedures will be followed; and feel confident that concerns will be addressed promptly and confidentially.

5. Provide personal counseling through an employee assistance program. Family, marital, financial, and personal issues can have a profound impact on employees' work performance as well as their social interactions at work. An employee assistance program (EAP) provides employees with a free, easily-accessible and confidential resource for addressing personal concerns. In addition, supervisors can be trained how to document and address work performance and attitude problems and refer employees for help. If a violent or threatening incident occurs at work, support services can be made available to help employees cope with their fears and concerns.

6. Implement security programs that protect employees. Employers have a variety of methods for ensuring workers' safety, such as full-time or after-hours security guards, high-tech monitoring systems, emergency warning systems, limited access key cards, strict visitor sign-in policies, new employee background screening, and safety awareness and training. Companies that regularly evaluate their security programs can best determine if they are meeting company and employee needs. Also, employers need to make sure that employees are aware of and understand existing security policies and procedures.

7. Provide employee safety education programs. In addition to making workers aware of company safety policies and employee support services, employers can provide educational materials and seminars about ways to maximize safety at work.

8. Provide job counseling for employees who have been laid off or fired. Because a job is often closely tied to one's identity, being laid off can be traumatic. Employee counseling and support services can help workers develop job-seeking skills, learn how to cope with life changes, and personally and financially prepare for the future. These services also help exiting employees feel that the company cares about them. It is helpful to train supervisors to sensitively communicate layoffs or firings.

9. Train supervisors on how to recognize signs of a troubled employee. One way to reduce the potential for workplace violence is to intervene before an incident reaches a flash point. Supervisors can be given training on how to recognize signs and symptoms of a potentially violent employee, such as threatening behavior or pre-occupation with violence. Also, supervisors can be instructed on how to be sensitive to signs of possible abuse among employees, such as frequent absences or depression.

10. Set up a crisis plan. Employers may want to consider developing a crisis plan for dealing with violent incidents. The plan can include details on how to report the incident, which key internal managers and external authorities should be alerted, how to maintain the safety of unaffected workers and security precautions to prevent further trouble. Companies also can arrange to provide individual crisis counseling and support groups for affected employees soon after the incident occurs.

About the Survey

"Fear and Violence in the Workplace" is a national survey of a representative sample of 600 full-time American workers. The survey was designed and analyzed by the Employee Benefits Division of Northwestern National Life (NWNL) and reviewed by a blue-ribbon panel of violence and stress experts. NWNL commissioned N. K. Friedrichs, an independent research firm based in Minneapolis, to conduct 15-minute telephone interviews with 600 full-time American workers in July 1993.

The workers polled were drawn from a national random sample of adults who work full time. Workers who are self-employed or enlisted in the military were excluded. The sample was drawn to accurately reflect the male-female ratio of the work force and the distribution of the work force among the four census regions in the United States.

Tests of significant differences were conducted at the 95 percent confidence level. The poll has a sampling error of plus or minus four percentage points. In conducting this survey, NWNL used common—not legal—definitions of harassment, threatening behavior and physical attack. Projections of the working population affected by harassment, threats and physical attacks are based on survey findings and work force data supplied by the U.S. Department of Commerce, Bureau of the Census.

About the Researcher and Panelists

Research design and analysis were conducted by Peggy Lawless, research project director, Northwestern National Life Insurance Company, Minneapolis. Lawless conducts major research projects on a broad range of health care and employee benefit issues, focusing on U.S. workers and

Profile of Respondents

Gender	
Male	57%
Female	43
	100%

Census Region	
Northeast	21%
Midwest	25
South	34
West	21
	100%

Age	
19 to 24	10%
25 to 34	30
35 to 44	34
45 to 54	19
55 to 64	7
	100%

Race	
White or Caucasian	84%
Black or African American	10
Hispanic or Latino	4
Native American	1
Other	1
	100%

Occupation	
Managers and Professionals	39%
Technical, Sales, and Administrative Support	28
Craftsmen, Operators, and Laborers; Farming, Fishing, and Forestry	26
Business and Personal Services	7
	100%

Union Affiliation	
Non-union	80%
Union member	20
	100%

Supervisory Responsibility	
Non-supervisor	52%
Supervisor	48
	100%

Working Hours	
8:00 a.m. to 5:00 p.m.	89%
5:00 p.m. to midnight	5
Midnight to 8:00 a.m.	4
Other	2
	100%

Workplace Location	
Central city of metropolitan area	37%
Suburb	27
Small town	26
Rural area	10
	100%

Worksite Size	
Fewer than 50 employees	42%
50 to 249 employees	29
250 to 999 employees	17
1,000 or more employees	12
	100%

Employer	
For-profit business	66%
State or local government	16
Non-profit organization	11
Federal government	7
	100%

Columns may total more than 100 percent due to rounding.

their employees. Her research helps employers solve current problems and identify future trends.

Eight experts on violence and workplace stress reviewed the research design and analysis:

Mark Braverman, PhD
Susan Braverman, MEd, MSW

Principals of Crisis Management Group in Boston. Experts on the prevention of workplace trauma and intervention strategies.

Lynn Curtis, PhD
Keith Baker, PhD

Dr. Curtis is President of Evaluation and Dr. Baker is Deputy Director for the Milton F. Eisenhower Foundation in Washington D.C. Dr. Curtis is also author of *American Violence and Public Policy*, *Criminal Violence*, and *Violence, Race and Culture*. The foundation explores the causes of violence in the United States.

Richard Price, PhD

Professor of Psychology for the Institute for Social Research at the University of Michigan in Ann Arbor. An expert on the prevention of job stress.

Michael Resnick, PhD

Sociologist and director of the National Adolescent Health Resource Center at the University of Minnesota in Minneapolis. An expert on children and violence.

Steve Sauter, PhD
Naomi Swanson, PhD

Dr. Sauter is Branch Chief of Psychology and Ergonomics, and Dr. Swanson is Chief of Motivation and Stress at the National Institute for Occupational Safety and Health in Cincinnati. Experts on the identification, treatment and prevention of organizational stress.

Appendix B _____

Guidelines for Preventing Workplace Violence for Health Care and Social Service Workers

U.S. Department of Labor
Robert B. Reich, Secretary

Occupational Safety and Health Administration
Joseph A. Dear, Assistant Secretary

Introduction

For many years, health care and social service workers have faced a significant risk of job-related violence. Assaults represent a serious safety and health hazard for these industries, and violence against their employees continues to increase.

OSHA's new violence prevention guidelines provide the agency's recommendations for reducing workplace violence developed following a careful review of workplace violence studies, public and private violence prevention programs, and consultations with and input from stakeholders.

OSHA encourages employers to establish violence prevention programs and to track their progress in reducing work-related assaults. Although not every incident can be prevented, many can, and the severity of injuries sustained by employees reduced. Adopting practical measures such as those outlined here can significantly reduce this serious threat to worker safety.

OSHA's Commitment

The publication and distribution of these guidelines is OSHA's first step in assisting health care and social service employers and providers in preventing workplace violence. OSHA plans to conduct a coordinated effort consisting of research, information, training, cooperative programs, and appropriate enforcement to accomplish this goal.

_____
Reprinted with permission of the authors.

The guidelines are **not** a new standard or regulation. They are advisory in nature, informational in content, and intended for use by employers in providing a safe and healthful workplace through effective violence prevention programs, adapted to the needs and resources of each place of employment.

Extent of Problem

Today, more assaults occur in the health care and social services industries than in any other. For example, Bureau of Labor Statistics (BLS) data for 1993 showed health care and social service workers having the highest incidence of assault injuries (BLS, 1993). Almost two-thirds of the nonfatal assaults occurred in nursing homes, hospitals, and establishments providing residential care and other social services (Toscano and Weber, 1995).

Assaults against workers in the health professions are not new. According to one study (Goodman et al., 1994), between 1980 and 1990, 106 occupational violence-related deaths occurred among the following health care workers: 27 pharmacists, 26 physicians, 18 registered nurses, 17 nurses' aides, and 18 health care workers in other occupational categories. Using the National Traumatic Occupational Fatality database, the study reported that between 1983 and 1989, there were 69 registered nurses killed at work. Homicide was the leading cause of traumatic occupational death among employees in nursing homes and personal care facilities.

A 1989 report (Carmel & Hunter) found that the nursing staff at a psychiatric hospital sustained 16 assaults per 100 employees per year. This rate, which includes any assault-related injuries, compares with 8.3 injuries of **all** types per 100 full-time workers in all industries and 14.2 per 100 full-time workers in the construction industry (BLS, 1991). Of 121 psychiatric hospital workers sustaining 134 injuries, 43 percent involved lost time from work with 13 percent of those injured missing more than 21 days from work.

Of greater concern is the likely underreporting of violence and a persistent perception within the health care industry that assaults are part of the job. Underreporting may reflect a lack of institutional reporting policies, employee beliefs that reporting will not benefit them, or employee fears that employers may deem assaults the result of employee negligence or poor job performance.

Risk Factors

Health care and social service workers face an increased risk of work-related assaults stemming from several factors, including:

- The prevalence of handguns and other weapons—as high as 25 percent[1]—among patients, their families, or friends. The increasing use of hospitals by police and the criminal justice systems for criminal holds and the care of acutely disturbed, violent individuals.
- The increasing number of acute and chronically mentally ill patients now being released from hospitals without followup care, who now have the right to refuse medicine and who can no longer be hospitalized involuntarily unless they pose an immediate threat to themselves or others.
- The availability of drugs or money at hospitals, clinics, and pharmacies, making them likely robbery targets.
- Situational and circumstantial factors such as unrestricted movement of the public in clinics and hospitals; the increasing presence of gang members, drug or alcohol abusers, trauma patients, or distraught family members; long waits in emergency or clinic areas, leading to client frustration over an inability to obtain needed services promptly.
- Low staffing levels during times of specific increased activity such as meal times, visiting times, and when staff are transporting patients.
- Isolated work with clients during examinations or treatment.
- Solo work, often in remote locations, particularly in high-crime settings, with no back-up or means of obtaining assistance such as communication devices or alarm systems.
- Lack of training of staff in recognizing and managing escalating hostile and assaultive behavior.
- Poorly lighted parking areas.

Overview of Guidelines

In January 1989, OSHA published voluntary, generic safety and health program management guidelines for all employers to use as a foundation for their safety and health programs, which can include a workplace violence prevention program.[2] OSHA's violence prevention guidelines build on the 1989 generic guidelines by identifying common risk factors and describing some feasible solutions. Although not exhaustive, the new workplace violence guidelines include policy recommendations and practical corrective methods to help prevent and mitigate the effects of workplace violence.

The goal is to eliminate or reduce worker exposure to conditions that lead to death or injury from violence by implementing effective security devices and administrative work practices, among other control measures.

---

[1]According to a 1989 report (Wasserberger), 25 percent of major trauma patients treated in the emergency room carried weapons. Attacks in emergency rooms in gang-related shootings as well as planned escapes from police custody have been documented in hospitals. A 1991 report (Goetz et al.) also found that 17.3 percent of psychiatric patients searched were carrying weapons.

[2]OSHA's *Safety and Health Program Management Guidelines* (*Fed Reg 54*(16), 3904–3916, January 26, 1989), provide for comprehensive safety and health programs containing these major elements. Employers with such programs can include workplace violence prevention efforts in that context.

The guidelines cover a broad spectrum of workers who provide health care and social services in psychiatric facilities, hospital emergency departments, community mental health clinics, drug abuse treatment clinics, pharmacies, community care facilities, and long-term care facilities. They include physicians, registered nurses, pharmacists, nurse practitioners, physicians' assistants, nurses' aides, therapists, technicians, public health nurses, home health care workers, social/welfare workers, and emergency medical care personnel. Further, the guidelines may be useful in reducing risks for ancillary personnel such as maintenance, dietary, clerical, and security staff employed in the health care and social services industries.

Violence Prevention Program Elements

There are four main components to any effective safety and health program that also apply to preventing workplace violence, (1) management commitment and employee involvement, (2) worksite analysis, (3) hazard prevention and control, and (4) safety and health training.

Management Commitment and Employee Involvement

Management commitment and employee involvement are complementary and essential elements of an effective safety and health program. To ensure an effective program, management and front-line employees must work together, perhaps through a team or committee approach. If employers opt for this strategy, they must be careful to comply with the applicable provisions of the National Labor Relations Act.[3]

Management commitment, including the endorsement and visible involvement of top management, provides the motivation and resources to deal effectively with workplace violence, and should include the following:

- Demonstrated organizational concern for employee emotional and physical safety and health.
- Equal commitment to worker safety and health and patient/client safety.
- Assigned responsibility for the various aspects of the workplace violence prevention program to ensure that all managers, supervisors, and employees understand their obligations.
- Appropriate allocation of authority and resources to all responsible parties.
- A system of accountability for involved managers, supervisors, and employees.
- A comprehensive program of medical and psychological counseling and debriefing for employees experiencing or witnessing assaults and other violent incidents.

---

[3]Title 29 U.S.C., Section 158(a)(2).

- Commitment to support and implement appropriate recommendations from safety and health committees.

Employee involvement and feedback enable workers to develop and express their own commitment to safety and health and provide useful information to design, implement, and evaluate the program.

Employee involvement should include the following:

- Understanding and complying with the workplace violence prevention program and other safety and security measures.
- Participation in an employee complaint or suggestion procedure covering safety and security concerns.
- Prompt and accurate reporting of violent incidents.
- Participation on safety and health committees or teams that receive reports of violent incidents or security problems, make facility inspections, and respond with recommendations for corrective strategies.
- Taking part in a continuing education program that covers techniques to recognize escalating agitation, assaultive behavior, or criminal intent, and discusses appropriate responses.

Written Program

A written program for job safety and security, incorporated into the organization's overall safety and health program, offers an effective approach for larger organizations. In smaller establishments, the program need not be written or heavily documented to be satisfactory. What is needed are clear goals and objectives to prevent workplace violence suitable for the size and complexity of the workplace operation and adaptable to specific situations in each establishment.

The prevention program and startup date must be communicated to all employees. At a minimum, workplace violence prevention programs should do the following:

- Create and disseminate a clear policy of zero-tolerance for workplace violence, verbal and nonverbal threats, and related actions. Managers, supervisors, co-workers, clients, patients, and visitors must be advised of this policy.
- Ensure that no reprisals are taken against an employee who reports or experiences workplace violence.[4]
- Encourage employees to promptly report incidents and to suggest

---

[4]Section 11 (c)(1) of the OSH Act, which also applies to protected activity involving the hazard of workplace violence as it does for other health and safety matters: "No person shall discharge or in any manner discriminate against any employee because such employee has filed any complaint or instituted or caused to be instituted any proceeding under or related to this Act or has testified or is about to testify in any such proceeding or because of the exercise by such employee on behalf of himself or others of any right afforded by this Act."

ways to reduce or eliminate risks. Require records of incidents to assess risk and to measure progress.

- Outline a comprehensive plan for maintaining security in the workplace, which includes establishing a liaison with law enforcement representatives and others who can help identify ways to prevent and mitigate workplace violence.
- Assign responsibility and authority for the program to individuals or teams with appropriate training or skills. The written plan should ensure that there are adequate resources available for this effort and that the team or responsible individuals develop expertise on workplace violence prevention in health care and social services.
- Affirm management commitment to a worker-supportive environment that places as much importance on employee safety and health as on serving the patient or client.
- Set up a company briefing as part of the initial effort to address such issues as preserving safety, supporting affected employees, and facilitating recovery.

Worksite Analysis

Worksite analysis involves a step-by-step, commonsense look at the workplace to find existing or potential hazards for workplace violence. This entails reviewing specific procedures or operations that contribute to hazards and specific locales where hazards may develop.

A "Threat Assessment Team," "Patient Assault Team," similar task force, or coordinator may assess the vulnerability to workplace violence and determine the appropriate preventive actions to be taken. Implementing the workplace violence prevention program then may be assigned to this group. The team should include representatives from senior management, operations, employee assistance, security, occupational safety and health, legal, and human resources staff.

The team or coordinator can review injury and illness records and workers' compensation claims to identify patterns of assaults that could be prevented by workplace adaptation, procedural changes, or employee training. As the team or coordinator identifies appropriate controls, these should be instituted.

The recommended program for worksite analysis includes, but is not limited to, analyzing and tracking records, monitoring trends and analyzing incidents, screening surveys, and analyzing workplace security.

Records Analysis and Tracking

This activity should include reviewing medical, safety, workers' compensation and insurance records—including the OSHA 200 log, if required—to pinpoint instances of workplace violence. Scan unit logs and employee and police reports of incidents or near-incidents of assaultive behavior to identify and analyze trends in assaults relative to particular departments, units, job titles, unit activities, work stations, and/or time of day. Tabulate these data to target the frequency and severity of incidents to establish a baseline for measuring improvement.

Monitoring Trends and Analyzing Incidents

Contacting similar local businesses, trade associations, and community and civic groups is one way to learn about their experiences with workplace violence and to help identify trends. Use several years of data, if possible, to trace trends of injuries and incidents of actual or potential workplace violence.

Screening Surveys

One important screening tool is to give employees a questionnaire or survey to get their ideas on the potential for violent incidents and to identify or confirm the need for improved security measures. Detailed baseline screening surveys can help pinpoint tasks that put employees at risk. Periodic surveys—conducted at least annually or whenever operations change or incidents of workplace violence occur—help identify new or previously unnoticed risk factors and deficiencies or failures in work practices, procedures, or controls. Also, the surveys help assess the effects of changes in the work processes. The periodic review process should also include feedback and followup.

Independent reviewers, such as safety and health professionals, law enforcement or security specialists, insurance safety auditors, and other qualified persons may offer advice to strengthen programs. These experts also can provide fresh perspectives to improve a violence prevention program.

Workplace Security Analysis

The team or coordinator should periodically inspect the workplace and evaluate employee tasks to identify hazards, conditions, operations, and situations that could lead to violence.

To find areas requiring further evaluation, the team or coordinator should do the following:

- Analyze incidents, including the characteristics of assailants and victims, an account of what happened before and during the incident, and the relevant details of the situation and its outcome. When possible, obtain police reports and recommendations.
- Identify jobs or locations with the greatest risk of violence as well as processes and procedures that put employees at risk of assault, including how often and when.

- Note high-risk factors such as types of clients or patients (e.g., psychiatric conditions or patients disoriented by drugs, alcohol, or stress); physical risk factors of the building; isolated locations/job activities; lighting problems; lack of phones and other communication devices, areas of easy, unsecured access; and areas with previous security problems.
- Evaluate the effectiveness of existing security measures, including engineering control measures. Determine if risk factors have been reduced or eliminated, and take appropriate action.

Hazard Prevention and Control

After hazards of violence are identified through the systematic worksite analysis, the next step is to design measures through engineering or administrative and work practices to prevent or control these hazards. If violence does occur, post-incidence response can be an important tool in preventing future incidents.

Engineering Controls and Workplace Adaptation

Engineering controls, for example, remove the hazard from the workplace or create a barrier between the worker and the hazard. There are several measures that can effectively prevent or control workplace hazards, such as those actions presented in the following paragraphs. The selection of any measure, of course, should be based upon the hazards identified in the workplace security analysis of each facility.

- Assess any plans for new construction or physical changes to the facility or workplace to eliminate or reduce security hazards.
- Install and regularly maintain alarm systems and other security devices, panic buttons, hand-held alarms or noise devices, cellular phones, and private channel radios where risk is apparent or may be anticipated, and arrange for a reliable response system when an alarm is triggered.
- Provide metal detectors—installed or hand-held, where appropriate—to identify guns, knives, or other weapons, according to the recommendations of security consultants.
- Use a closed-circuit video recording for high-risk areas on a 24-hour basis. Public safety is a greater concern than privacy in these situations.
- Place curved mirrors at hallway intersections or concealed areas.
- Enclose nurses' stations, and install deep service counters or bullet-resistant, shatter-proof glass in reception areas, triage, admitting, or client service rooms.
- Provide employee "safe rooms" for use during emergencies.
- Establish "time-out" or seclusion areas with high ceilings without

grids for patients acting out and establish separate rooms for criminal patients.

- Provide client or patient waiting rooms designed to maximize comfort and minimize stress.
- Ensure that counseling or patient care rooms have two exits.
- Limit access to staff counseling rooms and treatment rooms controlled by using locked doors.
- Arrange furniture to prevent entrapment of staff. In interview rooms or crisis treatment areas, furniture should be minimal, lightweight, without sharp corners or edges, and/or affixed to the floor. Limit the number of pictures, vases, ashtrays, or other items that can be used as weapons.
- Provide lockable and secure bathrooms for staff members separate from patient-client, and visitor facilities.
- Lock all unused doors to limit access, in accordance with local fire codes.
- Install bright, effective lighting indoors and outdoors.
- Replace burned-out lights, broken windows, and locks.
- Keep automobiles, if used in the field, well-maintained. Always lock automobiles.

Administrative and Work Practice Controls

Administrative and work practice controls affect the way jobs or tasks are performed. The following examples illustrate how changes in work practices and administrative procedures can help prevent violent incidents.

- State clearly to patients, clients, and employees that violence is not permitted or tolerated.
- Establish liaison with local police and state prosecutors. Report all incidents of violence. Provide police with physical layouts of facilities to expedite investigations.
- Require employees to report all assaults or threats to a supervisor or manager (e.g., can be confidential interview). Keep log books and reports of such incidents to help in determining any necessary actions to prevent further occurrences.
- Advise and assist employees, if needed, of company procedures for requesting police assistance or filing charges when assaulted.
- Provide management support during emergencies. Respond promptly to all complaints.
- Set up a trained response team to respond to emergencies.
- Use properly trained security officers, when necessary, to deal with aggressive behavior. Follow written security procedures.
- Ensure adequate and properly trained staff for restraining patients or clients.
- Provide sensitive and timely information to persons waiting in line or in waiting rooms. Adopt measures to decrease waiting time.

- Ensure adequate and qualified staff coverage at all times. Times of greatest risk occur during patient transfers, emergency responses, meal times, and at night. Locales with the greatest risk include admission units and crisis or acute care units. Other risks include admission of patients with a history of violent behavior or gang activity.
- Institute a sign-in procedure with passes for visitors, especially in a newborn nursery or pediatric department. Enforce visitor hours and procedures.
- Establish a list of "restricted visitors" for patients with a history of violence. Copies should be available at security checkpoints, nurses' stations, and visitor sign-in areas. Review and revise visitor check systems, when necessary. Limit information given to outsiders on hospitalized victims of violence.
- Supervise the movement of psychiatric clients and patients throughout the facility.
- Control access to facilities other than waiting rooms, particularly drug storage or pharmacy areas.
- Prohibit employees from working alone in emergency areas or walk-in clinics, particularly at night or when assistance is unavailable. Employees should never enter seclusion rooms alone.
- Establish policies and procedures for secured areas, and emergency evacuations, and for monitoring high-risk patients at night (e.g., open versus locked seclusion).
- Ascertain the behavioral history of new and transferred patients to learn about any past violent or assaultive behaviors. Establish a system—such as chart tags, log books, or verbal census reports—to identify patients and clients with assaultive behavior problems, keeping in mind patient confidentiality and worker safety issues. Update as needed.
- Treat and/or interview aggressive or agitated clients in relatively open areas that still maintain privacy and confidentiality (e.g., rooms with removable partitions).
- Use case management conferences with co-workers and supervisors to discuss ways to effectively treat potentially violent patients.
- Prepare contingency plans to treat clients who are "acting out" or making verbal or physical attacks or threats. Consider using certified employee assistance professionals (CEAPs) or in-house social service or occupational health service staff to help diffuse patient or client anger.
- Transfer assaultive clients to "acute care units," "criminal units," or other more restrictive settings.
- Make sure that nurses and/or physicians are not alone when performing intimate physical examinations of patients.
- Discourage employees from wearing jewelry to help prevent possible strangulation in confrontational situations. Community workers should carry only required identification and money.
- Periodically survey the facility to remove tools or possessions left

by visitors or maintenance staff which could be used inappropriately by patients.

- Provide staff with identification badges, preferably without last names, to readily verify employment.
- Discourage employees from carrying keys, pens, or other items that could be used as weapons.
- Provide staff members with security escorts to parking areas in evening or late hours. Parking areas should be highly visible, well-lighted, and safely accessible to the building.
- Use the "buddy system," especially when personal safety may be threatened. Encourage home health care providers, social service workers, and others to avoid threatening situations. Staff should exercise extra care in elevators, stairwells and unfamiliar residences; immediately leave premises if there is a hazardous situation; or request police escort if needed.
- Develop policies and procedures covering home health care providers, such as contracts on how visits will be conducted, the presence of others in the home during the visits, and the refusal to provide services in a clearly hazardous situation.
- Establish a daily work plan for field staff to keep a designated contact person informed about workers' whereabouts throughout the workday. If an employee does not report in, the contact person should followup.
- Conduct a comprehensive post-incident evaluation, including psychological as well as medical treatment, for employees who have been subjected to abusive behavior.

Post-Incident Response

Post-incident response and evaluation are essential to an effective violence prevention program. All workplace violence programs should provide comprehensive treatment for victimized employees and employees who may be traumatized by witnessing a workplace violence incident. Injured staff should receive prompt treatment and psychological evaluation whenever an assault takes place, regardless of severity. Transportation of the injured to medical care should be provided if care is not available on-site.

Victims of workplace violence suffer a variety of consequences in addition to their actual physical injuries. These include short and long-term psychological trauma, fear of returning to work, changes in relationships with co-workers and family, feelings of incompetence, guilt, powerlessness, and fear of criticism by supervisors or managers. Consequently, a strong followup program for these employees will not only help them to deal with these problems but also to help prepare them to confront or prevent future incidents of violence.

There are several types of assistance that can be incorporated into the post-incident response. For example, trauma-crisis counseling, critical incident stress debriefing, or employee assistance programs may be provided to assist victims. Certified employee assistance professionals, psychologists, psychiatrists, clinical nurse specialists, or social workers could provide this counseling, or the employer can refer staff victims to an outside specialist. In addition, an employee counseling service, peer counseling, or support groups may be established.

In any case, counselors must be well trained and have a good understanding of the issues and consequences of assaults and other aggressive, violent behavior. Appropriate and promptly rendered post-incident debriefings and counseling reduce acute psychological trauma and general stress levels among victims and witnesses. In addition, such counseling educates staff about workplace violence and positively influences workplace and organizational cultural norms to reduce trauma associated with future incidents.

Training and Education

Training and education ensure that all staff are aware of potential security hazards and how to protect themselves and their co-workers through established policies and procedures.

All Employees

Every employee should understand the concept of "Universal Precautions for Violence," i.e., that violence should be expected but can be avoided or mitigated through preparation. Staff should be instructed to limit physical interventions in workplace altercations whenever possible, unless there are adequate numbers of staff or emergency response teams and security personnel available. Frequent training also can improve the likelihood of avoiding assault (Carmel & Hunter, 1990).

Employees who may face safety and security hazards should receive formal instruction on the specific hazards associated with the unit or job and facility. This includes information on the types of injuries or problems identified in the facility and the methods to control the specific hazards.

The training program should involve all employees, including supervisors and managers. New and reassigned employees should receive an initial orientation prior to being assigned their job duties. Visiting staff, such as physicians, should receive the same training as permanent staff. Qualified trainers should instruct at the comprehension level appropriate for the staff. Effective training programs should involve role playing, simulations, and drills.

Topics may include Management of Assaultive Behavior; Professional Assault Response Training; police assault avoidance programs, or personal safety training such as awareness, avoidance, and how to prevent assaults. A combination of training may be used depending on the severity of the risk.

Required training should be provided to employees annually. In large institutions, refresher programs may be needed more frequently (monthly or quarterly) to effectively reach and inform all employees.

The training should cover topics such as the following:

- The workplace violence prevention policy.
- Risk factors that cause or contribute to assaults.
- Early recognition of escalating behavior or recognition of warning signs or situations that may lead to assaults.
- Ways of preventing or diffusing volatile situations or aggressive behavior, managing anger, and appropriately using medications as chemical restraints.
- Information on multicultural diversity to develop sensitivity to racial and ethnic issues and differences.
- A standard response action plan for violent situations, including availability of assistance, response to alarm systems, and communication procedures.
- How to deal with hostile persons other than patients and clients, such as relatives and visitors.
- Progressive behavior control methods and safe methods of restraint application or escape.
- The location and operation of safety devices such as alarm systems, along with the required maintenance schedules and procedures.
- Ways to protect oneself and coworkers, including use of the "buddy system."
- Policies and procedures for reporting and recordkeeping.
- Policies and procedures for obtaining medical care, counseling, workers' compensation, or legal assistance after a violent episode or injury.

Supervisors, Managers, and Security Personnel

Supervisors and managers should ensure that employees are not placed in assignments that compromise safety and should encourage employees to report incidents. Employees and supervisors should be trained to behave compassionately towards coworkers when an incident occurs.

They should learn how to reduce security hazards and ensure that employees receive appropriate training. Following training, supervisors and managers should be able to recognize a potentially hazardous situation and to make any necessary changes in the physical plant, patient care treatment program, and staffing policy and procedures to reduce or eliminate the hazards.

Security personnel need specific training from the hospital or clinic, including the psychological components of handling aggressive and abusive clients, types of disorders, and ways to handle aggression and defuse hostile situations.

The training program should also include an evaluation. The content, methods, and frequency of training should be reviewed and evaluated annually by the team or coordinator responsible for implementation. Program evaluation may involve supervisor and/or employee interviews, testing and observing, and/or reviewing reports of behavior of individuals in threatening situations.

Recordkeeping and Evaluation of the Program

Recordkeeping and evaluation of the violence prevention program are necessary to determine overall effectiveness and identify any deficiencies or changes that should be made.

Recordkeeping

Recordkeeping is essential to the success of a workplace violence prevention program. Good records help employers determine the severity of the problem, evaluate methods of hazard control, and identify training needs. Records can be especially useful to large organizations and for members of a business group or trade association who "pool" data. Records of injuries, illnesses, accidents, assaults, hazards, corrective actions, patient histories, and training, among others, can help identify problems and solutions for an effective program.

The following records are important:

- OSHA Log of Injury and Illness (OSHA 200). OSHA regulations require entry on the Injury and Illness Log of any injury that requires more than first aid, is a lost-time injury, requires modified duty, or causes loss of consciousness.[5] (This applies only to establishments required to keep OSHA logs.) Injuries caused by assaults, which are otherwise recordable, also must be entered on the log. A fatality or catastrophe that results in the hospitalization of 3 or more employees must be **reported to OSHA within 8 hours**. This includes those resulting from workplace violence and applies to **all** establishments.
- Medical reports of work injury and supervisors' reports for each recorded assault should be kept. These records should describe the type of assault, i.e., unprovoked sudden attack or patient-to-patient altercation; who was assaulted; and all other circumstances of the incident. The records should include a description of the environment or location, potential or actual cost, lost time, and the nature of injuries sustained.
- Incidents of abuse, verbal attacks or aggressive behavior—which

---

[5]The Occupational Safety and Health Act and recordkeeping regulations in *Title 29 Code of Federal Regulations (CFR), Part 1904* provide specific recording requirements that comprise the framework of the occupational safety and health recording system (BLS, 1986a). BLS has issued guidelines that provide official Agency interpretations concerning the recordkeeping and reporting of occupational injuries and illnesses (BLS, 1986b).

may be threatening to the worker but do not result in injury, such as pushing or shouting and acts of aggression towards other clients—should be recorded, perhaps as part of an assaultive incident report. These reports should be evaluated routinely by the affected department.

- Information on patients with a history of past violence, drug abuse, or criminal activity should be recorded on the patient's chart. All staff who care for a potentially aggressive, abusive, or violent client should be aware of their background and history. Admission of violent clients should be logged to help determine potential risks.
- Minutes of safety meetings, records of hazard analyses, and corrective actions recommended and taken should be documented.
- Records of all training programs, attendees, and qualifications of trainers should be maintained.

Evaluation

As part of their overall program, employers should evaluate their safety and security measures. Top management should review the program regularly, and with each incident, to evaluate program success. Responsible parties (managers, supervisors, and employees) should collectively reevaluate policies and procedures on a regular basis. Deficiencies should be identified and corrective action taken.

An evaluation program should involve the following:

- Establishing a uniform violence reporting system and regular review of reports.
- Reviewing reports and minutes from staff meetings on safety and security issues.
- Analyzing trends and rates in illness/injury or fatalities caused by violence relative to initial or "baseline" rates.
- Measuring improvement based on lowering the frequency and severity of workplace violence.
- Keeping up-to-date records of administrative and work practice changes to prevent workplace violence to evaluate their effectiveness.
- Surveying employees before and after making job or worksite changes or installing security measures or new systems to determine their effectiveness.
- Keeping abreast of new strategies available to deal with violence in the health care and social service fields as these develop.
- Surveying employees who experience hostile situations about the medical treatment they received initially and, again, several weeks afterward, and then several months later.
- Complying with OSHA and state requirements for recording and reporting deaths, injuries, and illnesses.
- Requesting periodic law enforcement or outside consultant review of the worksite for recommendations on improving employee safety.

Management should share workplace violence prevention program evaluation reports with all employees. Any changes in the program should be discussed at regular meetings of the safety committee, union representatives, or other employee groups.

Sources of Assistance

Employers who would like assistance in implementing an appropriate workplace violence prevention program can turn to the OSHA Consultation service provided in their state. Primarily targeted at smaller companies, the consultation service is provided at no charge to the employer and is independent of OSHA's enforcement activity.

OSHA's efforts to assist employers combat workplace violence are complemented by those of NIOSH (1-800-35-NIOSH) and public safety officials, trade associations, unions, insurers, human resource, and employee assistance professionals as well as other interested groups. Employers and employees may contact these groups for additional advice and information.

Conclusion

OSHA recognizes the importance of effective safety and health program management in providing safe and healthful workplaces. In fact, OSHA's consultation services help employers establish and maintain safe and healthful workplaces, and the agency's Voluntary Protection Programs were specifically established to recognize worksites with exemplary safety and health programs. Effective safety and health programs are known to improve both morale and productivity and reduce workers' compensation costs.

OSHA's violence prevention guidelines are an essential component to workplace safety and health programs. OSHA believes that the performance-oriented approach of the guidelines provides employers with flexibility in their efforts to maintain safe and healthful working conditions.

References

Bureau of Labor Statistics. (1986a). *A brief guide to recordkeeping requirements for occupational injuries and illness, 29. Code of Federal Regulations 1904.* 19 pp..

Bureau of Labor Statistics. (1986b). *Recordkeeping Guidelines for Occupational Injuries and Illnesses.* April 1986, 84 pp.

Bureau of Labor Statistics. (1991). *Occupational injuries and illnesses in the United States by industry, 1989.* Bulletin 2379.

California State Department of Industrial Relations. (1995). *CAL/OSHA guidelines for workplace security.* San Francisco, CA: Division of Occupational Safety and Health.

Carmel, H., & Hunter, M. (1989). Staff injuries from inpatient violence. *Hospital Community Psychology, 40*(1), 41–46.

Fox, S., Freeman, C., Barr, B. et al. (1994). *Identifying reported cases of workplace violence in federal agencies.* Unpublished Report, Washington DC.

Goodman, R., Jenkins, L., & Mercy, J. (1994). Workplace-related homicide among health care workers in the United States, 1980 through 1990. *Journal of the American Medical Association, 272*(21), 1686–1688.

Goetz, R., Bloom, J., Chene, S. et al. (1981). Weapons possessed by patients in a university emergency department. *Annal of Emergency Medicine, 20*(1), 8–10.

Liss, G. (1993). *Examination of workers' compensation claims among nurses in Ontario for injuries due to violence.* Ontario: Health and Safety Studies Unit, Ontario Ministry of Labour.

Novello, A. (1992). A medical response to violence. *Journal of the American Medical Association, 267,* 3007.

Oregon State Department of Consumer and Business Services. (1994). *Violence in the workplace, Oregon, 1988 to 1992—A special study of worker's compensation claims caused by violent acts.* Salem, OR: Information Management Division.

Ryan, J., & Poster, E. (1989). The assaulted nurse: Short-term and long-term responses. *Archives of Psychiatric Nursing, 3*(6), 323–331.

Simonowitz, J. (1993). *Guidelines for security and safety of health care and community service workers.* Division of Occupational Safety and Health. San Francisco, CA: Department of Industrial Relations.

State of Washington, Department of Labor and Industries. (1993). *Study of assaults on staff in Washington State psychiatric hospitals.*

State of Washington, Department of Labor Industries. (1995). *Violence in Washington workplaces, 1992.*

Toscano, Guy, and Weber, William. (1995). *Violence in the workplace.* Washington, DC: Bureau of Labor Statistics.

U.S. Department of Justice. (1986). *Criminal victimization in the U.S. 1984. A national crime survey report.* Pub. No. NCJ-100435. Washington DC.

U.S. Department of Labor, Bureau of Labor Statistics. (1995). *Census of fatal occupational injuries, 1994.* News Bulletin 95-288.

Wasserberger, J., Ordog, G., Kolodny, M. et al. (1989). Violence in a community emergency room. *Archives of Emergency Medicine, 6,* 266–269.

Wolfgang, M. (1986). Homicide in other industrialized countries. *Bulletin of New York Academic Medicine, 62,* 400.

Author Index

Numbers in italics refer to listings in reference sections.

Abrams, R. C., *194*, 197
Adams, J. S., 57, 58, *82*
Adams, K., 17, *23*
Akabas, S., 119, *148*
Akers, R., 18, *21*
Albrecht, S., 34, 43, *48*, 251, *258*
Alexander, B. H., 10, *21*
Alexander, D., 317, *325*
Alkus, S., 207, *215*
Allcorn, S., 111, 113, 118, 143, *146*
Allen, J., 116, *146*
Allen, J. G., 190, *197*
Allen, S., 233, *246*
Alpert, G. P., 232, *246*
Alutto, J. A., 141, *147*
American Academy for Nursing, 189, *197*
American Federation of State, County, and Municipal Employees, 317, *325*
American Psychiatric Association, 189, *197*, 232, *246*
Ames, G., 110, 114, 115, 119, 142, *146*, *147*, *149*
Ames, G. M., 110, 114, 124, *146*
Anderson, C., 114, *151*
Anderson, C. A., 55, 61, *82*
Anderson, W., 207, *215*
Anfuso, D., 29, 31, *46*, 268, *282*
Armao, B. B., 176, *188*
Arvey, R. D., 46, *47*
Ashford, S. J., 33, *46*, 119, 123, *146*
Associated Press, 51, *82*
Aussant, G., 231, *246*
Avenline, M. O., 233, *246*

Bachman, R., 8, 11, 12, 14, *21*, 154, *160*
Bachorowski, J. A., 55, *83*
Bailey, D. S., 111, 113, *146*
Baker, D. L., 89, *99*
Ball, G. A., 70, *82*
Ban, C., 110, *152*
Banaji, M. R., 113, *146*
Bandura, A., 32, 34, 36, *46*, 111, 118, *146*
Barbaranelli, C., 62, *83*
Bargal, D., 177, 184, *187*
Barker, T., 267, 268, 269, 279, *282*
Barling, J., 30, 32, 33, 34, 35, 36, 37, 38, 39, 41, 42, 43, 44, 45, *46*, *47*, *48*, *49*
Baron, R. A., 52, 55, 56, 61, 62, 69, 70, 77, 78, 79, *82*, 119, *146*
Baron, R. M., 67, *83*

Baron, S. A., 15, *23*, 271, 272, *282*, 315, *325*, 358, *365*
Barrier, M., 290, 291, *296*
Barry, B., 59, *84*
Bastian, L., 10, *21*
Bauer, B., 207, *215*
Baum, A., 37, 38, 41, *47*
Bayley, D. H., 235, *246*
Beattie, M. C., 110, 115, *146*
Beck, A. J., 207, *215*
Beehr, T. A., 45, *48*, 119, *146*, 243, *246*
Bellinger, S., 119, *148*
Bellingham, R., 116, *146*
Benjamin, G. A. H., 110, 112, *150*
Bennett, R. J., 69, *84*
Bensimon, H. F., 63, 64, 65, *82*, 167, *169*, 291, *296*
Bensley, L., 10, *21*
Berkowitz, L., 53, 70, *82*, 111, *146*
Berman, M., 55, 62, *82*
Bernstein, H. A., 176, 183, 184, *187*
Beyer, J. M., 110, 116, *152*
Bhagat, R. S., 119, *146*
Bickel, R. W., 291, *296*
Biener, L., 110, *152*
Bies, R. J., 58, 75, 77, *82*, *83*, *85*
Binder, A., 234, *246*
Blair, D. T., 327, 331, 334, 340, *340*
Blakelock, E., 221, *228*
Blander, B., 2, 4, 5, 12, *22*, 200, *206*
Block, C., 9, *21*
Block, R., 9, *21*
Bluen, S. D., 37, 38, *46*
Blum, R., 109, 110, *146*
Blum, T. C., 115, *151*
Blumberg, M., 232, 245, *247*
Blumstein, A., 16, *21*
Bobko, P., 33, *46*, 119, 123, *146*
Boje, D. M., 62, *82*
Bonafacio, P., 233, *246*
Bond, C. F., 109, 110, *149*
Bonnet, P., 53, *84*
Boswell, R., 43, 44, *46*
Bowie, V., 10, *21*
Boxer, P. A., 229, *246*
Boyatzis, R. E., 110, *146*
Brailey, K., 29, *49*
Branchey, M. H., 109, *147*
Braverman, M., 90, 94, *99*, 111, *146*, 229, 241, *246*
British Medical Association, 107, 108, *147*

Subject Index

About the Editors

Gary R. VandenBos, PhD, received his doctorate in clinical psychology from the University of Detroit. He is the Executive Director of the Office of Communications of the American Psychological Association. As a practicing clinical psychologist, he directed or served as consultant to various professional groups and organizations, such as research projects on treating violent schizophrenic patients, crisis intervention and child abuse, and family stress. He was an Executive Board member of the Michigan Jail Rehabilitation Service Association, a psychological consultant to several police departments, and a psychological consultant to courts in four states. He has participated in various panels, colloquia, and workshops on distressed professionals, on understanding and working with violent patients, and on psychotherapy with the violent criminal offender. He is a diplomate in forensic psychology.

After his strong investment in psychotherapy and his enjoyment of writing, a major organizing thread in Dr. VandenBos's career has been the translation of psychological research knowledge into application—whether that be its application in training, clinical practice, the shaping of public policy, or the dissemination of scholarly information to the professional community and the public. He is the author or editor of various publications including "Terror, decision-making, and professional conduct" (in *Ethics and Behavior*, 1991); *Professional Liability and Risk Management* (1990); "Professionals in distress" (with R. R. Kilburg and F. W. Kaslow in *Hospital and Community Psychiatry*, 1988); *Cataclysms, Crises, and Catastrophes* (1987); and *Psychotherapy with Schizophrenics* (1981). He received the Early Career Award for Contribution to Psychotherapy from Division 29.

Elizabeth Q. Bulatao received her Master's degree in sociology from Loyola University, Chicago. She is a communications dissemination officer in the Office of Communications, American Psychological Association, providing technical assistance and managing special projects. She previously managed special projects for child psychiatry, and international projects in women's health and family planning for development agencies. She has written on such topics as U.S. government initiatives in managed care and developing-country family planning programs.